COMMUNICATING IN GROUPS AND TEAMS

COMMUNICATING IN GROUPS AND TEAMS

Sharing Leadership

FIFTH EDITION

Gay Lumsden
California Polytechnic State University, San Luis Obispo

Donald Lumsden
California Polytechnic State University, San Luis Obispo

Carolyn Wiethoff
Indiana University, Bloomington

WADSWORTH
CENGAGE Learning™

Australia • Canada • Mexico • Singapore • Spain • United Kingdom • United States

WADSWORTH
CENGAGE Learning™

Communicating In Groups and Teams: Sharing Leadership, Fifth Edition
Gay Lumsden, Donald Lumsden, Carolyn Wiethoff

Publisher: Lyn Uhl

Executive Editor, Communication Studies and English Composition: Monica Eckman

Development Editor: Larry Goldberg

Assistant Editor: Rebekah Matthews

Editorial Assistant: Colin Solan

Media Editor: Jessica Badiner

Marketing Manager: Erin Mitchell

Marketing Coordinator: Darlene Macanan

Marketing Communications Manager: Christine Dobberpuhl

Content Project Management: Pre-PressPMG

Art Director: Linda Helcher

Production Technology Analyst: Emily Gross

Print Buyer: Justin Palmeiro

Permissions Editor: Mardell Glinski Schultz

Production Service: Pre-PressPMG

Photo Manager: John Hill

Photo Researcher: Jennifer Lim, Bill Smith Group

Cover Designer: Riezebos Holzbaur Design Group

Cover Image: © Sam Sharpe/Absolute Stock Photo

Compositor: Pre-PressPMG

For product information and technology assistance, contact us at
Cengage Learning Customer & Sales Support, 1-800-354-9706
For permission to use material from this text or product, submit all requests online at **www.cengage.com/permissions**.
Further permissions questions can be emailed to
permissionrequest@cengage.com.

Library of Congress Control Number: 2009925432

International Student Edition ISBN-13: 978-0-495-83346-8

International Student Edition ISBN-10: 0-495-83346-0

Wadsworth
20 Channel Center Street
Boston, MA 02210
USA

Cengage Learning products are represented in Canada by Nelson Education, Ltd.

For your course and learning solutions, visit **www.cengage.com**.
Purchase any of our products at your local college store or at our preferred online store **www.ichapters.com**.

Printed in the United States of America
1 2 3 4 5 6 7 13 12 11 10 09

Brief Contents

CONTENTS

PART THREE | SHARING LEADERSHIP THROUGH TASK PROCESSES

5 TASK QUESTIONS AND RESOURCES: LAUNCHING YOUR INQUIRY   113

PART FOUR | SHARING LEADERSHIP THROUGH TRANSACTIONAL PROCESSES

PREFACE

You may love working in groups, or you may hate it. Whichever way you feel, you can be certain of two things: First, you have company, because teamwork can be both gratifying and mind-boggling. Second, no matter how you feel about it, you *will* work in groups and teams extensively throughout school, career, and life in general.

We've written this book because we know that in your life and in your career, whatever it may be, you will be involved in cooperative group efforts by meeting together with other people in one place, and probably as virtual teams by linking with others electronically from multiple locations. Organizations—big and small, private and public, virtual and "bricks-and-mortar," for-profit and nonprofit—use groups and teams for everything from designing and implementing projects to managing improvement in overall quality of products and processes. That's because cooperative groups can be more effective than individuals at many tasks. When a team brings together people with different experiences and backgrounds to focus their attention on an issue, the team's diversity creates the potential for a wide range of ideas and approaches. However, groups also have the potential for breakdowns and misunderstandings; it takes wisdom to make teams work.

You can develop the wisdom to make your groups and teams work effectively by learning to understand them and by honing your communication skills. A cooperative group or team is more than the sum of its parts; when several people interact, communication among group members multiplies in complexity. Members need strong communication skills to make their ideas clear, to understand other team members, to build a team, and to work together through the task processes of collaborative problem analysis and decision making.

This book will help you learn how to create good team experiences. It will help you most effectively if you know how we've designed it. Therefore, we want to tell you about some changes in this new edition; about the philosophical premises on which it's written; about our assumptions about you, the student; about some new features that may help you learn; and about how the book is organized.

CHANGES IN THE FIFTH EDITION

In the fifth edition of *Communicating in Groups and Teams: Sharing Leadership*, we have updated research and resources. In particular, we've expanded coverage of how and when teams can be most productive, particularly when they are not physically together. In the workplace, people work extensively in virtual teams, and many of these platforms are being used in classrooms across the globe. In fact, some classes are conducted across multiple campuses and in different countries through the use of such innovative platforms as Second Life. In addition to updating information on technologically assisted meetings, we have eliminated some of the early computer information that is already old news.

New case studies appear in this edition, and all of the examples, boxes, etc. have been changed to reflect the vast array of team types. The definition of "business" has changed radically, and with it the definition of "team." Consequently, we focus on the many ways that teams form and run in everyday life. You'll see examples in medical surgeries, racetracks, and sports, just to name a few. The point we wish to emphasize in this edition is that teams don't merely meet . . . they DO. They create, they complete exciting and complex tasks, and they challenge each other to achieve better things than each individual could on their own.

PHILOSOPHICAL PREMISES

By philosophical premises, we mean beliefs that are basic to every part of this book. Let's begin by listing several of these:

A cooperative group should become a team. An effective task group builds a team by using the best abilities and talents of every member in a process that serves the needs of the individuals and of the task concurrently. This involves mutual commitment to vigilant, collaborative analysis as well as to team building.

Leadership is every team member's responsibility. Each person must take responsibility for influencing the team's transactions and tasks. Each serves as member, facilitator, contributor, participant; each has a responsibility for the quality of group transactions and achievements, for the satisfaction of the members, and for ensuring that the functions of leadership are served.

A designated leader is more than a manager. Leaders guide their teams over obstacles; they empower team members to take leadership; they activate quality contributions, interaction, and responsibility-taking within the team. And they link the team to parent organizations and outside systems.

The team is a system within a system. Teams today frequently cross departments, organizations, or public institutions to weave a number of systems, subsystems, goals, and objectives together in cooperative efforts. Learning how to do this can help you to bridge and to heal some of the chasms in your world.

The team is a microcosm. People of both sexes and of many sociocultural and racial backgrounds interact in groups. Diversity contributes to quality teamwork when members appreciate differences, actively seek different points of view, and understand that communication behaviors and norms are influenced by gender, culture, and expectations.

The team is an ethical system. Groups must consider ethical dimensions both in the transactions among the members and in the decisions that they make. Principled members and leaders who focus attention on ethical questions and their potential impact at every stage of a team's development and work will make better decisions and realize healthier consequences than those who do not.

ASSUMPTIONS ABOUT STUDENTS AND APPROACHES TO LEARNING

We think of you as one of our own students. We assume that, like our students, you have natural curiosity, an interest in becoming an effective group communicator, a desire to succeed, and some ideas about what teamwork is like.

You certainly have your own learning style; everybody does. You may also be like most people in that you learn best when you connect with the material in some real way. In the words of a Chinese proverb: "What I hear, I forget; what I see, I may remember; what I do, I understand." That's why:

This book is user-friendly. It is written for you, the student. It starts with you and your experience because we know that people learn, as Aristotle pointed out, from the known to the unknown. Learning works best when it starts where you are, with your experiences and your life.

The writing is directed to you and designed for your use. Throughout the book are clear checklists that will help you focus on exactly what works to make groups effective. Plenty of explanations, definitions, and examples clarify the ideas. Many of these come from our own experiences with students and with teams in organizations. If you interact with them, by creating your own examples and applying the definitions and concepts, the information will become more real to you.

The emphasis is on making your groups and teams effective. Theory and research are not emphasized for their own sake but are included as needed to make concepts clearer, to make a point, or to show relationships among different areas. The references contain excellent sources to which you can refer if you want to follow up on ideas for a research project.

Learning strategies are varied and interesting. We believe in varying learning experiences to meet a range of students' learning styles, so we've used a range of approaches. Because we also believe that learning about teamwork should be put in an applied perspective, the book has some real-life materials to show you how people are currently using what you are learning. Some of these are included in the text as examples, but some are in special formats.

These and other assumptions about you influence the features we have chosen to include in this book.

FEATURES

Boxes: Brief, inset boxes provide excerpts and synopses from newsletters and articles as well as teamwork examples from corporations and from nonprofit, public, media, and political organizations.

Case Analyses: In many locations, inset boxes give you case studies that apply principles developed in that chapter. Many of the end-of-chapter exercises also provide the bases for case studies. In addition, most photographs and cartoons throughout the book include questions guiding analysis, discussion, and recommendations, making each of them a mini–case study.

Exercises: Exercises at the end of each chapter provide opportunities for you to:

- *Observe and evaluate* others, in class and in outside situations, as they work in groups and teams. Many chapters include forms for observation and evaluation of groups to help you apply the information in the exercises.
- *Participate* in group and team experiences that focus on the content of the chapter.
- *Reflect* on and analyze your own experience and skill in relationship to the chapter's content.
- *Write* about your observations and experiences.

These exercises will make your learning real and applicable.

Glossary: Important concepts in the text are printed in **boldface** and listed in the glossary at the end of the book. As you read, if you can't remember precisely what a term means from a previous chapter, you can refer to the glossary for a reminder.

Instructor's Manual: Your instructor doubtless will use his or her own assignments and methods in the course. In addition, an instructor's manual contains assignments, exercises, case studies, evaluation forms, and test questions to help you work through the material in and out of class. Resources for students and instructors can be found on the book companion Website at http://cengage.com/communication/lumsden/communicatingingroupsandteams5E. In addition, InfoTrac® College Edition can be made available to students and instructors and accessed from the Web site as well. InfoTrac® College Edition is a world-class, online university library that offers the full text of articles from almost 5,000 scholarly journals and popular publications updated daily and going back more than 20 years.

ORGANIZATION

Learning *information* about groups and developing *skills* in working with them require you to deal with many things at once, and that presents a dilemma. Ideally, as students, you would know everything covered in the textbook before you began applying it. That isn't possible in a communication class. You must practice skills from the first moment of the semester, but information you need about these skills may be presented late in the book.

A textbook goes step by step through information that is intricately related throughout, and that doesn't always fit the way an instructor arranges the course. Your professor may rearrange the book to suit the way your course is designed. In whichever order you use the chapters, however, it will help to know how they are arranged. (We also have noted where you might want to skip ahead on your own to help you cope with problems or to plan projects.)

Part One (Chapters 1 and 2) starts with where you are—with your experiences in previous groups. It moves on into your future in groups and teams, your personal leadership responsibilities and roles, and the impact of ethics on your participation in groups and teams. This gives you a *thinking* foundation for the course.

Part Two (Chapters 3 and 4) introduces you to team processes—setting goals, getting the work under way. It gives you solid advice on developing positive climates for team communication, working with computer-assisted groupware, and facilitating your meeting processes. This leads to envisioning an excellent team and getting it started with your teammates. This part gives you a *doing* foundation; it gets you and your classmates started on activities and projects— and introduces you to what a developing team will experience.

Part Three (Chapters 5 through 8) guides you and your teammates through the task processes of goal setting, team inquiry, critical and creative thinking, problem solving, and decision making. This part focuses your thinking *and* your work on vigilance and collaboration.

Part Four (Chapters 9 and 10) develops verbal, nonverbal, listening, and questioning skills for team communication that share leadership and help achieve team goals. This includes assertive, confirming behavior that contributes to developing dialogue and healthy team climates. These chapters help you weave transactional processes to make a team.

Part Five (Chapters 11 through 13) addresses some sophisticated, and critical, problems and challenges in group interactions and thinking. These include the roles of designated leaders—what they do and why they do it that way. This part of the book explores both minor and major problems of group interaction, such as issues of deviance and conformity, competitive communication, groupthink, and conflict. (You may want to skip ahead and refer to Chapter 13 if and when you start to see problems in teamwork, either for this class or for some other one. This chapter is a great resource for solving team problems.)

Appendices A and B guide you through team projects, planning public meetings, and preparing and presenting written and oral reports. This part provides the key to finishing up course assignments effectively; it is also a valuable resource for future projects in other courses and your career. *(If you are involved in a project for this course—or any other course, for that matter—we suggest that you turn to these appendices to find suggestions for planning and implementing your assignment. They will help considerably.)*

The Glossary lists and defines all of the important terms that have been **boldfaced** in the text. It's a quick reference and review source.

The References list all the sources that you have seen in parentheses in the text, so you can see from whom, where, and when we have drawn quotations or references to research. You'll note that this edition has significantly more literature from business journals; since one of the new authors is a business professor, this perspective has been fully incorporated into the revision.

The Index lists information in two ways: It includes the sources quoted in the text and tells you on what page(s) they are quoted, so if you know a name but can't remember where it is cited, the index can tell you where to look. The index also lists subjects and numbers of pages on which they are discussed in the book, so if you want to find a specific idea or track a number of ideas about one subject, you can look it up in the index.

ACKNOWLEDGMENTS

Our approach to this book is influenced by our own research and learning about group communication, and that started in a class such as yours. We have been fortunate in having excellent professors and mentors to guide us along the way. We take this opportunity to express thanks to Dennis Gouran who, when he was at Indiana University, influenced the way we think about group communication and directed Gay's dissertation in group leadership. He continues to provide his sage advice and, occasionally, consolation. All three authors were part of the rich tradition in speech communication that was the hallmark of Indiana University, and we treasure the knowledge creation and dissemination that historically took place there.

Don and Gay also are indebted to the late Martin Andersen for immersing us in the study of groups during our years at California State University at Fullerton. Their thanks, too, go to Juliette Venitsky of Cerritos College for helping them develop their early understanding of the communication discipline we all have come to love. Similarly, Carolyn credits Norm Fricker of Orange Coast College for her love of teams and passion for communication.

We want also to acknowledge the influence of a person we never had the opportunity to meet and know. Henry Ewbank, who taught for years at the University of Wisconsin, had an enormous impact on our educational experiences through his writings and especially through his students, whom we later encountered as our professors. Jeff Auer, Bob Gunderson, Ray Smith, and Martin Andersen modeled for us, as Dr. Ewbank clearly had done for them, a love of scholarship and, even more important, human concerns for students, teaching, and learning. He is, to us, an academic grandfather who died before our "births." Ours is a rich heritage.

Although responsibility for the content is ours, a number of communication colleagues across the country reviewed drafts of the first four editions of this text. They helped us keep perspective on the book's material and on students as its readers. Freda Remmers, who was our colleague at Kean University, provided excellent suggestions for changes. Other reviewers include Diane Boynton, Monterey Peninsula College; Mary L. Brown, University of Arizona; David E. Butt, Penn State University; Patricia Comeaux, University of North Carolina-Wilmington; Isa Engleberg, Prince George's Community College; Charles J. G. Griffin, Kansas State University; Jean A. Groshek, Alverno College; Robert D. Harrison, Gaulladet University; Joan Holm, Northern Virginia Community College; James A. Jaksa, Western Michigan University; William E. Jurma, Texas Christian University; Steve May, University of North Carolina; Mary McComb, Marist College; John C. Meyer, University of Southern Mississippi; Susan Mitchell, University of Phoenix; Mary-Jo Popovici, Monroe Community College; Russell F. Proctor II, Northern Kentucky University; Kristi Schaller, University of Hawaii at Manoa; Joseph Scudder, Indiana University; Matt Seeger, Wayne State University; Sandra Pride Shaw, University of Texas at Austin; Brant Short, Idaho State University; Edwina Stoll, DeAnza College; Mike Wartman, Normandale Community College; and Tanichya Wongprasert, Washington State University. The reviewers of the fifth edition include Patricia Barnes, Monroe Community College; Polly A. Begley, Fresno City College; Keith Corso, Westminster College; Laurie Guttenberg, Suffolk and Nassau Community Colleges; Rosemary Kim, Cal Poly Pomona; Leigh Makay, Capital University; Don McCormick, California State University Northridge; Mark Meachem, Dominican College; Susan Miskelly, Bridgewater State College; William Price, North Country Community College; and Susan Wieczorek, University of Pittsburgh at Johnstown. The views of these reviewers support the idea that multiple perspectives can lead to an improved final product.

Finally, we dedicate this edition to our families, friends, students, colleagues, and to each other. All have contributed to our understanding of the importance of *Communicating in Groups and Teams.*

Gay Lumsden
California Polytechnic State University, San Luis Obispo

Donald Lumsden
California Polytechnic State University, San Luis Obispo

Carolyn Wiethoff
Indiana University, Bloomington

"I'd really rather work alone. . . ."
Forget it—the twenty-first century works in groups.

YOUR GROUPS AND TEAMS | 1

Communicating for Success

We're going to put this right up front: Working in groups and teams is unavoidable in twenty-first-century life. Sometimes, when we introduce the concept of group communication, either in the college classroom or in corporate training, people beam enthusiastically. Often, however, they wince. It all depends on their backgrounds and experiences. As one of our faculty friends put it, "There's a lot of group hate out there." Furthermore, you will work in teams that meet face to face, teams that work online across time and space, and teams that use a combination of both methods. For better or worse, you need to build skills in communicating in groups and teams in a variety of contexts.

In this chapter, we consider groups and teams that you have been a part of, how you felt about them, and what factors may have influenced your feelings. We then examine your future in various types of groups and teams, the power of team-work, and contemporary trends in the workplace. Finally, we provide some tips to get started on your work for this class. Thus, our goals in this chapter are to help you:

1. Understand how and why group experiences may both satisfy and frustrate you and other members of your groups
2. See how and why groups and teams—both real and virtual—will be involved in your future life and career
3. Understand a set of basic group and team concepts
4. Become aware of how communication operates in groups
5. Get started on your experiences for this class

Let's start with where you've been—and then move forward to where you are going.

YOUR GROUP AND TEAM EXPERIENCES

From day one of your life, you were in a group—your family—and this set your ex-pectations of how people act when they are together. Since then, you've added to your experiences. Perhaps you've been in study or support groups, or perhaps you've worked on special problem-solving groups, management or staff committees, or proj-ect teams; or you may share information, interests, and/or work projects online with specialized groups. Any of these experiences may connect with larger systems, such as corporations, schools, workplaces, communities, religious groups. You may have competed on teams in areas as diverse as scholastics, livestock judging, basketball, or even automobile racing. Many students have formed their clearest vision of what a group or team should be from these kinds of experiences.

Your vision of groups and teams may be shiny or it may be dim. On the shiny side, it's a great feeling to be part of a winning team or a super committee. It also can be more fun, more stimulating, and more motivating to work with other people than to work alone. Just belonging to a group can feel pretty good. The dim picture, however, is that working in a group can be a pain. It's demanding. It requires you to work on many levels at once—with people, with relationships, with information, with ideas—and many things can go wrong. It takes leadership and commitment to make a group work well.

Looking back, how do you feel about your experiences? We want your future groups and teams to give you great success and satisfaction, so it's worth consider-ing what some of the factors behind those feelings might be.

Expectations. People tend to generalize from their experiences, to decide that what was true of one will be true of all. These expectations color their perceptions of future events. If a study group helped you to improve a grade, then you may look forward to participating in other groups. If you once worked hard on a project team when others slacked off, and your grade or income suffered because of their irresponsibility, then you may dread groups. The loudest groans in our classes come from students who have had these negative experiences—and who do not want to repeat them.

Investment. Previous groups may have taught you that the more people become involved, the more time, energy, and money the job takes. For a corporate team, each person's salary and work time—as well as the space, materials, and other resources needed for the group—factor into the costs of that team. Group projects represent investments for their members and their organizations.

Pressures. You may have felt a lot of stress during previous group experiences from the work and from the group. Sometimes people conclude an experience with a thought such as, "The pressure was so great that I just didn't say what I really thought." A group may pressure members to go along with what others think. This can lead to dishonest, unethical, or at least foolish decisions. It takes leadership and wisdom to keep a group open and to eliminate the dangers of conformity.

Personal characteristics and preferences. Each individual brings a personal approach to his or her work. Are you an individualist—confident, creative, and competent in doing things by yourself? If so, then you may not trust a group of people to do as well. You may agree with the old line that "a camel is a horse put together by a committee." Or perhaps you dislike working alone and find the social interaction of a group more motivating and stimulating for your own thinking and creativity.

Gender. Your attitude toward groups could be affected by how you've been socialized as a male or a female. Gender expectations are changing, but differences still remain. Males may be more likely to approach groups with a competitive, let's-get-it-done orientation, whereas females may be more cooperative and concerned with the well-being of the group (van Engen & Willemsen, 2004). Good teamwork needs both approaches.

Culture. Cultural influences are vitally important, but making generalizations about them is risky. Even characteristics that generally are true of a culture may not fit everyone within that population. The point is not to stereotype individuals but to recognize that their culture can influence how they approach groups. For example, individualistic Europeans and North Americans may be frustrated by groups, but Latin Americans may like working in groups as a method of supporting each other and improving outcomes (Rodriguez, 2005). And, while the collectivist nature of many east Asian countries promotes group work, the Chinese in particular are often conflict-avoidant, which can result in a lack of robust discussion (Brew & Cairns, 2004). A team of diverse people, therefore, presents some challenges. The good news is the rich gold mine of ideas and creativity each member provides. The bad news is the minefield of interpersonal frustrations and conflicts that occur among diverse human beings who, after all, are just being human.

BOX 1.1	VIRTUAL TEAMS MAKE LOYALTY MORE REALISTIC

There's another twist to the concept of virtual teams, which are made up of telecommuters in different locations: Some teams now are ongoing, rather than being created only for temporary projects.

KPMG, the international accounting company based in New York . . . [with] revenue of $13.5 billion for fiscal year 2000 and 108,000 employees worldwide . . . is a risk-taker. And Pat O'Day, team leader of knowledge management training for the firm's state and local tax practice, is a beneficiary.

"We communicate through email and conference calls and meet in person only four times a year," said O'Day, of Hollywood, Md., who manages five people living in Washington, Maryland, and Texas. The Team creates Web-based management and training tools. Three of the "virtuals" have children under the age of 6. Though one member works full time in the Washington office, the others work from home.

O'Day started out working three days a week from home reviewing documents for the tax practice. "I'm delighted to tell you the job evolved within six months into strategic planning for maintaining a Web site, and soon I found myself in charge of a team—and able to achieve balance in my life," she said. The team's work is called "a success" by the firm and its programs are "well-used."

O'Day said virtual teams are "the wave of the future. I already see them expanding and changing the way we think about work." And more proof of her success: O'Day recently was named head of another virtual team with 13 members in two regions.

Source: Excerpt from Carol Kleiman, "Virtual Teams Make Loyalty More Realistic," *Tribune* (San Luis Obispo, CA), January 24, 2001, p. D1.

YOUR FUTURE IN GROUPS AND TEAMS

Unless you plan to become a hermit or some highly eccentric and wealthy genius, you will work frequently in groups and teams. This is true even in your private life. There's the family, of course, with all the activities that families have. You often hear the complaint that parents are "nothing but chauffeurs" for the kids: Little League, dance, theater, scouts, soccer team, gymnastics team, 4-H. Not only are the children involved in multiple group activities, but so are the parents, with advisory groups, planning groups, and support groups.

There also are group activities in the community, in recreational centers, and even—especially—in places of worship. More and more, churches, synagogues, mosques, and temples assign work to special groups and teams. We know one church member who is on an interdenominational task force to provide housing for the homeless, a special corps of laypeople who help with family crises, the church planning committee, and more. This man also serves in community groups and works with teams in his professional life as a sales representative.

Your private life and your work life (whatever your career) will involve you in many groups and teams. First, let's look at some examples of teamwork in various careers, then describe some different types of groups and teams on which you might serve, and finally examine the power of teamwork and current trends in the workplace.

CAREERS AND TEAMWORK

Consider your future career. You may have your sights set on a communication, scientific, or medical field. You may be aiming for archaeology, history, or meteorology. You may want a career in a technological field or in sales, agriculture, or the arts. In any of these careers, you will likely work with teams of other people in your field or with specialists in related fields.

If you're a communication major, your career may be in mass communication, telecommunications, or media. Alternatively, it may be in organizational communication, public communication or public relations, or even performance. As with other majors, you could also become a teacher or pursue a career in management, business, research, or a helping profession.

To get an idea of how groups and teams might be a part of your future, let's look at some applied career examples:

- A graduate in mass communication, telecommunications, business, art, or electronics might work on a team to design a communication system for a corporation or on a task force to develop guidelines for local, state, or national advertising. A graduate in media, marketing, art, or education might work on teams to design, produce, shoot, edit, and market training tapes, advertising tapes, and so on. Some of our own recent graduates followed precisely this path and now operate their own media businesses—as teams.

- A graduate in organizational communications could work on a corporate team to design and implement training programs, one of which might be to train managers how to work effectively in teams. One of our graduates followed this path in a large corporation. He began by producing training materials, but his responsibilities soon expanded to coaching executives in communication skills.

- A graduate in political science or public communication might work on a team to design and implement an election or a political-issue campaign. One of our graduates who was passionately interested in animal rights has made her career designing campaigns against animal abuse.

- Graduates in public relations cooperate closely in teams to coordinate advertising, public appearances, press relations, and legal responses for clients. One of our recent graduates began her career as a public relations intern for a pharmaceutical company, then moved on and up to another company. Recently, as an assistant account executive, she served as part of a special team to introduce to the market a product on which she had worked from its inception.

- A graduate in performance, radio, television, film, or theater will probably work almost constantly in team situations. Just ask any actor or director who has worked in repertory theater, and you will hear glowing accounts of "true teams." One of our graduates, a dancer, went to work in a small, tightly organized children's theater troupe that does everything from planning publicity, selling tickets, and making sets to performing at schools and parties.

- As a teacher, a graduate in education cooperates closely with administrators, other teachers, support staff, students, and sometimes parents to create and implement programs and policies. Another of our graduates became a history teacher and soon created and led a team of faculty and parents to design an entirely new curriculum for his school.

- A graduate in art works with creative teams to develop designs for a wide range of commercial purposes. One freelance artist and her team designed a huge mural to decorate a halfway house for teenaged alcoholics, and once the mural was designed, she led teams of the youngsters to paint and hang the mural.

- Graduates in many majors—business, communication, science, technology, liberal arts, psychology, English—may become managers who work in teams with other managers and with numerous other groups and teams of superiors, subordinates, and related departments on issues such as customer satisfaction and workflow improvement. One of our graduates who worked on a management team for a retail store went on to develop her own small business, for which she forged a tight employee team that makes her business work.

- Graduates in many majors—communication, liberal arts, behavioral sciences, sciences, marketing—become researchers who work in teams with other researchers, clients, and representatives from related areas. A marketing researcher, for example, might test the market for a new product in collaboration with teammates representing departments of research and development, finance, sales, production, and advertising.

All these people use their understandings and communication skills in numerous other group and team situations. And so will you.

TYPES OF GROUPS AND TEAMS

Your private life and work life will put you in many different types of groups and teams, each with its own distinct purpose and mode of operation. Some groups may be **ad hoc** (meaning "to this" in Latin), which are groups formed to deal with specific issues and then disband. An ad hoc group could be a committee or task force that meets at work or school to investigate a problem or make recommendations or create a program—or it could be a virtual group that "meets" electronically. You may, for example, have a professor who team-writes with one or more authors, each of whom teaches at a university in another state or country. Although they write their drafts separately, they communicate online to plan, share information, read drafts, and share ideas about improving and integrating their efforts. When the book is ready, their writing team expands to a publishing team that includes editors, designers, and marketers (among others) with whom the authors will "talk" online.

Here are some other types of groups and teams with which you may work in the future:

Informal groups. Even now, you may be about to meet with an informal group of friends or people with similar interests. Football fans who get together for tailgate parties and games may be considered an informal group.

Study and support groups. A **study group** focuses on learning information or skills; a **support group** focuses on learning to cope with various situations. Both are ongoing groups of peers who get together to help one another. These groups may be self-starting or may be sponsored by larger organizations. Meetings address the needs of their members, whether this means passing a course in biochemistry or surviving life with an alcoholic parent or mate.

Staff groups. A **staff group** consists of people who work together and meet periodically to discuss information and policies. Often the staff group uses both face-to-face and virtual meetings. In many organizations, face-to-face staff meetings have some systematic organization and approach; in others, they are loose and unstructured. When staff meetings are run badly, the people involved complain about how much time and energy are wasted. When staff meetings are run well, however, the group contributes to its members' satisfaction, cohesiveness, and quality of their work.

Task forces. A **task force**, which often is an ad hoc group, brings people together face to face or online to work on a specific problem. Members may be appointed to represent different interests or expertise within an organization or from multiple organizations. The task usually involves investigating an issue, gathering information, and making proposals that other groups may—or may not—implement. As a rule, such groups meet a number of times and have specific goals to accomplish.

Governance groups and committees. The gears of a democratic system are **governance groups and committees** that represent larger populations or organizations. These groups meet regularly to consider issues, gather information, make proposals, and report to larger groups. You may have participated in or observed such groups. If not, tune in to C-SPAN on cable television and watch your government at work, or attend a meeting of your student organization or faculty senate. The processes of these groups grind slowly and embody all the problems of group communication and bureaucracies, but they also are the way that we protect our rights and strive for justice in this society. Maybe we can't live with them, but we won't live without them, either.

Focus groups. A **focus group** pulls together representatives of a specific population who, with the help of a professional facilitator, discuss questions relating to anything from marketing a new product to evaluating a college curriculum for general education. During presidential campaigns, you occasionally see focus groups on television in which facilitators invite people of differing political persuasions to express their feelings about the candidates.

Self-managing teams. A **self-managing team** (SMT) is a group of people who work together in any area—in media production or on an assembly line, for example—and who are responsible for all aspects of their efforts. This includes everything from personnel decisions and budget allocations to project planning, coordination with other teams and departments, and assessment of their own success. A self-managing team may use a lot of e-communication as well as face-to-face communication for their work.

Management teams. A **management team** consists of managers from various departments and areas whose real and virtual meetings serve to coordinate their efforts, make decisions, allocate resources, and so on. Contemporary managers are responsible for coordinating various employee groups, including self-managing teams, who participate in directing their own activities.

Quality teams. A **quality team** is a group of employees, often drawn from different departments and areas of an organization, who work together to improve quality in some way. Quality teams are used at many levels of organizations, whether public or private, large or small, and they work in both real and virtual formats.

Project teams. A **project team** is a group of people with varied backgrounds and skills who work together to accomplish a specific task. A project could be developing a new product, getting it manufactured, and marketing it; moving an organization from one area to another; or establishing a corporation-wide training system.

Creative teams. In a **creative team**, people who have specific talents work together to do research, formulate ideas, and carry through an entire creative project. This approach is growing as creative work becomes more expensive and riskier to produce. A creative team might include a marketing research analyst, a public relations professional, a writer, an artist, a director, and a producer who design and produce a television commercial for a product or a political candidate. The high energy and sharp wit in one of the all-time most popular television series, *M*A*S*H*, resulted from the intensive, intimate teamwork among all members of that creative team (Hastings, Bixby, & Chaudhry-Lawton, 1986, p. 68).

Health care teams. Although you may or may not serve on a **health care team**, chances are that you and people you love will someday be the clients of one. Teams are a potent force in delivering care to patients by bringing together the entire range of professionals necessary for an individual's treatment and reha-bilitation. One team that we observed included geriatric, infectious disease, heart, and cancer specialists; nurses at various levels of specialization and care; physical, occupational, speech, and respiratory therapists; a nutritionist; a chaplain; and a social worker. Their tightly coordinated diagnoses and care saved the life of their patient. At the same time, each member of this team also served on other teams to provide care and rehabilitation to other patients. Their teamwork was the key to their success.

All these groups and teams have one thing in common: specific goals and ob-jectives or tasks toward which their members work. That's what this book is about: groups and teams that have tasks to accomplish.

TRENDS IN THE WORKPLACE

The workplace is changing fast as organizations respond to the vast social, economic, and technological pressures that affect their very lives. The baseline, of course, is competition, national and international. To compete, today's organizations need just the right information at just the right time to make just the right decision. The old days of memo blizzards and telephone tag up and down (but mostly down) the vertical hierarchy of management levels just won't meet the current needs.

In fact, not only do many teams do some or all of their work via electronic communication, but increasingly they work within virtual organizations. [Read about KPMG in Box 1.1.] "Touted as the answer to increased competition and demanding technological change, virtual organizations represent an approach to strategically managing business that is dependent on technology, opportunism, and excellence" (Ellingson & Wiethoff, 2002).

Both in virtual and in traditional structures, however, organizations are catching on that people perform better when they are full participants at every level of data gathering, problem solving, decision making, and assessment. This is because people involved in doing their own learning and making their own decisions are more satisfied and committed to the group's decisions.

Research has shown that when people know (probably more thoroughly than if they had worked alone) why and how a decision was reached, they achieve greater consensus and satisfaction (Tangirala & Ramanujam, 2008). That's why participative management, the quality movement, teamwork, and computer technologies are knocking down old structures and barriers in organizational culture.

Teams and Teamwork   The potential power of group communication was recognized long ago. Research going back more than fifty years has documented how effective cooperative groups can be. When competent, motivated, and trained individuals work as a team, they forge a more powerful instrument for problem solving than any one individual can provide. One study found that such groups outperformed their best member 97 percent of the time (Michaelson, Watson, & Black, 1989), and more recent research continues to support this premise (van Mierlo, Rutte, Vermunt, Kompier, & Doorewaard, 2007).

Diversity among members in age, gender, culture, expertise, political perspective, or level and status within the organization is one factor contributing to a team's increased performance. Heterogeneous teams profit from the various members' different perspectives, because the more diverse the members of a group, the more angles from which they can see a problem (Kruger & Mieszkowski, 1998). For instance, teams that consist of both males and females profit from the different approaches that men and women sometimes take toward group communication (Carson, Tesluk & Marrone, 2007), and both male and female members are more satisfied on the job when they work in mixed-gender instead of single-gender groups (Bligh, Pearce & Kohles, 2006).

Our own classrooms are extremely diverse. For example, the eighteen students in one class hailed from eleven different countries. We see firsthand how rich the results can be when classroom teams include differing races, cultures, backgrounds, genders, and orientations.

Communicating among diverse people, however, is a lot of work. The range of perspectives is only useful when members commit to making that extra effort to listen to one another's contributions. When teams listen to divergent viewpoints, they tend to find more and better strategies for solving problems—and to arrive at better solutions—compared with teams in which members listen primarily to the majority view (Staples & Zhao, 2006).

Of course, sometimes one individual can do a better job than a group in solving a problem. For example, if you have a math problem and just one mathematical genius available, don't bother with a group. Let the genius solve it. Or if a group is composed of members who are incompetent, unmotivated, and untrained in group communication skills, that group probably cannot do any better than its best member could alone.

Organizational consultant Sue DeWine (1994) goes so far as to say that building a team is sometimes inappropriate and even counterproductive (pp. 219–220). From her experiences, we have derived this list of times when a team approach is not going to work:

- When the work is better done by an individual
- When management, policies, or both are in the process of changing
- When a designated leader is controlling and insensitive to team needs
- When the organizational climate is hostile and competitive

Quality and Customer Satisfaction   Much teamwork today derives from the goals of **Quality Management** (QM). QM seeks the full involvement of employees throughout an organization to focus on providing high-quality goods and services that satisfy their customers' needs. Originally developed in the United States, these ideas were adapted by W. Edwards Deming to help Japan get back on its feet after World War II (Walton, 1986, pp. 10–21). The focus on quality in organizations initially brought people together in quality circles to identify areas for improvement as well as to create and implement plans.

As often occurs with new methods, QM advocates did not always know how to make their quality circles work, so the approach fell into some disrepute. General Motors and Xerox, among others, had trouble at the beginning. Katzenbach and Smith (1993) conclude, "More often than not, such failures lie in not adhering to the discipline of what makes teams successful" (p. 22). When members are properly prepared and trained, quality teams (and other organized approaches to teamwork) have succeeded in developing quality organizations and in improving customer satisfaction (Bligh et al., 2006).

Information and Technology   We should note here that most of your group experiences probably have been face to face, and the knowledge and skills you will develop through this course are essential to such face-to-face group communication in any context. They also will provide a foundation for the many group and team projects in which you will combine electronic assistance with actual meeting time, as well as for the virtual teamwork that you will most likely do. You will need the skills for operating in and adapting to these varied contexts. In today's global environment, virtual teams provide organizations with the ability to save travel costs, take advantage of global talent, and create new products and services. In 2001, it was estimated that 8.4 million employees in the United States alone were members of virtual teams (Ahuja & Galvin, 2001) and by 2008 that number had grown to nearly 20 million (Bergiel, Bergiel & Balsmeier, 2008).

Probably you already have some—or perhaps a lot of—experience with electronic discussion groups, chat rooms, research sites, and so on. You may have

| BOX 1.2 | **BUSINESS TEAMS WIN PROFESSIONAL AWARDS FOR EXCELLENCE** |

How valuable are teams in American business? Several professional societies hold annual contests to determine which organizations have the most effective work groups.

In the 2007 American Society for Quality contest for team excellence awards, Boeing Company's five-person C17 Stuffed Tailcone team won the gold award. This team innovated methods for solving unsafe working conditions while installing the tailcones and, in the process, improved quality and lowered costs for the company. In that same year, three teams tied for the silver award: two other Boeing Company teams—a six-person team that solved a problem with jet fuel tanks and an eight-person team that improved workers' safety on the job—and a five-person team in the Suncoast Region Department of Children and Families. This Florida social services team developed, piloted, and implemented an electronic imaging system for storage and retrieval of the paperwork generated by the region's 190,000 public assistance cases. The team saved $269,816 the first year and more than $300,000 annually thereafter. Finally, a CSX Transportation team won the bronze award by saving the railroad company $29 million worth of diesel fuel—that's 14 million gallons—by developing more efficient use of idle locomotives.

A team from Progress Energy, a *Fortune* 250 company with headquarters in Raleigh, North Carolina, won the 2007 HDI team excellence award. HDI is the world's largest association for information technology service and support professionals. Other nominees included teams from Automatic Data Processing Inc., Cablevision Systems Corporation, Delta Dental, Discover Financial Services, Monsanto, Nemours, Novell, Perot Systems, Sprint, and Verizon Wireless.

And the list goes on and on.

Source: World Conference on Quality and Improvement, http://www.wcqi.asq.org/team-competition/team-winners-2007; and HDI Team Excellence Awards, http://www.thinkhdi.com/hdi.aspx?c=186

worked on projects with several people at different locations, using e-mail or setting up sites for your exchanges of ideas and information. Or you may have taken or currently are taking an online course—even this one. Not long ago the idea of learning such skills as public speaking or group communication online was inconceivable to folks in the communication discipline. Today it's happening and apparently very effectively, too.

There are other ways of using electronic assistance for group projects as well. One is in computer-assisted meetings with programs known as **groupware**. Opper and Fersko-Weiss (1992) defined *groupware* as "any information system designed to enable groups to work together electronically" (p. 4). With this kind of assistance, teams can do everything from scheduling meetings to making decisions, because the software allows members to organize data, generate and analyze ideas, as well as to plan and design solutions. Groupware helps create a computer-mediated team culture (Alge, Wiethoff & Klein, 2003). That's an important notion: that the technology and the team processes are bound to alter each other. Inevitably, these changes will affect both organizational and team cultures.

Technology has certainly modified the way people interact at work, even changing the meaning of "work relationships." Even the term *workplace* suddenly becomes metaphorical, because your "virtual" workplace may be defined more by electronic communication than by physical boundaries. You may have face-to-face

President Obama relied heavily on the collective expertise of his economic advisors during his presidential campaign.

meetings, but you also may exchange information at any time through your computer (linked to your organization's local area network) or by communicating with teammates around the world. Alternatively, your team could meet in an **electronic meeting room** (EMR), which is set up for remote teleconferencing through computer, video, or telephone connections (or some combination) and for face-to-face groupware meetings. Or, you and your teammates could create personal avatars and meet in a virtual world (www.secondlife.com).

You also might confer by video with another team, gathered in a similar room in another city or another country. With desktop **videoconferencing**, your team could be spread across several states, using Google documents to collaborate and chat in real time about a project or report and seeing the facial expressions of your teammates as they discuss your work.

You may notice that these technologies allow groups to expand the typical boundaries of time and space. Your communication may be a **synchronous meeting** or real-time communication, in which members communicate at the same time through face-to-face exchanges, computer, telephone, or videoconferencing, or it may be an **asynchronous meeting**, in which you and your teammates enter and review computer messages at different times. Your team may meet in the same room, or you may be spread across the world. As you can imagine, these technologies require both skill and flexibility in communication.

KEY CONCEPTS FOR YOUR TEAMWORK

Your work in this course—and your effectiveness later—rests in part on your understanding some key concepts used in this text. All these ideas will be explored in greater detail in later chapters, but a few basic terms and definitions will help to get you started.

GROUPS AND TEAMS

A *group* is more than a bunch of people in the same place, and a *team* is more than a group. There are three important issues in understanding groups and teams: the nature of the *relationships* among members, the *processes* that they use, and the *purposes* for which they are together. If you brainstormed terms that defined each of these aspects, you might start with:

> *Relationships.* Interacting, influencing, sharing, cooperating, interdepending
>
> *Processes.* Communicating, collaborating, organizing, leading, supporting, developing, analyzing, thinking, creating
>
> *Purposes.* Goals, vision, tasks, activities, outcomes

You can probably think of many more, but these are a beginning. A group may have varying kinds and degrees of each component, and its purposes may range from having a good time together to creating a plan for universal peace. A classic definition of a **group** is "*two or more persons who are interacting with one another in such a manner that each person influences and is influenced by each other person*" (Shaw, 1981, p. 8).

Is a team different from a group? Yes, according to Deborah Mackin (2008), consultant and author of teambuilding books. She pinpoints decision-making norms as one way to differentiate the two. "In a group, the dominant viewpoint is represented; in a team, multiple, diverse viewpoints are represented. Decisions in a group are made by voting or implied agreement; decisions on a team are typically made by consensus." She continues, "To achieve a real team is difficult and time-consuming. There is no magic bullet that will transform a group into a team overnight. It takes time to develop the skills to work well together and understand how to solve problems and make decisions effectively."

We will discuss this topic further in Chapter 4 when we talk about building a team. For now, however, it is enough to consider some characteristics that help to create a team:

> *A team is a diverse group of people.* In a team, more than in a casual group, specific and different resources and abilities are needed from each individual to accomplish the task.
>
> *Members share leadership responsibility.* All members help the group to interact and make progress on the task at hand. Because of the diversity of contributions and the specificity of the task, every member, whether there is a designated leader or not, must guide the team.

A team creates an identity. Much more than an ordinary group, a team develops a particular self-image that becomes a cohesive and motivating force for its members.

Team efforts are interconnected. The team continually weaves and coordinates the contributions of each member to develop a tighter energy and focus than in ordinary groups.

Members work to achieve mutually defined goals. Members of a team communicate intensively to develop a consensus on their goals and how to achieve them. Larson and LaFasto (1989) count a "clear, elevating goal" as a distinguishing feature of a successful team.

A team works within the context of other groups and systems. A team both affects and is affected by the context, environment, and system within which it works. Although this often is true of other groups as well, the relationships among the team, the task, and the other systems are more likely to be critical to the team's successful functioning.

Putting all these factors together produces a working definition: A team is *a diverse group of people who share leadership responsibility for creating a group identity in an interconnected effort to achieve mutually defined goals within the context of other groups and systems.* To visualize this definition in a simplified form, look at the model in Figure 1.1. To simplify these concepts, we assumed a team with only three members, although most teams are larger than this. Each individual focuses on a goal that all the members have set together. To reach that goal, the members communicate and work together through task and transactional processes, which are defined and discussed in the following section.

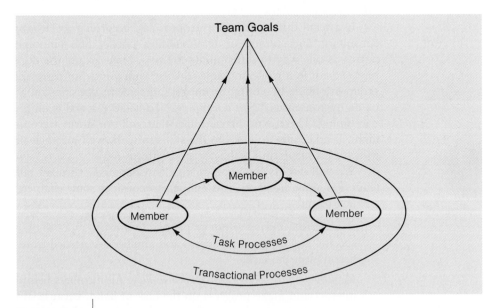

FIGURE 1.1

Model of a three-member team using transactional and task processes to reach team goals.

TRANSACTIONAL AND TASK PROCESSES

Transactional and task processes are essentially what this book is about; they make the relationships among people work, which enables them to achieve their goals. Transactional and task processes focus on the give and take of communicating in task groups and teams. Traditionally, group theory uses the terms *group-maintenance* and *task-maintenance* to describe messages. These terms are similar to transactional and task processes, but this idea of group versus task implies that communication occurs along two distinct tracks. We prefer, therefore, the idea of transactional processes as involving task as well as interactive messages, feedback, and adaptations that members go through to establish meanings about themselves and their relationships to each other.

Transactional processes are give-and-take interactions that involve concurrent communication about three possible topics: messages about individuals, messages about the team, and messages about the task processes. In transactional processes, members use verbal and nonverbal communication to develop a team. Positive transactional processes create a climate in which members are comfortable taking the necessary risks in communication to share information and ideas, to develop new ideas and approaches with others, to analyze ideas, and to make decisions. Poor transactional processes, however, create an uncomfortable climate that diverts the task processes with tides of negative messages.

Task processes are specific interactions that focus on the job at hand. These include gathering and sharing information; analyzing problems; designing solutions; analyzing and testing evidence and reasoning; and making, implementing, and evaluating decisions. In task processes, the roles and functions of the members are focused on the work.

Let's look at the relationship between transactional and task messages with an example. Your team is to consider whether the college should build a new student center. Sean has brought in some statistics, gleaned from a local newspaper, that indicate college populations are shrinking. The team needs to decide (1) whether the statistics are valid and (2) whether the statistics apply to the team's goal and, if so, how. That discussion moves through a task process.

The transactional process, however, determines how members interact when analyzing the statistics. It affects how supported or defensive Sean feels, which, in turn, affects the team's ensuing transactions. Suppose Rhonda says to Sean, "You want us to believe something printed in that rag?" Todd then says, "Sean, is that the best you can do?" At this point, Sean might snap back, "Hey, I don't see anybody else with data!" What then?

Although the topic of these comments is Sean's information and as such they relate directly to the group's task, the messages also carry other implications— about Sean and his competence—so Sean reacts to those implications by defending himself. The transactional processes, therefore, have made the task processes ineffective. Task processes are a specific, focused, and interactive set of behaviors, but they work within the flow of transactional processes (see Figure 1.1). Both transactional and task processes rely on all members' leadership, role taking, and communication skills. At the same time, these processes make possible every interaction and accomplishment of the team.

COMMUNICATION IN GROUPS AND TEAMS

If transactional processes make it possible to accomplish task processes, then communication makes it possible for transactional processes to work. A useful way of defining **communication** is *the process of using verbal and nonverbal cues to negotiate a mutually acceptable meaning between two or more people within a particular context and environment.*

Process suggests that understandings constantly develop and change through transactions. When people communicate, they engage with a dynamic, moving set of variables that have been interacting and will continue to interact. If you had a fight at home, for example, that may color your transactions with your team.

Verbal and nonverbal cues are given through language and voice, body, face, space, touch, and other personal cues. Sharing the same language does not ensure understanding, however, because each person has different connotations for even simple words and gestures that come from his or her own personal, identity group, or cultural experiences. For example, suppose that you introduce yourself to a new team member while looking her in the eye and touching her arm as you say, "I'm glad you've joined us—this is an exciting project." To you, this may be open and welcoming, but she may have been raised to believe that direct eye contact and touching are invasions. To top it off, she also may think the project is boring. You speak to her in her language, but the way that you put the message and the way that she "hears" it may be very different.

Negotiate a mutually acceptable meaning between two or more people indicates that communication is *not* the transfer of meaning or information from one person to another. It has been said that discourse is a field of contest, that communication is largely about difference and not about "sameness." So negotiating a mutually acceptable meaning involves people giving and taking bits of meaning to and from one another in a dialogue until each can work with an agreed-on interpretation. A mutually acceptable meaning, therefore, does not imply that people's perceptions will match perfectly but that dialogue can lead them to an understanding all parties can accept.

A particular context means that any communication is defined in terms of circumstances and situations. "How's the job going?" has a different meaning if you ask it of someone who just landed his or her first big job or of someone who expects to be fired soon.

Environment refers to the physical, social, and emotional conditions within which the communication occurs. "How's the job going?" is different in the physical setting of a crowded elevator and in an intimate, private office. Equally, the social and emotional climate affects the nuances of a message. For example, this same question may be whispered out of the boss's earshot in a workplace permeated with distrust, or it may be shouted across the room in a workplace where openness and friendliness are the norms.

Take all these communication variables and processes, visualize them as being compounded by the numbers of people involved, and you have communication in a group. If you make a statement, there are as many possible interpretations as there are possible interactions between and among people in the group. Add to that the influence that each person in the group may have on a given individual's understanding of your message, and you begin to see how very difficult negotiating a consensus of understanding can be. A classic quantitative analysis of possible relationships in a group, starting with one relationship between two individuals, found that there are 966 communication relationships in a group of seven people (Kephart, 1950). Even these numbers do not convey the full complexity of the situation, however, because each individual in the group brings in and also takes out information, opinions, attitudes, beliefs, values, and interpretations both to and from other individuals and groups. The real number of potential interactions truly is incalculable.

RISK IN GROUP AND TEAM COMMUNICATION

Communication often presents a dilemma between need and fear. One side of this dilemma is that human beings absolutely need to communicate for physical as well as emotional survival. The opposite side, however, is that when you communicate, you take a risk. The risk may be very small, but it's still there. For example, "I have to tell her the meeting time's been changed. She's going to be mad at me." This dilemma may not present heavy consequences, but it still presents a risk. (After all, maybe you really hate being snapped at.)

Sometimes the risk is greater. A person who speaks up may risk rejection, ridicule, and perhaps even failure. You may want very much to speak up for what you believe in, but you may fear others will think you're silly—or dumb—or whatever. So you keep silent, or perhaps you phrase your thoughts in vague, ambiguous terms. That way, if you feel rejected, you can back off with minimal damage. That's one response to the dilemma.

In a group, however, the extent of the risk is compounded by the number of people and the possible interpretations and interactions that can result from communication. If one person might reject your ideas, what might seven people do? This personal dilemma becomes critically important to transactional and task processes because it may cause a person to censor what she or he says—and what that person censors may be important.

This is one problem with groups: It is much too easy for members to talk themselves into ignoring issues—or even into rationalizing immoral or unethical choices. If members fear rejection or ridicule and, therefore, are so afraid to address these issues that they keep silent—or, worse, pretend to agree with the majority—then the team may make mistakes that the members will later regret.

Understanding this dilemma, both in yourself and in others, can help you in two ways. First, it will help you to comprehend and have patience with the risky give-and-take process of negotiating a shared meaning. Second, it will help you to ensure that transactional processes enable people to think for themselves, take risks, and express their thoughts freely.

SYSTEMS AND SUBSYSTEMS

A team usually works within an organization and with other units, and this interdependency affects everything the team does. A good way to understand these effects is in terms of **systems theory**, which was first introduced by Ludwig Von Bertalanffy to explain how biological systems interrelate. This theory also provides an excellent way to look at how teams work in organizations and communities (Ancona, 1990).

Systems theory is easy to understand by applying it to a family. Each member of the family is one intrapersonal system, or a **subsystem** of that family. Each individual subsystem plays various roles in the greater family system. The mother or father may have primary responsibility for decision making, but other members may influence decisions and family interactions as well. The members are interdependent. They work for mutual goals, support each other, and have both conflicts and problems. The family has unwritten definitions of how relationships, responsibilities, power, and influence are conducted—and by whom.

Outside of this family system are other systems and subsystems—other families, friends, schools, workplaces, the community—to which family members relate. Influences both to and from those other systems are carried by family members as they interact with other members of their family system.

Essentially, this is what systems theory describes. Applied to a team, it shows us the system within the team, its relationships with other teams and systems, and its relationships with its parent organization as well as with outside organizations.

These internal and external relationships are easier to understand in terms of the following six concepts:

1. *Interrelationships and interdependency.* A decision made within any part of a system may affect other parts of that system. If the decision is made without considering those relationships, then the effect may be negative. For example, suppose that the marketing department distributes product samples without consulting the production department. As a result, the production workers could be annoyed when inventory suddenly plummets without explanation.

2. *Linking communication.* Relationships among subsystems are both created and maintained by the communication flow. Each unit depends on the others for information, and all units interact in processing ideas, making decisions, and building relationships. Without linking communication, each unit would function independently, not interdependently.

3. *Open systems.* Information, ideas, and influences flow into and out of the system both from and to other systems and the environment. Efforts to keep the system closed, or exclusive, only make that system insensitive to its environment and insulated from the information it needs. Closed-off systems often go awry and cannot be repaired, and the consequences can be disastrous.

4. *Norms.* Accepted ways of doing things govern both systems and subsystems. People live by norms as if they were rules: members of the system know when and how to behave and when and how to communicate because of the norms in the group. For example, a friend you've invited to your political task force asks, "How should I dress?" You know the answer to the question, because you know how the group dresses. It's a norm.

5. *Roles.* **Roles** are ways of behaving or contributing that individual members use in the transactional and task processes of the team. Roles may be positive, thus facilitating behaviors, or they may be negative, thus blocking behaviors. The unit or subsystem also may have roles that it serves within the larger system. You may serve your team by bringing data, helping others to compromise, or using humor to relieve tension, all of which are roles that help the transactional and task processes. You also may act as a contact person for an outside identity group or serve as a public relations source for local newspapers.

6. *Cybernetic processes.* Feedback and assessment methods help open systems with their own development and improvement. **Cybernetic processes** are like that used by a thermostat to assess whether the temperature is correct and, if not, to adjust it to the right level. These processes are different from simply reading the temperature (as a thermometer does). Another analogy might be receiving back a paper with only a grade on it as opposed to one that also has comments and suggestions for improving the next one. The grade is a thermometer; the comments are the cybernetic thermostat (that is, of course, if you use the information for improvement).

A TEAM PROCESSES MODEL

Remember Figure 1.1, the model of a team? How that team acts as a subsystem of a larger system is illustrated in Figure 1.2 (page 20).

The three cone-shaped figures represent separate teams within an organization. (Remember that each team consists of members using both transactional and task processes to reach a mutual goal.) Each team has a goal that works toward the vision of the parent organization, and each team functions within the organizational culture. As the arrows leading in and out of the teams indicate, teams communicate back and forth with one another and with their parent organization.

The arrows to and from the government, community, other organizations, and other people indicate the influence that continually flows back and forth between outside systems, the teams, and the parent organization. Any given organization may have many teams, each interacting with departments, management, and numerous outside systems. You can see from this illustration how important communication is to making teamwork effective.

PREPARATION FOR YOUR TEAMWORK

So far, this chapter has introduced essential concepts regarding groups and teams. Now, however, it's time to get started on your actual work. If you skipped the Preface, please go back and read those sections outlining the philosophical and learning premises of this book and describing its main features, including the exercises, case studies, and special boxes. This overview will make using this book both easier and more productive.

With that bit of homework done, it's now time to start your group experiences in this class. These should be good experiences, but we recognize that you and other members may feel some anxiety at the beginning. Richmond and McCroskey

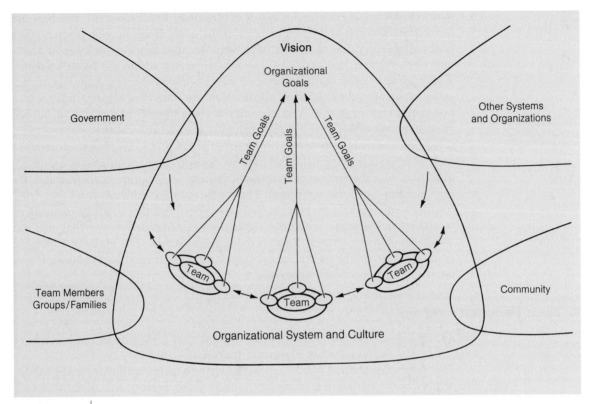

FIGURE 1.2

Model of teams as subsystems interacting with the larger system and with other systems and subsystems.

(1995) report that almost 95 percent of the population confess to "being scared about communicating with a person or group at some point in their lives" (p. 46). There is some risk involved as well, as we pointed out earlier; in this case, you're about to embark on group exercises, or perhaps a project, in which you and other people will be interdependent in achieving course credit and grades.

To minimize the risk and maximize the chances of a great experience, we suggest that you start by thinking about transactional and task processes. Those processes begin the moment you and your group sit down together. A group that meets just once may have only 5 minutes to make connections among the members, but even those 5 minutes are important. For a team that will meet for weeks—or perhaps for months or even years—taking enough time and effort to get to know one another is essential. We suggest that you make a conscientious effort to move the group through a getting-acquainted process, which goes like this:

1. *Start the process.* If the new group seems to be moving too fast toward its task, you can provide leadership by suggesting that everyone take a few

minutes for introductions. Say something like, "Could we take time to find out something about one another? It probably will help us work together."

2. *Learn one another's names.* A name, after all, is the first step toward seeing another person as a distinct individual. This may seem obvious, but how many times in how many classes have you come to the end of the term still designating someone as "You know—the smart senior who sits over there in the front?" (If you had gotten to know the "smart senior," she or he might have helped you with those sticky concepts that knocked your grade down a full point.)

3. *Create a dialogue.* You can take some of the stiffness and formality out of the discussion by asking people questions and showing some interest in them. Start, of course, with basic information, such as where you're from, what you do, and what your major is. This can lead to people disclosing bits of personal information—likes and dislikes, attitudes, and opinions—that begin building interpersonal credibility and trust.

4. *Identify special strengths.* Each individual brings particular strengths to the group. These may be everything from access to resources to interests and talents relating to the task to skills in research, analysis, organization, writing, creative projects—almost anything. Many individual attributes emerge naturally during the getting-acquainted discussion, but it's also possible to raise the subject by saying something like, "Why don't we each make a list of what we think we can provide? For example, I have some contacts with people who can give us information on the subject." Exploring individual possibilities will help the members to recognize what they can do early enough to actually do it. It's infuriating to reach the day of a project presentation and then hear a teammate groan, "I just realized I could have made a great visual for our presentation on my brother's computer." Too late! So explore the members' strengths early in the game.

5. *Share your expectations.* Individuals start out with a set of personal feelings about the team and its task. These may relate to how much time they have to put into it and how important the work is to them, their own particular needs or wants, and their expectations about how they want to interact.

These feelings and expectations often reflect values that affect the transactional and task processes again and again. An early sense of what people believe and value provides a starting point for members to understand one another and to communicate about value-laden issues. At this early stage, exploring values can focus on questions such as: What do you think is important about the issues facing the team? What kinds of ethical issues will we face? How will we deal with them? By tentatively exploring these basic issues, members can begin to understand one another's perspectives. This does not mean that everyone will see values in precisely the same light, however. In fact, a diverse membership ensures that everyone will not. What it does mean is that later, when the team inevitably faces some conflict, the knowledge of one another's values will make it easier to manage that conflict.

Through this process, sometimes you can get an idea of each member's **personal agenda**, his or her individual goals and objectives, for the experience. Often, these agendas are hidden, based on motives that the individual would rather not talk about but that will affect every interaction in the team. People rightfully hesitate to disclose private motives too early; however, some understanding of personal agendas helps your team to meet its members' needs and to achieve its goals. One of our students, at the first meeting of her project team for the semester, looked her teammates in the eyes and said, "I want an A out of this project. I hope you all do, too." Naturally, everyone agreed, and knowing this member's personal agenda helped later when the team confronted problems with two members who were slacking off on their share of the work.

Be aware, however, that very often people want to keep their personal agendas private. Sometimes people aren't even fully aware of their own personal agendas. For example, one of us worked on a team in which one member blocked every idea. After months of frustration and conflicting undercurrents, the team finally found out that he was angry at the organization because he had not received a deserved promotion. Talk about relationships among systems and subsystems! When we got this man's issue out in the open, the team members were empathic and supportive—and he stopped throwing boulders in our way and started participating as a team member. He probably couldn't or wouldn't have discussed this issue earlier, but if he had, we would have saved a lot of wasted time and energy.

To the extent possible, an early discussion of individual issues and expectations can begin the transactional processes that allow a team to meet both individual and team needs throughout the life of the team. How do you do this at the beginning? First, suggest that team members discuss what each person wants to accomplish from the experience. Second, understand and state your own agenda as openly as you can. Finally, listen carefully to the other team members and ask intelligent, nonthreatening questions.

Here's a checklist to help you make your first meeting a solid beginning:

1. Be interested in each other.
   - Get acquainted.
   - Find areas of compatibility and interest.
2. Assign someone to take notes.
   - Summarize any key decisions the group makes about its tasks, needs, and scheduling.
   - Plan to have a copy of these notes for each member at the next meeting.
   - Plan to rotate note taking among members at future meetings.
3. Take time to figure out what the group is supposed to do.
   - Identify the task or goal.
   - Determine the assignment's learning objectives, or agree that you will discover them from the experience.
4. Plan a systematic approach to reaching your goal.
   - Estimate how much time you will need.
   - Decide what steps you will take.
5. Plan ahead if the assignment will take more than one meeting.
   - Exchange telephone numbers and schedules.
   - Assign work among members.
   - Set the next meeting time and place.

6. Help each other to meet your goals.
- Fulfill your personal responsibility.
- Be on time, prepare materials, and share ideas.
- Support each other in the work.

SUMMARY

In both your private and your work life, you will participate in group and team communication, both in face-to-face, real meetings and in virtual teams or groups. Your experiences, personal preferences, characteristics, culture, and gender all may affect how you feel about working with others, and the skills you develop will influence the success of your participation and leadership. Groups can involve frustration and conflict, commitment of resources, and pressure to conform (possibly even pressure to unethical and harmful positions), but they also can have enormous advantages.

You may work in a wide variety of groups and teams. The power of teamwork is that it takes advantage of the diversity of group members to develop creativity and exploration, encourage logical and ethical examination of questions, and achieve good solutions with high member involvement, group identity, and commitment. Trends in the workplace are moving toward more and more technology, including the development of virtual organizations and virtual teams as well as on-site real work teams and self-managing teams. This

emphasis developed because, through technology, organizations can produce better, faster, and more economically sound results, and because it's known that through participatory management and cooperative teamwork groups can achieve better quality, maximize the participation of diverse members, and lead to greater employee satisfaction and commitment.

A team is different from a group in that a team is more focused and its members are more interdependent, thus achieving outcomes greater than the sum of the individuals' abilities. Groups and teams both use transactional processes, which communicate about persons, the task, and the team itself, and task processes, which focus on achieving the goals. The team is best understood as being part of a system that involves interdependency, interaction, and influence among subsystems as well as among outside systems.

At the beginning, any group or team, whether on-site or online, needs to establish connections and working understandings to develop positive transactional and task processes for developing their relationships and achieving their goals.

Exercises

1. Look at the advertisements for career positions in a large, metropolitan newspaper or a national publication such as the *Wall Street Journal* or *National Business Employment Weekly*. Identify those advertisements that include phrases like "works well with others," "team player," "excellent oral and written communication," "leadership ability." Bring some examples of these to your group, and discuss with your teammates what specific attitudes and abilities these employers seek. Then, based on the

introduction to this course that you have received from the Preface and Chapter 1, identify which of these attributes you might be able to develop through your work in this class.

2. Think of the best and worst groups that you've ever experienced (work, school, church, sports, and so on) and rate them on Form 1.1. Then, with a few other students, discuss what common characteristics you found that distinguish "best" and "worst" groups. Together, create a list of the five to

ten most important characteristics for group success. Report these to the class.

3. Form a research team to discover how groups are used in local organizations. You can do this as an on-site meeting group or you can set up a virtual team if you have computer access. Two sites that can help you create your team are www.groupvine.com or www.intranets.com.

   With several other students, make a list of local organizations that might use small groups or teams (businesses, churches, communities, schools, and so on). Have each member take responsibility for contacting one organization to find out if and how it uses groups and teams (approximately how many, their purposes, the way they function, and so on). Report to your team in one week, share your information, and then report what you've learned to the class.

4. Compeer Corporation, a management communication consulting firm, is planning to open its first international office in Tokyo. Your management team is to appoint a project team and charge it with three basic tasks: deciding where in Tokyo to put the office, creating the office, and establishing the initial contacts and organizational scheme to get the office under way.

   Draft a list of qualifications and personal characteristics that members of the project group should possess. Also, speculate as to how the project team fits into and relates with the other systems. Discuss your decisions with the class.

5. Consider your experiences in groups and teams (sports, work, community, church, family). Make a list of what you believe that you do well in transactional processes and in task processes. Then make a list of what you would like to improve in your group communication. Keep this list, and as the semester wears on, check back to see how you're doing.

FORM 1.1 | BEST AND WORST GROUPS ASSESSMENT

Think about your experiences (past or present) in groups or teams. Decide on the *best* and the *worst* group experiences you've had. Then check whether you agree or disagree with each statement as it applies to the best group and to the worst group.

	Best Group		Worst Group	
	Agree	Disagree	Agree	Disagree
1. Members were committed.	☐	☐	☐	☐
2. Good results came of conflicts.	☐	☐	☐	☐
3. Members listened to each other.	☐	☐	☐	☐
4. Members were equal regardless of sex, culture, race, or status.	☐	☐	☐	☐
5. Everyone participated.	☐	☐	☐	☐
6. People could disagree without fear.	☐	☐	☐	☐
7. Members liked each other.	☐	☐	☐	☐
8. The group discussed its goals.	☐	☐	☐	☐
9. Members helped one another.	☐	☐	☐	☐
10. Each member took responsibility.	☐	☐	☐	☐
11. The leader guided the group's processes.	☐	☐	☐	☐
12. Meetings were organized.	☐	☐	☐	☐
13. The group got information that it needed.	☐	☐	☐	☐
14. Members used humor.	☐	☐	☐	☐
15. Members considered questions of good/ bad, right/wrong.	☐	☐	☐	☐

"I'm not a leader—I'm a follower!"
Wrong. You have a leadership role, even when you're not
"the leader."

YOUR TEAMWORK RESPONSIBILITY

Sharing Leadership

2

CHAPTER CONTENTS

The Meaning of Leadership

Your Success and Your Leadership
- Short-Term Success
- Long-Term Success

Leadership and Personal Qualities
- Preparation
- Involvement
- Credibility
- Principles
- Adaptability
- Responsibility

Leadership and Teamwork
- Roles People Play
- Team Processes
- Obstacles to Leadership

Leadership and Ethics
- Ethical Dilemmas and Conflicts
- Ethical Issues for Teams

Leadership Development
- Developing Credibility
- Building Confidence

Summary

Exercises

You may not be the designated leader, and you may not want to be. Still, you have a personal responsibility for providing leadership to your team. Imagine you are on a jury that must decide an accused person's guilt or innocence. The foreman and two other jurors loudly assert the guilt of the accused. You're disturbed by the foreman's—the leader's—railroading, however, and you believe some of the evidence was biased. Even so, because you are not the leader, you raise neither of these issues. No one else raises them, either. All of you go along with what you assume is the majority view. In the end, a possibly innocent person is convicted because the members did not share leadership to make sure the process was just.

Is this an extreme example? Yes. Could it happen? Again, the answer is yes. That's why this chapter is so important. It lays the foundation for leadership—leadership that can avert disappointment, frustration, and even guilt from bad team experiences and wrong decisions. As a good team member, you can gain the understanding and skills necessary to help teams move through their work and ethical decisions with both credibility and confidence.

Developing that foundation begins with knowing the difference between being the leader and providing leadership. In a later chapter, we will develop the duties, theories, and research relating to the role of designated leader. For now, we think it is essential for every member of a group or team to recognize how sharing leadership affects the experience and the effectiveness of a group project. Your own leadership develops as you focus on your responsibilities to integrate ethical principles into team processes and decisions and as you consciously practice the necessary skills.

Through your work in this chapter, you will enhance your ability to:

1. Perceive team leadership as your responsibility
2. Understand how your leadership affects the success of both you and your team
3. See how your leadership helps your team with transactional and task processes
4. Identify and adapt roles for better leadership
5. Understand the qualities that contribute to effective leadership
6. Use your leadership to ensure ethical group processes and decisions
7. Understand how your leadership relates to your credibility
8. Begin developing your credibility, confidence, and leadership effectiveness

THE MEANING OF LEADERSHIP

Yes, it's true that many, if not most, groups have a designated leader. It's also true that groups and teams that function well have members who share leadership, consciously or otherwise. It's better to be conscious about what you're doing.

What is leadership? We define **leadership** as *verbal and nonverbal communication that facilitates a team's transactional and task processes in achieving members' and the team's needs and goals.* This definition recognizes that communication is how leadership is exercised, that transactional and task processes are how needs and goals are met, and that both individual members' interests and the team's interests are important.

In today's teams, leadership is seldom the responsibility of only one person. The complexity of team assignments makes it difficult for a single person to have sufficient knowledge and experience to successfully manage all elements of the work (Day, Gronn & Salas, 2004). Moreover, most teams are formed because members bring specific knowledge and expertise, and such individuals are likely to prefer to work autonomously rather than under constant supervision (DeNisi, Hitt & Jackson, 2003). You share leadership when your communication facilitates your team's processes, thus providing motivation, direction, orientation, and member satisfaction.

Let's begin by clarifying the difference between *providing leadership* and *being the leader*. Providing leadership is a set of behaviors; being the leader is a position. Leadership must be developed and exercised, but the title of "leader" can be elected or conferred. Providing leadership implies responsibility and facilitation. Being the leader may depend on some degree of status and power.

Of course, designated leaders should provide leadership. Sometimes they do, sometimes they don't. As one CEO explains, "Every team has a natural leader—and often that leader is not a team's official manager" (Mitchell, 1999, p. 178). Even a really good designated leader, however, cannot do it alone. Good teamwork requires every member's leadership in transactional and task processes. When people simply follow a leader because of his or her title, they may abdicate their responsibility for what happens, and this can lead to stupid—and sometimes even harmful—decisions and actions. Businesses and bureaucracies often initiate time-wasting and people-frustrating policies because no one dares to point out weaknesses when those policies are proposed. Followers do what "Simon says." At a far more deadly level, lynch mobs and riots occur when forceful leaders emerge to exploit people's baser motives and inclinations to follow mindlessly.

To prevent such consequences, every member of a group or a team must be responsible for what happens—both in the members' interactions and in group decisions. What, then, do we mean by leadership? What are the qualities that contribute to leadership? What are your responsibilities as a team member? How do you effectively share leadership of your group?

YOUR SUCCESS AND YOUR LEADERSHIP

Your leadership is important both to your short-term success with your team and to your long-term success in your life and career.

SHORT-TERM SUCCESS

In the short term, you may simply want to get through a project as efficiently and as smoothly as possible. If you take responsibility for ensuring the team works effectively, you will avoid frustration. You also will gain satisfaction from being part of a mutually supportive, creatively functioning team that gets results.

One of our students, who was irritated with teammates not doing their job, said, "I used to think I was a follower. From now on, I'm using my own leadership so I don't have to go through this frustration anymore." After she made that decision, her team improved, the project turned out well, and her grade was an A.

When your team wins, you win. Almost any work group serves some larger organization or the community; therefore, your team may have at least three sets of goals. Some of those goals serve the larger interests of the organization, some serve the group itself, and some serve you personally.

For example, if you are part of a creative team designing an advertising campaign, your client's goal obviously is to sell the product. As part of an agency, your creative team shares the client's goal and, furthermore, would like to impress other clients through this particular campaign's success. Each team member also has personal goals to make the client and the agency happy and, by so doing, to further his or her career, get a raise, increase self-esteem, and possibly reach many other goals as well. When you share the team's leadership, you can help to achieve all levels of success.

LONG-TERM SUCCESS

In the long term, exercising leadership builds a foundation for your future effectiveness in teams and career opportunities. Almost every request for a letter of recommendation that we, as faculty, receive includes a space for evaluating the leadership, interpersonal, and communication skills of the applicant. Corporations, businesses, service institutions, and graduate schools are interested in any activity for which you actually served as the leader, but that isn't what they mean by "leadership skills."

People who might hire or admit you to their graduate program are looking for a leadership orientation—in other words, for motivation, thinking, and communication skills that you can offer. Ironically, your entry-level career position may provide you with little opportunity to exercise those skills, but they do become apparent in how you work with others, problem-solve, and take responsibility. When you demonstrate these skills, you are marked for advancement and opportunity.

The working world emphasizes leadership so much that many organizations put potential managers into simulated team situations and observe how they perform. A candidate's leadership thus becomes a key to his or her advancement. Just ask the people cited in Box 2.1. What qualities help you to provide leadership, even—especially—as an equal member of a group?

LEADERSHIP AND PERSONAL QUALITIES

Alas, the qualities of leadership do not always reside in the person designated as leader—this makes it that much more important for members of teams to possess and exercise those qualities. In real life, people with dubious qualifications may be designated as leaders, and sometimes situational influences within an organizational culture determine the choice. For example, seniority is key in many organizations, because unions and guilds guard fairness.

Organizational politics also can impact the choice of a leader. People may choose one person because she has political leverage, or they may choose another to reward him for previous favors to someone in power. A team also may elect someone with connections to influential people in the hope they will then support

BOX 2.1	LOOKING FOR LEADERS IN "STRETCH ASSIGNMENTS"

PPG Industries, a leading international manufacturer of coatings, glass, fiberglass, and chemicals, began a program called Aggressive Career Management in 2001. The program facilitates the development of leaders within the corporation, very often through stretch assignments. In these assignments, employees with leadership potential are promoted to positions of greater responsibility than these employees had previously. As Harvette Dixon, PPG's director of Learning and Development, observed: "We need multitalented people. We need broad thinkers. We need people who can move across business units. Most of our 15 business units are global. We need people who can navigate through that complex business portfolio."

Bruce Nelson learned firsthand the challenges of a stretch assignment. His background was in sales, transportation, and logistics for PPG's commodity chemical business, but he was promoted to director of Business and Operations for Matthews Paint,

one of PPG's coating businesses. Nelson reflected on his stretch assignment: "At the end of the day, what I do impacts people's careers. My learning can't come at someone else's career expense. I take that responsibility seriously."

Tim Knavish has drawn several stretch assignments at PPG and, in 2005, was promoted to general manager of the company's Australia and New Zealand coatings businesses. Knavish said: "You are constantly learning and you don't have a lot of history to fall back on. It takes a lot more effort to handle the everyday things. But I've enjoyed the rush of the steep learning curve. It's obviously helped me from a career standpoint."

The lesson to be learned is, when you demonstrate leadership skills, you are marked for advancement and opportunity.

Source: Adapted from "Putting Industrial Leaders on the Fast Track," available at http://www.ddiworld.com/pdf/ppg_cs_ddi.pdf.

the team. Such choices may make political sense, but they don't guarantee a leader with the ability to actually lead.

Most theories about what makes a leader are inconclusive, outdated, moderated by the situation, or just plain wrong. An old cliché describes the business leader as a "40 long," referring to suit size—a definition that effectively excludes most men and women, and many ethnic groups. Far from suit size, however, it is a person's communication that suggests leadership qualities. We believe these qualities include preparation for the task, credibility, adaptability, ethical principles, and personal involvement.

PREPARATION

An individual may be designated as leader because members or a team's founder recognizes his or her ability to lead. Conversely, the appointment may reflect nothing more than a person's proven skill in doing a job—but not necessarily in leading a team. Perhaps you create great training films, so you're made assistant manager of the human resources and training department. Are you then ready to lead a department? Could be, but maybe you also need training to lead others so they can do the job as well as you can.

Often, however, preparation simply means doing your homework. For example, if you're a member of a classroom group, you come to the meeting organized, supplied with information the group needs, and ready to talk about it. You are then perceived as a leader because you're the one ready for the task.

INVOLVEMENT

Personal involvement is essential to being a leader. We see involvement in terms of an individual's proactivity and the "three Cs" of leadership: confidence, commitment, and concentration.

Proactivity means reaching beyond the moment and creating opportunities. Compare proactivity with reactivity. The reactive person waits for something to happen and then knee-jerks a response without any reasoned decision. The proactive person anticipates, thinks of possibilities and contingencies, plans ahead, and acts. A leader needs to move beyond the reactive point of view. Proactivity shows in preparation, in coming to meetings with information and ideas, in caring about and enjoying people as well as processes, in being able to play with ideas, and in seeing the humor in a situation.

Confidence, commitment, and *concentration* are essential qualities, combined with sensitivity to the needs of the team. According to Warren Bennis (1989), still one of the most influential writers on leadership today, "Leaders know themselves; they know their strengths and nurture them" (p. 22). Bennis recounts the story of Karl Wallenda, who was the leader of the Flying Wallendas, a world-famous family of aerialists and tightrope walkers. The secret to Karl's continued success—and existence—was total concentration and commitment to what he was doing. One day, for the first time ever, he personally supervised the installation of the lines stretched between two buildings in Puerto Rico on which he later would walk. That day, Wallenda fell to his death. Later, his wife said it was the only time in all those years that he "had been concentrating on falling, instead of on walking the tightrope" before his performance (p. 22).

As long as he was fully confident in his skills, concentrated on his performance, and committed to its outcome, Karl Wallenda was invincible. When he lost that, he died. Leadership is the same: a leader must be confident in his or her skills, fully concentrated on the team's processes, and committed to the team's vision and goals.

CREDIBILITY

Credibility has been investigated by many researchers who have found several factors that seem to influence how a communicator is perceived. We define **credibility** as *the extent to which people perceive you as being competent, objective, trustworthy, and cooriented with them.*

Competence is the degree of expertness, qualification, authoritativeness, and skill a person demonstrates. It is an essential component of teamwork, in which each member must contribute some expertise, information, analysis, and creativity to solving the problem.

Objectivity is the ability to look at both sides of an issue, to suspend any personal biases, to be reasonable and dispassionate, and to examine evidence, reasoning, and value questions before taking sides. In Western societies, where issues are decided by discussion and debate, the ability to be an objective judge is particularly crucial.

Trustworthiness is how consistent and honest a member's behavior is understood to be. It is the confidence other people have in your sincerity and your ability to behave ethically even under pressure.

Coorientation is other people's sense that you are similar to them, that you are concerned for their well-being, and that you share their interests, values, objectives, and needs. They can identify with you, because you can identify with them. Credible communicators care about how their actions might affect others, not just about their own personal objectives. Someone who wants a team to excel so that he or she will look good is perceived by members as having far less credibility than someone who wants all members to succeed.

To a great extent, a person's culture will influence how she or he perceives someone's credibility. For example, most cultures particularly value competence or expertise and trust. Particularly in collectivist cultures, such as those found in southeast Asia, a trustful interpersonal relationship is a precondition of successful interactions (Huang & Van de Vliert, 2006). Interestingly, employer/employee relationships in collectivist cultures show a great resemblance to child/parent relationships, suggesting that trust in authority figures may be something taken for granted in these arenas (Earley & Gibson, 1998; Huff & Kelley, 2003). Chinese see credible leadership coming from people who show interpersonal competence, personal morality, goal efficiency, and versatility (Ling, Chia, & Fang, 2000). For many Native Americans and Asians, elders are credible because they are imbued with great wisdom from life experiences, whereas people from other cultures tend to dismiss elders as being "too old." Likewise, a strong, loud voice may seem credible, authoritative, and dynamic to a North American, but to a Thai, it may seem angry (Merritt, 2000).

Unfortunately, stereotypes of people on the basis of ethnicity, gender, or status often affect how people judge others' credibility. In several studies, the *same messages* were attributed to high-status (Anglo-American, male) speakers and to low-status (female or minority) speakers. Subjects rated the high-status speakers as having higher credibility (Pearson, Turner, & Todd-Mancillas, 1991, p. 225). And in a survey of North American media stories, it was found that women of status, competence, and power were not called leaders as often as were men with lesser achievements (Bridge, 1994, p. 16). These labels show a cultural pro-male bias that even today may keep women from being perceived as leaders—even when they are. Even so, as women and minorities take more leadership roles and advance further in society, their credibility increases. Additionally, many stereotypically feminine behaviors have increasing value for teams because they nurture cooperation as opposed to competition. Women's communication conveys coorientation using verbal and nonverbal communication that might appear to be less dynamic but that increases feelings of trust and relationship.

You can see how culture affects interpretations of credibility in the selection of negotiating teams in different countries. Status is important to French, British, Chinese, Japanese, and Saudi Arabian teams, but not to North Americans, who base team selection more on technical expertise. French teams also are based on "social, professional, and family ties" as well as on interpersonal similarity among the team members, whereas British negotiators don't put much stock in interpersonal similarity. In addition to status, Japanese teams value knowledge, but they set age as a top priority. Mexican negotiation teams are most influenced by personal attributes and *palanca* (leverage, connections, clout), which may or may not be connected with formal status (Hellweg, Samovar, & Skow, 1994, pp. 289–290).

Even perceptions of competence or expertise may vary. In Western societies, someone is seen as an opinion leader only in a specialized area of expertise. In many other more traditional societies, however, people perceive that if someone is an expert in one area, they are generally knowledgeable and deserving of respect. Thus, in the United States, an expert in physics might be rejected as a team leader in some other arena, whereas in Africa, a credible leader might be someone people revere simply as an elder—someone whose wisdom is more important than his or her expertise.

PRINCIPLES

A **principled leader** is guided by internal ethical standards and helps his or her teammates to use processes and to make decisions that are ethically sound. Adaptability, however, raises an interesting ethical question: Is it ethical to adapt to others' responses? Our answer is a firm "Yes and no." For example, if you avoid using profanity because it would prevent your teammates from listening to your ideas, you've adapted with principle. If you lie to get someone to agree with you, however, then you've adapted without principle.

To provide principled leadership, you avoid manipulating others to do something that violates their personal standards and values, and you discourage teammates from taking advantage of or injuring others. A principled person chooses messages by asking, "Is this fair? Is it honest? Will it foster the team's efforts in the best, healthiest, and most ethical directions?"

Principled leadership encourages a sense of equity and procedural justice. Even when teams do not have the final decision, they are willing to endorse leaders who objectively and openly encourage members to have their say. Members see these leaders as being fair and just, and also report being more committed to the team because they believe justice is inherent in the team's processes (Carson, Tesluk & Marrone, 2007). Furthermore, leaders who reason with principle apparently influence their teams to do the same. Their influence seems to be a lasting one as well, because after working with such a leader, members continue to use more principled reasoning themselves (Wageman, 2001).

ADAPTABILITY

Styles of leadership that work for one team might not work for another. Successful leaders need to adapt their behaviors to be consistent with the goals and values of the team in order to effectively meet their expectations (Cohen & Bailey, 1997). In fact, not only do good leaders adapt to the situation, they remain leaders only if they adapt. How do you adapt? You watch, listen, and use the skills of self-monitoring, coorientational accuracy, and creating person-centered messages.

Self-monitoring is watching others' responses as well as your own behavior and being able to identify and act upon environmental cues. In short, these individuals can be counted on to act in an appropriate and socially adept way, regardless of the situation. Individuals who are effective self-monitors are

- Concerned about the appropriateness of social behavior
- Attentive to social comparison information
- Relatively adept at acting
- Able and willing to control behavior and to optimize self-presentations—even if this means portraying themselves very differently across various contexts (Fletcher and Baldry, 2000)

Coorientational accuracy is the ability to gauge another person's position or feelings. How clearly and accurately leaders assess their teammates' responses obviously affects how well those leaders can adapt to them and coorient with their teammates. This may be easier for some people than for others. Women may tend to be more coorientationally accurate than men (Tannen, 2001). In addition, people from lower-status groups tend to be more coorientationally accurate than people from dominant groups, simply because subordinated people must interpret and satisfy the requirements of those to whom they answer.

Person-centered messages focus on the other person rather than on oneself, thus showing a recognition of "the other as a unique person, and a sensitivity to the other's unique qualities, goals, feelings, and concerns" (Zorn, 1991, p. 183). For example, if you greeted a teammate's suggestion with "Nah—stupid idea. Too expensive," then your message would discount that person. If you said, "Interesting idea—but it seems to exceed the budget," however, you would raise the same objection but also recognize your teammate's worth.

RESPONSIBILITY

As we use the term, *leadership* assumes each individual's ability, right, and responsibility to think and to make choices. In a team situation, mutual respect and influence among members transform individual responses into team choices and actions. Thus, every team member has the *responsibility* to share leadership, to affect the thinking of others, and to influence the team's processes and outcomes.

The concept of *shared leadership* is not new, but every member's responsibility for practicing shared leadership has increased in importance as teams assume more and more management and decision-making roles. Certainly, the advent of virtual teams and virtual organizations increases the need for each participant to share leadership across space and time. As far back as 1948, Benne and Sheats wrote that "no sharp distinction can be made between leadership and membership functions, between leader and member roles" (p. 41). In 1976, Potter and Andersen defined effective group communication as "the systematic, purposeful, primarily oral exchange of ideas, facts, and opinions by a group of persons who *share in the group's leadership*" [emphasis added] (p. 1). In 1978, Weick suggested that leadership works as a medium to help a group manage environmental, social, or procedural obstacles. In 1986, Fisher recognized leadership as being present when any member helps the group to adapt to "shifts in situational demands, group composition, and developmental trends" (p. 205). In 1989, Barge tested a model of leaderless group discussion and found that "an individual leader's behavior does not necessarily aid groups in achieving their goals but that group leadership behavior does" (p. 245).

Today, we know that leadership is every individual's responsibility because group communication is complex. One leader cannot see or do everything that must be done, and members rely on one another in working toward their goals.

As path–goal leadership theory notes, many individuals must provide leadership to counteract problems blocking a group as it works along the path toward a goal. When such leadership is absent, groups often make bad decisions and take harmful actions (Northouse, 2004). That's why *you* have a responsibility for leadership.

LEADERSHIP AND TEAMWORK

You recall that Chapter 1 talks about how people function on two levels in group interaction, those of task processes and transactional processes. In task processes, members talk about and focus on information and ideas that will help to achieve the goal of the group. In transactional processes, members develop relationships, work through interpersonal issues, and try to create a sense of "teamness." These transactional processes are essential to achieving the task even though the transactions may or may not address the task issues directly at any given time.

As you share in the team's leadership, you must be able to facilitate task and transactional processes and, often, overcome obstacles to leadership. A first, and essential, step to facilitating these processes is to understand how people play certain roles in their group interactions.

ROLES PEOPLE PLAY

Of course, you know you play roles all the time by behaving in specific ways that seem to distinguish your function or character in a situation. In fact, you play a wide variety of roles in your life, and you probably also switch roles even within a given situation. Everyone has definitions, often unconscious, of how to behave in roles such as wife, husband, son, daughter, student, or teacher. Or a person's self-description may include a role such as, "I'm a comedian," or "I'm a helper," or "I'm a procrastinator."

In groups, members take on roles as well; some of their group roles may reflect their other roles. For example, a life-of-the-party person may take a distracting role in a work team, and someone who is in the habit of being the boss may take a dominating role in a group. An individual who thinks of herself or himself as a parent may carry that role into the team—and nurture everybody else to death.

Individual roles, however, are only part of the story. Many roles serve task and transactional needs. Some roles are traditional roles, such as leader or secretary. In this sense, a role is a job or a function that an individual fills, formally or informally, but any individual may switch roles at any time to meet specific needs.

Working together can result in decisions that are more technically complex and creative.

Some roles are more process-oriented than job-specific; in other words, they influence transactions among the members. One leadership skill is recognizing needs and adapting your own role to meet those needs. Another is helping others to switch their roles to eliminate problems and to facilitate processes. These skills require you to identify various role options.

Traditionally, role definitions are divided into three groups: those that serve group-building-and-maintenance, group-task, and individual needs:

Group-building roles focus on feelings and harmony. When you're playing these roles, you are interested in managing conflict within the group and ensuring that everyone participates and is heard. The focus here is on the emotional reaction group members are having to one another.

Task roles focus on doing the job. Here, you work to help the group make the best decisions, perhaps by playing devil's advocate. You could also help keep the group's discussions organized, take notes, or whatever else it takes to keep the group moving forward toward its goals.

Individual roles focus attention on individual problems or behaviors. These distractions are contrary to leadership functions because they play out at the expense of transactional and task processes.

A note of warning: *Beware of thinking about roles as personality types that tie people into one characterization. Remember that roles fulfill functions and that you can choose your own role according to what function you perceive is needed.* Still, understanding the various roles can help you to diagnose a group situation. At the end of this chapter is a condensed list of specific roles along with definitions and an observation form to use in analyzing a meeting. You may want to observe a small group and use those categories to identify the roles each person plays. When you do, observe how often people play more than one role and how members who share leadership may switch roles to meet the group's transactional or task needs.

TEAM PROCESSES

Role definitions reflect people's transactional and task processes as they develop a team and pursue their goals. Those processes, however, are much more dynamic and interdependent than you would think if you looked exclusively at the roles people play in them.

A given exchange may carry a message about the task at hand, for example, but it also may confirm or disconfirm an individual and thereby build or diminish the team. Suppose Lou is talking about the relative merits of a proposal and someone says, "Oh, shut up, Lou. It's time to vote." The comment is related to getting the task done, but the "slam" is directed at the individual—and both the individual and the team are hurt. This example shows how transactional processes occur within, through, and around task processes.

Transactional processes may seem to take time away from the task itself, but you can't accomplish most goals without them. When transactions involve individual roles that upset or alienate people, those transactions interfere with pursuing the task; when transactions help people to feel excited about their teamwork, those transactions advance the task. If the task is frustrating and seems to be unattainable, the transactions among people in the group reflect that pain. If the task is exciting and achievement is high, however, the transactions are easier and more rewarding. It's up to every person to provide the kind of leadership that enables the group to have positive transactional and task processes.

Transactional Processes   Transactional processes carry the task processes by working through the communication, negotiations, and understandings among the team's members. When transactional processes work well, they develop a positive climate in which group-building and task functions can be served, individual and team needs can be met, and problems created by individual roles can be handled so that they do not damage the team's effectiveness.

What does it "feel" like when effective transactional leadership establishes positive climates? Not much has changed since Kinlaw reported in 1991 that "hundreds of statements" reveal that members have strong feelings of inclusion, commitment, loyalty, pride, and trust in their teams. Members commented that "nobody was left out," "we respected each other," "if [other people] said they were going to do something, they did it," "it felt like a family," "people went out of their way to make somebody else look good," and if someone needed help, "we all jumped in" (pp. 48–50). Johannesen (1996) notes that a supportive climate is essential to a dialogical ethic of group communication (pp. 72–73). Only in this positive climate can people maintain their own ethics, dialogue openly, and make ethically acceptable decisions.

Such a climate encourages diverse and different ideas, expressions of disagreement as well as agreement, change, and growth. Every member is part of the whole, and all are concerned for one another and rewarded in emotional as well as material ways for their teamwork. A climate like this is so productive, in fact, that one team member commented, "It felt so important to get the job done that you sometimes forgot about anything else" (Kinlaw, 1991, p. 48).

Your transactional leadership depends on being intensely involved and highly committed to the team process while simultaneously seeing the interactions from enough distance to know what needs to be done. This sounds difficult, and it is challenging. It also is a skill you can develop. We'll work on the necessary verbal, nonverbal, and listening skills in Chapters 9 and 10, but the following list will get you started on how to use your leadership in transactional processes:

> *Suggest and encourage positive norms.* Establish an expectation of openness, mutual concern, cooperation, and responsibility. Openly state your preference for this climate, and ask for agreement from other members.
>
> *Encourage each member's involvement.* Ask for information, ideas, opinions, and feelings. Support others with agreement or open questions. Confirm the worth of others through your verbal, nonverbal, and listening communication.
>
> *Encourage trust and openness.* Take a few risks and disclose a little about yourself. State norms for confidentiality, expect those norms to be followed, protect confidentiality, and support others.
>
> *Help to manage conflicts.* Remind the team that conflict, when it arises, is normal. Recognize it can be helpful, and stay objective. Find ways to support negotiation and compromise.
>
> *Make connections.* Help people to support each other. Look for things they have in common, and state your appreciation for others' contributions. Encourage open-mindedness and interest in other members' points of view.
>
> *Create a sense of "teamness."* Orient members toward mutual goals. Support the team process, and discuss the ways in which the team works. Comment on what it does well, and suggest positive ways to assess and improve the quality of teamwork.
>
> *Deal actively with team stress.* Acknowledge stressful situations. Help to diagnose causes of such stress, and find ways to relieve it. Use humor, a "time out," and negotiation to ease conditions.

Task Processes   Task processes focus specifically on the job at hand. Contributions that produce information, cooperative analysis, critical and creative thinking, problem solving, decision making, and task achievement are part of these processes.

In an effectively functioning team, task processes are characterized by an appropriate agreed-on structure, flexibility and adaptability, and clarity of goals and objectives. The team has both the commitment and the ability to acquire and use necessary information and resources, and it maintains a norm of openness to creativity and to critical analysis. Members use various problem-analysis and decision-making approaches, and they continually evaluate—and reevaluate—their progress.

To make such a process work, every member must provide leadership through specific behaviors. The following guidelines should help you to get your team started on solid task processes:

Orient the team toward task processes. When the team's attention wanders, call it back. Summarize what's been done, suggest next steps, and check to see if people agree before moving on.

Be sure meetings are organized. Suggest and confirm meeting arrangements, agendas, records, and assignments. Remind people when the discussion gets too far off track.

Discuss and confirm team goals. State goals for the team, and ask for confirmation that everyone agrees with them.

Identify the team's requirements for its work. Suggest the team consider needs for information and resources, and propose ways to get what's needed.

Help the team to divide the work. Guide the discussion of expertise, information needs, and interests, and suggest ways to divide research and other outside work.

Make sure information is shared. Request, summarize, review, and analyze information. Ask for others' analyses and opinions, too.

Provide information and ideas. Take responsibility, get good information, and bring it to the team with clear explanations.

Contribute creativity and critical thinking. Help others to get ideas, ask questions, and make suggestions. Use your analysis to evaluate logic, reasoning, and proposed solutions.

Test conclusions for ethicality. Ask questions that stimulate thinking about the ethics of team considerations and decisions. Examine the value and acceptability of suggestions, decisions, and actions.

OBSTACLES TO LEADERSHIP

It may be up to every person to provide leadership, but we all know things don't necessarily happen that way. Some members may just sit, virtually silent, and do nothing to guide or encourage the development of a team. You even may have done that yourself at some time.

A few of these silent members may appear to be uninvolved, uncommitted, and uncaring, but they probably are none of these things. Often people are blocked by obstacles to their participation. When any member is excluded—or excludes herself or himself—the team loses. It loses information, ideas, insight, and analysis. It loses a point of view. A team needs every member. You can exercise leadership by recognizing and overcoming any obstacles that may stand in the way of anyone's participation.

Have you ever felt "left out" of a group activity because of your age, gender, etc.?

Recognizing Obstacles   People often are blocked by the perceptions of other members—or by their own perceptions—of who they are and what roles they should play. These perceptions stereotype, label, and put people into boxes, and it's hard to exercise leadership from a box. Some common pigeonholes are

- *The shy box.* Shy people may be thought of as being uninterested or dull. They may be able to provide good leadership, but nobody makes an effort to find out.
- *The point-of-view box.* This box encloses someone whose political, religious, or professional point of view is in the minority. Others simply ignore or put down this individual until she or he remains silent.
- *The different box.* This box is reserved for those whose gender, race, culture, or ethnic traditions are different from the majority. The majority members may not even consider that a "different" individual could provide leadership. In fact, when men are in the group, some women of high leadership ability may fail to assert their leadership roles (van Engen & Willemsen, 2004).
- *The too-much-effort box.* If it takes a little extra effort to communicate with someone who, for example, is disabled or speaks with an accent, members often just won't bother.
- *The disapproval box.* A group may cut off leadership from someone because he or she lives a different lifestyle. Even if the group is open and receptive, some people (gay or lesbian, orthodox religious, punk rockers—anyone whose lifestyle is a little off the norm) may withdraw because their previous experiences have made them fear being stereotyped and labeled.

Please note that none of this assumes there is anything wrong with the person in the box, nor does it assume you have to approve of or like everyone in a group. What it does assume, however, is that every member—no matter who or what she or he is—may be able to contribute something important. One of your leadership responsibilities is to help overcome these obstacles—for yourself and for others.

Overcoming Obstacles   People erect obstacles to leadership, consciously or unconsciously, because their own stereotypes and expectations are deep-rooted. Someone—either the boxed-in member or another person—needs to do something if these obstacles are to be overcome. For example, you might:

Confront the obstacle. Confrontation can be tough. It takes tact, determination, and guts to work through an issue, but sometimes it's the only way. (We talk about conflict management and confrontation in Chapter 12.)

Persuade the group. Call attention to the group's norms, discuss them, and then suggest ways of changing them. You may want to talk to members outside the meetings to get their cooperation in changing the norms and attitudes that exclude an individual.

Act as a mentor. Help the restricted member to connect with the group. Encourage, coach, and help this person to understand the team and how it works. Others may follow your example. Either way, the boxed-in individual will slowly become more confident and credible as she or he contributes.

LEADERSHIP AND ETHICS

From the moment a team forms—from the very first words you exchange—you are invested in that team and its outcomes. This is an investment both of self and of conscience. Your **ethics** are involved. Ethical issues arise, according to Johannesen (1996), when "behavior could have significant impact on other persons, when the behavior involves conscious choice of means and ends, and when the behavior can be judged by standards of right and wrong" (p. 1). Choosing between right and wrong can be particularly difficult for a group.

Several things make it harder to make ethical choices in a group, particularly a work group or team. One pressure to make expedient choices even if they violate members' ethics comes from outside the group—from the organization in which the group functions, and from the often contradictory attitudes about ethics in business, coupled with management's expectations of profitable decisions. Another comes from within the group transactions themselves. Yet another problem for rapidly increasing numbers of teams today may be that, as virtual teams, their communication is all verbal—they cannot look into one another's eyes or work out their issues face to face.

The current business climate exerts pressure for power and profit that leads to corrupt practices that are revealed by the news media almost on a daily basis. Business and political institutions *talk* a lot about ethics as a consequence. One Harvard Business School publication (*From the editor's desk*, 1999) notes that, "today, companies are hot for what are known as ethics/compliance programs—that

| BOX 2.2 | DEVELOPING CREDIBILITY AND BUILDING CONFIDENCE AT WHOLE FOODS MARKET |

Whole Foods Market is a long-time leader in using teams to run every department in its national chain of organic grocery stores. Continued success has made Whole Foods one of the most popular companies to work for in the United States. A 2007 advertisement for a produce department supervisor in the company's Bellevue, Washington, store illustrates how a successful applicant would have to develop credibility and build confidence on the job.

The general summary of the produce supervisor's position stated: "Works together with other Team Members to assure that all objectives and goals of the department and store, as communicated by the Store Leadership/Coordinator, are met or

exceeded." In addition, a successful applicant for the position would have to "work well with others and convey enthusiasm." Note how valuable coorientation and dynamism would be to develop credibility. The produce department supervisor would also have to "train and inspire Team Members to excellence in all aspects of the department." Note how valuable visualization would be to the successful applicant. Especially if the person had no experience in training others—much less inspiring them—painting a mental picture and writing a self-affirmation could be instrumental in building confidence.

Source: Whole Foods Market Career Opportunities. http://www.wholefoodsmarket.com/jobs/43297.html.

is, programs designed to discourage wrongful behavior among employees and thereby protect the organization from lawsuits (or worse). Once again, some executives seem to think that an off-the-shelf solution will suffice. Write down a code of conduct! Set up a compliance office and a telephone hotline!" (p. 11). The article concludes, however, that "off the shelf doesn't work"; ethical choices must have a firmer (and more sincere) foundation than guidelines written merely to protect the organization—or the team—from legal action or bad public relations.

In a brief survey of articles on business ethics, it's easy to find bewilderingly ambiguous positions. For example, one *Fortune* magazine article details a cleverly successful career and asks, "Is lying ethical? Nope, but it clearly has a hallowed role in business" (Useem, 1999, p. 1). Yet another article in a health care journal states that "integrity is integral to career success" and describes how hiring personnel carefully scrutinize applicants' resumes and interviews for the quality of their ethics (Gauss, 2000, p. 89).

The other pressure for ethical compromise can come from the realities of group communication. The enthusiasm of others, the sense of being part of something beyond oneself, and the pressure to conform sometimes may separate people from their personal responsibility and conscience.

Do virtual teams have greater or fewer pressures toward unethical practices? Does the lack of face-to-face communication create less or greater discussion of ethical standards and issues? We don't know yet; the virtual world of work is too new. But it's a question worth considering when you find yourself on a virtual team, as you probably will sooner or later.

Philosophers since Plato have probed the implications of one person's influence on another, and communication has long been examined regarding the ethical questions it involves. You make internal right-or-wrong choices about what you will say and how you will say it. For example, "Is it truthful if I say it this way? But will it then have the effect I want?"

Team processes involve making choices—individual choices and group choices. When leadership (either from a designated leader or from members of the group) guides the analysis of those decisions to include ethical concerns, all members stay on more solid ground. The old expression, "If you don't stand for something you'll fall for anything," applies to groups as well as to individuals. In fact, ethical choices are even more complicated in a group, because they highlight differences among group members' likes and dislikes, values, and priorities. In fact, some people will keep quiet in a group when they learn that others disagree with their ethical positions, just so they don't "rock the boat." Unfortunately, this means that the group loses the opportunity for an ethical debate, and may even ultimately make an unethical decision.

It takes guts to speak out against the majority even when you think the majority is wrong. It takes tolerance and understanding to comprehend another's point of view. It takes patience to handle the disagreements that ethical analysis creates. That's why it takes excellent shared leadership to ensure that all team members— including you—understand your ethical obligations and how to fulfill them.

To fulfill those obligations, you must identify ethical dilemmas and conflicts and then protect the ethics of individuals, team processes, and team decisions.

ETHICAL DILEMMAS AND CONFLICTS

Not all choices have ethical consequences. Whether a report has a blue or a green cover, for example, may involve conflicts over preferences but not necessarily over values. What if you must choose, however, between including information in the report that advances a worthy cause but is not quite accurate or information that is accurate but does not support that cause?

Toffler (1986, p. 20) makes an important distinction between an **ethical issue**, which can be considered in abstract, right-or-wrong, good-or-bad terms, and an **ethical dilemma**, to which we must apply standards and make decisions between two real choices. Even for an individual, these choices may present a dilemma among conflicting needs, desires, and ethical criteria. For a team, however, they may present multiple dilemmas among individual and team ethics.

Teammates may clash over distinctly different values that are deeply held within their respective cultures. Such differences can be extreme. What does a team do— what do *you* do—when ethical positions conflict? Suppose you must choose between two alternatives, neither of which meets your ethical standards or which meet some standards but not others.

Hackman and Johnson (1996) point out that "standards vary from culture to culture, but the dilemma of establishing the measure of right and wrong remains constant" (p. 335). To recognize and then solve a team's ethical dilemmas entails raising questions of right and wrong, of good and bad. It requires discussing the implications and consequences of an action in terms of how they affect the team, the task, and others on the outside. You must strip away the emotional language, focus on the issues, and allow others to have their own perspective while you defend yours.

Suppose you're a member of a campus group that can get the answers to an upcoming exam. Those answers would give the group members a definite edge in passing the class with good grades. Some members, however, including you, oppose cheating. They don't want to compromise their ethics, and they don't want their group to do so, either. Other members justify this cheating by pointing out the professor is unfair anyway and getting the answers will equalize the situation. Still others can't imagine what the big deal is—they don't even think of it as cheating.

What do you do? You lay the cards on the table, discuss the issues, and listen. You learn to understand where the others are coming from, and you try to persuade them. In the end, you may have helped to forge a team with an ethic that includes honesty. Either way, you will have learned something about how others think, and you may have managed to teach them something, too.

What if the majority still favors cheating after this discussion? Do you necessarily accept their decision? Do you cheat? Do you refuse to cheat but remain a member of the group? Do you leave the group in protest? It depends. You make these decisions based on your own strength of character, the group's importance to you, the degree to which you share its other values, and whether you hope to help the group evolve ethical standards more acceptable to you.

Jaksa and Pritchard (1994) make what is, at least to us, a very important point: You can tolerate disagreement without giving up your own standards. "Tolerating differences of choice and refraining from automatically labeling opposite choices as immoral are essential. At the same time, seeking exact points of difference can help solve disagreements by eliminating false distinctions and evasions" (p. 17).

Some people fear that listening to and respecting differences in values and ethics means that they must take a relativistic point of view, that they can never take a stand. Jaksa and Pritchard (1994) point out, however, that people can be nonrelative—that is, they can know what they think is right or wrong—and still be tolerant, see shades of gray in issues, and respect others' beliefs and ways (pp. 18–23).

ETHICAL ISSUES FOR TEAMS

If making choices with ethical implications is so much a part of a team's work, then understanding and analyzing ethics are incredibly important to team processes and outcomes. This is because:

1. Teams are made of individuals, each of whom applies his or her own moral and ethical standards to making choices and interacting with others.
2. Communication choices and interactions involve ethical questions of good and bad, of right and wrong.
3. In a team, individuals interact and influence each other to make many group choices and decisions.
4. The ethical systems and standards of individuals, which are used to assess and determine team choices and decisions, frequently come into conflict.
5. Ethical, moral, or value questions can be ignored or overlooked during transactional and task processes.
6. Individuals can lose sight of and even abandon ethical standards under pressure in group processes.

7.   Unethical decisions can be made and unworthy actions taken in the name of the team.

Ethical concerns of groups, therefore, involve making mutual choices in light of differing morals and standards—choices about sources of information and quality of analysis, about the transactional processes of the group, about the impacts of decisions, and about the freedom of each member to dissent. The list of such choices is endless.

With all these choices, it is possible to override or distort ethical decisions. It also is possible, however, to exert superior analysis and to make better ethical decisions, because the team's shared leadership examines issues from a wider perspective. As a team member, you have three broad sets of leadership responsibilities when dealing with ethical choices and dilemmas: to protect your own personal standards, to develop an ethic of team processes, and to guard the ethics of team decisions and outcomes.

Personal Standards   It's difficult enough to make decisions affecting you alone, and when you work with a group, it's all too easy to be pushed in directions you would not choose. Therefore, it's important to think about what your ethics are and to get a perspective on how they influence you.

The *standards*, or criteria, you apply to making your own choices are complicated. They relate to your value system, to learnings from your earliest childhood. Some you know consciously and could write as a list, but some are unconscious assumptions about the way things should be.

Standards may be clear moral rules, such as Tell the truth, Be fair, or Don't cheat. Others may be ethical guidelines for how you behave and make choices, such as Always do your best, Be positive, Be kind, Be smart, Win, or Be the best.

People get their ethical standards from a variety of sources. Religions teach perspectives on life and moral "Thou shalts" and "Thou shalt nots." Families and cultures, through both examples and norms, also teach their ways of doing things. Even subcultural or professional groups develop rules and codes of honor that distinguish their particular images. Any—or even all—of these may influence how you approach your ethical choices.

These influences help to mold a person's ethical point of view, which is the perspective from which he or she makes ethical judgments. There are many ways to describe points of view. Here, we look at those most important to teamwork: legalistic, situational, and philosophical.

The Legalistic View   The *legalistic view* uses some code or set of rules as the basis for making decisions. In this view, if it isn't illegal, then it isn't unethical. Likewise, if it isn't legal, then it is unethical. Legalistic views may be based on statutory law, a religion, or a code of ethics. The American Bar Association, the Public Relations Society of America, the American Association of Advertisers, and the National Communication Association, for example, all have a code of ethics formulated by their members.

Laws and rules are essential to a society, but they are not sufficient for ethical choices. Relying exclusively on a legalistic point of view assumes that all ethical issues are included and that the law is inevitably right. Such a position legally kept African Americans as second-class citizens until Martin Luther King, Jr., argued effectively that our body of laws included some that were just and others that were unjust. He established clear criteria to identify which law was which and proposed that just laws should be obeyed but unjust laws broken. In this case, conscience finally overcame the irrational rationalization of the law.

The Situational View   The *situational view* is ad hoc: every ethical question is weighed in terms of the context and the situation. A number of viewpoints may come into play here. For example, a member of a communication training team was asked to provide stress management training for a cosmetic company's customer relations representatives, who were under fire from animal rights activists because the firm tested its products on animals. Although not an activist herself, the trainer believed that unnecessary animal testing was wrong. Neither her religion nor the law would have prevented her from providing this training, but her personal ethical standards created a dilemma. She was sympathetic toward the stressed representatives and wanted to help, but she would also have been helping a corporation she believed was cruel toward helpless animals. She and the team decided to confront the issue with the company and, after examining the situation, decided to forego the contract.

The situation might have been much more difficult had the consultant desperately needed the income. Would she still have foregone this opportunity? Situational ethics are not considered in a vacuum. They are considered in terms of real situations and issues—and the more complicated the circumstances, the more difficult the decisions.

The Philosophical View   The *philosophical view* may be personal or cultural, and it may draw from religious, cultural, family, political, professional, and life experiences. It rests on assumptions about human beings, their position in the universe, governments, and God. Often these sources are intertwined in the ethical structure of a society as well.

The philosophies of the men who drafted the U.S. Constitution and the Bill of Rights, for example, influenced the content of those documents. In turn, their assumptions influenced the development of the U.S. political system, which in turn influences the assumptions that Americans make about what is right or wrong in political and in personal decisions.

The result of this view is a society in which people can take diametrically opposed positions that are ethically right to them. In addition, there is a social imperative to discuss, evaluate, and decide on the best alternatives for society as a whole.

Team Processes   Ethical issues are easy to see in task processes, such as using good data and making correct decisions. They are equally important, but perhaps even more complex, in transactional processes. Transactional processes involve standards—moral choices about how people treat one another and how they help one another to communicate, learn, develop, and be a team. Only through those processes are the ethics of task processes and decision making made possible.

Our philosophical point of view is described by Johannesen (1996) as a dialogical perspective on communication. This approach is especially important to ethical processes in groups. Think of dialogue in contrast to monologue. A monologue occurs when someone's communication is centered on himself or herself as the giver, but not receiver, of ideas. A dialogue, however, involves commitment, give and take, listening, and negotiating new meanings both between and among people. A dialogical perspective considers the attitudes of people toward each other in dialogue "as an index of the ethical level of that communication. The assumption is that some attitudes (characteristics of dialogue) are more fully human, humane, and facilitative of self-fulfillment than are other attitudes (characteristic of monologue)" (p. 64).

A dialogical ethic creates a climate that enables people to be authentic about who they are, to include and confirm the worth of others, to be "present" (that is, accessible and attentive), and to share a spirit of mutual equality (Johannesen, 1996, pp. 67–68). These are the values and assumptions teams must integrate when they establish their ethics for team processes. Brown (1990) clearly shows the relationship between ethics in task and transactional processes when he states that when teams evaluate information or ideas, "members must know that their views will be taken seriously and that the analysis will focus on the strengths and weaknesses of their arguments rather than on their character. For differences to become productive, participants . . . need to become mutually engaged in an open inquiry into the materials that all members contribute to the discussion" (p. 7).

When a team uses dialogical ethics, everyone has equal responsibility. Members act in ways to fulfill that responsibility, and they encourage others to do the same. Each member believes in the rights and the worth of every other member, and he or she works for the best results for every member—and for the team as a whole. The team rejects the concept that any individual must win points or triumph at the expense of others. Instead, the team values each member for his or her unique qualities, and members both listen to and encourage one another to share those qualities. It takes every member's leadership to create and then maintain this dialogical ethic of team process, thereby enabling the team to make ethical choices and decisions about its task.

As you work in a team, you can assess your transactional and task processes by asking some of the following questions:

- Did we identify everyone who might be affected by our decision, and show proper concern for their outcomes and/or point of view?
- Did we explore the discussion question as fully as we could have? Did we gather all relevant information?
- Did we interpret the information we received in an appropriate way?
- Did we say or do anything that unnecessarily affected any group member's positive sense of self? Did we respect everyone's opinions and positions throughout our discussions?

We will talk more about these attitudes throughout the book. For now, however, we hope that you think of them as guidelines for how your team conducts its transactions and accomplishes tasks together.

Throughout this section, we've talked about how important ethics are to the decisions your team makes. Behind every decision, however, are many choices that also have ethical implications. These choices may be important to the individual, to the team, or to someone on the outside. A team needs to know what criteria it will use when considering these dilemmas.

LEADERSHIP DEVELOPMENT

This entire book is written to help you, as a now-and-future member of groups and teams, to develop your leadership skills. Obviously, you have to start somewhere, and the best place is by developing your credibility and your confidence.

DEVELOPING CREDIBILITY

Your credibility is one factor involved in your leadership abilities. What do you mean, however, when you say someone is credible? Do you mean honesty? Accuracy? Competence? Likability? Whatever the answer, it determines how others respond to your influence. Credibility is a set of perceptions in the minds of those with whom you interact (Figure 2.1). What kind of perceptions are they, and how do you make those perceptions positive?

Given what you now know about the five elements of credibility, you can begin developing your own credibility, both in your self-perception and in the perceptions of others. Let's look at each element as it relates to you. See Box 2.2.

Competence One key to being perceived as competent is, of course, actually to be competent. Start by recognizing what competencies you have. For example, you may be excellent in math but mediocre in literary analysis. You may be strong in face-to-face communication but terrified and bumbling in a presentation. You may know much about the Spanish-American War but little about World War II. Everyone is more competent in one area than in another, which is why "more heads are better than one."

Think of competence in terms of content and process. In content, if you have knowledge of the subject, organize it and share it with the team. If you do not already have knowledge, get it. Do research, learn about the subject, organize your information, and present it to the team. You may not be an expert, but you are seen as being worth listening to—because you have something to contribute. For

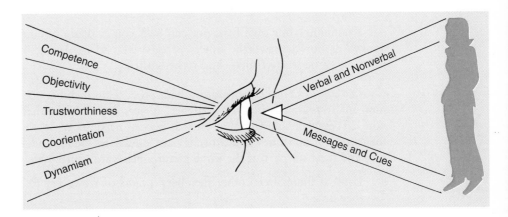

FIGURE 2.1

How one person perceives another's credibility.

process competence, develop your skills in careful listening, thinking, questioning, observing, and analyzing. As you do this, you help the team as well as establish your competence.

Objectivity   Developing your objectivity is a matter of disciplining your thinking and phrasing your thoughts. It's something you can practice even as you read or interact with people in a social situation. Try looking at every issue from more than one side. Even when you feel strongly about a topic, anticipate how someone who feels differently might argue or justify his or her position. Look for reasons and evidence to support various points of view. What you are doing is developing a habit of open-mindedness and fairness.

In dialogue, listen receptively to what others say, and phrase your own statements to acknowledge their points of view. As you develop these habits, you become more objective and are perceived by others as being objective.

Trustworthiness   To be trusted, one must be trustworthy. Trust—such a fragile commodity—is essential to relationships in general and to leadership in particular, and it can be measured in some very specific—and easily violated—ways. You can evaluate your own trustworthiness by looking at how you communicate it:

- Do you live up to what you say? Can you be trusted to follow through on a promise or commitment?
- Do you protect another's confidentiality? If you hear a rumor, do you pass it on or stop it? If someone tells you something personal, do you keep it to yourself? If you observe something embarrassing or distressing to someone, do you share it with the world or remain silent?
- Do you speak up for the ethical action when choices need to be made? Do you waver between advising the ethical path and taking the easy one?
- Do you consistently give the most truthful information you can? Do you choose the truth even when telling a lie would be easier?
- Is your communication straightforward and open? Do you avoid manipulating others? Do you deal with issues in a straightforward manner?

Examining your own behavior can help you evaluate how trustworthy you are as well as how trustworthy others perceive you to be. Using these guidelines can help you to be trustworthy—and to be trusted.

Coorientation   Your coorientation with other team members begins with the common interests that bring you together. It goes beyond just that, however. To see you as being credible in this regard, people need to sense that you care about them, that your values and attitudes are similar to theirs, and that, in some way, you and they are part of the same picture. Here are some ways to start:

- Look at things from other members' points of view. Try to understand who they are.
- Find ways in which you and the other members are similar. Examine backgrounds, attitudes, values, beliefs, and goals to find areas of agreement.

- Find ways to express coorientation, and confirm your common goals and common feelings.
- Express your opinions and ideas in ways that connect with those of others.
- Listen carefully to others and express your support, if not your agreement.
- Confirm statements that reflect others' coorientation with you.
- Show, both verbally and nonverbally, the kind of openness, friendliness, and supportiveness that says, "We're part of the same team, and we have the same vision."

Such communication carries a sense of mutuality that makes coorientation easy. We do not mean you should pretend, however. We mean you should express concern for others' positions and similarities when there are genuine bases for them. This may seem obvious, but people often take the things they share for granted and assume others know they sympathize with a point of view when the other person may not know that at all.

Dynamism   As we have already noted, dynamism can be important to credibility, but its impact can be hard to predict. If you are competent, objective, trustworthy, and cooriented with the team, dynamism probably is not too important. Some very soft-spoken, gentle people are powerful group members.

Our advice is to be as open and naturally enthusiastic as possible. Be sensitive to others' feedback, and adjust to it. If the group needs energizing, express your feelings with a little extra strength. Use humor to enliven or energize a discussion, and allow yourself to use gestures and vocal variety to give your communication energy and expressiveness. Use eye contact and body language to connect with others and to intensify your messages.

If you think you're a little too low-key, work on these skills to come across as being more dynamic. If being dynamic is natural and easy for you, however, be careful. Watch for responses from others. Don't bowl people over. Don't dominate, and don't keep the emotional pitch of the team at a constant high. The idea is to let dynamism energize your messages, not to overwhelm the team.

BUILDING CONFIDENCE

Nothing is more important to your leadership than for you to believe in it. At this moment, you may be very comfortable with leadership. If you are, keep it up. Continue adding to your skills and looking for objective feedback on areas in which you can develop. If you're not yet confident with leadership, you will be soon.

We suggest an approach to building confidence we know to be successful. It involves visualizing yourself the way you want to be, relaxing, and practicing what you visualize.

Visualization   Visualization is one of the most important techniques you can learn. Actually, you already do it, although perhaps not in quite the way we hope you will in the future. You visualize to tell yourself you're good at something or to tell yourself you're bad. Furthermore, you believe yourself—you see yourself as being the person you've described. Then you go forth and do what you've predicted.

The human mind is incredibly powerful. You can make yourself sick and make yourself well. When you want to become good at something—or better, or the best—using the power of your mind and your imagination can help you develop that ability.

An excellent technique for using your mind to develop a skill and to increase your confidence in it is to visualize the way you want to be. With **visualization**, you start by creating a specific mental image of your successful performance. Athletes have used this technique for some time. Dr. Fran Pirozzolo has worked with professional golfers since 1983. He instructs his clients, many of whom have won major championships, to visualize the shots they'll be facing during any upcoming tournament. He advises them to "Get yourself ready with the right pictures or stimuli that access the good swings. Try to see in your mind's eye the ninth fairway. Start doing that a month out, so it's not a new shot when you get there" (Nichols, 2005).

Before you dismiss using visualization because communication is not an athletic event, think again. You use your body and your voice (both of which are physiological) to convey the messages you create with your mind. When you imagine yourself saying or doing something, you are actually programming your brain to produce the results you desire. In other words, when you go through a mental rehearsal, your body also practices silently what you want it to do.

Try using the following visualization techniques to build confidence in your leadership:

1. View yourself as you would be in a leadership role, seeing both transactional and task needs, stepping in, and filling those needs with credibility. Paint yourself a mental picture. Hear yourself speaking and others responding to you.
2. Write down, in a sentence or two, an affirmation of how you feel and act in that picture. An affirmation is a positive, present-tense, and descriptive statement. For example: "I feel confident about my ability, and I give the team good, direct information about the topic we are discussing. I listen carefully to be sure I understand my teammates accurately. I answer questions confidently and easily because I know what I am talking about."
3. Keep picturing yourself in that positive scene, and occasionally read your affirmation to yourself. Use positive self-talk. Soon, you will begin to act in accordance with the visualization in your mind. You will make it happen.

Sports organizations as well as businesses currently employ people to train their managers and workers in visualization techniques. We've seen self-talk and visualization improve the communication and leadership of many people. It also has worked for us, and it can work for you, too.

Relaxation Another method for improving your performance is to consciously relax before you go into an event—in this case, before you meet with a group. Using relaxation techniques *before* an event helps you to develop confidence and effectiveness in your communication (www.mindtools.com, 2004). Relaxing slows your breathing, lowers your pulse and blood pressure, eases your muscles, and focuses your attention on what you are about to do.

There are several approaches to relaxation. Here is one called deep-muscle relaxation:

1. Get comfortable, close your eyes, and concentrate on relaxing your muscles.
2. Breathe slowly and deeply. Imagine the oxygen flowing through your blood-stream and reaching all parts of your body.
3. Now begin to relax your body, starting with your toes. See them in your mind, and imagine them relaxing. Think of the blood as circulating freely around your toes, making them relaxed, warm, and comfortable.
4. Move your concentration up to your feet, your ankles, your legs. Work slowly, thinking of each muscle relaxing, all the way through your body.
5. Concentrate on areas where you have the greatest tension—perhaps your back, shoulders, or neck. Tell yourself you feel them relaxing, and feel the blood circulating and the tension flowing out of them.
6. When your entire body and mind feel relaxed, allow yourself a few moments of floating in that easy, comfortable state.
7. Now tell yourself that the muscle relaxation will continue and that you feel comfortable, at ease, and energized for your communication. Picture energy flowing back into your body.
8. Open your eyes, and you're ready to communicate with confidence.

As you work through your relaxation exercise, your adrenal glands calm and pump out less stimulation. This reduces your physiological stress and increases your level of comfort. With practice, you can learn to relax yourself in a matter of seconds, even as you go down the stairs or across campus. We use both visualiza-tion and relaxation techniques all the time—especially on the way to a meeting we know will be difficult. It helps a lot.

Practice   The obvious next step is to practice your skills. It may be helpful to identify one or two abilities to develop at a time rather than trying to change too many habits at once. For example, you may decide to improve your task process skills by periodically summarizing a group's discussion more effectively. Look for opportunities, and try it in your group. Ask the members for feedback to see if you have adequately described the ideas. Your leadership practice has many benefits, in-cluding your team being more effective, you being more effective, and—definitely— your teamwork being much more fun. Leadership is both gratifying and rewarding.

SUMMARY

Although you may not be the designated leader, your responsibility in a team is to provide leader-ship by understanding and influencing both trans-actional and task processes. To do so effectively, you must understand the group, the task, and the individual roles people play in these processes. Your leadership affects your own short-term and long-term satisfaction and success as well as the team's processes and success.

Certain qualities and skills can help you pro-vide leadership to a team. Leadership requires you to prepare for meetings, to be involved in both task and transactional processes, to demonstrate credibility through your objectivity, trustworthiness, competence, coorientation with other members, and your dynamism. Leadership as a member involves understanding and acting according to your principles, adapting to members and situations, and acting with responsibility toward members and toward your goals as a team.

Through your own leadership, you can help eliminate obstacles to other members' leadership and to effective transactions, such as the stereotyping "boxes" into which people sometimes are put because of culture, race, or gender. As you participate in a group or team, you can recognize the roles people play in task and transactional processes, and understand how individual roles and objectives might affect your team's transactions and goals. You can also protect your personal ethics, help to develop a dialogical ethic of team process, and influence the ethics of team decisions. These ethical issues are crucial because groups face conflicts and dilemmas among ethical choices in both task and transactional processes.

Developing your own leadership and building confidence are critical to becoming an effective group or team member. Two ways to start on this development process are, first, to consciously analyze and develop your objectivity, trustworthiness, competence, coorientation with other members, and your dynamism. Second, you can build your confidence through self-talk and visualization to see yourself influencing the transactional and task processes of your team.

Exercises

1. Assess your leadership skills using Form 2.1. Make an extra copy of the form. On one copy, rate how you perceive yourself, and on the other, ask a friend to rate your behavior. Discuss the completed forms. What does your friend see that you do not? How can you use this feedback? List your strengths and the skills you'd like to develop.

2. Select one behavior from the leadership survey you think you could use more often. Then, for several weeks, consciously use the new behavior in meetings of groups or classes. Keep a journal of how you use the behavior, how you think it affects the group, and how you feel about expanding your repertoire of group behaviors this way.

3. With several other students, observe a meeting of no more than seven people, such as a small group in your class, a student organization, or a faculty committee. Using Form 2.2, tally the number of times each member behaved according to each role during the meeting. (Sometimes one person may play several roles.) Discuss the questions at the bottom of the form, and report what you observe to your class.

4. A self-managing team is discussing its budget. With a group, discuss the ethical issues raised in the following transactions:

   a. Harold suggests padding the budget. This violates Clarissa's moral code, but she remains silent.

   b. Ron keeps silent, because he thinks the group looks down on his race.

   c. Shelley says the whole thing is bogus anyway, because the team doesn't have enough information to create a realistic budget.

   d. Lenny says that Harold is right and calls for a vote.

      How do you think these ethical issues relate to the transactional and task processes of this team?

FORM 2.1 | SELF-ASSESSMENT OF LEADERSHIP

Mark the extent to which each statement represents what you believe to be true of yourself, and then ask a friend to complete the same form as she or he perceives you to be.

	Often	Sometimes	Rarely
1. I enjoy interacting in groups.	☐	☐	☐
2. People listen to me when I speak.	☐	☐	☐
3. I can get quiet people to talk.	☐	☐	☐
4. I am a good listener.	☐	☐	☐
5. I help people work out conflicts.	☐	☐	☐
6. It's fun to work with different kinds of people.	☐	☐	☐
7. I express my thoughts well.	☐	☐	☐
8. I am a credible person.	☐	☐	☐
9. I prepare ahead of time for meetings.	☐	☐	☐
10. When a group is off track, I bring it back to the subject.	☐	☐	☐
11. I can analyze ideas clearly.	☐	☐	☐
12. When tension is high, I use humor to ease it.	☐	☐	☐
13. I support my positions with logic.	☐	☐	☐
14. I am sensitive to others' feelings.	☐	☐	☐
15. I raise issues of ethics and morality.	☐	☐	☐
16. I work toward achieving goals.	☐	☐	☐
17. I keep a balance between the needs of people and the needs of the task.	☐	☐	☐
18. I summarize ideas to help the group.	☐	☐	☐
19. Doing what's right is important to me.	☐	☐	☐
20. I'm good at building team spirit.	☐	☐	☐

FORM 2.2 | OBSERVATION OF MEMBERS' ROLES

Observe a small group meeting. Enter the name of each member at the top, and tally each time someone acts as a facilitator for transactional or task processes or as a process blocker by playing individual roles. Where possible, record specifically which role is involved. The next page provides descriptions of these roles.

Members' Names

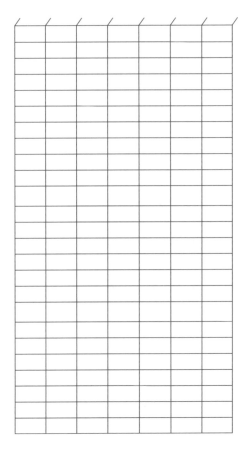

TASK PROCESSES FACILITATOR
    Initiator/contributor
    Information/opinion seeker
    Information/opinion giver
    Elaborator
    Coordinator
    Orienter
    Evaluator/critic
    Energizer
    Procedural technician
    Recorder

TRANSACTIONAL PROCESSES FACILITATOR
    Encourager
    Harmonizer/compromiser
    Gatekeeper
    Standard setter
    Observer
    Follower

PROCESS BLOCKER
    Aggressor/blocker
    Recognition seeker
    Self-confessor/help seeker
    Player/fun seeker
    Dominator
    Special interest pleader

Discuss:
    How did roles seem to combine for each member?
    In what ways did role behaviors contribute to the leadership of the group?
    Which members provided leadership?
    What roles were they filling?
    How and when did members take roles to balance the roles others were taking?
    When and if members played blocking roles, how did others respond?
    How did roles people took reflect ethical issues or decisions?

FORM 2.2 | CONTINUED—OBSERVATION OF MEMBERS' ROLES

TASK PROCESSES FACILITATOR'S ROLES

Initiator/contributor ... ... Proposes ideas or solutions
Information/opinion seeker ... ... Asks for facts, information, opinions, values, clarification
Information/opinion giver ... ... Offers facts, statistics, examples, opinions, beliefs
Elaborator ... ... Develops examples, extends ideas
Coordinator ... ... Pulls ideas, relationships together
Orienter ... ... Summarizes, calls attention to task
Evaluator/critic ... ... Analyzes data, reasoning, conclusions
Energizer ... ... Tries to motivate the group
Procedural technician ... ... Runs errands, distributes materials
Recorder ... ... Keeps records

TRANSACTIONAL PROCESSES FACILITATOR'S ROLES

Encourager ... ... Gives understanding, support
Harmonizer/compromiser ... ... Smooths, suggests ways to manage conflict
Gatekeeper ... ... Encourages participation, curbs excess
Standard setter ... ... Sets standards for tasks, ethics, goals
Observer ... ... Observes, gives feedback on processes
Follower ... ... Goes along with others

PROCESS BLOCKER'S ROLES

Aggressor/blocker ... ... Puts down others, takes issue, bulldozes, is negative
Recognition seeker ... ... Uses group to boost his/her ego
Self-confessor/help seeker ... ... Unloads personal woes, uses group for sympathy
Player/fun seeker ... ... Uninvolved in group, creates distractions
Dominator ... ... Manipulates, tries to control
Special interest pleader ... ... Uses team to serve own or another group's interests

Source: Based on K. D. Benne and P. Sheats, "Functional Roles of Group Members," *Journal of Social Issues, 4* (1948), 41–49.

"Groan, mutter, gnash—I hate meetings that drag and splutter."
Really? Then let's do something about those meetings.

THE "WORK" IN TEAMWORK

Planning the Process

3

Quotations from anonymous sufferers about the length, frustration, and ineffectiveness of meetings are legion. Some of our favorites include:

> *Meetings are groups that take minutes and waste hours.*
>
> *A camel is a horse put together in a meeting.*
>
> *To kill a project, hold a meeting.*

Are meetings really that bad? Well, ineffective ones are certainly costly. A typical eight-manager meeting can cost up to $700 an hour, not to mention the money that could be made if those managers were doing other things in support of the organization (Chaney & Lyden, 1998). Managers spend from 60–80 percent of their time in formal and informal meetings (Volkema & Niederman, 1996), and approximately one-third of that time is categorized as unproductive (Chaney & Lyden, 1998). You might be thinking, "Well, that's unacceptable," yet the need for meetings in the workplace increases as the corporate ladder becomes more of a stepstool, with organizations flattening out and more decisions being made by teams of people from all levels. Eventually there may be fewer face-to-face meetings, what with the increasing use of technology (virtual organizations, virtual teams, e-mail, groupware that guides on-site discussions electronically, videoconferencing, and so on). Nonetheless, the need to make meetings, whether online or on-site, more productive will continue to plague groups and teams.

How can you make meetings both productive and satisfying? The operative term is the *work* in *teamwork*. Funny thing about work: it's a four-letter word. It's said that some people don't mind work—they can sleep comfortably right alongside it. Americans even have been accused of having lost the work ethic. To the contrary, people in this individualistic society are accustomed to rolling up their sleeves and tackling a hard job alone. The problem is that when these individuals get together on a task, they don't always know how to work together as a team.

You may be on a work team for your job, this class, or some other activity even now. For a project to succeed, the team's meetings require solid planning—understanding the context and purposes of the team; deciding about a leader and about a recorder; identifying the expectations and responsibilities of the organization, the leader, and the team; and designing meetings so that interaction can flow along a reasonable agenda.

With all this in mind, our goals in this chapter are for you to:

1. Understand how a team relates to the context of the organization and to other systems
2. Know the advantages and disadvantages of—and alternatives to—designating a team leader
3. Know what qualities distinguish a person's potential as a good leader
4. Help a team to set norms and commitments for working on the task
5. Write clear, attainable goals and instrumental objectives for the task
6. Ensure that accurate records are kept of meeting actions and decisions
7. Be committed to preparing thoroughly for meetings
8. Know how to create and use agendas effectively

KNOW THE CONTEXT OF YOUR WORK

Teamwork doesn't happen in a vacuum. It's a focused, collaborative effort within a specific context. At the very beginning, you need to picture your team's relationships with and responsibilities to other systems.

ANALYZE THE SYSTEM

In a work team, some relationships are obvious. For example, the team usually is created by a parent organization to meet some organizational goal. Members may represent various levels and departments of that organization, thus bringing individual expertise to the team. The members are responsible for reporting to their managers, cooperating with all related departments, and contributing to the team's goals.

Sometimes, however, the context is not quite so obvious, and your team then must analyze the possible interdependencies. You may work in a team defined as a *collaborative alliance*, "a structure comprised of members from several different organizations . . . for the exchange or pooling of resources" (Heath & Sias, 1999, p. 357). Sometimes members meet at alternative sites, and/or they may meet online as virtual teams. In a collaborative alliance, team members must work together to achieve the goals of the parent organizations, yet they must share a sense of the mission of their team and create the structure and processes to achieve their goals.

Interdependence among systems even affects your work in this class. That is, your student groups function within the larger system of the class—which makes the class your parent organization and, we suppose, makes the professor your chief executive officer (CEO).

If your group wants to do a student survey, and it's okay with the "CEO," can you simply go out and do it? Maybe. The class operates within a larger system— the department—which in turn functions within the college and interacts with other academic departments, schools, and support systems. The college also functions within and interacts with other systems, such as state and federal systems, various accreditation systems, and legal systems. For example, your college may have a human research committee that would need to approve your survey, or you may need clearance from the public relations office. Each system and subsystem affects the other systems.

IDENTIFY RESPONSIBILITIES

The interdependence of teams in systems underscores an omnipresent issue: Teamwork is about responsibility. It's about the parent organization's responsibilities to the team and about the team members' responsibilities to one another, to their team, and to the parent organization.

Organizational Responsibilities   The system that creates a team has a responsibility to "do it right." That doesn't mean, sad to say, it always will. Doing it right means preparing and training members for their teamwork, a step that all too often is neglected in forming a workgroup or team. Doing it right also means giving the team the freedom—in other words, the autonomy—and the organizational support to do some key things (Gratton & Erickson, 2007):

1. Define the task as being different and distinct from those of other groups
2. Control both physical and social conditions without interference from outside management
3. Choose the processes for accomplishing and assessing its job

4. Develop a culture where managers mentor employees and support team members both in their technical work and in their interactions with others

Similarly, researchers have identified essential elements for success in a collaborative effort. These include a collaborative spirit (that is, "general principles regarding acceptable goals, values, and behavior that underlie and guide the collaborative alliance"), a shared mission or purpose, and shared power in developing information and making decisions (Heath & Sias, 1999, 358–359).

When organizations show their commitment to teams in this way, those teams are more likely to make risks pay off, both for themselves and for the organization or alliance. People who have the opportunity and the responsibility for creating their own work are more creative, more energetic, and more committed. They also simply do a better job (Ng & Van Dyne, 2005).

Team Responsibilities   A really gung-ho team can sometimes overlook interdependent responsibilities and get itself in trouble. To deserve autonomy and support, a work team must keep the confidence of the parent organization and other groups. That's why a team should identify its responsibilities:

To one another and to the leader, if there is one, for preparation, participation, and sharing leadership;

To the team, for ensuring transactional processes are dialogical and ethical, task processes are thorough and analytical, and decisions are ethically defensible;

To related departments or groups, for sharing information and reporting actions;

To the parent organization, for developing a team that justifies the organization's support and trust, that fulfills its task, and that reports on its progress and outcomes.

DECIDE ABOUT A LEADER

Sometimes management appoints a leader, sometimes not. For example, some self-managing teams in organizations are supervised and coached by an outside manager whose goal is to lead the teams until they can lead themselves. A specific team, however, may choose its own approach to leadership.

There are several approaches to leadership. Depending on the nature of the team and its goals, members might consider the following choices:

- Distribute leader functions among the team members according to their inclinations and talents. For example, a member with proven organizational talent might be responsible for meeting preparation, and a member with strong people skills might be responsible for reporting to the boss.
- Take turns being the primary leader according to a specific schedule. Self-managing teams often do this so that one person isn't stuck with the administrative tasks of leading for too long at a time. Some teams switch leaders every month or so.

- Share leadership among the members, and rely on good mutual planning and communication to fulfill the leader functions.
- Share leadership, but then allow a leader (or leaders) to emerge as the team works together over time. Someone frequently emerges in this role by filling leader functions and gaining the members' endorsement as leader.

Some people believe it is essential to begin with a designated leader. They reason that someone must take charge immediately to organize the meetings, get resources, represent the team, and facilitate participation. Although having a designated leader may be efficient, such tasks can be distributed among the members. A stronger argument is that a designated leader may be important when the task is very complex, interpersonal conflicts seem to be inevitable and someone must manage them, or the team's relationships with a parent organization and other systems are complicated and demand a strong spokesperson.

One argument against immediately designating a leader is that it takes time to select the right person, and you surely don't want to give that responsibility to the wrong one. Another drawback is that in a work team, saddling one person with handling all the paperwork, representing the team in outside meetings, following through on decisions, and so on in addition to his or her regular work duties may be unfair. It also may be too easy for a team to leave all responsibility up to the leader and then fail to do the work needed to develop a real team.

Wolff, Pescosolido, and Druskat (2002) studied 48 self-managing teams and found that leaders emerged as their skills and abilities best matched the task at hand. Given this flexibility, leaderless groups can be more productive than groups influenced by a single leader (Barge, 1989). Read about Zine Zone in Box 3.1.

It's often best to share functions and see if a leader emerges naturally as the team develops. Bormann (1990) reports that leaders emerge by "residues" (p. 205). In other words, members are eliminated as potential "leaders," one by one, until the sole remaining person assumes the leader role. Groups, Bormann finds, sometimes discover it is easier to decide who should *not* be the leader than who should be— although Schultz (1986) finds that individuals' communication shows who will probably emerge as leaders. In one study, Schultz had group members evaluate one another's communication behaviors after their first meetings, and on the basis of those ratings, she predicted correctly the emergent leaders in eight of nine groups. What did those people do? Their teammates rated them highly on goal-directedness, direction giving, summarizing, and self-assurance (p. 64). Those who emerged as leaders in this study, therefore, tended to demonstrate qualities that contributed to positive task and transactional processes in the group.

Important choices need to be made about a designated leader. If your team decides you want to designate someone, consider the qualifications for leadership we discussed in the last chapter. Keep in mind that whether you designate a leader or not, *all members* must share leadership through filling task and transactional roles in the day-to-day functioning of the team.

CHOOSE A RECORDER OR SECRETARY

It's entirely possible to get along without a designated leader, but having someone to take and report the minutes is essential. As a group, you will need to look back

BOX 3.1 | START THE DAY WITH COFFEE AND A SCRUM

Employees at Zine Zone, a fast-growing Internet company based outside of Boston, work in an environment filled with pressures and deadlines—many of which are intrinsic to the world of the Web. Every day brings new chat sessions to run, new software features to test. Look beyond the specifics, though, and you see challenges that plague startups in every field. How do people focus on their work, but still keep their colleagues informed about what they're doing? How do leaders enable crisp execution without imposing bureaucratic oversight?

Enter the Scrum. Zine Zone's core production team (along with a few people from other departments) gather at 9:30 A.M. to scope out that day's work and to identify obstacles that may interfere with specific projects. The Scrum takes its name and its inspiration from a rugby formation in which players from opposing teams lock themselves in a circle and battle for the ball. In this case, though, everyone is trying to move the ball in the same direction. "This is not a coffee klatch," says Cristen Bolter, production coordinator at Zine Zone. "Gathering as a team every day reminds us that we're all in this together."

Guiding Principle: Radical minimalism. "Our aim is modest: to identify short-term obstacles. The agenda is minimalist: What does the day look like? Are your projects on track? We want to fix problems both quickly and informally: People volunteer to help out, or they suggest a solution on the spot. If the problem requires more attention, we take it offline."

Best Practice: Face-to-face. "We're open, democratic, and extremely dependent on our computers. Even though we all work in one big room, we're still as likely to e-mail the people sitting next to us as we are to talk to them. But after a while, e-mail becomes a blur. Building in the face-to-face meeting provides daily glue, which helps to hold the team together."

Talking Stick: "The team stands in a circle. I go through a master list of projects, and each project owner gives an update and describes problems. People know they have to stick to the facts, or else we could end up standing around for hours."

Setting: "Standing is crucial. We sat down once, and 30 minutes sped by! The next day, several of our people boycotted the Scrum."

Source: Cathy Olofson, "Meeting I Never Miss," *Fast Company*, February–March 1999, p. 60. Reprinted with permission.

---

at what you discussed and decided at previous meetings. Given the unreliability of human memory, good records are essential. After all, team members may be distracted and miss important information, or they may hear and remember only what is most convenient for them.

With this in mind, someone needs to record an accurate summary of your team's work during each meeting. These notes, or meeting minutes, become the legal record of actions and decisions in formal groups, and some committees are required to send copies of these minutes to their parent groups. In groups governed by parliamentary procedure, keeping and submitting a record of the meetings is an absolute requirement. Most important, however, is that good notes help all teams progress smoothly from meeting to meeting.

You may elect a secretary for this job, but the recorder can be a volunteer or an appointee by the chairperson or leader. Alternatively, members can take turns as recorders, in which case they should have a clear understanding of when they will take the job and what they are to do. Generally, the secretary or recorder of any group should complete these tasks:

- Take the minutes of the meeting
- Write up and duplicate the minutes
- Distribute the minutes by mail or e-mail, and/or present the minutes to the group at the next meeting for approval
- Make corrections to the minutes at the direction of the group
- After approval, enter minutes into the records of the group

Not everyone has the skills to be a good recorder. Recording good minutes demands objectivity, perceptive listening, accurate note taking, and the ability to summarize proceedings both promptly and accurately. If the members agree, you might tape-record the sessions to provide a check on accuracy.

The team needs to support the recorder's effort, so he or she should be free to ask for clarification whenever necessary. Still, the point is not to write down everything that is said. Normally, all that appears in the minutes is:

- Who attended
- Who called the meeting to order
- Information reported for each item of business
- The precise wording of each motion
- The outcome of a vote on motions (passed or failed) and the type of vote (voice, show of hands, or by ballot)

A particular group or team may want more specific details in its minutes; often a member will request that information be included that can be referred to later. Generally, minutes are better if they are accurate but somewhat terse. In fact, a recorder who scribbles too frantically often inhibits members from saying what they really think. The objective is to record only the major information and decisions for future reference. For example, suppose the team is in conflict over an issue. The minutes need not include any personal remarks, but they do need to include the specific issues raised and what the decision was.

Here's an example of poor notes: "Tom said Genelle was an idiot for thinking we could possibly spend money on hiring a consultant, and Genelle said Tom obviously hadn't looked at the budget or he'd know we had enough money, so we are going to get a consultant." These notes are much too word-for-word and not an objective account.

Better minutes might go like this: "We found the budget includes $600.00 for a consultant, and Tony volunteered to get a list of consultants who would work for that amount. He will bring the list, with résumés of the candidates, for the team to consider on October 25."

SET WORK EXPECTATIONS

Most norms—from ways of dressing to ways of thinking to ways of interacting—develop over time as part of the team culture. This is fine, but expectations about commitments, goals, and meetings need to be discussed early in the life of the team.

TIME AND RESPONSIBILITY COMMITMENTS

Imagine you've knocked yourself out for several weeks, and then a teammate who is consistently absent, late, and unprepared breezes in saying, "Well, I just don't have the time," or even more endearingly, "Well, that's just the way I am!"

These things happen all the time in face-to-face groups. Imagine how much more difficult it will be to develop a good working relationship in virtual teams. Platt (1999) talks about how "distance, boundaries, and reliance on communication technology add levels of complexity that ordinary teams just do not have" (p. 4). In a virtual team, you will not be able to use facial expressions and vocal expression to understand one another, you may be working across vast cultural differences, and you will not have the day-to-day chances to develop relationships with one another that you have when you work in the same environment and can see each other in meetings and in informal settings. Before this problem arises, the team needs to discuss and define what they expect from one another.

For example, take the commitment of time. North Americans are driven by time: "Time is money," "Don't be late," and "Don't waste my time." When someone arrives late for an appointment in the United States, others often think the late person is irresponsible, incompetent, rebellious, or manipulative.

Other cultures, however, might think North Americans are slaves to time. Bruneau (1988) suggests that a culture so obsessed with time suffers from "chronophilia," in which life is dictated by clocks and schedules. Contrast this attitude with that of the Hopi, who believe each person, plant, and animal has its own time system. The Hopi don't impose one entity's deadline on another (Porter & Samovar, 1994, p. 18). In the Masai culture, the wisdom of the past guides life, and the present and future are irrelevant. Public transportation in Kenya, for example, has no schedule. When Masai tell a nervous American the bus will leave "just now," they actually mean "when the bus is full, of course," and not before (Skow & Samovar, 1991, p. 95).

Hall (1994) describes the time concepts of different cultures along a range from *monochronic* to *polychronic*. In a **monochronic culture**—like most of those in North America—people generally attend to one thing at a time. In a **polychronic culture**—like most of those in Latin America—people do many things at once. In a business meeting, monochronic members might be prompt and stick to the agenda so they can finish on time, but polychronic members might be late because their previous meeting ran long. Why? Because the polychronic members, unlike the monochronic folks, were willing to override the agenda to deal with other concerns and social relationships in addition to the explicit goals of the meeting.

Porter and Samovar (1994, p. 18) note:

> Even within the dominant mainstream of American culture, we find groups that have learned to perceive time in ways that appear strange to many outsiders. Hispanics frequently refer to Mexican or Latino time when their timing differs from the predominant Anglo concept, and African Americans often use what is referred to as BPT (black people's time) or hang-loose time—maintaining that priority belongs to what is happening at that instant.

This is why time can be such a huge issue, with some team members feeling unreasonably pressured and others feeling frustrated by the former group's slack attendance and apparent indifference toward deadlines. Therefore, at the very beginning, the team must negotiate their approach toward time and work. The members need to explore, individual by individual, how much time—per day, per week, per month—each can reasonably commit to meetings and outside preparation. They need to consider what problems with time other members may have and how much time each member is willing to give. They also need to negotiate ways to fit their schedules together to produce feasible blocks of time in which to work as a team. This process should help the team to:

- Agree on team norms for time and work, such as being on time to meetings, not missing meetings, and meeting work deadlines
- Agree on ways to keep ahead of problems, such as by systematically checking progress at each stage of the task instead of waiting until the end
- Agree on ways of dealing with exceptions, such as by communicating among members and sharing information with those who are absent or late

One team we knew fervently wished they had set some norms on these issues when, near the end of the project, they discovered one member had "just assumed" the others would "pick up" the work he had not done. In the end, the team managed to produce a good project because the other members pulled together—with no thanks to the errant member.

MEETING SCHEDULES

We urge teams to share their phone numbers and schedules and to identify potential meeting periods. Next, set specific meeting times—and a few alternatives in case of unforeseen glitches—for the entire stretch of the team's work. Get those meeting dates on everyone's calendar, but also have someone remind members by phone or by note to avoid any unnecessary misses. As the work proceeds, you may cancel some meetings and add others, but at least you have a basic plan from which to work.

Regular meetings often are essential, because members need to develop full communication, mutual understanding, information, and cohesiveness by being together. Do all groups need to meet regularly, however? No. Some—such as groups of people who live a great distance apart or teams of specialists who work mostly apart and communicate by e-mail—might meet face to face only when necessary.

Even with groups that meet regularly, sometimes a meeting is pointless. Myrsiades (2000) notes that meetings aren't necessary when all they contain is a series of announcements or reports. In fact, this information is probably better disseminated to individuals before a meeting so they have time to absorb and think about it before the group comes together.

Alternatively, you need a meeting when the team needs to:

- Work on goals, norms, and approaches
- Develop plans, timelines, work distribution, and assignments
- Work on team building and connecting
- Resolve problems with transactional and task processes

PURPOSES AND GOALS

We all need to know where we're going if we're to know that we've arrived. Even when we change destinations in the middle of a trip, knowing where we were going gives us a point of comparison for where we wind up in the end. Any work team has three important reasons to set its goals quickly:

1. To clarify both team and organizational expectations.
2. To develop a plan for doing its work. (Good plans are flexible, but they map out a route to the desired results.)
3. To develop strategies for evaluating team processes and outcomes.

When a team gets down to business, it needs to know what its purposes are; then it can define its goals. As your team works toward its goals, it may reassess and change them based on new information or insights.

Understanding Purposes   When setting goals, begin by considering who created your team and for what purposes. In your class, the team founder may have been the professor. In a public institution or a private corporation, it may have been the CEO, a task force, or a management team. Perhaps you and several others organized your group for reasons of your own. Whoever started the whole thing, however, probably made some statement—or **charge**—to the team regarding what it was to do. Charges fall into several overlapping categories:

Information gathering asks for research and investigation focusing on a specific problem or issue, and this charge usually involves preparing a report. Gathering information also is a component of all other team purposes.

Problem analysis requires the team to analyze causes and effects and, possibly, to make recommendations about possible solutions. In a college setting, a problem-analysis team might focus on anything from a parking problem to plagiarism.

Decision making usually completes the information-gathering and problem-analysis charges and requires the team to make specific decisions they or some other group will then implement.

Which of the five "needs" might have saved this meeting?

Project might be a specific goal, such as to design and build a new-model automobile, or a vague goal, such as "to identify and implement ways to improve quality." A group with the latter charge might select consumer feedback to study, and then develop, implement, and assess ideas for improvement.

All these charges are legitimate and desirable uses for teams. Unfortunately, however, organizations can use, misuse, and even abuse groups. Organizations may initiate groups for purely political—and sometimes unethical—purposes. They may create teams to deceive people into believing they are participating in decisions that management has already made. Sometimes, too, organizations establish groups only to soothe angry people or to defuse a given crisis. We've seen institutions create task forces to "study the issue" when enough people got mad but then impose restrictions on timing, resources, support, and personnel that created insurmountable obstacles to progress. When organizations abuse their teams like this, people become cynical, and everybody loses.

To us, these abuses of group purposes are both unethical and reprehensible. If your team is being misused and abused, however, don't panic. You may feel your best ethical choice is to refuse to serve; however, your team still might accomplish excellent results despite the manipulative intent. On occasion, you *can* make lemonade out of the proverbial lemon, but you need to know early on that it really is a lemon and not a peach, so that your team can set goals they will be proud to reach.

Defining Goals   With teams, you can't just "wing it" without knowing your goals. As professors, we have seen faculty and administration team projects fail because the members just didn't want to deal with setting goals and objectives. For example, curriculum-development teams often fail to develop cohesive study units for students "because the goals of study are not explicit" (Traver, 1998, p. 70). If you've ever taken a class in which the goals were unclear, you probably understand why goals are so important—they give you a target for which to plan a logical approach.

Any work team needs to set its goals quickly to clarify both team and organizational expectations, to develop a work plan, and to develop strategies for evaluating the team's processes and outcomes. Granted, sometimes a little ambiguity isn't all bad. For example, the less definition, the more room to be creative and to meet individual members' preferences. An ill-defined charge, however, can doom a team to failure. For example, your boss may put you on a task force charged to "interface with the academic community." Now, how can you find out what that actually means?

1. *Examine the language of the charge.* Look carefully at the specific language. What does your boss mean by *interface*? Could it mean "communicate"? If so, about what? Could it mean "collaborate"? If so, on what? Perhaps *interface* means to develop mutually beneficial, cooperative programs, but who is to interface with whom? And what does *academic community* mean? A local university? Colleges? High schools, junior highs, or elementary schools? And what elements of the "academic community" are included? Teachers? Students? Support personnel? Administrators?

2. *Request clarification.* If the charge is unclear, your team might need to outline its understanding of the task to present to the founder to either clarify or confirm. Even then, however, you may get more of an overview than a direct answer: "Well, more and more corporations are reaching out to schools, helping with programs, even influencing curricula. We just thought it was time for us to do something with the local colleges." Perhaps the organization hopes to improve community relations, influence college programs, or employ better-prepared graduates. The more you find out about these expectations, the better prepared you are to write your goals.

3. *Visualize the outcome.* Try to specify the final products of your team's work. Again, your founder may not be very specific: "We want a report." But on what topics? "Uh, maybe, what other companies are doing, what the colleges want, what we want them to do to prepare students for jobs with us . . . oh, and some ideas for things we could do." A written report or an oral report? "Yes." Yes, what? "Yes, both." Your team must boil all this down into some possible goals, and your discussion might lead to goals such as:
    *   Get information on what colleges see as a helpful corporate role.
    *   Get information on current "interfacing" between business and academia.
    *   Find out what businesses want colleges to do better.
    *   Prepare a written report.
    *   Prepare an oral report.
    *   Suggest ideas for what your company can do.

    In this example, you now have six goals: three information-gathering tasks, one problem-analysis and idea-generating task, and two reporting tasks. Now you want to work out each specific goal so that you can reach it.

4. *Consider criteria for success.* How will you measure your achievement? Taking the written report as an example, ask yourselves the following questions:
    *   What do you want the report to do? (Provide complete information? If so, about what areas? Document information clearly and accurately? If so, how?)
    *   What do you want the report to be like? (Present information professionally? Be well written, clear, and readable?)
    *   When do you want to submit the report? To whom?
    *   How long should the report be?

With this information now established, it's time to write your major goals. This may be touchier than it sounds, however. It's necessary for goals to be open enough that everyone can commit to them, perhaps for different individual reasons, but also specific enough that your team knows precisely what they want to achieve. The perfect goal statement is both clear and measurable. An example might be:

> *Major goal.* On October 1, to present to Ms. Sorensen, director of community relations, a written report on the investigation and recommendations of the V.V. Video Company Task Force on Corporate and College Interfacing.
>
> *Criteria.* The report will be approximately twenty pages long, complete, well written, documented, and professionally prepared.

Even with these criteria, however, we can almost guarantee individuals will interpret adjectives such as *well written*, *documented*, and *professional* differently. Soon the team will need to look at examples of written reports so that you can agree more specifically on what these criteria mean—and that's for just one of your six goals.

Identifying Instrumental Objectives   It takes a number of steps to reach each goal, and these steps are known as **instrumental objectives.** Identifying these steps is critical to creating a path toward your goal. To find out what colleges and corporations are now doing, instrumental objectives might include:

1. Design a survey.
2. Survey local organizations and institutions.
3. Analyze the results of that survey.

Planning these steps is critical. We've seen teams plan and duplicate surveys only to discover they skipped the instrumental objective of getting permission from the institution to conduct the survey. This meant delays, rewriting the survey to meet the institutional requirements, and missing deadlines. The better you plan your instrumental objectives at the outset, the fewer times you will slap your foreheads and wail, "Why didn't we see that before?"

A timeline for achieving instrumental objectives can show the path to your goal. Figure 3.1 shows a timeline that a group might use to create a videotape as a class

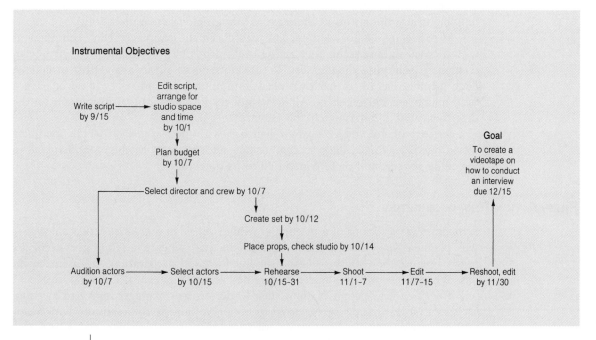

FIGURE 3.1

The path of instrumental objectives to goal achievement.

project. Note how each step is identified relative to the other instrumental objectives necessary to reach the goal. The timeline can show you where you need more—or less—time, and it can reveal the need for contingency planning as well.

Confirming Understanding and Commitment   It's painful when you believe team members are standing together and suddenly come to the rueful realization that your feet aren't even on the same planet. The team may need to confirm its members' mutual understanding of what the goals are as well as their commitment to achieving them. It helps to paraphrase team goals and to hypothesize what they mean operationally.

For example, suppose one of your goals is "To find a solution to the parking problem." Someone might paraphrase (badly, in this case) your goal as "So we want to get the board to approve new parking lots," and a teammate might hypothesize, "That would include getting parking closer to the buildings." As members clarify their meanings, they might note that "a solution" might involve ideas other than parking lots (so the member who paraphrased jumped the gun). They also might note that their hypothesis provides one criterion they might want to adopt.

When everyone can express close to the same ideas about what the goals are, you've negotiated a meaning for those goals. You still may need to negotiate everyone's commitment to those goals, however. If some believe the goals are worth working for and some do not, or if three members can give great time and energy to achieving them and four are willing to commit little, then success is improbable. You get commitment from team members in two ways: by asking for it, and by building it into the norms of the team as you go along. You need both.

At this stage of goal setting, you can check the team members' commitment with a census-taking technique: asking each member to what extent she or he can commit to achieving these goals. We are not suggesting loyalty oaths, of course. Each member has his or her own needs and approach, and you will never have a total match among members. All you want to do is ensure that everyone's on the same boat with approximately the same rowing pace.

Degrees of commitment often increase with performance. As the members work together and see some success in their efforts, they become more involved in the entire process and more committed to its outcomes.

PREPARATION RESPONSIBILITIES

Sometimes we walk out of a meeting crowing over what a great experience it was—well planned, smooth, interesting, and productive. When a meeting goes well, it's partly because the team took responsibility for good preparation and useful agendas. When a meeting goes badly, it may be because the team planned poorly.

You often hear people blaming their leader or their manager for a bad meeting. Of course, a leader may be expected to obtain resources, communicate with members and the parent organization or other related systems, solve problems, and generally "run" the meeting. The team should not assume a designated leader will do all this, however, and the leader should not make such assumptions, either.

Recall that designated leaders may not necessarily know how to lead a team or manage a meeting, and many teams choose not to designate a single leader but to distribute or share leadership. That's why, at every meeting, members need to share leadership, summarize what they've accomplished, and project what they will need to cover in the next meeting. This means the following:

- Before a meeting ends, plan objectives and needed resources for the next meeting.
- Designate someone to ensure meeting arrangements and resources are ready.
- Designate someone to create an agenda that considers time, participants, issues, and order of discussion.
- Designate someone to publish and distribute the agenda before the next meeting.

All this is useless, however, if the members haven't done their homework. Too frequently, the meeting time goes on a member's calendar, but the preparation period does not. We cannot say this strongly enough: Every member must set aside time to prepare before the meeting! Successful meetings require that each member arrives fully prepared, both materially—with any needed information, resources, and assignments—and mentally.

Think about the meeting. Take the time to organize and to understand important information. Get a mental set for moving the processes along productively. As Box 3.2 illustrates, that is leadership.

Hastings, Bixby, and Chaudhry-Lawton (1986) write that ideally, "before the team splits up to work apart, they [members] will have a clear idea of what each person is mandated to do. Each team member acts with delegated authority. Team members see that their roles are central to others, and develop a greater sense of responsibility to do what they have said they will do. Each person is seen as a team ambassador" (p. 119).

BOX 3.2	GETTING A JUMP START

Experts stress that all good meeting leaders share one characteristic: preparation. A lack of preparation will spell certain failure in the meeting room.

"Usually people will just dive into a meeting without thinking," said Ann Rice, a senior vice president with the Forum Corporation, an international training and consulting firm in Boston. "People have to figure out what is the purpose and objective of a meeting. What do we want people to walk out of a meeting with?" said Rice. "Too many times, a meeting strays off course and hours are wasted."

Good meeting leaders don't meet unless there's an absolute need; they decide what their goals are, and then go about reaching them in an efficient manner. . . . Beyond the logistical rules, personal leadership styles are critical—and highly variable. . . .

"Good meeting leaders do not always put themselves into so-called power positions," said Rice. "Power has this connotation of ego, charisma, and dominance. There are times when it's wise to turn over a part of an agenda to the group or to someone who can create more power in the group."

Source: Condensed from Dean Chang, "The Makings of a Powerful Meeting Leader," *Corporate Travel*, Winter 1991, p. 30. Used with permission.

PLAN AGENDAS

A good meeting is based on an **agenda**, a structure guiding transactional and task processes so that members can focus their discussion. The type of agenda and the way it is created depend on what needs to happen at a specific meeting.

AGENDA TYPES

An agenda can be simple and straightforward, or it can be creative and artful. An agenda can be extremely informal or quite formal and rigid. It all depends on what your specific meeting needs.

Informal and Special Agendas   An informal or special agenda is custom designed for a given meeting, which could be anything from an ad hoc, one-time meeting to a workshop extending over several days. For example, a classroom exercise gives a group limited time to accomplish a specific task, so students rarely talk about their agenda. They just start. It saves time and trouble, however, if the group first discusses what they will do. Their ad hoc agenda might look something like this:

1.   Introduce yourselves.
2.   Ask someone to take notes.
3.   Decide on what we need to do by the end of the meeting.
4.   Plan steps to reach the goal.
5.   Get all information about our task on the table.
6.   Work through the process to the goal.
7.   Summarize what we've accomplished.

Of course, this agenda must be adapted to the specific meeting's purpose, but using it as a checklist helps your group work through its task efficiently.

Formal Agendas   Some agendas follow a traditional list of procedures, perhaps because the members are more comfortable with a predictable structure or the parent organization requires parliamentary procedures, such as the most recent revision of *Robert's Rules of Order* (Robert III, Evans, Honemann, & Balch, 2000). These rules guide the processes for writing bylaws, electing officers, making motions, voting, and so on. Written for democratic bodies that are adversarial and political, parliamentary rules recognize that members will engage in every possible means of persuasion. If their interaction is not structured carefully, however, the weakest voices will not be heard and the meetings will be bedlam. Although the content under each category varies from meeting to meeting, the predictable format is as follows:

1.   Meeting called to order by chair or president
2.   Minutes distributed or read by secretary
3.   Approval of minutes
4.   Committee reports from standing committees and special committees
5.   Old business (motions being discussed when the last meeting adjourned)

6. New business (motions not previously introduced)
7. Announcements by members or officers
8. Adjournment

AGENDA PLANNING

Woe betide the manager who calls a meeting without planning a workable agenda. The result is a lousy meeting.

NetCatalyst, a high-tech firm with thirty-six employees, was having problems with its meetings. Derek McLeish, COO of the company, found that company meetings were "haphazardly scheduled. . . . Rounding up participants was a problem. Agenda items didn't always get addressed. Decisions seemed to take eons to reach." He corrected the problem by setting regular Monday morning meetings with coffee and doughnuts (always an incentive!) and, more important, by having his employees e-mail him in advance about their projects. From that he created an agenda that guided the team's discussion (Vaughn, 2001).

A team that meets over a period of time usually needs custom-designed agendas. This means choosing, ordering, and phrasing the necessary steps to be covered in the meeting in ways that facilitate both task and transactional processes.

Selecting Items   Suppose you've volunteered to create the agenda for a team meeting. Last week, the members talked about expectations. For the next meeting, however, your purpose is to open discussion and to set goals, so your agenda might include only four items:

1. Review the background and charge to the team.
2. Brainstorm to identify possible goals.
3. Draft and revise specific goals.
4. Discuss members' agreement with and commitment to those goals.

In contrast, suppose your project team is to create a marketing plan for a specific product, and at the last meeting, you shared the data you need. Thus, your agenda for the next meeting might have only two items:

1. Brainstorm ideas.
2. Discuss ideas.

Planning the agenda requires understanding what members need to accomplish by the end of the meeting and what issues must be discussed. You need to estimate how many issues are pending, how straightforward or complex each one is, and how much discussion (or hot debate) it will take to resolve each of them.

Developing the Order and Time Allotments   Each item we've discussed so far helps you to decide how to order the items on your agenda. Ordering may be a logical progression of steps, but it also may be management of conflicting priorities. For example, suppose the organization is currently suffering through management upheavals, and your teammates are anxious. They need information and time to talk about the issues. The team also must make an immediate decision about a proposed project, however. You know you can get someone in to talk about the management changes, but you also know the team will want to ask questions and discuss the potential impact of these changes. Both will take a lot of time. So, when planning the agenda, you would consider the following questions:

- Should the speaker on management changes be first? (If we discuss these changes first, however, it might agitate the team too much—and take too much time—to deal with the project proposal.)
- Should the project proposal be discussed first? (If we haven't discussed the hot topic of management changes first, the team might be too distracted to concentrate on the project proposal anyway.)
- Should the team have two separate meetings and, if so, in which order? (Can we find a way to postpone the project decision? Can we have two meetings in one week?)

You would need to make these decisions partly on the basis of what you know about your teammates. In this example, we would guess that two meetings might be the better way to allow full discussion of both issues—and then you would need two different agendas. And so it goes.

Phrasing the Steps   You can take any number of approaches to phrasing agenda items. In Chapter 8, we develop agenda steps that guide the problem-analysis and decision-making processes. Here, however, we only mention two ways to phrase agenda items: topical format and question format.

If everyone has a clear sense of where the team is going and your only purpose is to review and then discuss some information, the agenda needs only to order the topics. A simple topical format can be terse and to the point, such as:

1. Review notes from last meeting.
2. Hear report from Raul.
3. Hear report from Jan.
4. Discuss info relating to Dale's proposal.
5. Plan agenda for next meeting.
6. Schedule time and place for next meeting.

If you need to think through the implications of a given proposal, however, a question format can analyze the recommendation:

1. How well does the proposal meet our goals?
2. What are the advantages of the proposal?
3. What are the disadvantages?
4. What are the ethical implications?
5. What are the legal implications?

Several other questions are possible, but you get the idea. The question format guides the order and kicks off the discussion, but it leaves wide open spaces for thinking both critically and creatively.

Distributing and Modifying   If people have the agenda early, it helps them to do their homework, so distributing the agenda in advance can save a lot of blithering around at the meeting. The team may want to require the agenda to be duplicated and distributed to members at a certain time before each meeting.

An agenda is only a plan, however, not a manifesto. Any agenda can be modified at the beginning of a meeting. A member might propose adding items, shifting items, or even suspending the agenda to cope with an emergency. The agenda should facilitate team processes, not stifle them. There must be room for spontaneity and adjustment, and modifying the agenda is one way of providing that.

SUMMARY

Beginning the work of a team requires that you know the context for your task. You need to analyze the system, the purpose your founder had in mind for the team, and the interdependencies between and among parts of the system. It's also important to recognize both the organization's responsibilities to give the team sufficient autonomy and support to do its job and the team's responsibilities to the organization, to one another, and to the development of the team.

Within that context, your team has several decisions to make at the outset. One is whether to designate a leader, to share or distribute leader functions, or to wait for a leader to emerge. You also need to select someone to take, record, and report minutes of the meeting. You may elect a secretary (a requirement for a group governed by parliamentary procedure), or you may ask for volunteers or appoint someone. Whoever does the job must be reliable and accurate. Minutes should cover only the essentials of the meeting, rather than be a word-by-word record of what was said by whom and why.

Early in the life of a team, members also need to set norms or expectations that will advance the task processes, particularly those regarding time and responsibility commitments. The team needs to articulate quickly the task goals and the instrumental objectives required to reach those goals, and it must also confirm the teammates' understanding of and commitment to those goals. In addition, it is important to create meeting schedules so members can plan for and commit to the team's work.

Making meetings work for your team is everyone's responsibility—the team's, the individual members', and the leader's. Although a designated leader may fulfill specific functions, the team must assign responsibilities and individuals must prepare for their own participation. Part of this preparation involves planning meeting strategies, including creating either informal or formal agendas, depending on the purpose of the meeting as well as on the type of parent organization. Consider the purposes of the meeting as well as the interests of the members when developing the order and phrasing of the items on the agenda. To be most useful, agendas should be distributed early and be readily open to modification.

Exercises

1. As a team, locate a working committee or task force, such as one of your college's faculty or student organizations or committees. Using Form 3.1, find out about the group from someone connected with it—the founder, the leader, or a member. Get permission and observe several meetings. How do aspects of the group's development seem to affect the meetings? How effective do you think the group is, and why? Once

you've identified the development of the team, report what you've learned to the class.

2. Meet with a group of students. Assume you work for Families, Inc., a nonprofit organization that keeps troubled families together with counseling, seminars, activities, and financial assistance. The president of your organization has assigned your task force to investigate how Families, Inc., can cooperate with businesses and colleges to reach more families in trouble. Using Form 3.2, set goals, instrumental objectives, and criteria for your task force.

3. Your job is to create an agenda for a future meeting of your class. The purpose of that meeting is to create a list of test questions to include in a special examination for high school teachers who work with student groups. Don't make the list—just create the agenda for the meeting. Use Form 3.3, be realistic about information, resources, time limitations, and such.

4. Critically analyze a task group meeting in which you've participated. How well did the group understand its relationships to other groups and systems? To what extent were the goals—and the criteria for achieving them—clear to the group members? How did the goals affect the transactional and task processes? How did they affect accomplishing the task? What were the group norms? Did these norms facilitate or impede the group's work? How was the meeting? Was there a written agenda? Did the agenda work? Did it help the members to focus on the task and discuss issues effectively? What worked well? What would have made the meeting better?

FORM 3.1 | TEAM IDENTIFICATION ANALYSIS

To identify the who-what-why-where-when-how of your team, complete the grid with this information:

Reasons For members, why they were chosen for the team; for others, what their relationships to the team might be

Goals For members, what each would like to get from the teamwork; for others, what they expect the team to produce

Resources For members, what each can contribute (talents, skills, abilities, resources, and so on); for others, what they can/will provide for the team's work

Limitations For members, how each may be limited (time, resources, and so on); for others, how their involvement may be restricted

	Reasons	Goals	Resources	Limitations
Members				
Founder				
Related Teams or Units				

Note below any other history, circumstances, or comments that are important to understanding the team and its context:

FORM 3.2 | TEAM GOALS ANALYSIS

Together, set the *goals* for the team's work. Then identify the *instrumental objectives* the team must accomplish to reach each goal and the *criteria* the team will use to judge its success in reaching each goal. (Duplicate this form for additional goals.)

Goal #1

_____

_____

Instrumental objectives to goal #1

_____

_____

_____

_____

Criteria for reaching goal #1

_____

_____

_____

_____

Goal #2

_____

_____

Instrumental objectives for goal #2

_____

_____

_____

_____

Criteria for reaching goal #2

_____

_____

_____

_____

FORM 3.3 | AGENDA PLANNING

Step 1. Survey these planning data before creating the agenda.

Purposes of the meeting

_____
_____
_____

Special concerns of members

_____
_____
_____

Time limitations

_____
_____

Special equipment/resource needs	Persons responsible for arranging for/ obtaining item

Step 2. Using the above data, arrange your agenda to allow time for members to discuss issues and arrive at goals. If an individual is responsible for reporting a given item or facilitating a discussion, indicate that responsibility on the form. Be sure to include time to prepare for the next meeting.

	Person Responsible	Approximate Time
Item #1		
Item #2		
Item #3		
Item #4		
Item #5		
Item #6		
Item #7		

Notes to remember for the meeting:
_____

"Make a team out of this group? Nah—can't be done!"
Sure it can. You just have to "get it together."

THE "TEAM" IN TEAMWORK

4

Bringing Individuals Together

CHAPTER CONTENTS

A Superteam Model

Organizational Environments

- Organizational Cultures
- Organizational Strategies

Individual Members

- Why People Join Teams
- What Individuals Bring

Team Development

- Developing by Stages
- Creating Team Attributes

Teamwork Through Electronics

- Virtual Teams: The Good News and Bad News

Teamwork Improvement

- Sources of Feedback
- Uses of Feedback

Summary

Exercises

It's one thing to get a group together, but it's quite another to forge that group into a team. Everyone has experienced ho-hum meetings or, worse, left a group muttering, "Not on pain of dismemberment and death will I ever work with those people again." Not a pretty picture, obviously, but in this chapter, we start with a different one—a model of the "superteam" toward which your group can strive. We then take you through the processes of building a team. A team develops in the context of an organizational culture, either real or virtual, and it includes individual members whose characteristics and motivations help to shape it. A team creates its own identity and develops through a series of phases, changing and growing through feedback and analysis.

By the end of this chapter, you should:

1. Have a mental picture of the ideal team
2. Know how organizational culture affects a team's development
3. Understand how individual members' motivations and characteristics affect a team's development
4. Know the ways a team develops its own characteristics
5. Understand the phases a team goes through as it develops
6. Know means and impacts of electronic teamwork
7. Know how to get—and use—feedback to help a team develop

A SUPERTEAM MODEL

When writers get started on the "ideal," they sometimes make it sound like metaphysical hocus-pocus or, worse, pure hype. Much writing about teams seems to be "Rah, rah, sis boom bah," cheerleading for the good old team concept.

That's not what we want to do here. We do, however, want to start with a vision of what the ultimate team would look like, a model for which to strive. Teams like those we describe here are possible. We know because we have experienced them and, in contrast to more ordinary teams, have found the experiences rich and productive. Hastings, Bixby, and Chaudhry-Lawton (1987), a British consulting group, coined the term **superteams** for groups that "weave together a rich fabric of competencies, experience, attitudes, and values which create a tightly woven, integrated cloth suitable for many purposes" (pp. 10–12).

Members of outstanding teams can and do describe precisely how their teams work together, and researchers who have observed such teams have described what they have seen. We have rephrased and subdivided the characteristics identified by Hastings and colleagues in terms of transactional processes, task processes, and systems relationships to place them in the context of this book.

In their *transactional processes*, superteams are:

Success-driven. They have energy, excitement, and commitment and thrive on the recognition success brings.

Committed to quality; never satisfied. They have very high expectations of themselves and others and constantly look for ways to improve.

Flexible but consistent. They work best with principles and guidelines rather than with rules, but they also consistently maintain communication, working apart as well as together.

Active. They are quick to respond, positive, and optimistic, and they make things happen.

Leader-valuing. They value leaders who maintain direction, energy, and commitment, and they expect the leader—with their help—to fight for support and resources.

People-valuing and cooperative. They respect knowledge, competence, and contributions over status and position, and they focus on cooperation and problem solving.

In their *task processes*, superteams are:

Vision-driven and goal-oriented. They are persistent, obsessive yet flexible, and continuously asking, "What are we trying to achieve?" as well as devising strategies for turning that vision into reality.

Analytical, tenacious, and inventive. They distinguish priorities, confront issues, and choose flexible, creative, or routine approaches appropriately to remove obstacles.

Creative and innovative. They take legitimate risks to achieve significant gains.

In their *systems relationships*, superteams are:

Networking. They build formal and informal networks, and they include people who matter to them and can help them.

Visible and accessible. They communicate what they are and solicit feedback and help from outside the team.

Committed. They understand the larger system's strategy and philosophy and want to achieve the organizational goals. They thrive in an open culture where responsibility and authority are delegated to them to produce agreed-on results.

Mutually influential with their organization. Teams share power with their founder, because the members' influence is based on credibility rather than on authority.

We've seen members of highly motivated, strong teams turn to each other and say, "Damn, we're good!" When this feeling motivates the members to reach for bigger and better things, that's a positive outcome.

It is true that sometimes superteams have such success that they get a little carried away with themselves: "Superteams sometimes seem arrogant—and this can be the cause of their downfall!" (Hastings et al., 1987, p. 12). Feeling too good—being too cohesive—can lead to excesses of ego, blind spots, declines in productivity, and even arrogance. We examine the dynamics of that phenomenon—and what to do about it—in Chapter 12.

With that said, we see an accurate image emerging from this list. The superteam achieves its goals, and then some. It's something for which to strive, but getting there takes understanding and work. A superteam doesn't just happen. And it doesn't happen in a vacuum. The organization (or organizations) that put it to-gether provide an environment—good or bad—in which it can grow.

ORGANIZATIONAL ENVIRONMENTS

You may already have experienced the impact an organization can have on the way its employees feel and the way they interact. They work in an environment that either helps them or hinders them in their work. That environment influences a team's development through the culture of the organization and its management strategies.

ORGANIZATIONAL CULTURES

As Taormina (2007) observed, an **organizational culture** is the "attitudes, values, beliefs, and behaviors that are shared by a particular group of people" (p. 86). You won't find an organization's culture written down in a manual. Instead, people work together to create and perpetuate ways of thinking and behaving that become norms for the group. Newcomers to the group learn about the culture in subtle ways. In addition to watching how people interact to learn about culture, newcomers are often told stories about the organization's heroes, usually as they embody a core value of the organization. At the Nordstrom department stores, a new employee might hear about a staff person who ran out of the store and used her own quarters in a parking meter to allow a customer to shop longer without getting a parking ticket. Southwest Airlines employees tell stories about employees who used their own cars to drive stranded customers to their destinations. In each case, a newcomer would understand the importance of going "above and beyond" to give excellent customer service.

Organizations develop norms, expectations, and responses that become part of their culture, and this culture guides how people in that organization act and what they do. We recently observed the organizational culture of a large hospital. It was unmistakably one of care and concern. No matter how rushed or exhausted from 12-hour shifts, people spoke with compassion and focused on the patients' well-being. We were startled when one nurse was abrupt and rude; later, we found out she was not a permanent employee. This hospital's culture was so strong that we, as outsiders, could tell when one individual simply wasn't a part of it.

ORGANIZATIONAL STRATEGIES

Taormina (2007) identifies three types of organizational culture: bureaucratic, innovative, and supportive. Although you can find evidence of all three types in most organizations, usually you'll see one emerge as the predominant culture. Familiarity with these types of organizational cultures can help you understand what's happening to a team.

- A **bureaucratic organization** is power-driven, hierarchical, and tightly controlling. It has an adversarial, nontrusting relationship with its people and the union, so management doesn't trust people to work in groups or teams.
- An **innovative organization** deliberately reduces layers of authority and control, commits to quality, and adopts methods that make its culture open,

receptive, and participative. It uses teams extensively, gives them support and autonomy, trains and nurtures the members, and empowers them to make decisions for quality results.

- A **supportive organization** puts its people first. You'll likely first notice its social working environment. Managers show strong consideration for their employees, and the organization is likely to have generous benefits that help employees balance their work and personal lives. However, this isn't a country club—managers in a supportive organization are often very focused on production quotas, perhaps to balance their efforts in human resource development.

Teams perform more effectively in innovative and supportive organizations because they can be more creative, more satisfied, and more productive. In an old-fashioned, bureaucratic organization, teamwork is limited to what people can create with coworkers, on the job, and without organizational help.

Because of the current explosion in information technologies, organizations are under increasing pressure to adopt innovative strategies. Management cannot bring individuals and teams so intimately into the information loop via computers and groupware without trusting and involving those individuals and teams.

Virtual or real, how an organization sees its culture inevitably affects how a team sees itself. If the organization is controlling, suspicious, and mean, it's hard for the team to get beyond these barriers. If the organization cares about people and dares to make progress, the team can be that way, too.

INDIVIDUAL MEMBERS

Regardless of where a group starts—an organization, athletic program, community, or academic institution—building it into a team requires changing loosely connected individuals into something with a life, a culture, and characteristics all its own. A team is shaped, consciously and unconsciously, by members who are assembled from across some system. What is it about individuals that induces them to join groups, and what attributes do they bring to a team?

WHY PEOPLE JOIN TEAMS

Of course, you may be on a team because your professor or boss assigned you to it, perhaps for your specific expertise or to represent an outside group's interests. In your career, you may serve on many teams, both face to face and virtual, because your organization assigned you to them. Other times, you may join—or even create—a group to meet your personal interests or needs.

Interests and Attractions   You may join a sports team because you want to play, a study group to succeed in a class, or a support group to cope with some heavy burden. You may form a coalition to achieve some community or political purpose because you feel deeply about that goal. You may even join a particular group simply because you are attracted to its members—you like them.

What attracts you to other people? Their physical appearance? Their likes and dislikes, intellect, or sense of humor? The degree to which they are similar to you?

BOX 4.1 | **FAMILY HISTORY CAN AFFECT YOUR CAREER**

Do you come from a family who believed that any-thing could be accomplished with hard work? If so, chances are that philosophy is a basic tenet of your management style.

Did your family solve problems through consen-sus, by holding a family meeting? If so, that may be one reason why you seek the opinion of your group before making a final decision. Did your family insist on cooperation among the members, that siblings help each other to finish chores faster? That may be why a team approach to problem solving is the one you choose.

As these examples illustrate, your family history—who you are and how you were raised—can affect how you approach your job. . . .

- **High expectations**. Some families expect the best from their sons and daughters—high marks in school, artistic talent, or athletic prowess. While setting high goals for children can be inspiring, it can also be demoralizing

when any attempt falls short of the mark. A series of misses may result in an individual developing low self-esteem, something that can carry over into a career.

- **Low expectations**. Families who failed to en-courage their children produce workers who are ambivalent about success. . . . Someone who does achieve success may suffer the "imposter syndrome" and be unable to accept that success. . . .

- **Make negatives positives**. A perceived weak-ness may be an area of strength if applied properly. Your family may not have appreciated your penchant to pursue a task doggedly until completed. But that habit could be used to your advantage at work.

Source: Condensed from *Working Smart: Personal Report for the Executive*, September 1, 1990, pp. 1–2, published by National Institute of Business Management, Inc. Used with permission.

The degree to which they are different from you? Despite the cliché "Opposites attract," it's long been known that people often are attracted to others by similarity as well as appearance (Krebs & Adinolf, 1975). People feel safer with others who seem to be like themselves because there are fewer unknowns, fewer surprises, about similar people. Furthermore, people are attracted to those who meet stan-dards of beauty and style acquired through a lifetime of socialization.

Still, physical attraction and similarity may become less important as you get to know others (Phillips, Northcraft & Neale, 2006). After a period of time with a group, you may discover that you really respect and enjoy a person you thought was boring to begin with or that you really dislike someone you originally thought was attractive.

Drive Reduction   Whether you are appointed to a team or join one on your own, your personal motivations affect the quality of your teamwork. Anderson and Martin (1995) note that "why people communicate should explain, to some extent, their perceptions about general satisfaction with the group experience. People's motives influence how much attention and time they spend listening and respond-ing to others" (p. 12). Other researchers (Rubin, Perse, & Barbato, 1988; Rubin & Rubin, 1992) have identified six motives behind people's communication:

1. Pleasure (fun)
2. Affection (caring)

3. Escape from other issues
4. Relaxation
5. Control (power)
6. Inclusion (sharing and avoiding loneliness)

Several classical **drive-reduction theories** suggest people are motivated to act in ways that help them relieve some need. For example, suppose you're on a community task force charged with recommending changes in police coverage for the town. Other members of the task force include a representative of a city-supported housing project and the principal of an elementary school on the "better side of town." The housing project representative keeps saying the town needs more police protection and seems not to hear anything else. The elementary school principal keeps insisting the task force must produce a truly high-quality report. Neither person understands the other. What's going on here?

The housing project representative may be terrified by crime in that area. The school principal, who lives and works in a secure, affluent part of town, may be more concerned that the task force reflect well on its members. These two people may have joined the task force for very different reasons, which affect how they perceive the issues. Here are three theoretical explanations:

1. *Drives are felt according to their fulfillment in an ascending hierarchy of importance.* Abraham Maslow's (1970) hierarchy of needs theory could account for each person's motives in our example. Maslow proposed that an individual moves up a ladder of needs, driven to satisfy one level before being able to notice the next. The steps go like this:
   - *Physiological* needs for food or sleep. Once these needs are met, a person can attend to:
   - *Security* needs for safety and predictability. (Our housing project representative may be unable to think about anything but whether the family is safe at home.) With security satisfied, it's possible to feel the need for:
   - *Love and belongingness* needs for social interactions with others. Once a person is comfortable with relationships, attention can move on to:
   - *Self-esteem* needs to feel worthwhile as a person. (This is probably where the principal is.) With a strong sense of self-esteem, an individual can attend to:
   - *Self-actualization* needs to develop oneself, to reach beyond present accomplishment and achieve his or her full potential. Not many people reach self-actualization—most mere mortals are struggling up the prerequisite steps.

2. *Individuals' drives interact, through communication, with the drives of other individuals in the group.* Schutz (1966) saw needs for affection, inclusion, and control as motives that drive an individual's interactions with others. *Affection* and *inclusion* are similar to Maslow's hierarchical need for love and belongingness, but *control* could involve almost any level of Maslow's hierarchy. A teammate who is lonely, needs to feel included, and needs to receive affection may have a strong drive to participate but not be willing to buck the majority

on a controversial issue. Another teammate may try to force his or her opinions down other members' throats because of a strong need to control.

How this affects the group's transactions depends on the individual's competence as a communicator and whether the members' needs are in harmony or in conflict. If members want someone to take control, they may accept another's controlling communication. If, on the other hand, some members resent this dominance or want to control the group themselves, watch out. They may lock horns in a power struggle. In fact, Graham, Barbato, and Perse (1993) found that people who communicate for control often are dominant, argumentative, and dramatic—and this behavior may diminish members' satisfaction with their group experience (Anderson & Martin, 1995).

3. *Individual drives may focus on personal or professional objectives.* McClelland (1989), for example, identifies a human *need to achieve*. People with a high need to achieve "set moderately difficult, but potentially achievable goals for themselves . . . setting challenges for themselves, tasks to make them stretch themselves a little" (p. 86). A high achiever can set a standard and help to motivate others, leading them to create a high-achievement team that seeks challenges and improvement for the sake of the growth provided. (We've experienced such teams, and we've liked them.)

Each of these views provides insight into why people join groups and behave as they do. The important concepts to remember from these drive-reduction theories are

- Motivational drives, as Maslow believes, may be hierarchical. Recognizing these levels of needs can help you to understand how another member can make assumptions very different from yours.
- The need to control, as Schutz proposes, may be balanced or imbalanced during interactions between or among people. Recognizing this can help you understand some seemingly strange affiliations and conflicts among people in groups.
- The need for achievement, as described by McClelland, explains why individuals have certain expectations that can be met through involvement with the team.

Reinforcement   Reinforcement theories propose that people do things for some reward and don't do things because of some threat or punishment. For example, if you make a joke and the team laughs, that's a reward, but if you make a joke and the team glares, that is a punishment. Theoretically, the reward causes you to continue making jokes, whereas the punishment keeps you from doing it again. Immediately, of course, you can also think of the individual who seems to love being glared at and who turns right around and offends you again.

Rewards and costs are perceived individually. You could look at this example in terms of both drives and reward. If your drive is for love and you can't seem to get it from being "good," then perhaps getting attention from being "bad" is reward enough. Therefore, you'll keep on playing the "fun-seeker" role in your team—preventing work, frustrating people, but getting the attention you need.

People may weigh the possible results of their actions either consciously or unconsciously. In their **social exchange theory**, Kelley and Thibaut (1978) hypothesize that people weigh three factors when selecting their behaviors:

1. How they predict the interaction will come out. (Will the rewards outweigh the costs?)
2. How that result compares with what they minimally will accept.
3. How it compares with other possible choices.

Suppose you're trying to decide whether to join the debate team. You're motivated to join because you would feel good about yourself and believe you would win trophies and opportunities (rewards). You also know it would take an enormous amount of time and energy (costs). You then compare the expected satisfactions with the amount of time you dare give up from your schedule (comparison level), and you decide the rewards outweigh the costs. Now you compare the rewards of joining the team with those you calculate for taking an extra job (comparison level for alternatives). If the debate team seems to promise more rewards, you go with it, but if you want the paycheck more than the rewards of the debate team, you take the job.

In this example, you have gone through a social exchange process—computing your possible rewards and costs, aligning those comparisons with your motivations and needs—and come up with a decision you predict will be a good one for you. A team goes through the same comparison of rewards to make decisions, but parent organizations often send contradictory signals. Long ago, Steven Kerr (1975) addressed this dilemma in an essay entitled "On the Folly of Rewarding A, While Hoping for B." Kerr pointed out the contrariness of organizational policies that punish desired behaviors and reward undesired behaviors. For example, suppose an organization hopes for intensive cooperation among team members—but gives large bonuses to individual members on a competitive basis. The organization may hope for cooperation, but it rewards competition. Management then wonders why teammates are cutting one another's throats rather than building teams. If an organization wants good teamwork, it must support and reward the team as an entity of its own.

WHAT INDIVIDUALS BRING

Various personal motives cause people to join groups, but when you are *selected* for a team, it's specifically for what you, as an individual, can bring to it. The diversity individuals bring to their team can become a strength, or it can create barriers. The outcome largely depends on understanding why two or more people may perceive something so differently and on appreciating the contribution those divergent viewpoints may make to the team as a whole.

Ways of Perceiving   Picture this: You and a teammate have the same magazine article in your hands. You see it as supporting your position, but your teammate sees it the opposite way. Who is right?

Try this one: Your team is stymied. You've worked on a report for hours, and you just can't seem to make it clear. One member then exclaims, "Map! We'll draw a map showing how the data lead to our conclusions." Of course! What you couldn't do with words alone, you can do with a diagram. Why did one member see this when the others did not?

One more: Imagine you are uncomfortable with a teammate because you believe she doesn't like you. Another member then tells you privately that the person you thought didn't like you believes that *you* don't like *her*.

Perception is a funny thing. It's the way people do—or do not—pay attention to a stimulus and how they interpret that stimulus for themselves. The previous examples point to three facts about how people perceive that are particularly important for understanding transactional and task processes:

1. *People perceive selectively.* Their motives, needs, drives, wants, and experiences actually may keep them from seeing things that are unacceptable or unknown to them. They may find in a ten-page essay the one—and only—statement that supports their biases. It isn't just a matter of consciously ignoring something, although people do that, too. The point is they may not even know that a message has been given because they've screened it out.

2. *People perceive what their backgrounds permit them to perceive.* Culture, language, gender, and experience all affect how a person can see and think. The teammate who thinks of a diagram may be more visually oriented than others—perhaps an artist, or maybe a chemist who sees things in structures. Once, as a student, Gay gave a report on Aristotelian logic, whereupon a Japanese classmate looked puzzled. "In my culture," he explained, "we do not think this way. We have no 'logic' in the way you use the term." He was a very competent, bright person, but our backgrounds prepare us to perceive things in different ways.

3. *People multiply their misperceptions regarding other people.* Just as you cannot really be sure how another person perceives objects or ideas, neither can you be sure how teammates perceive you or others. For example, Briana may be perceived as creative by Len, as flaky by Raquel, as weird by Todd, and as bright by Sandi. In addition, Darrel may have selectively screened Briana out and can't even think of her name. Furthermore, Briana undoubtedly perceives each of these people differently and misunderstands how they perceive her.

Abilities and Backgrounds   Suppose you find yourself appointed to a team with people who see things—and each other—in a wide variety of ways. What on earth inspired someone to put you all together? A discussion of whom to include on a team may go something like this: "Let's put Bobbi on the team; we need her expertise." "That's true, but she's so abrasive." "Right. Well, what if we ask Ron to be on it? He's good at smoothing out rough edges." "Okay, great . . . yeah, he really is. But sometimes he smooths things out so well you don't get at some of the problems." "True. What if we add Janet? She can go straight to the heart of an issue— great critical analysis—and she also gets along well with Bobbi. . . ." In this way, a team with different yet complementary abilities and backgrounds begins to form.

Some considerations that traditionally go into creating teams are:

Specific talents and abilities to meet the needs of task and transactional processes

Resources such as knowledge, networks, or special qualifications

Differences of background and experience that can enrich the group's thinking

Representation of gender, ethnic, special- or related-interest groups

Authority, status, and influence of a manager, administrator, or person with clout

Would organizations want the same qualifications for people who serve on virtual teams? Ellingson and Wiethoff (2002) suggest that workers in virtual organizations should have the relevant cognitive ability and job knowledge; communication skills; interpersonal skills; conscientiousness; extraversion (again, an ability to communicate with others proactively); agreeableness; openness to experience; self-efficacy (a belief in your ability to organize and execute a course of action; tolerance for ambiguity (you don't get flustered when people or issues are inconsistent); risk-tolerance (you can identify and accept risks that may provide rewards); and an intercultural style (oriented toward adapting to diverse cultures and differences). We'd suggest that all these abilities fit together to make a good team member in any context.

The choice of team members is vital to good task and transactional processes. A manager who is there to make the final call, for example, may inhibit the way the team considers ideas. Or, if someone is there because of a strong legal background, the team may look to that person exclusively on legal issues. Equally, the team may look to one member as the authority on his or her identity group.

It can be tough, for example, if you're the only African American member. Your teammates may expect you to speak for the entire race and to know precisely what every African American thinks about every issue. Outside people may expect you to get the team to do what they want. You may feel shut out of the chance to make observations about anything not seen as an African American issue because other issues are not perceived as being your concern—no matter how worthy your analysis may be. Such pigeon-holing seriously limits your potential contributions.

An aware and effective team enables its members to fulfill the unique purposes for which each was appointed. At the same time, it empowers all members to go beyond their expected roles, to contribute the full range of their talents and abilities, and to exercise leadership in developing a strong team.

TEAM DEVELOPMENT

You will find that participating in or observing the development of a team is absolutely fascinating, sometimes nerve-wracking, often both. So many factors influence the process, whether the team is to work face to face or electronically or in some combination of contexts.

DEVELOPING BY STAGES

It is traditional to talk about phases of group development, as if each group or team followed a nice, linear growth sequence. Most teams, however, are not that predictable. Each develops through its own process, but each also must manage issues that bring its members together, drive them apart, push them to accomplish goals, hold them back, and move them forward. Although these issues arise in

| BOX 4.2 | GROUP EMPATHY |

Futurist Maureen O'Hara, psychologist, dean of faculty at the Saybrook Graduate School in San Francisco.

Scenario "Don't believe all the recent buzz about the rise of the individual. . . . Both our work and leisure activities will require stronger team, organizational, or community affiliations. At the same time, basic identity is splintering.

"All of this puts pressure on people to be a lot more psychologically flexible than ever before. People need what I call group empathy. That encompasses a whole set of higher-order mental skills: openness to learning, a capacity for self-criticism, low defensiveness, and the ability to process multiple realities and values."

So What? "Coping with this level of complexity using mental equipment designed for a much sim-

pler world creates massive stress. Failure to grasp the nuances of the group mind has real consequences for businesses: Group empathy is critical for effective teamwork and for getting a whole organization behind a new idea."

Futurology Decoder Key "Everyone must become a student of human nature in all its glorious complexity. Exercising new psychological muscles— tolerance, flexibility, empathy—becomes part of developing competence at work. That takes practice. Any coach can sense when a team is clicking. And he or she understands that the way to get a group to click is not by training individuals but by putting the whole group through its paces."

Source: From Danyel Barnard, "Report from the Futurist," *Fast Company*, September 1998, p. 54. Used with permission.

different sequences for different teams, being aware of them can help you to share leadership as you recognize developmental issues in your team. We suggest you consider the following "phases" not as specific periods but as developmental issues that vary from team to team.

Phases as Developmental Issues   One researcher has noticed that short-term groups (not teams) proceed through orientation to the group, conflict, emergence of a proposed decision, and mutual reinforcement as well as commitment of the group to a decision (Fisher, 1970). Other observations have similarly classified stages as forming (orienting to one another), storming (conflicting), norming (becoming a team with processes for managing strife), performing (getting the job done), and adjourning (saying good-bye) (Tuckman & Jensen, 1977).

Poole (1983) saw that groups move concurrently along three activity paths, which deal with task, relational, and topic issues, at differing rates and times according to the type of group. Using a form of the **adaptive structurational process,** some groups follow a linear path, talking straight to a decision, and others begin talking about solutions before examining the problems or causes. Most observed groups went around and around, repeating cycles of discussing a problem, arriving at a solution, and then circling back again (Poole & Roth, 1989a, 1989b).

Developmental Issues for Specific Teams   The developmental patterns just discussed help you understand the processes a group might experience, but the most useful information is that how your team develops depends in part on its type and its purpose (or purposes). Gersick (1988) observed real-world project teams, fund-raising committees, corporate and health care teams, and university teams. All had specific projects and tasks, used shared leadership, and met for an extended period of time. Thus, Gersick's observations directly relate to the kinds of teams most people experience.

Each team had its own distinctive pattern of development depending on its purposes and members, but all experienced a **punctuated equilibrium**—that is, periods of seeming inertia broken by bursts of energy and change. In addition, for every team, precisely at the midpoint of its life, a period of crisis struck. This is consistent with our own observations of a **midpoint crisis**: members suddenly wake up and realize that half the time is gone and only half is left to finish the job. Sometimes they panic, but then they get down to work.

Gersick found a general pattern:

1. At their first meetings, teams' activities varied with their respective tasks.
2. Several meetings (Phase 1) dealt with conflicts, getting information, and working through issues.
3. The midpoint-crisis meeting was focused according to the team's purpose. Various teams dealt with decisions about goals, revising drafts of reports, outlining programs, or managing conflicts. It was a point of tension, management, and direction. The same kind of period involving crisis and change hit each team at precisely the midpoint of its experience. One team even dissolved, reconstituted, and redefined itself at this meeting.
4. After this transition, teams went through another series of meetings (Phase 2) to work out details of their tasks.
5. This led to the final completion meeting, in which each team finalized its work according to the type and purposes of the team.

If you can identify what your team is going through, you can help the process along. It helps to remember that emotional highs and lows are normal in group development, but so are some periods of inertia. This doesn't mean you should ignore developmental issues, however. If the group abbreviates working through a transactional or task problem because it is too anxious to get the job done, the members aren't willing to work through their conflicts, or they simply won't take developing the group seriously, then the team and its quality may be torpedoed.

It also helps if members realize the potential—almost inevitability—of a midpoint crisis. If you understand what's happening, the team can use its midpoint crisis as an effective fulcrum to promote creative, productive fulfillment of its goals.

CREATING TEAM ATTRIBUTES

Just like individuals, groups also have unique characteristics. As individuals bring their complementary abilities into play, they begin to develop a team culture and team character.

Team Culture   We've already talked about how a team is affected by the organizational culture in which it functions, but any team also develops a **team culture**. This team culture is a newly woven fabric of threads from the larger society, the parent organization, and the various cultures or subcultures of the members.

Different as they may be, team members develop shared values, beliefs, and assumptions. They create mutually understood and accepted rules and norms that influence their behaviors in—and often outside of—the group. They also develop a team ethic that governs their transactions and influences their tasks. For example, does the team culture encourage the open exploration of ideas, or does it stifle the members' efforts to look at various viewpoints? Does the team culture emphasize honesty and equity in decision making, or does it communicate that the highest value is profit or advantage? Does the team culture encourage dialogue, trust, and cooperation, or does it foster competition and suspicion?

Team cultural norms are reflected in the myths, stories, images, and symbols that members tell and use. For example, do members tell stories about moments when the team pulled together and created something positive, or do they exult in taking advantage of another group or in playing "dirty tricks"? One way to understand the team's culture is to see how these elements are reflected in the shared image and vision of the team.

Shared Image   A team that works together for any period of time develops, as part of its culture, a **team image**. The team image is a strong sense of its own identity that helps motivate and direct the members, just like a strong sense of personal identity may shape an individual's behaviors.

An excellent team can—and will—develop a positive self-image. The foundation often consists of moments of humor, bits of fantasy, or metaphors that members use to describe how they feel about the team's task or work. (In Chapter 7, we will talk about fantasy chaining, which is one way that teams develop this image.)

For example, if someone says, "I feel like I need spikes on my shoes, we're climbing so many mountains," another might respond, "Yeah! I've got my little pick and rappel rope handy." A few more comments such as these, and the team has created an image of a carefully coordinated team of skillful climbers, mutually dependent on one another, scaling a difficult peak but determined to plant their flag at the top. The image becomes a metaphor for the entire experience, and the symbols become refined through frequent reference. Sooner or later, in discussing a difficult problem, someone may say, "Wait a minute—I've got to get my spikes in," and everyone will know exactly what that means.

Such an image is positive, mutual, and healthy. When problems must be overcome, this team is more motivated to meet the challenge—to get to the top of their mountain—than is a team with a weaker image. Unfortunately, it also is possible for teams, like individuals, to develop negative or destructive self-images. Members who share positive leadership detect and discourage negative images, but they recognize and seize moments to encourage strong and healthy team images.

Sometimes the culture of a small group can be so strong—and its image so clear—that even nonmembers can identify a member of that group without having any information other than the person's behavior, dress, or speech. You might see this in fraternities, sororities, professional groups, and sometimes in departments of an organization. This may or may not be a good thing; it can lead to the arrogance mentioned earlier and to excessive conformity. It does, however, indicate how strong and important a group image can become.

Shared Vision   People who have experienced excellent teamwork feel they shared a **team vision** of what they were doing and where they were going. This vision is more holistic than the goals and objectives; it is something total that the team sees ahead as the result of its work.

The principle is closely akin to visualization, described in Chapter 2. When an individual has a clear mental picture of what she or he is striving for, both the goal and the steps to be taken become more vivid and more attainable. Just as visualizing a goal and strategies for achieving it helps an individual, it also helps group members know what they're striving for and to behave in ways that will get them there.

Character   Groups and teams become very specific entities, developing what Tajfel and Turner (1986) call *social identification*. As they commit to the team, members willingly make their membership more important than their individuality, going through "a transition from feeling and thinking like a distinct individual, to feeling and thinking like a representative" (Lembke & Wilson, 1998, p. 30).

Syntality   As a team develops this sense of "teamness," it takes on a **syntality**, which is to a group what personality is to an individual (Cattell, 1948). Your personality reflects who you are to yourself and to others; your team's syntality communicates what that team is to itself and to others. It includes what members have created as a team culture, ethic, image, and vision, as well as what they themselves are. You can't add up the personalities of each member and come out with the team's syntality; the whole is much more than the sum of its parts.

Your team's syntality reflects the entirety of its traits—the ways members interact, share ideas, solve problems, and feel about and respond to one another. Teams can be introverted or extroverted, open-minded or closed-minded. The team's entire approach to transactional and task processes is reflected in its syntality.

Synergy   As team members work together, their energies and talents fuse into **synergy**, which is a special kind of energy that moves your team. It is a combination of the drives, needs, motives, and vitality of the members. When all members are committed to the team and its vision—and when their individual needs and drives motivate them to work for the goals of the team—then the interactions of the team create synergy. Synergy is what makes it possible to be a team and to do the work of the team.

The importance of synergy to a team's effectiveness is obvious by looking at a group with poor or nonexistent synergy. Some members drag the team back with their negative energy. Other members, motivated to do well for a grade or a promotion, work themselves to a frazzle, do other people's work for them, and meet frustration at every turn. These members function as loose-knit individuals, not as a team.

Cohesiveness   Good teams feel like more than just a bunch of people. A team's **cohesiveness** is the degree to which its members are attracted toward one another and to the group. It is a team's *esprit de corps*, "groupness," or team pride. Cohesiveness involves loyalty, commitment, a certain like-mindedness, and a willingness to sacrifice for the group. It is the glue that holds the members together.

The quality of a team's performance relates to its cohesiveness. Obviously, you want your team to develop cohesiveness—a "one for all and all for one," good feeling about the team and its work. Cohesiveness helps you do great things.

It's important, however, to distinguish the positive from the negative effects of cohesiveness. It can give members an unrealistic view of things, keep them from thinking for themselves and from investigating issues, and lead to illusions and bad decisions. Cohesiveness is something to think carefully about as we work through this book. It comes up again in Chapter 12.

TEAMWORK THROUGH ELECTRONICS

"Whether your organization has 10,000 people or just ten," according to Katzenbach and Smith (2001), leading authorities on teamwork, "you will *face* the challenge of working virtually with people down the hall, around the corner, as well as across continents and oceans. As a result, your work group will need to develop new and different rules of engagement—including when and how to interrupt one another's dinners" (p. 1).

Electronic systems to assist people in **virtual meetings** range from the familiar to the esoteric; they serve groups from very small to very large; and they provide minimal meeting guidance to elaborate meeting structures to achieve very specific goals. Your team might meet or share information through the already ubiquitous e-mail, telephone, and fax. Or it might use one of the following:

Teleconferencing allows a few people to meet concurrently over telephone lines or large groups to meet on-site and with people at a distance by using telephone lines and public address systems to ask questions or express ideas. The system is good for sharing information but not effective for real discussion, analysis, or decision making because the transactions are so limited.

Videoconferencing allows groups or individuals to be at different sites, using whiteboards and other aids for visual communication, so that members of the conference can see one another, the relevant graphics, and discuss issues. DeTienne (2002) says that videoconferencing is a good method when you need to save travel money and time but need face-to-face contact, or when you want to provide information; it's not so good when the time lag will be distracting, when people really need the social contact of being in the same room, or when discussions need to be in depth, focus on sensitive issues, or develop ideas in subgroups (p. 79). Often, a team is dispersed over great distances and the expense in time and money of bringing them together on one site is prohibitive.

Online meeting systems can be nothing more than a chat or discussion room, which can operate either in real time or asynchronously. However, many communication companies now offer online systems that enable a variety of meeting objectives to be met. If you use an online search engine to find such opportunities as you read this book, you will find many options.

On-site groupware or *CSCW (computer-supported collaborative work)* are elaborately designed systems for meetings. GroupSystems.com (http://www. groupsystems.com), for example, provides systems through which the meeting is conducted in a specially equipped room, with a facilitator guiding the steps of the discussion as participants enter their ideas on computers that are screened so no one else can see what they are writing. Contributions are projected on a screen that everyone can see and respond to—again, anonymously. This presumably gives members of the group freedom from pressure to conform to the boss's or to the group's opinion. The system is created to guide such processes as information sharing, idea creating, categorizing, outlining, evaluation, decision making, even drawing and writing. And the site might be linked to one or more identical sites at dispersed areas around the country or the world, so that the range of ideas, expertise, and information can be sifted and evaluated systematically with the aid of elaborate computer programs. Each site may also be equipped for videoconferencing and/or teleconferencing so that team members might exchange ideas with members at another location with the benefit of visual information as well as verbal cues.

Then, again, computer assistance may be as simple as a guided program to help a team create an idea, write a proposal, draw a plan, or examine its analysis of an issue. The possibilities truly are endless.

At one time people who studied group discussion or group dynamics thought of the processes as purely interpersonal, the objectives as the face-to-face development of a civil and constructive exchange of ideas to achieve a goal. It's comforting for some of us to know that probably the bulk of group communication still is face to face and still involves developing relationships in real time and space. Nonetheless, **virtual teams** and groups using CSCW are a vital and growing method for working together. That's what's happening now. The question is not whether you will participate in such processes, but simply how this technology will affect your transactional and task leadership and team development.

It might help you in preparing for future technological teamwork to think about the advantages and disadvantages of virtual teaming and CSCW.

VIRTUAL TEAMS: THE GOOD NEWS AND BAD NEWS

Virtual teams and face-to-face teams are the same and different. Researchers have noted that all teams are made up of individuals, exhibit task interdependence, possess one or more shared goals, and are embedded in a broader organizational setting; however, virtual teams also are not restricted by boundaries of time or space, communicate primarily through technology, and have a dynamic and adaptable membership (Horvath & Tobin, 1999).

The advantages of virtual teams are pretty obvious:

People are able to meet across distances, in real time or asynchronously. This eliminates scheduling problems, meeting space problems, and commuting and expense problems so that people can get together at the same place and time.

A team can bring together the people with the best qualifications, interests, and ideas. You can go any distance to bring in just the right expert for the job. And you can seek diverse opinions and outlooks more easily.

A virtual team can react quickly in a crisis. In coping with the Code Red virus, for instance, PriceWaterhouseCoopers in Atlanta created "an international

These students collaborate with one another and with colleagues across the globe.

team to share techniques for accessing switches and blocking traffic from affected servers, buying time for staff to commute in for the clean up" (Gaspar, 2001, p. 3)

The disadvantages of working in a virtual team are obvious—or not. Consider these problems:

Members are unable to see others' nonverbal communication in a shared environment. Even when there is a videoconferencing option, you get much less information from a videotaped image than from being physically close to the person, where you can pick up a range of nuances through eye contact, movement, posture, and so on. Members are unable to communicate as effectively because they must rely on written symbols and cannot use expressions of face, voice, and gesture to clarify their ideas or to communicate their emotions.

Members may not share the same language or cultural expectations and may need help in translating and understanding one another.

Time zone differences can make contact difficult. Katzenbach and Smith (2001) point out that the person you need to reach might not be there when you can send the message (p. 8).

Finally, virtual teams have some special requirements. An understanding of these needs is emerging as organizations gain experience with their teams and as researchers study them. For example:

Virtual teams need just the right people with just the right expertise for the project.

You don't want to bumble around bringing in new people as new needs emerge if you can help it. If you can determine who you need from the outset, you can build a team more efficiently and reach the goal more quickly.

Virtual teams need training, and most don't get it. True, all teamwork needs training, but developing a virtual team requires some special preparation (Katzenbach & Smith, 2001, p. 8). (We'll talk about some of this preparation in context as this text goes on.)

Correct tools are vital to the work of virtual teams. A quick e-mail is not sufficient.

A Houston firm's information technology (IT) department handles 1,100 projects per year, so their teams need project management software. In addition they use "e-mail, Outlook scheduling, Documentum for content management, and videoconferencing to keep projects going" (Gaspar, 2001, September).

Virtual teams need to develop trust in one another, usually without the benefit of face-to-face experience. This requires careful steps in ensuring commitment to the team and its goals, starting with a contracting discussion of norms, expectations, and online courtesy. When at all possible, virtual teams need an initial meeting where people can actually see and talk to one another; some teams need occasional face-to-face meetings even though most of their work is done online (Katzenbach & Smith, 2001, p. 7). That first meeting face to face seems to be enormously helpful in establishing trust and a sense of "teamness" (Alge, Wiethoff, & Klein, 2003).

Computer-Supported Collaborative Work (CSCW): The Good News and Bad News

Here are some of the ways groupware is helpful:

Participants are equalized and empowered to contribute more freely. Coleman (1992) points out that "the anonymity inherent in [CSCW] allows ideas, rather than personalities or hierarchical positioning, to dominate a meeting. The result is equal participation, so the expertise of even the most junior members can be heard to the company's benefit" (p. 10).

Communication among diverse members is easier and more accurate. Coleman (1992) also notes that decision-making teams often draw from many levels and areas; furthermore, many meetings involve people who speak different languages. "This necessitates better group interaction to produce not only a satisfactory result, but also one that is completed in a more timely and cost-effective manner, compared to traditional meetings. CSCW can answer these needs by linking a group together in a better environment" (p. 10). The University of Hawaii, for example, has hosted successful problem-solving meetings between North American and Japanese representatives, in which groupware provided the opportunity for participants to share their ideas effectively across differences in language and culture. The "group dictionary" function of the groupware provides for group-designed, mutual definitions of important terms to be used in the discussion, and the capability of typing in ideas as they occur to a participant helps alleviate the pressure to translate what you mean quickly into another language (Chidambaram, 1995).

Ideas are accurately and completely recorded and accessible. Rao (1995), writing in *Financial World*, enthusiastically summarizes the effects of a meeting using the Group Systems software package: "Simple but effective. In a typical 10-person, one-hour, flip-chart-and-marker meeting, each person has the floor for a maximum of six minutes. Someone is designated to take notes, and what is recorded is sometimes different from what was actually said. In animated discussions, some points may escape recording altogether. In an electronic meeting, by contrast, each person can potentially use all 60 minutes and recording is complete, totally accurate, and immediate. You can leave the meeting with a disk containing the full transcript" (Rao, 1995, p. 72). What an advantage this could be!

Better decisions can be made. Groupware programs make information more accurate, more quickly available, and more readily analyzed than people's memories and a flip chart can manage. In addition, the technology speeds organizational learning by providing a context for knowledge and a record of actions (Opper & Fersko-Weiss, 1992, p. 47).

Expenditures can be reduced. You can find EMRs in some major corporate offices, at some universities, or at Kinko's. Costs vary. Organizations that have no EMR of their own might rent a university EMR at an hourly rate, or groups of five to eight people can go to one of Kinko's EMR locations, where they can confer by video with teams in other locations across the country (Hamilton, 1995, p. 180). The costs are considerably less than sending just one participant across the country to a face-to-face conference.

Time is saved. A groupware meeting takes about 30 percent less time than a nonassisted meeting (Opper & Fersko-Weiss, 1992, p. 45) because the computer organizes, records, and feeds back information so efficiently. Between meetings, related software lessens project delays by tracking work flow and revealing problems in time to manage them easily, by ensuring that all information is available to every member, by keeping a chronological record of ideation and decision making, and by making the entire picture available to new members (Opper & Fersko-Weiss, 1992, p. 46).

Groupware (on-site or online) does, however, have some drawbacks:

Management and employees may resist the idea. Effectively functioning teams have access to information, but control-strategy organizations are uncomfortable when employees have the information they need because information gives them power. Nonetheless, "in a company where everyone is connected electronically and groups work together on-line regularly, top executives must get involved or be left out" (Opper & Fersko-Weiss, 1992, p. 57). Team workers, on the other hand, may appreciate the accessibility of information and team-working possibilities, but still be technophobes afraid even of a PC. Surely not too many people fit into that category anymore, but many may still have to learn how to use the technology to its fullest extent.

Groupware potentially can structure group interaction very tightly. Will the structure actually impede, rather than encourage, full exploration of ideas and development of a team? It is important for a team to have the program that is best suited to its goals and its situation. And virtual teams are learning they are most effective when they do not limit themselves to a CSCW system. Initial or occasional face-to-face meetings, if possible, help people to get to know and trust one another; supplementing the program with direct phone, e-mail, and fax helps, and occasional videoconferencing may be helpful, as well.

Teams may forget their communication skills. Used properly, groupware may provide all of the benefits suggested by its proponents. Groupware does not, however, guarantee success, nor does it excuse members from responsibility for their communication. In fact, transactions in a groupware meeting require the same skills in transactional and task processes that face-to-face, non-mediated teamwork does, but with much greater attention to clarity because there are no nonverbal cues.

Team communication may become too structured—or too loose. If you're using an elaborate on-site groupware room, with a facilitator and a tightly structured program, you may find yourselves following such strict protocol that your teamwork is compressed into boxes and not allowed to flow freely. On the other hand, if you're e-mailing freely and loosely, you all may become so informal that you overlook important checks and balances both on courtesy and on clear thinking and analysis.

Non-collaborative work patterns may actually be encouraged by groupware designed for collaboration. It becomes too easy and convenient to divide up tasks into individual assignments without the benefit of multiple ideas and viewpoints, without discussion and cooperative analysis of the issues. In this case, CSCW may aid in sharing information, but actually block the goals of teamwork (Katzenbach & Smith, 2001, p. 6).

CSCW teams can "grow like weeds." Katzenbach and Smith (2001) observe that "rarely have we observed more than 10–12 people team up effectively without subdividing in favor of smaller numbers. . . . Too many contributors create communication and integration nightmares."

A control-strategy organization certainly may resist computer assistance and groupware because upper management doesn't trust its people with information. Clive Holtham, professor of information management at City University Business School in London, notes that "the failure to improve the effectiveness of work-groups often lies far less in any technical dimension than deep in the management style and culture of an organization. . . . If key strategic steps are not taken from the top of the organizations, no amount of effort at middle levels can compensate for this" (Cheek, 1993, p. 89).

If this is true for traditional teams, it's even more important for virtual teams. The virtual environment lacks the information about one another that people gain from face-to-face communication. There are no nonverbal cues, no eye contact, no shared environment. The effectiveness of the team and the responsiveness of the organization are perceived through constricted sets of electronic cues. As virtual

BOX 4.3	VIRTUAL TEAMS

You can use virtual teams for problem solving, quality assurance, product development, information sharing, and a variety of team-oriented activities—just like in the physical world. We also know that virtual teams can be more innovative than their physical counterparts. But there are some rules you need to follow.

- **Rule number one**. There should be a clear purpose and focus. If you don't have this, even having virtual technology doesn't help you get the job done.
- **Rule number two**. Unless all the participants have worked together before, you'll have to allow for a time when they get to know each other. That can be in a physical meeting or in a series of virtual ones. If you use virtual meetings for this, you will have to have more contacts than you might if you can have a physical meeting.
- **Rule number three**. Participants on a virtual team need to be aware that there are different kinds of communication rules when communicating online. We know that people in online communication often are more brusque, and sometimes even rude, than they would be in face-to-face conversation. If team members are aware of this tendency early on they can watch it in themselves or be called on it by other members.

Source: Copyright 2003 by Wally Bock, http://www.bockinfo.com.

teams become more and more prevalent, researchers have found that organizational commitment is particularly vital to their success. There must be "the appropriate physical, financial and social support," such as "evaluation and compensation systems that encourage competent task-and-group behaviors; training and development programs that provide the appropriate task and group process skills; information systems that provide relevant, accurate, and timely information for the group; and a corporate culture that encourages and supports collective activities" (Furst, Blackburn, & Rosen, 1999, p. 8).

Clearly, successful computer-mediated meetings absolutely require excellent facilitation and excellent technography to ensure that benefits accrue. The need for sharing leadership becomes more pronounced if teams are going to avoid the potential pitfalls technology could create.

TEAMWORK IMPROVEMENT

Remember the cybernetic processes mentioned briefly in Chapter 1—feedback, observation, discussion? These processes are essential for helping teams develop.

After a meeting, you might hear someone say, "That was great. Did you notice how so-and-so came out of his shell?" This sounds good until so-and-so tells you privately that the meeting was a nightmare. It's only natural for people to judge things based on their own limited perceptions.

That's why teams need systematic approaches for getting and using feedback to assess and improve their accomplishments. In this section, we talk about principles, sources, and uses of feedback to improve a team's processes and outcomes.

There are two critical principles for feedback: it must be non-threatening, and it must be team-generated (Lumsden, Knight, & Gallaro, 1989). All members must plan—and want—the feedback before they can use it freely. That means the feedback must be exclusively for the team's use.

As a team, you need to agree to collect information on how you're doing, and as a team, you need to choose your methods, timing, and use of that feedback. Then your assessment belongs to your team.

SOURCES OF FEEDBACK

Your team needs feedback from all relevant sources throughout its life, and everyone involved with the team can help. A constant feedback loop can get information from the parent organization (or boss or teacher), from team members, and from related sources (other teams or departments, clients, or customers). You can also seek feedback on ways team members actually conduct both transactional and task processes, how the team interacts with other systems and subsystems, and the effectiveness or quality of the outcomes.

Here are some useful techniques for assessing your team's transactional and task processes:

Feedback forms. On a regular basis, members individually complete short questionnaires about their teamwork and then analyze them together. Feedback forms can focus on any aspect of the team experience: individual, transactional, or task.

Objective process observers and consultants. An outside person can observe and analyze the team at work and then help members process the observations and design ways to improve their quality. In a classroom, the observer may be a member of the class. For an organizational team, a team communication consultant may come from a corporate training and development department or be hired from outside.

Videotaping or audiotaping. Taping a session and playing it back for discussion can help team members see how they are working together. It highlights both strengths and weaknesses—and it can be played back as many times as needed.

Groupware programs. If your team uses computer-supported systems, a groupware program can provide instant feedback and a record by which to check what the team has done. The program also can survey how members feel about the process, what they think they need to improve, and how they can go about improving their transactions.

If these methods are combined, a very clear idea of what's working—and what's not working—can emerge.

USES OF FEEDBACK

All team members must participate in getting and analyzing feedback, because it takes mutual commitment for any changes to be effective. Teams can follow these steps to make feedback work most effectively:

1. Focus on the team's successes and accomplishments. Identify those processes that are working well and the positive feelings members have about the team's

work. All teams do some things well, and starting with this perspective provides a foundation on which to build future successes.

2. Discuss what the feedback means to the team. Is it valid? Was the technique used to gather it objective, complete, and consistent? Is the information supported by and consistent with other knowledge the team has of itself? Does it provide important insights into the way the team is functioning?

3. Design a method for implementing the insights gained from the feedback. This method could be structural—changing the format, location, or times of meetings. It could be constitutional—modifying the team's task, adding or deleting members, or changing the leader. It could also be transactional—changing specific communication behaviors, such as agreeing to be more assertive.

4. Agree on a method for achieving the change. Methods may require outside support or resources, new procedures, supporting and helping each other with behavioral changes.

5. Agree on times and methods for reassessing the issue to see if it is resolved or improving. This could mean simply repeating the original method of feedback and comparing the results, or it could mean adding new evaluation methods to the process.

6. Agree to implement and support the changes and to be open in giving and receiving feedback during the process of improvement.

Here's an example of the process: A consultant has observed four meetings of a corporate work team and noted that of the seven members, only three talked—an executive and two managers. In discussing this observation, the team notes it was consistent over all four meetings, is supported objectively by videotape and the observer's notes, and conforms with the members' own observations and evaluations.

Is this information important? In discussing the subject with the consultant facilitating, the four usually silent members—a supervisor and three workers—finally speak up. It seems they all had information to contribute but were intimidated by the status of the three more talkative members. The three more dominant members are shocked—they thought they had to talk because the others would not! Now they have an insight that may help. For it to make a real difference, however, the team and its consultant should explore how the team can change the imbalance of contributions and liberate the silent members.

After working out ways of changing their transactions, the team members need to practice their new behaviors. At an agreed-on point in the near future, they should reassess their transactions to see if they are working better. They might use feedback forms and discussion, or they might bring back the consultant, depending on what the team feels it needs to do.

Does this kind of feedback, assessment, adaptation, and reassessment happen in the real world? Yes, although not often enough. Too often organizations wait until the harm is done and only then provide team training and feedback. The point, of course, is to avoid problems by using feedback as you go along. You'll have that opportunity in this class and, we hope, on the teams in your future.

CASE 4.1 | VIRTUAL TEAMS

The following is taken from David Creelman's interview of Dr. Gina Walker, director of Research & Product Development for Harold Stolovitch and Associates.

DC: Take me through the specifics of one project involving a virtual team.

GW: In one project, a large global high-tech corporation needed a learning and performance support system to help their engineers implement a new software system. There were a lot of change management implications and we anticipated a lot of resistance . . . .nd we had a very short timeline. . . .

Our company has resources located all over so, as project director, I first talked to the client in France about their needs. One issue was that we needed somebody like myself in the same time zone to facilitate communication with the client. The client also had some key resources in California so we needed people there who could get some face-to-face contact. We also had some people in Vancouver who had experience doing this kind of work, so I wanted them on this project. And that's how I assembled the team.

We went through the usual planning phases like doing front-end analysis, making sure that we were in touch with the key people, getting an idea of who the learners were, and then launching the design and development phase where we had to deal with the subject matter experts. . . .

It was impossible to meet face to face, so, "We had to establish clear, unambiguous objectives for the project [and] to be very specific about budgets and timelines."

With e-mail and telephone, and without face to face contact, "There is a risk of ambiguity creeping into your work. With electronic communication . . . it's very important to be clear in all of our communication." And to "communicate frequently. We had, at least, a weekly discussion by phone where we would discuss the status of the work. Prior to this meeting, I would e-mail the client a status report. . . . Because of distance, frequent and regular status and review meetings are necessary to diffuse uncertainties or to redirect efforts."

One communication guideline we adopted was to request our project team members respond to any questions within 24 hours. . . . However, one thing that you have to be very careful of is burdening everybody with too much e-mail. . . . We learned to filter the excess and find out what was really important. . . .

With virtual teams, scheduling meetings is very important because people are in different time zones and coordination is important. . . . Try to establish specific time slots when individuals will make themselves available. . . .

[Although a face-to-face meeting was impossible] I do recommend [it]. . . . A meeting helps the team establish a sense of comfort with each other . . . [At least] have a phone launch where you work to create a sense of team identity. And I encourage people to get to know each other over the course of the project. . . .

We also had to build structures of teamwork—one was a set of team leaders to manage the resources at their individual locations. . . . Another structure is a "co-director." On a recent large project spanning time zones, I was the project director in Montreal and my co-director was in Vancouver. We had our own team members as well as those of the client located across the continent. We were able to pass work back and forth across the time zones, so work could be done and on the client's desk in the morning. We were able, in fact, to lengthen our work day. It's a very interesting way of working.

In order to avoid rough spots, you need to establish a common set of understandings . . . common standards and work practices. Shared templates and tools, samples, job aids, and process/output norms all help.

DC: What's your overall assessment of virtual teams?

GW: I think that they will become more and more routine. They provide a very positive means of accomplishing goals. . . . Overall, we have found that virtual teams operating in virtual environments produce as high quality results as they do in live, local contexts. Project management has to be more present, however.

Questions to Consider for this Case

1. In what ways would you say the team described here would be like the superteam model described in the chapter? In what ways would it be different? Why?

Continued

| CASE 4.1 | **VIRTUAL TEAMS** *Continued* |

2. How does the development and work of this team reflect organizational cultures and organizational strategies? How would a different organizational approach have affected the success of the team?

3. Each team member was selected for a specific reason; how would you say the composition of this team would vary from an on-site, face-

to-face team making strategic decisions about how to get the software up and running in this organization? Would such a face-to-face team be more or less effective than the virtual team?

Source: Excerpt from David Creelman, Interview with Gina Walker. Retrieved August 10, 2001, from http://www.hr.com.

SUMMARY

When you start developing a team, you're working toward an ideal "superteam," a work group that is success-driven and committed, flexible, active; they value effective leaders but share in the leadership; superteams value and respect one another and their visions and goals. They are analytical, tenacious, creative, inventive, and innovative. They are visible and accessible to those outside the team and build both formal and informal networks to advance their work. They interact influentially with their organizations and share power with their founder. They have to watch out for becoming arrogant, because they really are so good, and they flourish in an organizational environment in which they are trusted and supported.

Organizations have their own cultures, myths, ways of interacting, and their own management strategies. Some organizations function with a control strategy; such organizations are unlikely to nurture open, self-managing teams, in contrast to commitment-strategy organizations, in which the philosophy is a commitment to the growth and development of its employees and the quality of its achievements. Some organizations are in transition, working from a mixed control-commitment position.

Individuals join teams for many reasons, including shared interests, attraction to the group and its members, and personal drives, needs, and motivations for reward and reinforcement. Individuals are assigned to teams because of their

specific attributes. They bring diversity in ways of perceiving, thinking, and doing to their transactions within the team.

As members work together, they develop a team culture—influenced by the organizational culture and by their individual cultures and subcultures—that includes a team ethic; team myths, symbols, and beliefs; and team ways of doing things. Over time, they also develop a team image and team vision. In addition, the group develops syntality, the personality of the team as a whole, as well as synergy, the combined energies and drive of all its members. Through these elements, the team develops cohesiveness.

During the developmental process, teams often follow a predictable series of stages such as orientation to the group, conflict, emergence of a proposed decision, mutual reinforcement, leading to commitment of the group to a decision; or the group might go through stages of forming, storming, norming, performing, and adjourning.

Groups do seem to move concurrently along paths of task, relations, and topic issues, and some groups follow a linear path of adaptive structuration, talking straight to a decision, or talking about solutions before examining the problems or causes. Real-world teams that have specific projects and tasks seem to have their own patterns of development, but all experience a midpoint crisis, a point of panic in which they regroup and focus more intensely on the goal.

Much teamwork today is done through electronics, as virtual teams online, with dispersed members working synchronously or asynchronously on specific goals, perhaps using electronic conferencing programs, videoconferencing, or Computer-Supported Collaborative Work (CSCW). Electronic teamwork is advantageous in that it allows wide access to experts in specific areas, dispersed participants, use of real time or virtual time; it has disadvantages in the lack of nonverbal information and the need for training and clear methods to ensure trust in one another for commitment and competence. CSCW provides opportunities for anonymity and freedom, for guided activities and facilitation, for linking to other electronic methods as well as to other sites around the world. There are many programs for each venue that help teams to share information, categorize, analyze, create, problem-solve, and make decisions.

To guide its development through these phases, a team should use feedback, adaptation, and improvement for all its processes and outcomes. To be effective, however, these processes must be team-generated and used by the team for its own benefit. (Form 4.2 provides some guidelines for developing a team.)

Exercises

1. Your executive team at Foods, Inc., which handles farm products of all kinds, is meeting to decide on criteria for selecting a team that includes members from both inside and outside the company. This team will design strategies for educating schoolchildren about foods.

   What types of expertise should the members possess? What backgrounds, motivations, and special perspectives or abilities does the team need? Do any of your criteria conflict with other values? Are ethical issues involved? What similarities and differences among these members might cause misunderstanding or disagreement—or contribute to better thinking and valuing? How might the availability of electronic communication affect your decisions about whom to include on the team? Report your decisions to the class.

2. As a follow-up to the previous exercise, consider how the characteristics of your executive committee members affected your team processes. Then do the following individually:

   • Label a separate piece of paper or index card for each person in your group. Make a list of the individual attributes you think she or he can contribute to a team. Think of how that member interacts with others, approaches a task, thinks, or of what he or she values—anything that seems relevant to transactional and task processes.

   • On another piece of paper or card, list the attributes you believe that you contribute to a group.

   • Now exchange lists. Give each person the list you made for him or her, but keep the list of your own attributes along with those that others have made for you.

   • Still working individually, look over the lists to see the attributes on which people seem to agree. What trends do you see? How do others' perceptions of you agree with your own?

   • Now, as a group, discuss what you've found. Look for clarification, and talk about how you can develop and maximize your best qualities.

3. With a group of students, design a model or a picture showing the characteristics of a team, including culture, image, vision, syntality, synergy, and cohesiveness.

4. Using Form 4.1, assess a group or team with which you're presently (or recently have been) associated. What strengths do you see? What problems? How do you think the problems could be corrected and the strengths maximized?

5. Using the guidelines listed in Form 4.2, analyze the same team in terms of its development. What aspects has it accomplished well? What remains to be done? How do you see the team doing those things?

FORM 4.1 | EVALUATION OF TEAM SYNTALITY

After watching a team's transactional and task processes over a period of time, rate how true each statement is of that team.

	Very	Somewhat	Not at all
1. Members feel unified.	☐	☐	☐
2. Members bring diverse ways of thinking, valuing, and seeing.	☐	☐	☐
3. The team has norms, beliefs, and its own ways of doing things.	☐	☐	☐
4. Members know what the team's vision is.	☐	☐	☐
5. The team has an image that members and others can identify.	☐	☐	☐
6. Members are motivated for team success and achievement.	☐	☐	☐
7. Members are cooperative in critical problem analysis.	☐	☐	☐
8. Members support each other.	☐	☐	☐
9. Members work for the team when apart as well as together.	☐	☐	☐
10. Members share responsibility.	☐	☐	☐
11. The team analyzes ethical issues.	☐	☐	☐
12. The team maintains open communication with outside systems.	☐	☐	☐
13. The team has credibility with other systems and subsystems.	☐	☐	☐
14. The team seeks and uses feedback to improve transactional and task processes.	☐	☐	☐

In a few words, try to describe the team's syntality (use metaphors, images, analogies):

FORM 4.2 | GUIDELINES FOR DEVELOPING A TEAM

1. Get to know one another.
   - Who is on the team?
   - What does each person want from the experience?
   - What attributes does each person have to offer the team?
2. Look for ways to connect members.
   - What can members find in common?
   - How can the team share experiences and create bonds?
   - What can members do to enjoy one another as people?
   - How can members support one another?
3. Start to develop a vision.
   - What is the team striving to accomplish?
   - What will be the qualities of that accomplishment?
   - How does the team's vision relate to the parent organization's vision and goals?
4. Help the group develop its own character.
   - What norms and expectations will develop a strong, positive team culture?
   - How can you reinforce positive ways that create a strong syntality and synergy for the team?
   - How can you share stories, approaches, and traditions that make the team special?
   - What ethical standards will be part of the team's culture?
5. Make the team safe for participation.
   - What can members do to value and use their diversity?
   - How can members find shared values and orientations?
   - What norms will help members manage disagreements?
   - How will each member share leadership?
6. Discuss phases as the team goes through them.
   - How can the team identify phases and work through them?
   - What will the team do to handle inertia?
   - How will the team deal positively with a midpoint crisis?
7. Develop transactional and task processes.
   - What will keep communication open, clear, and supportive?
   - How can the team develop strong, analytical task processes?
8. Use cybernetic processes for self-assessment and improvement.
   - How will the team work out feedback approaches?
   - How will the team use information from feedback?
9. Celebrate the team and its accomplishments.
   - How will the team accomplish its vision?
   - What can the team do to recognize and reinforce its achievements?

"Well, maybe we could—like—do a video project...."
That's the end. How about starting at the beginning?

TASK QUESTIONS AND RESOURCES

Launching Your Inquiry

5

It's tempting to jump right to a plan without paying an iota of attention to what comes between the start and the finish. When people do this, they tend to fill in the middle as best they can and call it a job. They overlook important information, don't think of alternative possibilities, and miss serious drawbacks—all leading to flimsy thinking and poor results.

A team's potential superiority over a collection of individuals lies in the team's ability to accrue more information, to explore it together, and to collaborate on analysis and decision making. Consider what Millard Fulmer said about Habitat for Humanity teams in Box 5.1.

Of course, a team can meet without having facts—but having ideas and opinions without the benefit of data (or with poor data) only "pools the group's ignorance," leading to biased and unsupported decision making. Or you can circulate data through memos, fax, or e-mail, but deciding what that information means for the team's goals requires vigilant, cooperative analysis involving every member of the team. Quality decisions depend on quality evidence and vigilant analysis.

To obtain quality information, a team needs to plan its inquiry—to analyze and differentiate the questions the members want to answer, to plan their research and identify their resources, and to share the findings among members in ways that keep them focused and well informed. In this chapter, we help your group to develop the information base necessary for effective analysis and decision making by strengthening your abilities to:

1. Develop a work plan for your team's approach to its task
2. Analyze questions for a clearer understanding of the issues involved

---

| **BOX 5.1** | **TEAM BUILDERS** |

Millard Fuller, *Founder and president, Habitat for Humanity International,*

  Americus, Georgia

The most essential ingredient of a successful team is a cause that everyone agrees on. In our case, it's providing housing for low-income families—people who otherwise wouldn't be able to afford a home. We operate with what we call the "theology of the hammer." People may differ religiously or politically, but we can all agree on a hammer as a way to help people in need.

The second essential ingredient is preparation. In our case, that means doing all of the background work: having all of the materials, plumbers, electricians, and so forth scheduled to be on-site. That way, the work goes smoothly, because as soon as the volunteers arrive, they have something productive to do and someone there who is qualified to show them how to do it.

We've had so many different types of people working together to build Habitat houses as part of one team or another. A company's CEO and janitor can be on the same team. And you know what? It's good for both of them.

Nobody works for nothing. Some people work for money, and some people work for recognition. But I'll tell you this: People will stick out an unpleasant assignment, but they won't do it again. We have a great record because it's a good experience. Everyone who works on a Habitat house gets something of value out of it. That's an important part of building a lasting team.

Source: "What Makes Teams Work?" *Fast Company,* October, 2000, p. 109.

3. Phrase questions to focus on the issues
4. Identify data needs and resources to create an information base
5. Assign responsibilities among team members to maximize research efforts
6. Share information with team members in clear, useful ways

PLANNING THE TEAM'S INQUIRY

The process that takes you from setting goals to reaching them usually determines the success of the final achievement. Individuals work through a task process together better than they do alone, but only if they know what they're doing.

Nobel Prize winner Herbert A. Simon (1977), who worked extensively on decision making in organizations, identified four broad categories people use when they work through a problem:

1. *Intelligence*: The process of recognizing a need (or an opportunity) for a decision and gathering the necessary information to analyze the situation
2. *Design*: The process of developing alternative possible solutions
3. *Choice*: The process of analyzing, weighing, and selecting a plan of action
4. *Review*: The process of assessing the effectiveness of a choice and then adopting appropriate adjustments or changes

For now, think of these categories as an outline for a team work plan. Within each category, a team distributes that work into other categories. For example, your team receives an assignment. You see that the assignment requires decisions, so you set your goals. You then gather the information that you need—the intelligence phase (like the detective work of gathering intelligence). Next, you begin thinking of ideas and possible plans and tentatively evaluate each in relationship to your goals—the design phase. You then use critical analysis, debate the pros and cons of each alternative, choose a decision, and implement it—the choice phase. Finally, you look at your implemented decision to see if it's working well, and you assess it, test it, and correct any problems—the review phase. Simon's categories provide a simple outline of the processes your team goes through in reaching its goals.

Keep in mind, however, that real teamwork is not quite so linear. For example, your group might be in the middle of the design phase and suddenly realize you need more information. So you scurry back to the intelligence phase for that information and bring it back into the design. This is as it should be, and Simon's phases help you to know where your loops are taking you.

For our purposes, however, Simon's categories provide a clear way of examining your team's processes. We begin by concentrating on the intelligence phase in this chapter, and we focus on the other categories in the next three chapters.

IDENTIFYING QUESTIONS FOR ANALYSIS

We think it's essential first to examine issues as open *questions*, not as statements or pros and cons. That's because until you've inquired into the facts and possibilities, you don't want to close off information and analysis. Frequently, discussions are confused because team members don't recognize the underlying questions that

Team of metropolitan London detectives at the scene of a crime inspecting evidence.

relate to their tasks and purposes. Much like Russian dolls, one question may be nested inside another. Sometimes several questions are nested inside one, and some of these may represent controversial issues. Even a simple question may arouse strong opinions and feelings regarding issues about which your team will need both solid data and cooperative analysis to reach agreement.

For an example of analysis, Figure 5.1 provides a road map of four types of questions—fact, value, policy, and prediction—inherent in deciding a public policy on how social service agencies handle abusive parents. We'll start with a value assumption—that no one in his or her right mind would say child abuse is okay. Therefore, we begin this policy discussion with that value held in common. From there, the questions to be answered might interrelate as shown.

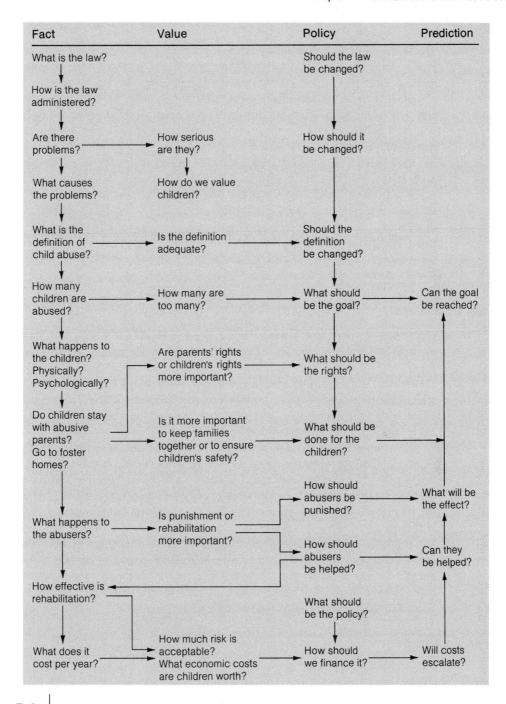

Figure 5.1

Relationships among questions of fact, value, policy, and prediction on the issue of child abuse.

QUESTIONS OF FACT

Questions of fact can be answered by data that prove, or support the probability, that a statement is true or untrue. When is a "fact," in fact, a fact? People often assume a statement is factual because something always used to be true, or always seems to be true, or somebody wrote that it was true, or it certainly ought to be true. To make good decisions, however, you need solid information. In Figure 5.1, you see the list of facts (starting with "What is the law?") that a team would need to research for their decision.

Of course, you need accurate and valid information. We'll talk about how you analyze information and assess its quality in Chapter 6, but for now, suffice it to say you need to look carefully at the evidence. Is the source objective or biased? Is the source credible? Is the "fact" 100 percent true? Few facts actually are. To be universally true, there must be no exceptions, so you usually must settle for something being *probably true*. But what probability that something is true will the team accept? Is it true 90 percent of the time? Or 80 percent? Or 50 percent? Are you 75 percent sure that it is ever true?

QUESTIONS OF VALUE

Questions of value seek answers about the worthwhileness, ethicality, and relative importance of a concept, act, or policy, and they are intrinsic to every task a team takes on. Sometimes they are very small questions, to be sure. "Is it okay to use Fred's boss's duplicating machine without permission?" is a question of ethics, which are grounded in moral and value assumptions. Using the duplicating machine without permission might not rock the world; nonetheless, this is a value choice the team might make.

At a more elevated level, a team dealing with the issues in Figure 5.1—policy recommendations for ways social service agencies should handle abusive parents—might ask, "How serious are the problems?" and later, "Which is more important, keeping a family together or protecting a child from possible harm?" Here you see the relationship between questions of fact and questions of value. Questions of fact: Is there a probability the child will come to harm? How strong is that probability? Questions of value: What risk is acceptable? How important is the child's safety? How important is it for children to be with their parents? As you consider these questions, you begin to play the third against the first two value questions. Combined with a number of other questions of fact and value, the questions begin to illuminate a controversial question of policy.

QUESTIONS OF POLICY

Questions of policy seek answers to what positions or actions should be adopted, enacted, or implemented. A policy question might propose laws, rules, or guidelines to be enacted by a governmental body, public institution, private corporation, or smaller organization or group of any kind. In Figure 5.1, policies regarding child abuse affect the actions of parents, neighbors, schools, police, courts, media, and social service agencies. The question of what policies already exist is a question of fact, and the question of whether the existing policies are good is a question of value. The question of what a policy *should be*, however, is a question of policy. The key terms to look for in policy questions are *should* and *ought to*.

Every policy question has several questions of fact and of value within it. One reason it's so hard to get people to agree on a policy is that such decisions are filled with conflicting data and values. Another reason is the difficulty of predicting what will happen in the future.

QUESTIONS OF PREDICTION

Questions of prediction ask about the future—to what degree will a fact be true, a value be worthwhile, or a policy fulfill its promise in time to come? "How will a new policy affect the incidence of child abuse in the future?" is a question that requires predicting the probability of a fact. "To what extent might the new policy be better than the present one?" tries to predict the value of the policy. "How will the policy need to be modified?" addresses the probability of policy change and ways to provide for it.

A question flowchart like Figure 5.1 helps you visualize the relationships among fact, value, prediction, and policy questions that your team must consider. In the end, a policy decision is the one the team decides is *probably* best—based on value choices, facts they believe are probably true, and predictions of probable effects and outcomes. Every insight the team can get to help it raise the right questions also helps that team make the best decisions.

PHRASING QUESTIONS FOR DISCUSSION

Questions of fact, value, policy, and prediction often arise without anyone ever phrasing them as such. You just find yourselves discussing the issues. Sometimes this is fine, but at other times, the questions need to be phrased more pointedly.

For example, suppose you're discussing demographic data indicating that middle-class students cannot get financial aid. This is a question of fact. As you discuss it, though, there seems to be a lot of anger in the air, and words such as *unfair* are tossed around the group. This tells you there really are two questions at issue:

1. What are the facts about financial aid for middle-class students?
2. How fair is financial aid for middle-class students?

By clarifying and separating these questions, you get a clearer, more pointed, and more effective discussion of both the facts and the values than if these two questions continued to blur together.

Another situation calling for specific phrasing of questions is when you want to use them as focus items for an agenda, either for a private or a public discussion. Careful selection and wording of the questions help a group to focus its analysis. Some guidelines for phrasing and disentangling discussion questions include:

- Focus on one idea per question.
- Phrase questions unambiguously and clearly.
- Phrase questions objectively.
- Phrase questions open-endedly.

When a question clearly centers on just one subject, it's far easier to keep the discussion on target. When a question is open-ended, it's easier to stay open-minded and think creatively because open-ended questions reduce the yes-or-no, right-or-wrong responses fostered by closed-ended questions.

Sometimes a closed-ended question is okay, if you're really dealing with exclusive alternatives. The problem is that dichotomies are often artificial. Take, for example, this question: "Is the campus policed by municipal or campus security?" If security really is handled by one or the other, this question is okay. The question overlooks the possibility, however, that each group may have different responsibilities or that another off-campus security organization does part of the work. Generally, you're better off with an open-ended question such as, "What group or groups are responsible for policing the campus?"

There are a few "tricks of the trade" to phrasing questions that meet the criteria of unitary focus, clarity, unambiguity, and open-endedness for each kind of question:

FOR ALL QUESTIONS
- Use terms that keep the question open-ended—*in what ways, in what respects, to what extent, how, how much, where, when, who,* and *why.*
- Keep the question short.
- Keep the language simple and concrete.

FOR QUESTIONS OF FACT
- Ask about things that can be measured or proved.
- Ask about things that can be answered in numbers.
- Ask about things that can be answered by historical records.
- Ask about things that can be answered by empirical research.
- Ask about things that can be answered by expert testimony.
- Avoid adjectives; they introduce subjectivity as well as other value and fact issues and also reflect conclusions about secondary questions.

FOR QUESTIONS OF VALUE
- Ask about the degree to which something is worthwhile.
- Ask about how concepts and actions should be prioritized.
- Ask about the degree to which an idea is consistent with moral, ethical, and value criteria.

FOR QUESTIONS OF POLICY
- Ask questions that contain "should" statements.
- Ask questions about possible actions as solutions to problems.
- Ask questions that subsume ideas of both values and facts.
- Avoid adjectives; they introduce subjectivity as well as other value and fact issues and also reflect conclusions about secondary questions.

FOR QUESTIONS OF PREDICTION
- Ask questions of fact, value, or policy that may arise in the future.
- Ask questions that must be answered in probabilities.

Careful analysis of your questions helps to avoid confusion. Too often, people include values and facts in one long question or statement. It then takes a great deal of talk to straighten out which is which.

Consider this question: "How should the college control the appalling lack of respect for college property?" This question meets the criteria for policy questions. It contains *should* and asks about solutions. But it assumes a question of fact—that there is a problem. It also biases the issue by using a value-laden adjective—*appalling*—and it assumes the college should be the controlling entity. Finally, it even makes a prediction assumption—that the college *can* control the alleged problem.

What you need is all four of these ideas in separate sets of questions:

Fact. What harm is being done to college property? How much harm is being done to college property? Who is harming college property?

Value. How important is the harm being done to college property? How do we weigh the harm compared with other issues requiring college resources?

Policy. What should the policy of the college be regarding protection of its property?

Prediction. To what extent will the proposed solution control damage to college property?

When you separate the questions in these ways, you begin to see other questions, too, and you're on your way to getting the information needed to address the issues involved.

PLANNING RESEARCH

Writing about the quality management movement, Walton (1986) begins her chapter on data with "In God we trust. All others must use data" (p. 96). That about sums it up.

Questions are answered with information. People must have material from which to draw ideas and with which to make decisions. Hamid (2008) notes that "often when users interact with information, new knowledge is created. The synthesis and analysis of information causes embedded knowledge to surface, thus emerging useful patterns, frameworks, or concepts" (p. 259). The bottom line: teams with quality information make better, more creative, and more complete decisions than teams without it (Patel & Riley, 2007).

A team's purposes dictate the specific information needs, but most teams find they need more information than they actually have. A quality task force, for example, may need data about employee satisfaction before it can recommend a company policy. Project team members also may need to develop personal learning—about a topic, skills, and other members' viewpoints—to proceed with their job.

IDENTIFY NEEDS FOR DATA

Early on, you need to talk about what information your team needs and decide who will find what. Your team may include experts in some of the fields relevant to the team's goals. Even with expert input, you will need to seek out additional information on those areas and on others. In addition to your experts, information can come from the following sources:

Historical data are summations and analyses of what happened, according to written and oral records. Teams need historical background—perhaps from yesterday or a thousand years ago—about issues, events, people, and processes.

Empirical research is scholarly investigation of ideas or behavior. Sometimes empirical research provides studies of limited variables, and sometimes reports are "meta-analyses," which are summaries and analyses of research and theories that link variables, causes, effects, and relationships. Empirical research starts with questions or hypotheses to be answered or tested. It follows research designs that (one hopes) are carefully selected to provide specific and focused information. Data are tested statistically to measure probabilities, not absolute truths. Empirical studies contribute to further questioning, hypothesizing, testing, and developing theories, but they also contribute to decision making about policies and actions. Empirical studies on the effects of smoking, for example, have provided data used in public advocacy and policy making.

Critical analysis is researchers' analysis and judgment about the qualities and effects of written or oral materials or processes. Critical analysis may be applied to plays, speeches, social movements, or policies and procedures. It should be conducted with objectivity and competence, provide clear definitions of criteria used, and offer new insights into the subject of the research.

Opinion research may investigate what experts or laypeople (nonexperts) believe about a subject. Experts provide bases for interpreting, drawing conclusions, and evaluating circumstances as well as facts. (The quality of their contributions relies on the quantity and quality of their expertise and their credibility, of course.) Laypeople cannot provide expertise, but they can tell you what ordinary people are feeling, thinking, experiencing, and observing.

Suppose you're on the campus multicultural task force with a goal to increase multi-cultural sensitivity and awareness. What information do you need? You might have a list that goes something like this:

1. Historical background and definitions of multiculturalism in the United States and other societies, on campuses in general, and on your campus in particular;
2. Empirically researched information about how people's attitudes are formed and how these attitudes can be changed;
3. Opinions from experts—anthropologists, sociologists, psychologists, and others—who have researched issues of multiculturalism;
4. Opinions from laypeople on campus with personal experience regarding these issues;
5. Critical analysis of events, communication, and activities on campus that relate to cultures and multiculturalism.

This list is a good starting point. Next, your team would break it down into specific units of research, and then you would figure out where to get the information.

MAKE A TEAM PLAN

Information gathering begins "at home." The members of a work team who have been chosen because of their expertise and competence need to share their knowledge with the team. Even in a group whose membership is less specifically selected for expertise, each individual brings personal knowledge, information, understanding, and resources.

An initial exploration, therefore, includes examining what people know, what they can do, and how they can share their expertise. Keep your antennae up for unexpected or unusual resources. In a group discussion of language acquisition, we remember discovering that one woman thought of American Sign Language as her first language and of spoken English as her second. She had learned to sign first—although she was a hearing child—because her older sister was hearing impaired. In fact, the entire family used signing from her earliest memories. An incredible range of insights about language acquisition became available to the group from this woman's personal experience.

Once you've explored what each member might be able to contribute personally, you can identify areas for each person to cover. Consider each person's talents, interests, contacts, and time, but also consider equity and balance in getting the work done.

Agree on how—and when—the work will be done. This is where many groups slip up. Everybody may get an assignment; half of the people do it, and half don't. Of the half who do it, half do it well and the other half only do it halfway. By the time those who do it halfway get what they've learned back to the team, you can cut it in half again. The team winds up without the information it needs, and that undermines its effectiveness.

What's the answer? Before anyone leaves the room (or the online meeting), do three things:

1. Divide the work, and make specific assignments to each member.
2. Establish guidelines for presenting the information to the team.
3. Set deadlines.

Each of these steps is essential for face-to-face meetings, but for online meetings they are absolutely crucial. There just isn't time for a virtual team to renegotiate at every meeting what each person is to do, and it's far too easy to misunderstand one another when you lack the nonverbal feedback of face-to-face communication. Online, you want to state each of the steps specifically, and confirm that you all understand it.

Guidelines for presenting information can be simple; your team can identify its own needs. But here are a few things we know can help:

- Get full documentation for sources—author; date; article, book and journal title; edition; publisher; page numbers; and if your source is on the Web, the full address and date of your visit. Always, always, always do this. The documentation is essential for two practical reasons and for one ethical concern. First, documentation shows the credibility of your source. Second, if you need to go back to that source for further information, you know where to find it. The ethical reason is that documenting sources helps avoid plagiarism. Communication ethicist Richard Johannesen (1996) explains that plagiarism "stems from the Latin word for kidnapper. It involves a communicator who steals another person's words and ideas without properly acknowledging their source and who presents those words or ideas as his or her own" (p. 308). People can fall into this ethical trap without ever meaning to do so, and all it takes to keep out of it is documentation.

- Get full data for experts you interview—the correct name, academic degrees, position held, and accomplishments relevant to the topic. This is another form of documentation and is the ethical thing to do, both because it enables you to trace information and because you are crediting the source properly.
- Provide the team with brief, concise handouts (or, for a virtual team, faxes or e-memos) that clearly summarize the critical information and define new terms.
- If you run across information that would be useful for someone else on the team, bring or e-mail that person a full bibliographic citation—or better yet, bring or fax a copy.

If all members know and accept the guidelines your team creates, they are more likely to bring back data the team can actually use. Much time and valuable information can be lost simply because people don't organize data and record them in usable ways.

When you know who will do what and how they will report it, create a work plan that includes both assignments and deadlines. Within the period before the final project or report is actually prepared, calculate the time available for research, discussion, and planning. Leave room for the unexpected. The only thing you can count on is that you can't count on anything. Set specific deadlines for having each piece of work completed and ready to report to the team, either in person or online.

Another practical hint: *Make a complete list of assignments*—that is, who is doing what and by when. Figure 5.2 provides a model to help you create such a worksheet, and many of the groupware systems provide online models that can be used for this purpose. Once the list of responsibilities and deadlines is complete, give everyone a copy.

Information Planning Form					
Information needed	Resource location	Reporting format	Possible resources	Date needed	Person(s) responsible

FIGURE 5.2

Information planning form.

IDENTIFYING INFORMATION RESOURCES

You and your teammates should start your research as soon as you have your assignments, because it always takes longer than you expect. A good beginning is to identify possible resources.

First, keep in mind that some sources will be primary and some will be secondary. A **primary source** is direct, perhaps from an expert or layperson in the first publication—which could be publication in print or online—of an item. The item could be an in-depth news analysis, a research study in a journal, or an original news report in a newspaper. When you can get primary sources, they are what you should use, because you know that the words are actually the ones spoken or written by that source. That doesn't answer the question of whether the originator is unbiased, honest, ethical, or expert—but at least you know the information is straight from the source.

A **secondary source** paraphrases, repeats, or quotes information from another source, so the material is at least one step removed from the original. This distinction can be important for two reasons. First, secondary sources often present an item as "new news" when it actually is not. Research quoted in a magazine may be years old or even obsolete, and the date and context may not be given. Second, whenever information is abstracted, summarized, and presented in a secondary publication, its message may be changed or even be misrepresented. The secondary source may put a spin on the information that distorts it in some way. Even when a newspaper reports the release of a research study, or perhaps a speech, the headline and lead paragraph may give you one strong impression that further reading contradicts. We all too often see a report (in the paper, on television, online) of "new research findings" that are, to our personal knowledge, not only not new, but sometimes outdated and inaccurately reported. Secondary sources usually are easier to find, however, and you can't avoid using them. Just watch them carefully.

With these points in mind, you can start planning your research. You will want to draw from your team's expertise, use external research sources for information, and develop a plan detailing responsibilities for every team member.

INFORMATION FROM INTERVIEWS

Directly questioning an expert or a layperson sometimes can give you wonderful information to supplement or illuminate your other sources. With an interview, you have the opportunity to probe ideas and to get data that are immediate and fresh.

When interviewing experts, brainstorm a list of qualified people you know personally or by reputation. Whether you're serving on a work team at your job, a campus task force or committee, or a project team—even one for this class—many experts on various subjects are easily reached by a telephone call, e-mail, or a short visit. For instance, consult the faculty list at your college (most college catalogs list faculty, along with their degrees and areas of expertise, in an index at the back). Or use a two-step process, such as asking people in the community or in the college if they know of someone.

Here are a few tips on interviewing an expert:

- Call well ahead of time. Whether you will meet the interviewee in an office, on the phone, or online, *make an appointment, and confirm the time and location.*
- Do your homework. Be familiar with the subject; plan a rough outline of what you want to know. You may want to e-mail the outline or questions to your subject ahead of time so she or he can be prepared.
- Be on time, whether you're meeting in real or virtual conditions.
- Use a tape recorder if the respondent is agreeable; otherwise, take notes. Ask probing questions, and verify what you think you hear.
- Leave before you wear out your welcome.
- Write a thank-you note, and call or e-mail to verify any information of which you are uncertain.

You can plan an interview with a good outline, but you should leave enough open space to follow spontaneous leads or to probe specific areas. Critical thinking expert Edward de Bono (1994) distinguishes between two broad categories of questions:

1. "'*The shooting question*,' in which we know exactly what we are aiming at. We usually expect a 'yes' or a 'no' for an answer" (p. 80). Or, at least, a specific fact for an answer. "Did you earn a college degree?" should get a "YES" or a "NO." "Where did you go to college?" should get a specific answer, too, although it won't tell you if the respondent graduated. Both shooting questions are closed-ended, aiming just for specific data or confirmation.
2. "'*The fishing question*,' [in which] we dangle the bait in the water and wait to see what we catch" (p. 80). An open-ended question leaves space for the respondent to answer. For example, "How would you evaluate this issue?" fishes for the respondent's feelings, opinions, and values about the topic.

Sometimes interviews give you both excellent information and contacts that might be invaluable in your future. Use them well.

INFORMATION FROM SURVEYS

To get the opinions, attitudes, or views of ordinary people—students at your college, coworkers at your job—your team may want to take a survey or distribute questionnaires. First, identify the broad categories you want to investigate, and then identify more specific questions for each category. Next, write your questions.

Giacobbi (2002) points out that the shorter the questionnaire, the better, but the questions must be friendly both to the respondent and to you as a data collector.

Questionnaires look deceptively simple, but creating good ones is an art form. Here are some hints:

- Plan who will administer the survey as well as where, when, and to whom it will be given.
- Write the questions so each is simple, unbiased, and (mostly) positive.
- Design the format so it's quick and easy for people to complete.
- Plan how you will tabulate responses.

- Place easier (or milder) questions at the beginning and tougher ones in the middle.
- Place questions about demographic data (age, sex, race, and such) at the end.
- Prepare your questionnaire so it looks neat and professional.

When respondents take your survey, they're doing you a favor. So the rule is to ask them logically, courteously, and persuasively to help you out. Take as little of their time as possible, and conclude the process courteously. Finally, tell them how they can find out the results of your research if they want to know. The same rules apply whether you are presenting the survey in person or online.

Tabulate your responses as clearly and honestly as you can, and draw only reasonable conclusions from them. Sometimes people think of a survey as a way to prove a point, but it really should be a way to find out honest information—even if you don't like the results!

INFORMATION FROM ORGANIZATIONS AND LIBRARY SYSTEMS

The times they are a'changin.' We used to talk about "print" versus "electronic" resources. Now that's a hard distinction to make. Sometimes you can find what you want in print from organizations and libraries.

Government offices (federal, state, and local) may provide good information. Your representative or senator probably has a well-trained assistant to help you with political issues, libraries often serve as government repositories, and government sites online can provide government-published information, of which there are tons and tons on just about every possible subject.

Organizations distribute information directly and online, supporting their points of view, corporations have public information offices, and nonprofit groups provide information on their causes. Specialized museums offer collections on specific topics—broadcasting, baseball, the Holocaust, women writers—to cover almost anything of interest to anybody. The curators are experts and willing to share.

Library indexes—print, online, or on disk—cover a wide range of academic disciplines and publications. *Books in Print*, for example, lists every book currently in print on any subject. Other indexes list various organizations and millions of government sources for every subject imaginable. Most libraries have indexes and databases available to provide printouts of sources or full texts of articles for an extremely wide variety of subjects. In addition to the usual offerings, many libraries maintain collections of professional research journals—and often even special or antique books; historical artifacts; letters and documents from historical figures; music, art, or drama; and collections of books, documents, videotapes, and artifacts dedicated to major eras or historical events.

Your best friends can be research librarians, almost all of whom respond to "Please" and a friendly smile. And they are expert in finding both print and electronic materials. "[Our] electronic library functions as an intranet," says Miriam Drake, dean and director of libraries at the Library and Information Center at the

Georgia Institute of Technology in Atlanta. "We have had many requests for the ability to search multiple databases across one or more servers" (Walker, 1998a, p. 1). New software also is appearing on an almost daily basis that "enables teams to gather and reuse data from disparate repositories and view the aggregate knowledge of the group within a browser interface" (Walker, 1998b, p. 14).

INFORMATION FROM THE INTERNET

And then there is the 'Net. With the advent of "at your fingers" data, the researcher's problem no longer is, "I can't find anything on this issue" but instead, "There's just too much data to process."

In pursuit of information about your topic, you can contact everyone—including the president of the country—by e-mail, or you can use a browser to locate the address and qualifications of an expert and then use e-mail to contact that person. You can go to multitudes of research sites, find lists of people and addresses, meet with people asynchronously or in real time through chat groups or discussion groups focused on your topic area. You can go to organizations' and individuals' home pages for information about their origins, purposes, services, and so on. For example, if you were a communication major, you might want to go to the National Communication Association forum, ComGrads. Through *Spectra*, the association's newsletter, an invitation to participate goes out to "students of communication within Comserve, a service of the Communication Institute for Online Scholarship (CIOS). ComGrads provides an open forum for discussing student issues, getting feedback on ideas, and networking with others from across the world" (Ratliffe, 1995, p. 4).

You probably use, on a regular basis, the many databases online that provide collections of information and references for everything from Dow Jones news/retrieval to the *Wall Street Journal* to "boutique" databases—though you may have to pay a fee for access to some. Then there are the encyclopedias on disc and online, not to mention Wikipedia.

Don't forget both print and electronic journals. Well, these days your school's library probably has access to print journals online, so for the user this distinction is growing dim. In fact, two recent studies undertaken in the University of Florida libraries confirmed a national trend: libraries are spending significantly more of their resources to make journals available online, and are less likely to purchase printed copies for their archives. The researchers found that, between 2004 and 2005, there was a significant increase—183 percent in the humanities, for example—in the number of researchers relying solely on electronic access to articles, and reported that libraries responded to users' preferences (Botero, Carrico & Tennant, 2008).

Just remember that using the Net presents you with three problems: information overload, the opportunity to procrastinate, and the difficulty of evaluating quality and sources.

Whether you're checking your e-mail, surfing the Net, downloading from a database, or blogging, you can get seriously overloaded and confused. Enthusiasm, curiosity, and serendipity might take you down an unknown path to a genuine discovery—or to a muddy morass that prevents you from reaching your intended destination. Be critical, be selective, and stay on target. And don't let the Net snag you and keep you trapped far from your scholarly goals. Chat rooms or discussion groups can be filled with inane comments from people who must not have a life, and since basically anyone can set up a Web site, often the weird or bizarre can sidetrack you from the really valuable.

As for issues of quality and sources in Internet research, stay tuned for the next chapter. These are crucial concerns in the critical thinking your team must do in order to achieve goals successfully, and we'll discuss them in Chapter 6.

SHARING INFORMATION AS A TEAM

If teammates have been thorough researchers, they may end up with a wheelbarrow full of stuff. Now they must share their findings and work through this information together. Excellent methods exist for sharing information with the team to gain the members' attention and understanding.

WORKING THROUGH INFORMATION TOGETHER

When your team meets to share information, this may be the only item on your agenda. You need to be clear about why you're meeting and get every member's commitment to be there and to explain their findings clearly and usefully. Follow the guidelines suggested earlier for presenting information—documenting, condensing into handouts, keeping information easy to follow.

This next point may seem obvious, but teams sometimes do overlook it. The results can be painful. *Be sure every member of the team understands the information that each member has uncovered.* Work it through, and allow time for feedback and questions. Because different people are responsible for discrete parts of the task, and some members have expertise that the others do not share, it is essential that all members understand the data.

This understanding is important for two reasons. First, if the membership changes or some personal crisis occurs—who knows?—it's far easier for the team to pick up the threads and weave the work back together. Second, information is essential not only for achieving the goals but also for developing the vision and cohesiveness of the team. When information is shared and understood by all, the team's base is strengthened, and the synergy of the group has a more consistent focus. It's one of the ways you become a superteam.

MAKING CLEAR REPORTS

Reporting to your team requires the same skills as presenting information to a class or other large group. It means organizing the material carefully, presenting it in an interesting and direct manner, and supporting what you say so that it is both clear and believable. The same advice pertains to reporting online—except, once again, you must take even greater precautions to be clear.

Organizing your material will require you to categorize ideas in some logical and memorable way so that people can discuss it. Some groupware provides structures for categorizing and outlining information for easier analysis, but you have to be aware that the very process of categorizing may cause you to overlook important aspects of the data or interactions among them. We once created a training manual for a very large shipping corporation whose in-house trainer told us that if an idea didn't fit he would just "malletize" it—that is, just pound the idea into the category whether it belonged there or not. The problem with that is that you can lose the shape of your data. In a free-wheeling, face-to-face meeting with a clearly thinking team, members probably are more likely to say, "Wait a minute; we've overlooked...." In a virtual team meeting or in a groupware-equipped meeting, information and ideas might get "malletized" to the detriment of your teamwork. Beware the mallet. Appendix B provides suggestions for preparing written and oral team reports; you may find it helpful to look ahead to those topics.

Posting Information   With a large audience, it may not matter if a few people don't understand you. In a team, however, all the members need to understand all the information well enough to analyze it, draw conclusions from it, and use it to achieve the team's goals. They must be able to talk about it together—to be "on the same page." One way to keep people's attention from wavering is to make the information visible by posting it. You can use flip charts, a blackboard, an overhead projector, online graphics, or PowerPoint. Visuals work for very good reasons, but they do need to be made and used well so everyone can see as well as hear what you're talking about.

Purposes for Visuals   Human beings are easily distracted by competing stimuli. If you can get people's hearing *and* vision involved, it's easier for them to pay attention and resist distraction. Furthermore, visual stimuli are important because everyone processes information differently. Some people learn more readily through hearing a lecture, others through hands-on experience, and still others through visual input. When an individual receives a variety of stimuli, it's more likely that one method will click than if information arrives via only one channel.

Another reason for using visual displays along with verbal explanations is that people can share specific visual stimuli in a way they cannot share the hearing and interpretation of words. When data are in front of people, they can discuss them, point to them, and understand them in a more directly shared frame of reference than if they're working exclusively with words.

Methods for Visuals   Visuals only help you get your point across if they are done well. We don't necessarily mean your visuals must be fancy. But if you're reporting to your parent organization, you want to be as professional and polished as you can. If you're reporting information you've found back to your team, however, you don't need to be elaborate—just good. To be good, a visual display needs to follow a few very important rules:

- Eliminate extraneous information.
- Keep messages big and easy to see.
- Keep messages brief.
- Keep language clear.
- Use only a few items (seven at most) per visual.

- Use vivid comparisons or contrasts.
- Round off numbers.
- Choose the most effective method for the purpose.

The graphic form you choose can make a huge difference in helping your listeners understand your information. Line graphs, bar graphs, matrices or grids, in particular, are excellent for clear presentation of facts and conditions. These are familiar territory and easy to read for almost everyone because they enable the viewer literally to see the data, making the information vivid, clear, and memorable. Please note, however, that visual displays also can be terribly deceptive. For instance, a mild upward or downward trend may appear exaggerated if the proportions of the graphic are distorted. If you're using a graphic presented by one of your sources, be sure it is accurate; if you're creating your own display, examine it carefully to ensure that you are giving your team accurate information.

A *line graph* displays the interaction between two things, so it's excellent for visualizing trends or changes over time. For example, if your self-managing team is trying to set up its personnel assignments to cover the workload, you might use a line graph like the one in Figure 5.3 to help decide how many people should be on duty each day.

A *bar graph* is another easy way of visualizing how one item relates to another. You can draw bars vertically or horizontally to demonstrate distinctions between units of time or categories. Such graphs often work well for showing trends and contrasts in statistical information or populations over time or by some other variable. Bar graphs appear in many reports because they show vividly how frequently something has occurred within certain brackets of time or circumstances. If your team is investigating the fund-raising activities of charitable organizations, for example, you might present data on

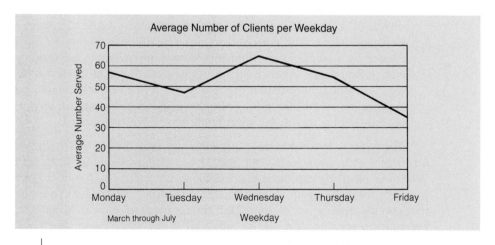

FIGURE 5.3

Sample line graph.

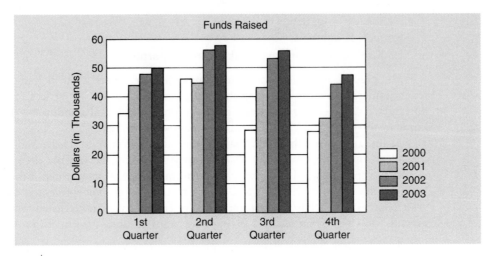

FIGURE 5.4

Sample bar graph (histogram).

contributions for each quarter over a 4-year period in a bar graph similar to that in Figure 5.4.

Matrices and *grids* help people see relationships and remember detail. These visuals show information spatially, in related blocks or cells, and they are powerful aids to analysis. A matrix can be created by hand to illustrate your information, or it can be computer generated. Variables that interrelate are labeled across the top of the grid and down the left side. Each cell of the grid then is filled in with the information about each variable. Common relationships and interactions emerge from this visual device. Figure 5.5 shows a grid created by a team investigating educational opportunities for southwestern Native Americans. After the types of questions the team needed to answer were identified, information needs were brainstormed and entered into the appropriate cells of the grid. This provided a clear picture of what was needed—and a way to see what might have been overlooked.

These forms for displaying information are presented here to help you share information with your team, but they are useful throughout your team's work. Whenever members explore ideas, it helps to use a flip chart, a board, an overhead projector, or if the group is small enough, a pad that all can see. You then can refer to a specific item or see relationships among ideas in ways that make it easier for everyone to stay focused and to recall what the ideas mean. We'll review some other specific visual techniques as aids in problem analysis and decision making in the next chapter.

TYPE OF INFORMATION	SUBJECT OF INFORMATION		
	System	Suppliers	Customers
QUANTITATIVE	Numbers of:	Numbers of:	Numbers of:
public records	schools	N.A. teachers	N.A. students
tribal records	tribal schools	Non-N.A. teachers	elem. school
	colleges near	N.A. support	middle school
		Non-N.A. support	high school
		N.A. admin.	college
		Non-N.A. admin.	post-grad
ratings	of each school	of teacher	students' scores
			% graduating
QUALITATIVE	Nature of:	Nature of:	Nature of:
	schools	teaching	student achievement
Surveys, interviews:	education	teacher prep	student motivation
personnel	support	teaching styles	learning styles
teachers			distractions
students			
families			
tribal elders			
Analysis:			lifestyles
stories			traditions
documents			values
legal code	Effects of:		beliefs
federal regs.	laws, rules,		needs
Experts:	historical influences		expectations
scholars			
gov't.			
PERSONAL			
focus groups	School personnel's	N.A. community's	N.A. students' ideas,
community forums	ideas, opinions	ideas, feelings, opinions	feelings, opinions

FIGURE 5.5

Sample information planning grid for information needed to study educational opportunity proposals for Native Americans.

SUMMARY

In this chapter, we've suggested using a systematic plan to help the team achieve success. Simon's four phases of group development—intelligence, design, choice, and review—provide a good basis, but a team will adapt these categories according to its purpose, task, and needs.

Analyzing and phrasing questions of fact, value, policy, and prediction that must be answered to reach the goal enable a team to begin identifying its information needs. The team may need both quantitative and qualitative data from historical, empirical, critical, and opinion research. Team members also may seek information from interviews, surveys, public sources, and electronic resources such as the Internet.

The team should use its members' expertise and all necessary research. This requires devising a complete work plan, including specific agreements as to who does what research and reports it to the team on what date. It also involves following guidelines for good reporting and for sharing that information with the team. Members should work carefully through the information together so that everyone understands and can use it when working toward their goals. Presenters must select and organize their information, using handouts and visuals to clarify the data and to help the team stay focused on the task.

Exercises

These exercises create a hypothetical team and goals. The activities can be used for your actual class team if you are working on a related assignment. If you want to do this as a virtual team, set up specific times for online meetings or time limits for responding to messages.

1. Analyze a topic. Suppose your team is a community task force investigating health care for the elderly. You are charged with deciding whether to urge the federal government to provide long-term health care for all its elderly citizens. Consider the proposition, and figure out what type of discussion question it is. What other questions (of fact, value, policy, or prediction) will your task force need to examine to reach a decision about the overall question? See how many you can identify.

2. Examine all the questions you identified in Exercise 1. How could you phrase these questions to make them appropriate for a discussion format? Write one well-phrased question of fact, one of value, and one of policy.

3. Plan your inquiry. As a group, identify sources of information for the questions you've identified. Think of specific sources in each of the following types:
   - Professional organizations
   - Governmental agencies
   - Scholarly journals
   - Newspapers
   - Periodicals
   - Experts

4. Select sources for information (Web sites, local organizations, library, interviews, and so on). Assign team members to gather some background information to answer your questions.

5. Design a survey to provide information on one of the questions you've identified. Consider the criteria given in this chapter for a good survey, and then test the survey by having your classmates take it and give feedback on it.

"We've got this stuff. Now, what do we do with it?"
That depends on whether it's garbage or gold.

LOGICAL AND CRITICAL THINKING

Analyzing Team Information

6

Rosabeth Moss Kanter (1990, p. 9), as editor of *Harvard Business Review*, reported the following incident:

> It was a meeting of the minds at a crossroads of world trade. In a Singapore ballroom, the British oil company head was about to reveal to managers from 37 countries the characteristics necessary for success in their global company. The audience squirmed in anticipation of the usual list of sensible—but—bland clichés about biases for action and putting people first.

"Brains," he said. "You need brains." And sat down.
How unexpected. How refreshing. How appropriate.

Brainpower is also essential for your team's success. You made a good start when you and your teammates went forth to do your research and brought back reams of data. As you know from any quick trip through a newspaper, however, not all information is equal. Your team's analysis can separate the garbage from the gold, and analysis involves using your brainpower to think logically about information and any conclusions you draw from it.

Your ability to think is more than just the genetic intelligence you were granted at birth. In fact, de Bono (1994) compares that innate ability to a car's horsepower, adding that "the performance of a car does not depend upon the horsepower of the car but upon the skill with which the car is driven. . . . Thinking is the operating skill through which intelligence acts upon experience" (p. 2). After all, everyone knows individuals who seem to have greater native intelligence but are surpassed by those with greater operating skills.

A team has many advantages over an individual when it comes to decision making. First, what one person misses, another might see. Second, teams have more collective knowledge to draw upon. Third, team members' differing perspectives allow a problem to be reviewed on a number of levels. However, in the real world teams don't always live up to their potential. They often fail to pool their collective knowledge (Stasser, 1999), or when they do, they may not take the time to integrate all members' information and perspectives in a meaningful way (van Ginkel & van Kippenberg, 2008). Additionally, groups have a tendency to focus most attention on the information they all have in common, in an attempt to avoid conflict (Wittenbaum & Park, 2001). In other words, teams accept norms for simply agreeing with one another rather than create a transactional climate in which the task processes of cooperative critical analysis—including constructive disagreement—can occur.

Logical, critical analysis doesn't prevent all decision-making errors; hindsight always provides a clearer view. But when members, like a team of detectives, cooperate in critical analysis, they can track causes and connections one individual might miss. To help you become a good critical detective, this chapter spells out norms, criteria, and methods for evaluating information critically. It then helps you to analyze ideas by examining how people reason from data to conclusions. Finally, it provides ways of testing the quality of your reasoning, of identifying fallacies, and of understanding people's underlying assumptions and values. Sometimes this means life or death, as noted in Box 6.1.

With these purposes in mind, our goals in this chapter are to enable you to:

1. Help your team set norms for critical analysis
2. Analyze data to determine what makes it trustworthy and usable or unacceptable and not useful
3. Find the strong points and the weak points of ideas and reasoning
4. Avoid illogical pitfalls and fallacies in thinking
5. Detect how assumptions and values affect a team's cooperative analysis

BOX 6.1	CRITICAL THINKING

Okay. You agree that critical thinking can be a valuable skill but, come on, it's not life or death. Or is it?

Nursing students and practitioners study the following textbooks, among others, as they try to improve their decision-making abilities—perhaps in life or death situations. In *Critical Thinking TACTICS for Nurses: Tracking, Assessing & Cultivating Thinking to Improve Competency-Based Strategies*, M. Gaie Rubenfeld, RN, and Barbara K. Scheffer, RN, MS, EdD, address the merging of critical thinking and quality health care. The authors emphasize interdisciplinary team work and evidence-based practice among their many recommendations. The text makes the concept of critical thinking tangible and manageable, and offers specific strategies for improving critical thinking in all aspects of nursing care. (This text won the 2005 American Journal of Nursing Book of the Year Award.) In the well-respected fifth edition of their *Medical-Surgical Nursing—Critical Thinking for Collaborative Care* (Elsevier, 2006), Donna D. Ignatavicius, MS, RN, and M. Linda Workman, PhD, RN, FAAN, offer related advice; as does Shelley Cohen in her text, *Critical*

Thinking in the Medical-Surgical Unit: Skills to Assess, Analyze, and Act (HCPro, 2006).

Priscilla LeMone, RN, DSN, FAAN, and Karen Burke, RN, MS, demonstrate that critical thinking remains a central skill in nursing with the recent edition of their text, *Medical-Surgical Nursing: Critical Thinking in Client Care* (Pearson Education, 2008). The authors answer the question, What do practical vocational nurses need to know and be able to do in order to deliver safe and effective medical-surgical nursing care?

You're probably not surprised at this point that several leading texts also address critical thinking skills for doctors! For example, look at *How Doctors Think* by Jerome Groopman (Houghton-Mifflin, 2007). Groopman pinpoints the forces and thought processes behind the decisions doctors make. This book is the first to describe in detail the warning signs of erroneous medical thinking and reveal how new technologies may actually hinder accurate diagnoses. *How Doctors Think* offers direct, intelligent questions patients can ask their doctors to help them get back on track.

EVALUATING INFORMATION CRITICALLY

No matter how bright and analytical team members may be, good analysis requires good information. If you draw conclusions from data that are incomplete, wrong, or false, you don't have much chance for your results to be complete, correct, or true. Evaluating your information, therefore, is crucial.

Good thinking doesn't just happen without conscious effort. Begley (2006) reports the distinction between having critical thinking skills and the willingness to deploy them. Curiosity, open-mindedness, and conscientiousness are some of the personality traits that often correlate with the desire to think critically. For most people, critical thinking is "context specific," meaning that they will use it in some areas, but not in others. If team norms discourage members from questioning and disagreeing, members are not likely to engage their critical thinking skills (Stasser, Vaughn & Stewart, 2000).

NORMS FOR CRITICAL ANALYSIS

We've already talked about norms that "just grow" and about norms that are set. Once you've gone through the process of setting goals, identifying your information needs, and establishing criteria for researching and reporting, your team may have established a norm for critical analysis. It is so important that a team be prepared to analyze critically and creatively, however, that team members should discuss and agree on some specific norms. We suggest beginning with these:

Quality of data is everyone's responsibility. All members share a mutual, hardheaded concern that any data used be worthwhile and of high quality.

Analysis is a collaborative activity. The team expects to analyze information and reason together. All members also expect to look for connections, fallacies, and problems as well as listen to and extrapolate one another's ideas and insights.

Analysis is objective and not personal. Members focus on the information and reasoning; they avoid bringing personalities or blame into the equation.

Disagreement and mind-changing are part of cooperative analysis. Members expect to disagree on points—and sometimes to change their minds—as they work through their analyses. They probe the sources of disagreement and listen carefully to one another to arrive at the best interpretation.

The team owns all information. Data can take on an emotional character, creating a barrier to good analysis. Members may start referring to "June's study" rather than to its source, the Gallup Poll. June then feels forced to defend the information because—heaven help her—the other team members will attack as if the data were her own creation. Members should avoid "killing the messenger" by agreeing that once information is reported, it belongs to the team as a whole. It can be quoted, praised, criticized, cut up, cut down, and even shredded without ego involvement or defense by anyone.

Set these as norms, practice them, and you'll develop a team that can handle information with good critical thinking.

CRITERIA FOR ANALYSIS

You can't analyze data critically without some standard of measurement. "Uh—well—it just doesn't look right to me" is a start, but it's certainly not a finish. Team members need to discuss and share criteria in two areas: the information's source and the information itself.

The Information's Source Suppose Jan brings in a tape and a summary of her interview with an expert. To decide whether the source is good, you evaluate the expert. Now suppose Dan brings in statistics from an article written by a freelance reporter based on an interview with an expert and published in a magazine. You now have three sources to consider: the expert, the writer, and the magazine. Fortunately, many of the same criteria apply to each of these sources, but the team cannot overlook one source as it analyzes the others.

We suggest three broad categories of criteria: (1) the external credibility of the source's expertise, (2) the habits of communication the source exhibits, and (3) the ethical inferences you can make from the content of the source's messages. Let's examine each category more closely:

Expertise. If the credibility of your source relies, in part, on his or her expertise, you start with that. To examine the source's observable expertise, ask these questions:

- *Qualifications.* Are the person's academic degrees, experience, and training sufficient? Are these qualifications relevant to the information in question? In other words, is the expert really "expert" on your issue?
- *Reputation.* Is the person acknowledged and respected by other experts in the field? Do other experts refer to or quote this person as a source?

Habits of communication. If the source of your information passes the previous tests, you then examine other aspects of communication to assess the source's credibility. Karl Wallace (1955) provides an excellent, and now classic, perspective by proposing the following four criteria for examining a communicator's ethics:

- *Habit of search*: The knowledgeable, thorough presentation of sound information. Does your source document information? Prove any assertions? Are the source's data complete? Is the source's habit of search ethically acceptable (such as by not abusing the environment or animal and human subjects)?
- *Habit of justice*: Fairness in presenting information so that an audience can assess it equitably. Is the source known to be trustworthy, honest? Is the source normally clear and direct in dealing with issues and people, or does the source have a history of manipulation and strategy in such dealings?
- *Habit of preferring public to private motivations*: Openly letting people know about the source's own sources, plans, and expectations. Are the source's previous actions consistent and reliable? Do contradictions in behavior or quality put this source in doubt?
- *Habit of respect for dissent*: The ability to remain objective and to encourage dialogue about opposing arguments and positions. Does the source have a history of bias toward a political, social, or philosophical position, or does the source typically present and listen to more than one side of an issue?

Ethical inferences. Messina (2007) suggests additional guidelines to use when evaluating persuasive messages. First is respect for the audience. Is the information presented in such a way that the audience can make a voluntary, informed, and rational judgment about it, or is the source using "bullying" tactics that try to force agreement? Second, does the source show respect for the material? Is the message presented in a way that both respects the audience's current views and adequately provides new information? For example, presenting a newly minted high school student with a 4,000-page U.S. tax code is not an ethical way of persuading him or her to comply with tax laws.

These criteria—the external credibility of a source's expertise, habits of communication, and inferences about respect for the audience and the material—can help your team decide how much to trust the information's source.

The Information Itself   When you start to accumulate information, you make an interesting discovery: Conclusions from data may be possibly true, or probably true, but are hardly ever *absolutely* true. As a team, you want to know how probable something is, so how do you assess probability?

As a team, you approach this question by weighing various pieces of evidence that seem to support—or refute—an idea. As you go through the information you've collected, the team becomes judge and jury. In other words, you assess each piece of information in terms of its quality, and then you weigh any contradictory pieces against each other.

The process is not that different from weighing evidence in a court of law or in a debate. Ask yourself, which evidence seems to have the most convincing characteristics? Which evidence pertains most directly to the issue or question at hand? Which conclusion has the most evidence on its side? The best conclusion—the one that is most *probably* true—is the one supported by the preponderance of *quality* evidence. In other words, there are more credible data backing that conclusion than backing other, alternative conclusions.

In most cases, a preponderance of evidence is enough to allow the team to draw a conclusion. If you were on a criminal jury, however, you would have to be even more critical in examining and weighing the evidence. A criminal court requires a conclusion "beyond reasonable doubt." This criterion demands not only greater evidence but leaves no room for any other possibility.

Most team decisions only need to rely on assessing the relative weight and value of your data. The criteria to evaluate such information are similar—but not identical—to those used to evaluate sources. Let's take an example: your team has been asked to improve the quality of student life. You've obtained the results of a survey conducted 3 years ago at ZU, another college. Here are some questions you might ask when analyzing that survey—and information in general:

- Is the information valid? That is, does it actually measure what it intends to measure? Does it apply to the issues and questions relevant to the students at your college? Would students today be different from those surveyed 3 years ago?
- Are the data reliable? In other words, to what extent are the data consistent with themselves or with other data? On this survey, if the question, "Are you comfortable at ZU?" gets a strong "Yes," but the question, "Do you feel at home at ZU?" gets a strong "No," then the reliability may be questionable.
- Is the information truthful and objective? Does the report present more than one side of the issues? Were the data gathered objectively? If the survey uses biased statements such as "ZU should reduce its excessive fees for activities," it lacks objectivity.
- Is the information sufficient? How much information is enough depends on the questions involved and what you need to know about them. Are the questions inclusive? Do they focus on facts, values, or policies? What more might you need to know?

Internet Information's Virtual Locations   Web sites are often cited as the source of information. Keep in mind that a Web site is just that—a site, a virtual location—not a source. Saying that information comes from a specific site is about the same as reporting which library a book comes from. You still need to know who wrote or prepared the material you found at that location, and you need to apply the criteria for analyzing the credibility of the source and the quality of the information that are developed in the previous sections.

Internet information raises these additional concerns:

Motives. Web sites are built for specific purposes; each has its own agenda. Material is prepared or selected to achieve those goals and not to provide an objective point of view. Approach Web sites expecting a bias, and evaluate all information with caution.

Accuracy. When you get information from the Internet, you need to know both that it's really coming from the source with which it's identified and that it's being accurately reported. Anyone can easily send fraudulent messages— and someone else can pick them up as accurate data. This issue is extremely important at both the personal and the scholarly levels and involves false information about anything from an inaccurate credit rating to false research data.

Just as top investigative journalists check for corroborating sources, Net users need to look for credibility of sources, documentation, and corroboration of information. Remmers (1998, p. 102) gives us some guidelines:

Abstracts from scholarly journals and Web sites of well-known professional organizations, news organizations, government organizations, corporations, and nonprofit groups should carry some degree of credibility. Moderated listservs will usually contain credible information (depending upon the quality of the moderators), but chat rooms, newsgroups, and unmoderated listservs will primarily contain the opinions of participants. Also, don't assume that just because a Web site is based at a college or university that the site is credible. Some institutions will give any professor or student (whether that person is the world's leading expert or the world's biggest idiot) a home page.

REASONING LOGICALLY

Inadequate—or inaccurate—analysis can lead to wrong decisions. And those wrong decisions can be costly. A study conducted by the market research firm Dynamic Markets analyzing businesses in the U.S. and United Kingdom reported that *Fortune* 500 companies collectively lose over $250 million annually as a result of poor decision making, mostly because their data are either flawed or misanalyzed (*Business Wire*, 2007).

The potentially serious impact of analytical errors underscores the need for teams to develop climates and habits that foster critical thinking. Four assumptions represent our beliefs about the uses of analysis in this society, as well as in teams:

1. Data don't prove; people do. How often have you heard statements like "Statistics prove . . ." or "Research proves . . ."? Statistics and research are only data that people need to analyze and then apply to conclusions. Teams need to apply the criteria for information and sources to determine if statistics and research findings support the conclusions.

2. Careful, objective, cooperative analysis is the essential tool of a democratic society in which people discuss, debate, argue, and try to persuade one another to make what they believe are the right decisions. Such analysis also is the essential tool of effective teams.

3. Human beings can make rational decisions, even though much of what people do and feel seems unconnected to rationality. Analytical techniques are ways to ensure disciplined thinking and to achieve a measure of rationality in decision making.

4. One objective of critical analysis is to make ethical choices. When care is taken to analyze evidence appropriately, use only credible evidence in crafting arguments, and present messages in a balanced and fair perspective, it becomes hard not to abide by ethical principles as well (Messina, 2007). Thus, ethical team decisions aren't just matters of etiquette or of avoiding wrongdoing. They are matters of choosing actions that are right.

With these assumptions stated, let's examine how people draw conclusions from data and how you can assess the validity of reasoning.

DRAWING CONCLUSIONS

We use critical thinking to "evaluate and analyze the contents of an issue . . . so as to understand its contents from a rigorous and robust perspective" (Natale & Ricci, 2006, p. 273). The evidence we gather will not draw conclusions for us. Instead, we have to use reasoning and thought to evaluate that information and come to our own understanding. Let's see how reasoning works.

Suppose your project team receives a charge from the corporation's human resources division to recommend ways of reducing health insurance expenses. Your research yields data showing that health maintenance organizations (HMOs) cost less than traditional, individual insurance coverage, so your team concludes all employees should become HMO members. In this example, your team simply looked at the data and reached a conclusion, as depicted in Figure 6.1. You can call this process "leaping to conclusions."

The mind is a wonderful thing. It makes an **inference**—a connection between the data and the conclusion—sometimes even without the individual being aware of the process. The line going from the data to the conclusion in Figure 6.1 represents the inference. This quick, invisible arc of inference between information and a conclusion is how people reason.

In a team, every member continually goes through internal, mental inferential processes, and the team's job is to bring those inferences together with some kind

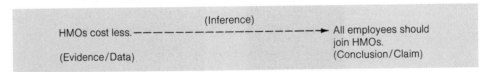

FIGURE 6.1

Inferring a conclusion from data.

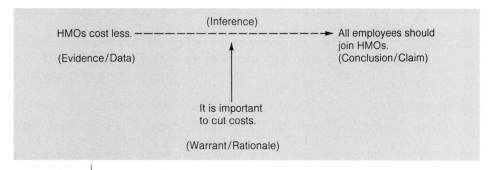

FIGURE 6.2

Identifying reasoning from data to conclusion.

of coherency. Critical analysis demands that a team identify the inferences—the relationships between data and conclusions—and evaluate them. What you need are ways of seeing these invisible relationships.

Toulmin (1958), a British philosopher, uses diagrams to describe how people think. Here, we have adapted his diagrams to help you visualize the processes of reaching a conclusion—or, in Toulmin's words, of making a **claim**. With more visible steps, it should be easier to analyze the reasoning.

What influences our inferences? Why do we leap to any particular conclusion from a specific piece of evidence? According to Toulmin, the thinking process includes a "because" clause—which he calls a **warrant**—that provides the reasons for the connection. The warrant in this example might be "It is important to cut costs." This certainly is consistent with the team's charge. Figure 6.2 shows how this warrant relates to the data and to the claim, providing the reason for the inference.

Analyzing Warrants   Warrants often are not stated out loud; sometimes they aren't even fully recognized. In discussion, members may assume that they perceive issues in the same way and that they share a common connection between data and the claim. These assumptions are critical because people probably make more errors in perception than errors in thinking (de Bruin, Parker & Fischoff, 2007). Therefore, team members need to examine potential differences in individuals' perceptions and assumptions; the warrant is a critical segment for understanding the logical processes members are using and for confronting the ethical implications of choices that are made.

Different reasons can motivate the same warrant, and examining these reasons frequently pinpoints ethical issues and dilemmas. Why is it desirable to have a health care delivery system that cuts costs? Obviously, it would save the company money. But consider these related issues:

- Does cost cutting have a higher priority than other warrants or rationales? What is the relative importance, for example, of health care quality or additional out-of-pocket costs for employees?
- Why is cost cutting important? Would it reduce the need to lay off employees, provide more money for salary increases, provide money to redecorate the board meeting room, or provide a better return to shareholders?

Critical thinking looks at these types of issues and examines them in relation to one another. By focusing on competing priorities for warrants as well as on the background for accepting any given warrant, you see the ethical implications. For example, your team may want to recommend that cutting costs on health care is desirable. If you avoid examining warrants, your conclusions may be logical—but they can still be wrong.

Identifying Reservations   Almost any claim has reservations to challenge it. Whether spoken or not, a **reservation** recognizes the possible arguments against a claim. These may in some way refute the data, the warrant, or the reasoning. In our example, although your team might agree that employees should belong to HMOs because reducing costs is desirable, some members might add, "Unless cutting costs results in lower-quality health care." Another might think the data are too limited and say, "Employees should join HMOs only if further data support the claim they're less expensive." If team members play devil's advocate and raise all possible reservations, you can develop a better understanding of the reasons for and against accepting a claim as logically and ethically acceptable.

Qualifying Conclusions   What degree of certainty do you attach to a conclusion? We have indicated that most decisions are based on probability—the degree to which you can be sure that any conclusion is true. For this reason, conclusions need to be qualified to indicate the level of certainty, and it is important to use these **qualifiers** appropriately:

Possible means the conclusion has only a small chance of being true but could still be so.

Plausible implies a higher probability of truth than possible but the conclusion still is not the most likely interpretation.

Probable applies to conclusions with a greater-than-50 percent likelihood of being true. (Be careful, however, with this one. Sound research methods recommend that levels of certainty should be in the 95 to 99 percent range to be accepted as being probable.)

Certain means the conclusion is 100 percent guaranteed; in this case, you may simply eliminate qualifiers. Remember, however, that not qualifying a conclusion implies certainty—and that's hard to arrive at for most claims.

Examining Complete Arguments   Let's go back to the Toulmin Model and add some of the elements we've been discussing. Figure 6.3 shows how the reasoning behind the warrant and the qualifier for your conclusion fit into the picture. If you diagram a full argument or statement this way, you can track and evaluate visually the thinking behind it, which can be helpful in several ways:

• The warrant and the reservation show how the inference connects the data and the claim; you can see the strength of this connection.

• When you actually see the reasoning, you may see other alternatives. For example, is this an either/or situation? Might other data and different warrants lead to a different conclusion?

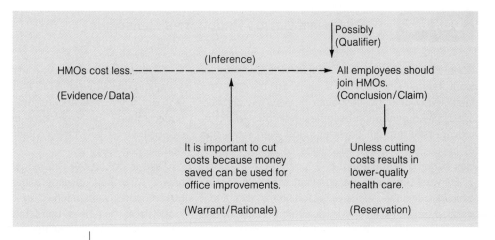

FIGURE 6.3

Examining an entire argument.

- You can see the degree of probability or possibility that modifies the argument. Is the claim probable enough to accept it?
- You can assess the ethical priorities involved with the decision. Is the warrant one that your team evaluates as ethically acceptable or desirable?
- You can examine the trustworthiness and competence of your sources. If you see that the data support only a qualifier of "probably" or "possibly" but that the information source has stated a conclusion as being absolutely true, then you have to question that source's honesty or analysis of data.

TESTING REASONING

Everybody's logical—it's just that sometimes a person's logic has holes in it. Consider "defensive" versus "productive reasoning in Box 6.2. Mending the holes in logic is much easier, however, if you understand how reasoning connects the parts in the diagram. These types of reasoning—inductive, deductive, and cause-and-effect—are not mutually exclusive. People move constantly from one form of reasoning to another. Seeing the distinctions, however, helps in analyzing warrants. Let's take a closer look at these three ways of reasoning—and at some of the fallacies people commit when using them.

Inductive Reasoning   Suppose your community water-quality task force learns that two small farms have problems with polluted springs (the data) and concludes there is an underground pollution problem. The warrant is, "If two springs are polluted, there is general underground pollution."

In this case, your team has used **inductive reasoning**. Inductive reasoning *draws a general conclusion from a sample of specific instances of an occurrence.* It relies on accumulating a sufficiently large data sample to justify making a generalization—or at least it should. Here, when your team examines its warrant,

| BOX 6.2 | **DEFENSIVE VERSUS PRODUCTIVE REASONING** |

Does this sound like your company, department or work team? Criticism is shaken off as "not our fault." New or opposite points of view are discouraged. The organization becomes geared toward protecting itself through cover-ups and even cover-ups of cover-ups. Misunderstandings escalate. Prophecies become self-fulfilling.

Harvard University management scholar Chris Argyris calls this the defensive reasoning mindset, and it leads to creation of an underground organization whose "existence is known, but where actions are rarely taken to correct its counterproductive effects, mainly because . . . those who share the defensive reasoning mindset believe they must continue doing so to prevent the organization from going out of control, from imploding."

By contrast, the "productive reasoning mindset produces validatable knowledge, informed choices, and transparent reasoning, so claims can be tested." In order to get rid of or reduce defensive routines, you need double-loop learning. Think of the thermostat in this room. It's programmed to maintain a constant temperature. Now, if the thermostat were ever to ask itself the question, "Why am I programmed this way, and why should I measure heat?"—that's double-loop learning.

If you have defensive routines and somebody says, let's tweak them a bit, that's single-loop learning. But if you ask a question, "How come they're underground?" or "How come people have this predisposition to say I'm a victim?"—that would be double-loop learning.

Take a look at the Challenger and Columbia disasters. After the Challenger disaster, there was a big government investigation. They found out that single-loop issues had been corrected, but the ones that really baffled them were the lack of openness and communication among engineers and the manager. They said, we're going to change this. I think they did their best, but they did it by looking at above-ground rules and regulations.

With the Columbia disaster we had the same problem, lack of connection, and so on. Yet [NASA] had gone through an intensive reorganization of the above-ground. None of the groups that studied the disasters took a serious look at the underground. That's where double-loop learning comes in.

Source: Excerpt from Mallory Stark, "Surfacing Your Underground Organization," *Harvard Business School Working Knowledge for Business Leaders*, November 1, 2004, http://www.hbswk.hbs.edu/archive/4456.html. Reprinted by permission of HBS Working Knowledge.

members may realize that two polluted springs probably are not enough data from which to draw a firm conclusion.

Figure 6.4 shows how a general conclusion is reached inductively from specific instances. To check whether inductive reasoning leads to a valid general conclusion, you can ask these questions:

- Are there enough cases in the sample to justify making a general conclusion?
- Did all cases in the population have an equal chance to be included in the sample?
- Do the cases represent the same population as that to which the generalization applies?
- Does the claim include a qualifier that reflects any exceptions to the general conclusion?

Deductive Reasoning   Suppose your water-quality task force has established—after thorough investigation—that there actually is an underground pollution problem. Based on that general conclusion, you notify the Swensens that their spring is

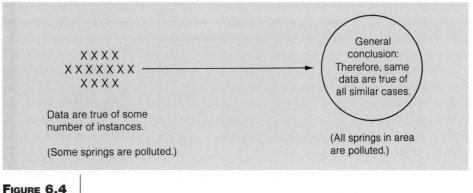

FIGURE 6.4

Model of inductive reasoning.

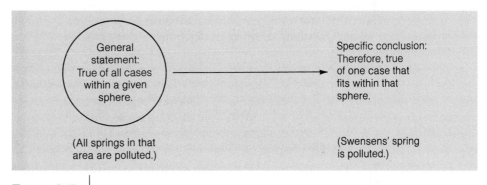

FIGURE 6.5

Model of deductive reasoning.

polluted. In this instance, you have used **deductive reasoning**. Deductive reasoning *draws a conclusion about a specific case from a general or universal statement.* Figure 6.5 illustrates the process of deductive reasoning, in which you move from a general premise—All springs in the area are polluted—to a specific conclusion—the Swensens' spring is polluted.

Like inductive reasoning, deductive reasoning may be invalid. Some questions you can ask to assess its validity include:

- Is the general statement accurate? Should the general statement have a qualifier, such as "some springs" or "most springs"? You may need to look at how the generalization was arrived at—that is, the validity of the inductive process that provided the general statement.
- Is the instance to which you're applying the generalization really the same as the ones covered by the general concept? (Is the Swensens' farm in the same geographical area?)

- Do other characteristics make the specific instance less likely to be affected by the generalization than the other instances were? For example, is the Swensens' spring fed from a different source?

Cause-and-Effect Reasoning   Suppose your water-quality task force discovers that farmers have been dumping waste into sinkholes (the data). These land-surface depressions allow substances to move into and through a wide underground limestone system (the warrant). Your team then concludes that dumping in the sinkholes pollutes the springs in the area (the claim). In this case, your team has used cause-and-effect reasoning—dumping is the cause, and pollution is the effect. **Cause-and-effect reasoning** *draws a conclusion that there is a relationship between two occurrences and that one causes the other.*

Much of teamwork involves analyzing problems to discover their causes. Few effects have single causes, however, and the actual causes may be many and complex. Thus, such analysis often demands careful and detailed examination to discover what the causes actually are and how to interpret both the causes and their effects. Cause-and-effect reasoning is critical to problem analysis, and teams must sort through many possible connections to determine how various circumstances relate. Questions that help in determining causes include:

- Has the suggested cause happened each time before the effect, or have there been exceptions?
- Did the suggested cause happen concurrently with other events?
- Could the other events be causes?
- Could all the observations actually result from some other, unidentified cause?
- Do other causes—or multiple causes—seem more probable?

There also may be a variety of effects or aspects of a problem that result from one or more causes. Examining such effects involves questions such as:

- How extensive are these effects?
- Who is affected, to what extent, and under what circumstances?
- How significant are the effects?
- To what extent—and in what ways—are the effects harmful?
- Could these effects also result from some other cause?

People tend to make quick inferences about causes and effects. After all, if one occurrence is followed by another, it's easy to conclude a causal relationship between them. Many myths and bad decisions have come about, however, because someone did not examine the relationship between causes and effects. "Fire the coach," says the alumni board. "The team didn't win enough games this season." In fact, the team may have lost games for other reasons, and the board may be firing a great coach.

Fallacious Reasoning   When people make mistakes in reaching a specific conclusion from a general premise—or when they irrationally draw a general conclusion from inadequate specific data, or mistakenly infer that one event has caused another—they are thinking fallaciously. Consider the investigation of crop circles in

Case Study 6.1. A **fallacy** is *an inference from data to a claim that circumvents sound, logical reasoning*. Here are some common fallacies (with tips for catching them):

Hasty generalizations are reasoned from too few examples or instances to broad conclusions. Go back to the earlier case of the polluted springs. Leaping from the data that two springs are contaminated to the conclusion that all springs are polluted is premature. Overgeneralizing from slim data often sweeps people or events from related categories under one, indiscriminate blanket. "You people are all alike" represents this fallacy. Carefully examining generalizations can avoid many "-isms"—racism, sexism, classism, handicapism—and guide your team toward making better decisions. For instance, a management team might conclude that tardiness is a problem and set up rigorous rules and penalties to deal with it. A thorough analysis, however, might have shown that only one or two employees were chronically late. You can minimize faulty generalizations by checking the quantity and quality of your data and by watching out for words like *always, never*, or other forms of unqualified conclusions. Look for exceptions to the generalizations, and qualify claims with *probably, possibly*, or *perhaps*.

False analogies are comparisons of one thing to another because of similarities when, in fact, they also have significant differences. Your college holds pep rallies before games and shows enthusiastic school spirit; my college concludes, therefore, that it should hold pep rallies, too. Yours is a small, residential campus with an active athletic program; mine is a large, urban, commuter campus with a limited athletic program. Both are colleges, but the analogy breaks down from there. Avoiding false analogies requires identifying the differences. If the two things don't compare on all significant issues, reject the analogy.

False dilemmas are artificial divisions of an issue into an either/or choice when both choices may be true or other alternatives may exist. For example, discussions about distributing condoms in high schools frequently reveal this fallacy. One side, advocating abstinence, argues that "condoms don't work very well." The other side argues that "teenagers who are sexually active shouldn't be denied the protection of condoms." People tend to line up on one side or the other, but the two positions are not mutually exclusive. The conclusion that condoms may provide "safer" rather than "safe" sex recognizes both arguments. Anytime you hear a dichotomous statement—or have an urge to make one—examine the alternatives to see what might lie between the extremes.

Special pleading is giving special consideration to one entity over others because of bias, prejudice, or other preferential factors. It seeks to apply a different standard to similar situations. Related fallacies include appeals to pity or to ignorance as special reasons for treating one situation differently from another. The classic example is the man who kills his parents, then asks for leniency because he's an orphan. Though not all circumstances are the same, you need to weigh suggestions for preferential treatment against established criteria and precedents. You also need to base decisions on the merits of the case and on your ethical evaluation.

CASE 6.1 | BLT RESEARCH TEAM, INC.: SCIENCE AND THE CIRCLES

BLT, Inc., was incorporated as a nonprofit, tax-exempt U.S. organization in 1999, although it has been working as a nonprofit institution since 1990, when Michigan biophysicist Wm. C. Levengood, with U.K. researcher Pat Delgado, began systematic crop circle plant comparisons with control plants taken elsewhere in the same fields. From there a worldwide, organized network of systematic field research, analysis, and reporting of crop circle phenomena by a growing number of scientific consultants has developed.

Between 1990 and 2000, more than 300 crop formations were investigated in the United States, Canada, England, the Netherlands, Germany, Australia, and Israel, with field workers sampling and documenting both affected plants and control study plants, and with laboratory analysis of seeds and soils. Research papers, published in peer-reviewed scientific journals, reported that a theory of causation attributing crop circles to "human pranksters with planks and boards, was inadequate."

The researchers concluded that "there are pervasive, re-occurring abnormalities in crop-circle plants and soils (as compared to the control plants and soils taken from the same fields and as compared with plants evaluated in the control studies) which are consistent with exposure of these plants and soils to an intense and complex energy system which emits heat (possibly microwaves) along with highly unusual electrical pulses and strong magnetic fields. . . . More than 90 percent showed the characteristic anomalous changes in somatic (nonreproductive) and/or reproductive plant tissues, and magnetic material was consistently documented in those formations where soil sampling had also been conducted."

BLT supports the validity of its research methods, pointing out that its work is the most comprehensive to date; hundreds of different field workers were mostly unacquainted with one another or with the previous results; and results of testing were remarkably consistent. Additionally, they compared their results to an evaluation of experimental fields in which crops had been downed manually (using pranksters' methods of trampling and compressing the plants) and found that the manually downed crop plants do not exhibit the same physical changes as in the crop circle plants studied over the years. "It seems probable, then, that the overall number of man-made crop circles is relatively small, compared to the total number of circles discovered and reported each year. . . . Although the media has [sic] made this progress more difficult by labeling the crop circle phenomenon as 'fringe,' hard data—obtained through rigorous scientific methodology—is difficult to ignore."

Questions to Consider

1. How did the BLT gather and evaluate their information? What evidence do they present for having used solid, scientific norms for their critical analysis?

2. How would you evaluate the validity of the organization's conclusions to date? Consider their evidence, their reasoning, their handling of warrants and qualifiers.

3. What has the team done to test its reasoning? How and where do you see the uses of inductive and/or deductive and/or cause-effect reasoning? Do you see fallacious reasoning in this report? What, why, to what effect on the report?

4. How do assumptions and values (of the researchers and/or of the environment in which they are conducting and reporting their research) affect the way the research is conducted or reported?

Source: Adapted from "BLT Research Team," http://www.bltresearch.com, retrieved January 31, 2003.

Red herrings are fallacies that divert attention from the real issue by presenting irrelevant arguments. The term comes from the practice of putting a strong fish smell across a tracking dog's path to divert the dog's attention from its prey. For example, a paralyzed former police officer who had been shot in the line of duty dramatically enters a courtroom during the unrelated trial of another police officer—who has been accused of shooting a teenager. The judge is outraged because he believes the paralyzed officer's appearance is a red herring: an attempt by the defense to focus the jury's attention on a different situation rather than on the merits of the case at hand. One way to examine this fallacy is to diagram the argument as Toulmin suggests. The lack of a relationship among the data, claim, and warrant reveals a red herring.

Circumlocution is reasoning that actually goes in a circle. Suppose we, as your authors, tell you that every word in this textbook is the final word on that topic. How do you know it's the final word? Because the authors say so in the book. How do you know the authors are correct? Because the book is the final word on the topic. (We would not make this claim, of course—and we hope you wouldn't believe us if we did.) Using a Toulmin diagram is a big help here. If you see that the claim and the data or that the data and the warrant are the same, you know you have circumlocution.

Appeal to authority is linking an advocated position to someone or something that has high status—whether or not that status is relevant to the issue. A corporate team member may argue that an idea is superior because it comes from the firm's president. The president's point of view may be important, but it is not necessarily better simply because of his or her position. To avoid fallacious appeals to authority, separate the issue from the appeal, and consider the issue on its merits.

Ad hominem, or personal attack, avoids an issue by attacking the individual or the information source. Labeling a newspaper as "that rag" or a person as a "reactionary" diverts the focus from what that source has to say. In organizations, proposals may be labeled as "management" or "union" without considering the potential usefulness of the ideas. Try to focus on the issue, and disregard statements about individuals—unless those statements relate directly to the information's credibility and to the issue at hand.

Your vigilant leadership helps to identify fallacies in your own thinking and in the thinking of others. Vigilance can separate issues objectively and isolate sloppy or deceptive thinking. Vigilance requires alertness, however, and separating the merits of an issue from the fallacies. Even fallacious thinking may lead to a conclusion that seems reasonable on other grounds. This type of leadership requires tact in confronting fallacies and maintaining open communication climates. The good part is that this process of analyzing thinking and spotting fallacies is energizing and challenging.

EXAMINING ASSUMPTIONS AND VALUES

What individuals feel—and what they think they know—pervades every transaction between and among people. When members bring their individual values and assumptions to their groups, these issues permeate every aspect of cooperative analysis. Warrants emerge—consciously or unconsciously—from values, and fallacious reasoning often results from assuming facts that are not in evidence. With this in mind, we want to look at the nature and effects of assumptions and values and how they are influenced by issues such as culture and gender.

NATURE AND EFFECTS

An **assumption** is *an untested belief, often unconscious and usually unstated, that something is true*. It can be a belief about anything—data, values, people, actions. In our thinking processes, as we have seen, many warrants are simply assumptions. How often have you said, or heard someone else say, "But I thought you'd agree," "I just assumed we had enough money for the evening," or "I figured you knew I was going to do that"?

Actually, people couldn't get along without assumptions. There simply is too much to know, too many decisions to make, for someone to check every assumption before proceeding. The problem is that an assumption often is treated as if it were a fact. Furthermore, one assumption may be based on another: he not only assumed she knew he was going, but he also assumed that if she knew, she wouldn't mind. The assumer believes the assumed fact is shared by others and, therefore, doesn't need to be discussed.

A **value** is different. It is *a personal, internal understanding about the worth and importance of an idea, action, or way of being*. Values are the foundation for human behavior, and they take on their character through the way a person ranks or prioritizes each value against others. Like assumptions, values often are unstated and may be unconscious.

Values and assumptions are easily confused, because frequently a person *assumes* that another person holds particular *values*. Group members sometimes stare at each other in complete bogglement when it comes time to make a decision and they realize they are coming at it from totally different value systems. They had assumed that they held basic values in common, but they were wrong.

The reverse can be true as well. People who know intuitively that they differ in their assumptions also may assume that they have radically differing values. Sometimes they are shocked when they agree on value-motivated decisions.

Here's an example. A task force consisting of corporate and nonprofit organizational representatives is charged with developing a low-income housing program for people who are homeless. The team members include Ann, a corporate manager, and Bernard, who works in a nonprofit organization. Ann assumes Bernard's top value is making life easy for the poor, and that *he* doesn't comprehend life's realities. Bernard assumes Ann's top value is corporate profit, and that *she* doesn't understand life's realities. When the time for a decision arrives, they find themselves agreeing on a plan for corporate sponsorship to help people rehabilitate condemned homes and buy them at extremely low prices.

Ann and Bernard may be surprised about agreeing when each assumed the other to be so different. What they don't realize is that they may be starting from different assumptions about "life's realities"—but not from such different values. Bernard assumes that corporations are indifferent to human deprivation and social injustice; Ann assumes that corporations are not indifferent and have a unique capability to intervene and to counteract human and social incompetence. Bernard doesn't know that Ann values opportunity for human beings even more highly than she values corporate success, and Ann doesn't know that Bernard values opportunity for human beings very highly but also values entrepreneurship and independence. In this case, their values lead them to favor a plan that meets their priorities and allows both sets of assumptions and values to operate comfortably.

We could say that Ann and Bernard live in different subcultures and that they are engaging in a cross-cultural negotiation. If they listen to each other and examine some of their own assumptions and values, they'll reach agreement faster—and with much less pain—than they would otherwise.

CULTURAL AND GENDER INFLUENCES

Today, many teams are multinational, with government and business drawing together decision makers from around the world. Even small, local teams involve people of differing genders and diverse backgrounds. It's clear that cultural, subcultural, and gender factors influence people's assumptions and values and that these, in turn, influence the ways people analyze data, reason, and arrive at conclusions.

For example, many U.S. managers working overseas express frustration at the length of time it takes to reach a decision. U.S. managers tend to express a sense of urgency in getting results, and are often taken aback when additional evidence and study is said to be needed for programs that have already proven to be effective (Jassawalla, Truglia & Garvey, 2004). Others with assignments in Japan report that pushing a team toward consensus, or talking about the issue too quickly before establishing interpersonal rapport, are each considered rude and may completely inhibit the team's problem-solving effectiveness, whereas in the U.S. those hard-chargers would be praised for their efficiency in meetings (Forster, 2000).

What do these differences mean? Suppose an international task force charged with creating cultural connections among countries is trying to choose between two proposals. One is to sponsor, in the capital of one country, an impressive international plaza to exhibit art from around the world. The other is to create a long-term, well-funded cultural exchange program among the countries. The warrants (perhaps unspoken) might be, "This action will reflect glory on the team" versus "This action will strengthen understanding among our nations." The different assumptions and values of the various cultures may affect members' preferences between those alternatives.

Some people think of gender as a subcultural variable, because within cultures there is evidence that women and men develop different value/ethical structures. Significant research confirms that women and men use "different cognitive styles or moral orientations to solve moral dilemmas" (Nguyen, Basuray, Smith, Kopka & McCulloh, 2008). Typically, men subscribe to an ethical decision rule of *justice*, whereas women are more likely to invoke an ethic of *care* (Jaffee & Hyde, 2000). The justice decision rule focuses primarily on issues of fairness, ensuring that everyone affected is treated equally. Here, decision makers strive to be emotionally detached from the situation so that they can make rational decisions. On the other hand, a care decision rule looks more closely at individual need, and argues that each person should be taken care of differently if their needs are different . . . and sometimes those needs are felt on an emotional level. As you can see, the two perspectives are in direct contrast. The "unemotional, treat everyone the same" philosophy of the justice perspective conflicts with the "emotional, think of everyone as individuals" mandate of the care perspective.

Studies indicate that both sexes can use both orientations, but men are more likely to focus on the justice orientation and women on the care orientation. There are differences, too, in the values and ethics people have derived from experience, education, their professions, and from their characters and personalities (Toussaint & Webb, 2005).

What do you do with this information? Well, we hope you won't look at an individual Korean, say, and assume she or he is not concerned with love, friendship, or health simply because one study, as summarized by one researcher, found that one group of Koreans rated these values as low priorities. We also hope you won't assume a woman can't apply an ethic of justice or a man can't apply an ethic of care.

Members of various cultures, subcultures, and genders may differ significantly in the values they bring to a group or team experience, but it's a mistake to assume that anyone has x, y, or z values. It is wise, however, to recognize that their values may differ radically from yours and to be willing to examine, probe, and learn to understand differences before making group decisions.

With some understanding of the reasoning process, common fallacies, and human assumptions as well as values, you now have a foundation for analyzing the information and ideas your team has generated so creatively.

SUMMARY

Once a team has collected information, its job is to analyze it cooperatively and critically. Toward that end, a team needs to set norms that enable it to collaborate objectively. To analyze evidence, a team needs shared criteria and skills for weighing the credibility of sources and the quality of data. The basic assumptions involved in critical analysis are that the purpose is to make good decisions and that human beings have the rationality necessary to make those decisions.

Making rational choices involves examining the inferential connections between data and conclusions. One useful way of visualizing these connections is to map them, showing the warrant (the reason that justifies connecting the data to the claim) and the qualifiers indicating the degree of certainty.

Problems of reasoning include overgeneralization in inductive reasoning; improper deductive reasoning from a general statement to a specific instance; unjustified inferences of causation in cause-and-effect reasoning; and fallacies in connecting data, warrants, and claims.

Problems also arise because people bring their assumptions and values—often influenced by culture, gender, and other individual variables—to their analyses without stating or, sometimes, even being aware of them.

Exercises

1. Using See Form 6.1, rate the way you think with a group of people. What do you do well? What do you want to improve? How could your leadership help a team with critical analysis?

2. Be a critic. Record a serious discussion among several people, perhaps in class or on television, and then write a brief summary that responds to these questions:

   a. To what extent did members work together to think critically?

   b. How thorough was the group in analyzing its reasoning?

   c. How well did the group analyze its data?

   d. How objective were the interactions in regard to data and reasoning?

   e. How rational were the group's conclusions?

3. Find an editorial or a short article that argues for some position, and map the relationships among the data, the warrant, and the conclusions. (The data and warrant may not be stated explicitly, so you may

have to infer them from what the author does say.) Did the writer analyze the background leading to the warrant? Were his or her conclusions qualified or stated absolutely? How complete, rational, and ethical was his or her communication? Based on this analysis, would you use this editorial or article as a data source for a group project? If so, why and how? If not, why not?

4. Cooperatively analyze reasoning. As a team, look over the following questions and use them to analyze the statements that follow:

What assumptions might the speaker be making?

What assumptions might other team members make about the statement?

What differing values might various members of a team bring to their analysis of the statement?

What reasoning (inductive, deductive, cause-and-effect) does the statement imply?

What fallacies does the statement reflect?

Here are the statements:

a. Abortion is a question of the right to choose or the right to life.

b. Only the United States can ensure world peace.

c. Educational excellence is declining because of television.

d. People who smoke infringe on other people's rights.

e. If executions were televised, the number of crimes would decrease.

f. When pornography is available, people buy it simply because it is available.

FORM 6.1 | SELF-ANALYSIS OF LOGICAL AND CRITICAL THINKING

Think about how you analyze information, reasoning, and conclusions when you're in a task group. Then rate the degree to which you think you are effective in each area.

	Good	So-So	Could Be Better
When I'm working with a group, I:	☐	☐	☐
1. Examine source credibility	☐	☐	☐
2. Show where reasoning doesn't make sense	☐	☐	☐
3. Analyze causes and effects	☐	☐	☐
4. Catch overgeneralizations and try to correct them	☐	☐	☐
5. Suggest alternative choice options besides either/or	☐	☐	☐
6. Examine connections among data, reasons, and conclusions	☐	☐	☐
7. Stay objective in analyzing data and reasoning	☐	☐	☐
8. Listen carefully to others' analyses	☐	☐	☐
9. Examine assumptions behind reasoning and conclusions	☐	☐	☐
10. Examine values in reasoning and conclusions	☐	☐	☐
11. Evaluate ethical issues in uses of data and reasoning	☐	☐	☐
12. Evaluate the ethics of decisions	☐	☐	☐
13. Point out fallacies	☐	☐	☐

"But I'm just not creative. . . .
I can't draw a straight line."
You don't have to—there are better ways to help your team be
creative than by drawing straight lines.

INNOVATIVE AND CREATIVE THINKING

7

Generating New Ideas

You work for an advertising agency team that is preparing a pitch for a valuable account. The present campaign is getting stale, and you think the advertiser may be ready to listen to new ideas. Your creative team has met off and on for weeks, but the concepts you've come up with are as dry as the ads now running. It's frustrating. You're not making any progress. (Maybe you should make an appointment for a root canal when the next meeting is scheduled.)

Your team needs a fresh approach—some creative ideas to get you out of your rut. The question, however, is, How do you get them?

Ideas, solutions, decisions, projects—they all need to come from somewhere. In fact, there is such a critical need for creativity in the business world that major business schools devote entire courses to it. In an increasingly competitive global marketplace, organizations have to be able to come up with new and different products and services in order to merely survive (Pil & Cohen, 2006). In fact, employee creativity is now recognized as one of a company's intangible, but most important assets (Petty & Guthrie, 2000).

That's the big picture. But right now and in the future, in both your personal and professional life, your ability to think creatively and critically can make your work fun and your decisions successful. As a team member, you need these skills as well.

To make the rigorous journey from recognizing a problem or receiving an assignment to making and implementing decisions, team members need well-exercised minds. An effective mind uses not only the critical thinking skills discussed in Chapter 6, but also creative skills that generate innovative ideas. That's why this chapter examines thinking processes, how you can facilitate creative thinking, and ways to tap your team's talents to generate new ideas. This chapter will help you to:

1. Become more aware of how people think when processing information
2. Develop your creative abilities by using approaches to open up your thinking
3. Use specific team techniques for increasing the number and quality of ideas

THINKING CREATIVELY

Thinking is both logical and creative, both analytical and artistic. It takes flexible thinking to work through information, ideate, analyze, and make decisions.

Immediately we can hear some students saying, "Forget it. I'm just not logical at all. I always lose arguments." Other students may have the opposite reaction: "Creative? Me? No way. I can't do music or art." Who says being logical means winning arguments? Who says creative thinking applies only in music or art?

Scholars have many definitions of creativity, but all of them share common characteristics. They agree that creativity involves the creation of something novel or uncommon that is also useful. When we think creatively, we see new uses for familiar things, or imagine new products that solve day-to-day problems. As DiLiello and Houghton (2008) put it, "… the value of creativity in organizations may relate to an ability to harvest novel yet appropriate ideas in order to increase organizational efficiencies, solve complex problems, and improve overall effectiveness" (p. 37). Whether you realize it or not, you use creative thinking all the time to solve all kinds of problems.

Just make sure you don't do what many people do—box themselves into just one thinking mode that fits some narrow concept of logic, of creativity, or above all, of themselves. Many times a person who says "I'm not logical" often turns out to be extremely bright and analytical, and often one who says "I'm just not creative" comes up with fresh ideas and innovative relationships. When these people recognize what they've done, their barriers begin to crumble.

Can people actually develop both critical and creative thinking? The U.S. Department of Defense (DOD) thinks so. It recognized that its mission to protect the country from terrorism depends on its ability to develop new capabilities. Consequently, the DOD has emphasized training in creativity and innovation, recognizing this as the most effective way to make the changes it needs for a competitive advantage (DiLiello & Houghton, 2008).

Obviously, this means that you, too, can develop your critical and creative thinking abilities. You can start by understanding how your brain works to accomplish both kinds of thinking.

UNDERSTANDING BRAIN PROCESSES

Traditionally, brain functions have been understood in terms of *hemisphericity*—that is, the left and right hemispheres of the brain. It's generally accepted that the left side mostly controls speech, language, writing, arithmetic, and reasoning, and that the right side of the brain mostly involves spatial, motor, musical, and touch abilities. The left brain processes information in a logical, linear, rational, mathematical, serial, and organized set of patterns. The right brain is more holistic, intuitive, and abstract, dealing with ideas in a more visionary, imaginative, and creative way. Box 7.1 offers you a chance to test your creativity.

There's evidence, however, that these processes are not as cut-and-dried as once thought. We now know the right brain does more language processing than previously thought, and evidence suggests a person's left and right brain functions may be determined by the conditioning of his or her culture and first language. Gender plays a role too: in children, boys tend to process information in the right hemisphere, whereas girls are more left hemispheric-oriented (Vengopal & Mridula, 2007).

BOX 7.1	JOE DOODLEBUG

As a team, figure this one out: Joe Doodlebug is a strange sort of imaginary bug that can—and cannot—do certain things. He has been jumping all over the place, getting some exercise, when his master places a pile of food 3 inches directly west of him. Once he sees this food, Joe stops in his tracks facing north. He notes the pile of food is a little larger than he is. After all this exercise, Joe is very hungry and wants to get to the food as quickly as he can. Joe examines the situation and then says, "Darn it, I'll have to jump four times to get the food."

Joe is a smart bug, and he is dead right in his conclusion. Why do you suppose Joe Doodlebug has to take four jumps to reach the food? The solution takes into account these five rules:

a.   Joe can jump in only four directions: north, south, east, and west. He cannot jump diagonally (northeast, northwest, southeast, or southwest).

b.   Once Joe starts in any direction, he must jump four times in that same direction before he can change his direction.

c.   Joe can only jump. He cannot crawl, fly, or walk.

d.   Joe can jump very large distances or very small distances, but not less than 1 inch per jump.

e.   Joe cannot turn. He always faces north.

Source: This exercise is based on a problem from Milton Rokeach in *The Open and Closed Mind* New York: Basic Books, 1960.

Another study found that the left hemisphere of the Japanese brain processes "non-verbal human sounds, animal sounds, and Japanese instrumental music (the opposite of the Western brain), while the right hemisphere processes Western instrumental music" (Lieberman, 1991, pp. 230–231).

So what does this mean for you? Many times people say, "I'm just left-brained," or "What do I know? I'm just right-brained," and thereby limit themselves. Today, however, the direction of your "braininess" is no longer an excuse, because research indicates that traits of both the left and right brain work collaboratively on creative problems (George & Zhou, 2001).

What does all of this tell us? Some tentative conclusions include:

- Each of us is capable of thinking both critically and creatively.
- Thinking processes may be very individual, possibly cultural.
- The brain hemisphere used more often may be influenced strongly by a person's language, gender, and cultural or subcultural shaping.

Some people are more inclined to use one side of the brain than the other, of course, and at any given time, one side predominates over the other. But look what happens when you work through a problem. For a while, you're analytical and rational—you sift through your information, and you seek out causes. Then, perhaps, you go off on a flight of fancy, imagining ideal, unrealistic solutions. Then you come back to thinking about what will really work—but you also go back to one of your fantasies and say, "Wait a minute. There is something there I can use. . . ."

What's the relevance of all this in a group communication textbook? The more you know about the way human beings think, the better you can learn to think clearly, analytically, and creatively. In turn, the better you learn to do that, the more satisfying and effective your team experiences will be.

Critical and creative thinking are used at all stages of a team's work. In fact, the more diverse the team members are, the more likely different members will be thinking in different modes—or using opposite sides of their brains—at any given time. This means two things to team members: First, others' thinking may operate differently from yours, so sometimes you'll have to work harder at understanding one another. Second, you have a richer range of creative possibilities among the team members.

FACILITATING CREATIVE THINKING

It takes work to tone your least-used brain muscles. Many people are task-oriented and feel uncomfortable when discussion gets too far from the goals. They may feel silly or inadequate; they may want to avoid creative efforts that could lead to better solutions to problems.

Once a team breaks through those barriers, however, members discover imaginations they may have forgotten—or never knew they even had. From those imaginations come ideas that are innovative, original, perhaps daring. A major objective is to make it acceptable, desirable, maybe even a norm to be playful and imaginative. By allowing members to "play," a team plants a rich field of ideas from which they can harvest good solutions during later rational analyses.

A group of clowns on tour with the Bertram Mills Circus playing a game of poker during an interval.

CREATING A SUPPORTIVE ENVIRONMENT

Teams in one organization may feel free to be creative, to take risks in trying out new ideas. Teams in another organization, however, may feel inhibited, unable or unwilling to risk innovation and possible failure. Team creativity is influenced by and, in turn, influences the organization within which it works. Amabile, Burnside, and Gryskiewicz (1999) identified the components of organizational support for creativity: "An organizational culture that encourages creativity through the fair, constructive judgment of ideas, reward and recognition for creative work, mechanisms for developing new ideas, and active flow of ideas, and a shared vision of what the organization is trying to do" (p. 15).

Creative thinking is most likely to thrive when both the team and its organization embrace the notion that great ideas entail risk—first to express ideas, then to make them happen. Some farsighted corporations expect a high percentage of their managers' ideas to fail; if all their ideas succeed, it suggests the managers are being too safe and not being innovative enough. This philosophy works: employees with strong creative potential are more likely to actually practice creativity when they perceive strong support from the organization (DiLiello & Houghton, 2006). Box 7.2 illustrates this practice. Moreover, when people have the opportunity to be creative on the job, they report higher satisfaction with their company and plan to stay with the organization longer (Shalley, Gibson & Blum, 2000).

BOX 7.2	THE BETTER PAINT CAN

How did Dutch Boy stir up the paint business? It's so simple, it's scary. They changed the can.

Paint cans are heavy, hard to carry, hard to close, hard to open, hard to pour, and no fun. Yet they've been around for a long time, and most people assumed there had to be a reason why they were so bad. Dutch Boy realized that there *was no reason*. They also realized that the can was an integral part of the product: People don't buy paint, they buy painted walls, and the can makes that process much easier.

Dutch Boy used that insight and introduced an easier-to-carry, easier-to-pour, easier-to-close paint jug. "Customers tell us that the new Twist & Pour paint container is a packaging innovation that was long overdue," says Dennis Eckols, group vice president of the home division for Fred Meyer stores. "People wonder why it took so long for someone to come up with the idea, and they love Dutch Boy for doing it."

Source: Excerpt from Seth Godin, "In Praise of the Purple Cow," *Fast Company*, February 2003, 74–85.

It takes every member's leadership to develop a nurturing environment for innovation. In fact, shared leadership can contribute much more than a designated leader can in this regard. Moore (2000) compared the creativity of groups with an assigned leader against those who shared leadership, and found that leaderless groups performed significantly better. When people are allowed to work in an environment that gives them autonomy and includes challenging activities, they are likely to be more involved and committed to the organization (Bandura, 1997). People are also more creative when they perceive encouragement from their managers to solve problems creatively (Tierney & Farmer, 2004). In fact, the most crucial determinant of creativity may well be perceptions of a supportive work environment (Amabile, Burnside & Gryskiewicz, 1999).

UNDERSTANDING CREATIVITY

To maximize the chances for creativity and innovative outcomes, it doesn't hurt to understand both the stages of a creative process and the "mind locks" that can block you from thinking creatively. Let's look at these aspects of creative thinking.

Stages of Creative Thinking   In *The Creative Brain*, Hermann (1988, pp. 187–188) describes the creative process—identified years ago by Graham Wallas—as involving four stages:

1. *Preparation*: Defining, motivating, gathering information, and setting up criteria for solving a problem.
2. *Incubation*: Stepping back, allowing the mind to play with ideas, "contemplate, work it through. Like preparation, incubation can last minutes, weeks, even years."
3. *Illumination*: Flashes of insight when "ideas arise from the mind . . . pieces of the whole or the whole itself. . . . Unlike the other stages, illumination is often very brief, involving a tremendous rush of insights within a few minutes or hours."

4. *Verification*: Analysis of the idea, implementation, and assessment of its completion.

Others have added to Wallas's concepts. People need to initially be motivated to engage in the creativity process, or they're unlikely to get started (Herzberg, Mausner & Snyderman, 2003). Additionally, Tierney and Farmer (2002) have suggested that creative self-efficacy, defined as "the belief one has the ability to produce creative outcomes," is also necessary (p. 1138). Research also suggests that having knowledge, both about the general subject area in which you're creating and about your organization's culture, is a prerequisite for effective creative functioning (Kijkuit & van den Ende, 2007).

Reading about these stages was a gigantic "Aha!" experience for us. Incubation and illumination describe exactly what happens to us, personally, when faced with a problem to solve. All of us go through a sometimes long and painful hiatus while everything we've learned or thought about a problem incubates, a point where we just look at each other and say, "Be patient, it's incubating." And then—suddenly—the idea is there, almost full-fledged and ready to fly. We surely experience that good feeling as ideas emerge, but they won't fly until we verify them, check them out, and maybe alter them to make sure their wings are ready.

In their classic work, Scheidel and Crowell (1964) describe idea development in a group as a spiraling process. They say that group members tend to follow a "reach-test cycle," in which someone suggests an idea (perhaps after incubation), some people then agree, someone gives supporting examples of how the idea might work, and the group finally agrees or affirms the idea (verification, perhaps). There's a process of suggesting, agreeing, clarifying, affirming, and deciding or "anchoring" the suggestion before the group moves on to other ideas.

"Mind Locks"   Roger von Oech wrote two amusing, accurate, and successful little books on creative thinking that organizations all over the country used to open up their employees' minds. In *A Whack on the Side of the Head* (1983), von Oech lists ten "locks" that people keep on their minds. **Mind locks** are *assumptions about how people should be that close off the ability to think creatively.* Do you ever snap closed one of these locks on your mind?

1. "The right answer."
2. "That's not logical."
3. "Follow the rules."
4. "Be practical."
5. "Avoid ambiguity."
6. "To err is wrong."
7. "Play is frivolous."
8. "That's not my area."
9. "Don't be foolish."
10. "I'm not creative." (p. 9)

Each of these, you'll note, is a message we give to ourselves *about* ourselves. Consider the positive alternatives listed in Box 7.3. As children, people probably

BOX 7.3   STRENGTHEN YOUR INTUITIVE POWERS

To get in touch with your intuitive ability and develop it . . .

- Believe in your intuition. What we believe we can do is one of the most important factors in determining what we can do.
- Pay attention to your intuition. Very often, intuitive people are not even aware of their skill.
- Practice the skill. One way to do this is to keep an intuition journal—individually or as an organization—of insights, how and when they come, by what means (for example, dreams), and keep a record of their accuracy.
- Share your experiences with others. Form an intuition club where you can compare your skills with colleagues and record your successes and failures.
- Explore ideas without a specific goal in mind.
- Reserve judgment on ideas, rather than looking for immediate or simple solutions.
- Learn to tolerate ambiguity so you can study a problem from many perspectives.

- Stay receptive to unknowns. Avoid depending on rules, procedures, calculations, and the status quo; this can inhibit flexibility.
- Think of unique solutions.
- Follow up on points that have no factual justification. Sometimes logical thinking prohibits the open-ended mental explorations that help to trigger fresh insights.
- Practice guided imagery by picturing a situation and considering various possibilities. Or try hypnosis.
- Improve your concentration by meditating or focusing on a problem in a relaxed state. Relaxation can take you into your creative space where your mind can free flow with options and choices.

Source: Condensed from "All About Intuition," an interview with Weston H. Agor, director, Global Intuition Network, University of Texas at El Paso, *Boardroom Reports*, December 15, 1991, pp. 13–14. Used with permission.

hear these scoldings at school or at home, and these mind locks reflect three assumptions people make about themselves:

1. *"To be worthwhile, I must be expert, logical, practical, and serious."* These criteria prevent a person from being playful, adventurous, foolish, or creative. How dull.
2. *"I have to choose between two extremes."* Always seeking one "right answer" and "avoiding ambiguity" sets yes/no, right/wrong limits on ideas and actions. Most things have many possibilities, but these locks hide them behind the either/or doors.
3. *"I have to do everything just right."* This is like "Don't color outside the lines." To always "follow the rules" or avoid risk because "to err is wrong" is to blind yourself to possibilities. Even worse, with these mind locks, someone may obey rules that don't even exist because of fear that they actually do.

   To be innovative and creative, team members need to turn some keys in these locks and open their minds. When you do, the interactions among you will increase the creative potential of each individual. This definitely is not a linear, 1–2–3 process. Instead, it's interactive, multidimensional, and magical.

ENHANCING CREATIVITY

You develop your personal creativity in many ways, but for a moment, let's look at the creative thinking of a team. Teammates who think together exert synergy—an energy bigger than and different from each individual's contribution—on their task. There are ways to liberate this synergy and enhance the creativity that results. If you are a virtual team or even if you work face to face, there are many software programs designed to help your team develop skills in critical and creative thinking. These programs take you step by step through many variations of the techniques we list, but you don't have to use software, unless you're working online as a team or unless you'd just like to use online programs for your individual development. You can use methods to develop creative and critical thinking skills with nothing more than your brain and, in the case of a group or team, your teammates. It helps to consider some of these norms and approaches before you start:

> *Encourage playfulness.* Make it okay to use the imagination, to play, to fantasize, to tease, to laugh. These are part of the energy and provide many stimuli to creativity.
>
> *Agree not to judge people or ideas.* Let it roll. Sometimes a person comes up with the weirdest idea—and it turns out to be a treasure. But nothing turns off imagination like criticism or judgment. Both have their place, but creative processing isn't it.
>
> *Look for different, even bizarre, idea relationships.* Encourage each other to stretch, reach, deliberately match up concepts you wouldn't normally put in the same ballroom.
>
> *Break down barriers.* Don't close on ideas too fast; don't stereotype ideas or people; don't worry too much about the "rules."

If you agree to these guidelines as a team and your goal is to improve your team's creative problem-solving skills, then team members can use a variety of activities, exercises, and problems to help one another open up their minds. These activities help you to begin thinking of different ways to see or to relate ideas. We'll look at approaches such as perception activities, puzzles, role playing, humor, imagery, and relaxation.

Perception Activities   Edward de Bono (1994) asks, "What is the main purpose of thinking?" He answers that the "main purpose of thinking is to abolish thinking. The mind works to make sense out of confusion and uncertainty . . . to recognize familiar patterns in the outside world. As soon as a pattern is recognized the mind switches into it and follows it along—further thinking is unnecessary" (p. 35).

When the mind perceives something, it immediately assigns the perception to some pattern. Therefore, to think creatively, it is necessary to see alternative patterns and consider multiple possibilities. Cooper (2000) described creativity associated with new imaging information technology in terms of radical changes in departments by facilitating the changing or eliminating of departmental boundaries, job descriptions, and work flows. Creativity requires the ability to look at things as they could be, rather than as they currently are.

Perception exercises provide stimuli that invite more than one perceptual interpretation, so different people see different things. As teammates compare their observations and discuss why and how their perceptions differ, they discover new ways to enlarge their repertoire of perceptual patterns.

For example, take a look at Figure 7.1. What do you see? Do you see a demon? A man? They're both there. When you know they're both in the picture, can you see them both? Which one did you see first? What influenced your perception? Are you thinking about demons? About men? Did your eyes first hit the black area or the white one? How did the first thing you saw affect the way your mind organized the rest of the picture?

Several factors influence how people perceive things. What we want, need, or are interested in; how close to or similar an object is to something else; how much contrast it has to its background; what detail draws the eye as a center of interest—all these influence what you see, hear, smell, feel, or think.

Puzzles   Puzzles, too, help people learn new problem-solving strategies. Most puzzles have a fairly direct and simple solution, but the foundation for that solution often rests in a pattern outside an individual's frame of perceptual experience.

FIGURE 7.1

What do you see?

FIGURE 7.2

Connect the dots by drawing a *square* without lifting the pencil from the paper.

For example, Figure 7.2 contains four dots. Without lifting your pencil from the paper—and without rearranging them—connect those dots to make a square by drawing only four straight lines.

Was this puzzle easy? Was it difficult? Here's a hint: The instructions don't prevent you from going outside the arrangement of dots.

To find the solution, you have to use what de Bono (1970) calls *lateral thinking*, or thinking that goes outside a single frame of reference. To do this, you have to be able to let go of standard operating procedures; to think randomly, provocatively; and to look at things from above, from the side, from underneath. You need to go beyond your childhood connect-the-dots experiences—and then you begin to see solutions you didn't see before.

Puzzles like this can help people break down some of these mind locks—get rid of the "rule" orientation, learn to be comfortable with ambiguity, not worry about logic or practicality, and be unafraid to make a mistake or look foolish for a moment. (In Box 7.1 on page 159, you'll find one of our favorite exercises: "Joe Doodlebug." Try it out with a group, and see what you can do.)

Exercises and puzzles are especially helpful when a team works on them together—as long as the members follow the guidelines set out earlier for making it comfortable to take risks. Members can help one another discover new strategies and approaches to solving their problems.

Role Playing If the team needs a sense of what someone else perceives or feels or a picture of how some idea might work, **role playing** is great. To role-play, create a situation with designated roles for individuals. Outline the situation and the characteristics of the individuals, but let the role players work out the interaction as they go along.

Suppose your team is a cooperative task force involving the school of education at your college and the local school system, and you are charged with investigating the effectiveness of English as a second language (ESL) programs. Although your team is multicultural, no member attended ESL classes as a child.

Therefore, to increase your awareness of what a child might experience, you set up a role-play situation. One member is given the role of a child whose first language is, for example, German. Another member is given the role of a teacher, and a third member is given the role of a parent who speaks only limited English. The situation is a first meeting of the teacher, parent, and child.

The role players act out this situation as they think it would happen, and the other team members observe. The team then discusses how each person must have felt and what variables seemed to get in the way of—or facilitate—communication among the three people.

Role playing is amazingly real for people. They don't have to be actors. Simply as human beings, they feel some of what the persons they are playing might feel, and they act somewhat as those persons might act. Their audience begins to see some of the "truths" of the interaction in ways they would not comprehend from hard data or experts' opinions. This "felt" reality then becomes a start for more thoughtful and creative solutions to problems.

Humor   Katherine Hudson, CEO of the Brady Corporation, suggests that humor in the workplace can "foster *esprit de* corps . . . spark innovation . . . increase the likelihood that unpleasant tasks will be accomplished . . . [and] relieve stress (Hudson, 2001). Humor takes the mind out of the logical, linear, predetermined tracks and into new patterns—and this allows us to think about things in new ways. (Does this sound like creativity? It is.) "Creativity," according to Winter and Winter (1997), "is good for your brain. It involves the release of tension, provides gratification, and generally aids your ability to cope. Expressing yourself creatively literally changes the chemistry of your brain and body" (p. 122). That's exactly what humor does as well. Humor promotes openness to new ideas by relaxing people and making them less likely to criticize mistakes or new ideas (Romero & Cruthirds, 2006).

C. W. Metcalf is a fine example of this. Once near death from alcoholism and despair, Metcalf reinvented his life—through humor. Today, Metcalf is a consultant and author who both uses and teaches humor as the way to create life itself. He often wears colorful undershorts over his trousers and a very large red bulb on his nose when appearing in front of serious-minded—and perhaps stuffy—executives. "Humor," Metcalf and Felible (1992) write, "can help you thrive in change, remain creative under pressure, work more effectively, play more enthusiastically, and stay healthier in the process" (p. 5).

They recall comments from de Bono at a conference (pp. 9–10):

> [de Bono] explained that humor and the creative process are actually one and the same thing. With both forms of thinking—humor and general creativity—he said, the brain recognizes the value of the absurdity or the creative idea only in hindsight. Prior to that moment, both innovation and humor seem "crazy." But it is the willingness to play with ideas, to risk foolishness without fear, that are the hallmarks of the creative thinkers. And it is the creativity which springs from humor that increases our effectiveness.

In teaching people how to use humor, for example, Metcalf and Felible warn against "terminal professionalism." They note that even in the most suffocatingly serious atmosphere, groups have found ways to keep their sense of humor. These authors talk about "secret silliness," as with "a group of particularly joyful Catholic nuns" who called their humorous underground "the Sisters of Secret Silliness," or the members of a Wall Street group who dared not let their employers see their humorous side—so they all secretly wore Mickey Mouse underwear to work every Friday and called themselves the "UU," or the "Underwear Underground" (p. 165). In such cases, the humor is a secret among members of a group, but it keeps them from sliding along the same old track. In so doing, their humor not only makes them healthier and more productive people, it also makes them more creative.

Some of today's most successful organizations provide strong evidence that humor is related to creativity . . . and profitability. Google, Pixar Animation Studios, and Yahoo! are all wildly successful, and all have spent significant time and effort to create playful and creative work environments (Newstrom, 2002).

Humor that switches your team onto a new track may take a variety of forms:

- A short story
- An exaggeration
- Facial expressions and body movements
- Quick responses to the unexpected
- Absurdity or irony
- A generalization obviously intended to be humorous
- Wordplays or puns

Humor should be outgoing, friendly, enthusiastic, positive, and open—aggressive, down-putting humor can turn a group dysfunctional and competitive (Holmes & Mara, 2002; Holmes, 2007). If humor tramples on any teammate's ethnic, racial, gender, or spiritual sensitivities, it will cut off the transactional processes and impair—or even terminate—your creative potential as a team. Used as a shared way of seeing new ideas, however, humor is invaluable.

Imagery   Can you imagine wonderful things? Then you can use imagery in developing creative solutions. Gibbs, Lima, and Francuzo (2004) contend that imagining mental images of words makes them more "real," and allows us to unleash our creativity because both our ears and our eyes are engaged in processing information.

Since the time of Plato, Aristotle, and Cicero, imagery has played an important role in helping people to remember concepts and to perceive new solutions. The art and science of imagery was lost for a time, but cognitive psychologist R. R. Holt (1964) revived imagery as a legitimate consideration in human perception and information processing. Since then, it has become increasingly obvious that mental images that evoke the senses—seeing, hearing, feeling, smelling, tasting—are important to creativity (Gibbs, Gould & Andric, 2005).

Developmental psychologist Jean Piaget identified two types of images: *reproductive* images, which evoke previous perceptions; and *anticipatory* images, which "envisage movements or transformations as well as their results, although the subject has not previously observed them" (Piaget & Inhelder, 1969, p. 71). You and your teammates may describe your previous images and then, to find creative solutions, use anticipatory imagery to envision new possibilities.

Many exercises can improve your ability to use imagery to envision possibilities. Eberle (1971), for example, brought together the concept of SCAMPER, which suggests that as you perceive a problem and, perhaps, recall previous images, you then generate new ideas and images by:

- Substituting
- Combining
- Adapting
- Modifying (and magnifying or minifying)
- Putting to other uses
- Eliminating
- Reversing and rearranging

Suppose your task force is asked to adapt three large classrooms and one small one into a learning center that will accommodate computer facilities, seminar spaces, and teaching-learning areas. Your first image might be of one large classroom for each purpose, with the smaller room being used for an office. This would provide no flexibility, however, for activities such as using the computer facilities for on-the-spot research in seminar discussions. So, as you discuss, you might substitute an image. Perhaps you could combine the three large classrooms, but how? Maybe you could adapt by knocking out the separating walls.

As you imagine the much-larger space now available, you might imagine modifying that space by erecting movable dividers and creating flexible pathways throughout the facility. You even might decide that an office isn't really essential and then imagine the smaller room could serve another use. Perhaps it could become a videotaping center to allow students opportunities to give presentations with feedback. As for eliminating, reversing, and rearranging—you've done that in your image of knocking out walls, creating new spaces, and so on.

Relaxation   Sometimes the best way to start the creativity flow is to just kick back and relax. Unfortunately, some folks think relaxation is only something you do in front of the TV or on the golf course—certainly not in your work team. For example, look at Box 7.4. "Purposeful" relaxation is too weird, maybe, or it's just wasting time. We hope these people get over that feeling, because using relaxation really does help creativity.

As Rampersad (2007) noted, "A calmer state of mind leads to clear thinking, which results in more creativity, less waste of energy, and a clearer view of reality" (p. 402). Our personal experience suggests that simply taking a deep breath and thinking about relaxing the body frees the mind and makes it easier to focus, and research supports this claim. Relaxation exercises can help you screen out distractions, which in turn facilitates your ability to create high-quality images (Kennedy & Ball, 2007). In freeing your mind of current distractions, both mental and environmental, you become more able to access images of past experiences and to create images of new solutions for the question you want to answer.

Here's one way to relax as a team:

1. Choose someone to be a guide. Have team members sit comfortably in a chair or on the floor, and then have them close their eyes and get comfortable.

BOX 7.4	FINDING THE BEST TIME OF DAY TO DO YOUR CREATIVE THINKING

Based on a nationwide survey by NFI Research, the majority of senior executives and managers say that when it comes to personal thinking related to business, the most effective location is at home. Most businesspeople find their thinking to be most effective between 7 A.M. and 9 A.M., followed by times before 7 A.M. Fewer than half of executives and managers find their thinking to be most effective in the office. "I have found that my mind is open to fresh ideas when I'm away from the office, but still on business," said one survey respondent. "I bring the ideas back and am able to jump on them when I return." For the majority, the least effective time for thinking is between 11 A.M. and 2 P.M. This is also the time that's the least productive for executives and managers, based on a separate survey.

Commuting time is the second most effective time for thinking, based on the survey. "My daily commute is just about an hour each way," said one manager. "I find that the end of the day, [when I'm] by myself in the car, is the best time to reflect and focus on either issues or direction of my business unit."

A quarter of managers say their most effective business thinking occurs on weekends as well as after 8 P.M. "I do a lot of business thinking when I go jogging after work in the 5 to 8 P.M. time range," said one respondent.

Survey respondents cited numerous activities that they use as thinking time. "The best place is at the gym when I am on the treadmill," said one. "I do my best thinking while mowing the grass," said another. "I seem to achieve my highest levels of creativity either while working out, or in the morning shower," said another respondent. "In fact, I keep a small voice recorder nearby to log my pearls of inspiration. Sad, but true." "I find the shower in the morning to be an excellent opportunity to prepare for the day's events or think about more strategic issues," another manager said.

And then there is golf, a favorite pastime for many in business. "Nothing like walking a couple of holes on the golf course to get my mind around a good business problem," said one executive. Since the least effective thinking and productive time is between 11 A.M. and 2 P.M., a little midday golf might not be such a bad idea!

Source: Excerpt from Chuck Martin, "The Best Times for Business Thinking," *CIO*, July 26, 2006. Reprinted by permission. Available at www.cio.com.

2. Have your guide talk through the following script in a slow and quiet voice, pausing between ideas to give everyone time to create the scenes and the actions in his or her mind:

> You're someplace that makes you feel relaxed and comfortable, someplace you always love to be. Maybe it's the beach, or the mountains. Wherever it is, you feel the peace and tranquility of the place washing over you . . . soothing you . . . taking away the stress and pain. You're comfortable . . . you're relaxed. Look around you . . . see the things you love . . . touch them . . . feel the relaxation that comes from them. You have all the time in the world . . . enjoy the tiniest little shell . . . the smallest leaf . . . the delicate little breeze . . . the sweetest scents. Now just explore your place for a while, go a little deeper into it. Feel it giving you energy . . . and strength . . . and imagination. Reach out to it . . . feel its peace and inspiration. Think about what you will be able to do and accomplish with this peace and strength and creativity.

3. The guide then allows the members to meditate in their special places for a few minutes and then says, "When you're ready, open your eyes and come back to our team and our meeting refreshed and ready to think together."

After this exercise, spend a few moments talking about where you've been, and use this sharing as a jumping-off point for generating ideas related to the group's objectives. Sound like hocus-pocus? It's not. It is a meditative way to shake off the shackles of stress and tension; it opens the mind so you can work with greater energy and openness. This is a technique anyone can use alone—and it's a helpful thing to do. When you relax this way as a team, however, it allows you to share some of your experiences, create a greater sense of syntality and synergy for the group, and move directly into generating ideas and solving problems related to the group's goals.

GENERATING IDEAS

We've looked at how the creative mind works and at some ways to facilitate innovative thinking and develop your abilities. Now it's time to put these ideas to work. Your team knows what its purpose is, has established its goals, and has gathered and analyzed its information. You've loosened up your creative processes, and you're ready to go—so how do you get some ideas to work with? We'll cover five approaches here: brainstorming, metaphorical thinking, fantasy chaining, and two techniques for use with larger groups. You may use any one—or some combination—of these techniques, depending on your needs and the time available.

BRAINSTORMING

Brainstorming is something you may have done many times—or, at least, that's what you called it. Too often, though, people don't know how to make brainstorming really work the way it should. It helps to have a facilitator to keep you from trampling one another and the process, and you absolutely must have someone record and post (on a board or flip chart) the ideas as they emerge. The goal is to think of as many ideas as you can. The emphasis is only on the number of ideas that you can list, not on their quality—that comes later. Reach to the outer limits for wild and crazy thoughts. Energy usually is extremely high when brainstorming, and people are free to be humorous and weird.

When the inevitable periods of silence settle on the group, wait them out. These painful quiets are incubation periods, and if everyone waits, eventually someone breaks through. When we conduct brainstorming sessions in corporations or in classrooms, we unobtrusively mark the list at the point when quiet periods occur. People start getting edgy and want to move on. After we've completed the session, we go back and ask the group to remember how they felt at that particular time. Then the group looks at the ideas that emerged after everyone thought they should quit. Most times, the more useful ideas came *after* the quiet periods. If we had quit then, we would have missed those ideas.

When you and your team brainstorm, the following guidelines are helpful:

- Have someone facilitate. Remind people not to stop and talk about the ideas but to keep it moving fast.
- Generate and post ideas as quickly as possible.
- Don't "own" ideas, whether good or bad.

- "Piggyback" or "hitchhike" ideas onto previous thoughts.
- Don't evaluate any idea; bizarre or ridiculous ideas are fine.
- Sweat out the silences and plateaus until someone comes up with something.
- After many ideas are on the list, discuss them and winnow them down.
- Start serious analysis of the remaining possibilities.

METAPHORICAL THINKING

Metaphorical thinking is a part of creativity—often, indeed, its foundation—at any stage. Metaphors are powerful because they phrase comparisons between two things as if one were the other. Metaphors are the bridges with which people think and learn new ideas. Seeing similarities between two things makes you consider other similarities—or differences. In your mind, you suddenly may see connections and relationships that you never saw before.

Suppose your team is having trouble working together, and someone says, "We're so discordant—we're all off key." Someone else then picks up the musical metaphor and says, "No—we're just all playing at a different place on the score." Someone else says, "Problem is, there's no conductor." Suddenly, the team sees what it needs—leadership. *Ta da!* Now you might ask some metaphorical questions: How does an orchestra get a conductor? What criteria should the conductor meet? How would your orchestra work with a conductor? Who should be your conductor? You're on your way to a solution—not there yet, but on your way.

Normally, metaphors just happen; sometimes they don't. You may just get *clichés*—once juicy metaphors that have dried up from too much air. You can use metaphorical thinking in two ways. One is simply to be alert to opportunities for exercising your leadership to get the process started and to guide it along. The other is to use metaphorical thinking consciously as a creative strategy. If your team wants to try it, the following guidelines may help:

- State the objectives of thinking in metaphors: to see comparisons between two ideas, and to gain new insights from those comparisons.
- Brainstorm possible metaphors for some aspects of the problem.
- "Piggyback" on metaphors; build on them.
- Choose the best metaphor with which to proceed.
- Examine all imaginable areas of comparison in that metaphor.
- Ask questions for which the metaphor might provide answers.
- Look for insights into causes, effects, and solutions for your problem.

FANTASY CHAINING

Although fantasy chaining traditionally is seen as a post hoc analysis of what actually happened in a group, it's useful to understand how members might engage in fantasy chaining as your team develops. **Fantasy chaining** is an imaginative, creative process that group members often start spontaneously. Bormann (1990, pp. 101–120) describes fantasy chaining as a series of ideas that members link together like a play.

Remember when you were a kid and you made up plays? "I'm the mother and you're the father and Tommy's the baby and Woof is the monster." "Yeah, and the monster comes in. . . ." "It's the middle of the night. . . ." "Yeah, and there's a full moon. . . ." "Yeah, and . . ."

Maybe you can think of a time in your adult life when you and your friends or family did something similar. Someone begins with a colorful idea—a pun or a play on words, perhaps a metaphor or an allegory—and, from there, the members create a series of fantasized events that "chain out" with heroes, villains, plot, action, settings, and scenes.

Fantasy chaining serves several purposes for team members. Sharing a dramatization may release tension or provide a way of indirectly addressing difficult issues. Like metaphorical thinking, fantasy chaining also can trigger insights and possibilities that don't show up in any other way. As members participate, they "create common ground that unites the participants" (Bormann, Knutson & Musolf, 1997, p. 255). Perhaps most important, as the fantasy chain develops, it provides members with a mutually understood, shared set of symbols. Sharing these special symbols creates closeness and makes communication easier among members.

Even though fantasy chaining is a naturally occurring process when people interact, it also can be used in developing an organization's plans, a team's vision, or creative ideas to meet a goal (Poole, Hollingshead, McGrath, Moreland & Rohrbaugh, 2004).

GROUP TECHNIQUES

Two other approaches for generating and evaluating ideas from groups are the **nominal group technique (NGT)** and the **Delphi technique**. These methods generally are regarded as decision-making tools. In reality, however, these techniques allow for freer exchange of ideas, which leads to the generation of more and better ideas. For example, consider Honda's creativity as illustrated in Box 7.5. The synergy created by these techniques helps to produce solutions that truly reflect the combined judgment of the group (Duggan & Thachenkary, 2004).

Both techniques ensure that individuals have opportunities to generate and evaluate ideas. Traditionally, the principal difference is that NGT takes place in face-to-face meetings, whereas Delphi is used without bringing the individuals together. Actually, both techniques can be used with computer-assisted technology or groupware, and both are especially useful when groups are too large for all members to be highly involved all the time. They even can be used to draw ideas from those who are not on the team.

Nominal Group Technique   In NGT, each group member writes down ideas on cards. The facilitator has each member read an idea, one at a time, and writes them on a flip chart or board for all to see. The group then works through the process of setting priorities and making decisions.

After discussing all the ideas, the group narrows down the list—much as it would in brainstorming—and settles on a few that might meet its goals. Members then multiple-rank the possibilities (we'll talk about that in Chapter 9) and, if a final decision is part of their task, take a final vote.

BOX 7.5	THE KNOWLEDGE-CREATING COMPANY

In 1978, top management at Honda began the development of a new-concept car with the slogan, "Let's gamble." A team of young engineers and designers was charged with two tasks: First, to come up with a product concept fundamentally different from anything the company had ever done before; and second, to make a car that was inexpensive but not cheap. Team leader Hiroo Watanabe coined another slogan to express his sense of the team's challenge: "Theory of automobile evolution." In effect, it posed the question: If the automobile were an organism, how should it evolve?

The "evolutionary" trend the team articulated eventually took the image of a sphere—a car simultaneously "short" in length and "tall" in height. This gave birth to a product the team called Tall Boy, which eventually led to the Honda City, the company's distinctive urban car.

Working on a team for this kind of knowledge-creating company poses special challenges, not the least of which is developing new strategies for innovation. Not surprisingly, recent research has turned to the investigation of how workers learn what they need to know in these kinds of organizations.

Source: Excerpt from "The Knowledge-Creating Company," by Ikujiro Nonaka, November/December 1991. Copyright 1991 by the President and Fellows of Harvard College: all rights reserved; and R. F. Poell and F. J. Van der Krogt, "Learning Strategies of Workers in the Knowledge-Creating Company," *Human Resource Development International*, 6.3 (2003), pp. 387–404.

The NGT is an orderly process for getting full participation, but it doesn't generate the variety or the quantity of ideas that brainstorming can. If you want to use NGT, follow these steps:

1. Get each member to write ideas on cards.
2. Collect ideas round-robin style, one at a time from each person.
3. Post the ideas so that everyone can see them.
4. Discuss each idea in order.
5. Have individuals privately select and rank the priority of these ideas.
6. Report and discuss the selections.
7. Take a final vote, possibly by individual rankings.

Delphi Technique Frequently, a team needs to involve a wide range of people, possibly from other groups or locations, who cannot attend meetings. The Delphi technique can be used for this purpose at any or all stages of the decision-making or the planning process. This technique does require time, effort, and either duplication or Internet time, however, to distribute the information and the responses.

To be effective, the Delphi technique has to be carefully done. At every stage, participants must know what is going on. They have to feel their participation counts, and they must be motivated to respond. Why? Because Delphi is conducted by repeated mailing, tallying, analysis, and reporting of questionnaires. When personal contact and transactions are limited—or even nonexistent—communication must be handled with extreme care.

Questionnaires must be written precisely and unambiguously to get exactly what the committee or team needs from the respondents. After receiving the initial responses, the committee redrafts the questionnaire to cover the next step of emerging ideas or issues and then distributes the revised questionnaire. As the process continues, it may be necessary to draft, send, and tabulate several different questionnaires. Depending on what the respondents are being asked to do, this technique can be carried all the way from fact finding through ideation and problem solving through voting for decisions. Multiple ranking generally is used to narrow down the final decisions, and participants must be kept fully informed all the way through the implementation and review of any decision in which they were involved through the Delphi method.

If you want to use the Delphi technique, follow these steps:

1. Identify the broad question areas, prepare an open-ended questionnaire, and send it to selected individuals.
2. Analyze the responses, redraft a more specific questionnaire, and then send it to the same people.
3. Tally the responses, and narrow down the options.
4. Send out ballots that list possible decisions for multiple rankings. If the decision list is long, repeat this step until a decision is made.
5. Follow up with a report to all participants.

CREATING WITH COMPUTER-SUPPORTED COLLABORATIVE WORK (CSCW)

You can do a great job of brainstorming and ideation without any technology but a flip chart or a blackboard. It's also true that the software exists to help you as an individual or to help your team develop skill in creative and critical thinking and to use these techniques for generating innovative ideas.

Both programs used in groupware facilities, with large screens where everyone can see the development of ideas, or those used online for virtual teams to generate ideas or for individuals to improve their own idea-generating skills, can work well. In fact, researchers have found that with CSCW, virtual teams generate more ideas than face-to-face groups, although they exchange fewer messages and take longer to complete their work (Furst, Blackburn & Rosen, 1999).

The software systems allow members to spill out their thoughts as quickly as they get them—and to keep a clear and accurate record. They also prevent the team from evaluating or judging ideas by keeping the focus on the brainstorming task itself. The danger, as with all innovations, is that participants will become so enamored of the technology they fail to exploit their own creativity fully. For the process to work well, it's important to have a facilitator who can encourage and support the process and who is in no hurry to move to the organization and evaluation steps.

Once a good list of ideas is generated, groupware can help the members to categorize, evaluate, and rank those ideas. Because the entire process is displayed for all to see, staying clear and making good decisions are easier. Again, however, if the process is hurried or someone's comment is brushed aside, the transactional processes will be blocked—and so will the task.

Whether your team sits in a classroom with nothing but a blackboard and chalk or in a corporate office equipped for elaborate CSCW meetings, complete with all the bells and whistles and trained facilitators, there's one main principle: Creative thinking can and should go on continually during the team's life. The techniques we have discussed can be used to define problems, identify questions, set goals, identify resources and ways to use them, think of solutions to problems or ideas for projects, find ways to implement plans, discover advantages and disadvantages, and find ways to assess your team's processes or outcomes as well as to overcome barriers or conflicts. The high energy and member involvement that creative thinking demands increase the quantity and quality of innovative possibilities; they also help to develop—and to intensify—individuals' effectiveness and team synergy.

We must add one more benefit of creative and critical thinking: Identifying problems and coming up with new ideas to solve them is just plain fun. Much of worklife is drudgery, repetition, and grind. But when your brain is firing at 100 percent and sending off sparks, that's when the work you do becomes play. We recommend it highly.

SUMMARY

In this chapter, we contend that both critical and creative thinking are essential to effective team communication—and that everyone is capable of both. Although the right brain is believed to control creative processes and the left brain logical processes, some evidence now suggests this hemisphericity is not as absolute as once thought. Brain processes are influenced by culture and language, and they also may adapt through experience or need.

People can expand their skills in either creative or critical thinking with practice. It helps to get rid of "mind locks" that limit people to thinking in terms of rules, either/or choices, or "logical"

self-stereotypes. A team can enhance creative thinking by making the members comfortable with taking risks and can develop the members' abilities through exercises and activities. A team also can generate ideas creatively through techniques such as brainstorming, metaphorical thinking, fantasy chaining, the nominal group technique (NGT), and the Delphi technique. CSCW programs can facilitate the creative process in all parts of a team's creative work. These methods involve all team members in generating a large number of ideas and then analyzing them for quality and appropriateness.

Exercises

1. Your team has been called together to design an ad campaign for Better Bricks, Inc. This company makes bricks—real, fake, big, little, all kinds, and all colors—which they sell to home-building companies as well as through retail outlets to "do-it-yourself" suburbanites.

Using brainstorming, metaphorical thinking, and fantasy chaining, create a campaign concept for this client. Use your critical thinking to refine it, and then present your campaign to the class and explain the processes used to create it.

2. Using Form 7.1, assess the group you worked with in Exercise 1. How did you function regarding these variables? What did you do well? What could you improve, and how?

3. Using Form 7.2, rate yourself on each statement the form includes. What do you do that you've never thought of as creative? What else do you do that is not listed on the form but that also might be creative? How can you expand on those abilities?

4. With your team, create your own brain-stretcher or puzzle in written or visual form.

The rules for designing your brain-stretcher are as follows:

a. It should have a simple solution.

b. It should not be deceptive, but should require lateral thinking and breaking through mind locks to solve it.

As a group, present your puzzle to the class. Can they solve it? Teach the class what mind locks may have kept them from solving it and how creative thinking could have helped.

FORM 7.1 | OBSERVATION OF GROUP CREATIVE AND CRITICAL THINKING

Assess how well your own team—or a group you observe—uses creative and critical thinking together.

	Well	So-So	Could Be Better
1. Members brainstorm many ideas.	☐	☐	☐
2. Members don't judge ideas as they brainstorm them—they wait until later.	☐	☐	☐
3. People have fun piggybacking ideas.	☐	☐	☐
4. People create metaphors and analogies.	☐	☐	☐
5. Humor helps the team to develop ideas.	☐	☐	☐
6. Members help each other break mind locks.	☐	☐	☐
7. It's a norm to fantasize and to play with ideas and solutions.	☐	☐	☐
8. When it's time to analyze ideas, the members focus on it together.	☐	☐	☐
9. Members cooperate in analyzing the logic and reasoning of ideas once they have some good ones in front of them.	☐	☐	☐
10. People appreciate one another's ideas and can be objective about their own.	☐	☐	☐
11. The team can be serious with analysis and have fun with ideas.	☐	☐	☐
12. The team values both creativity and critical analysis of data, reasoning, and conclusions.	☐	☐	☐

What could this group do to further stimulate its creativity and hone its critical analysis?

FORM 7.2 | SELF-ASSESSMENT OF CREATIVE THINKING

This assessment is a way to start thinking about your own creativity. Check off the extent to which you believe you do the following:

	A Lot	Some	Not Much
1. I think about what might explain people or events (I can imagine their stories).	☐	☐	☐
2. I enjoy playing mental games with an idea.	☐	☐	☐
3. If I cannot find the right tool to do something, I can think of some other way to do it.	☐	☐	☐
4. I enjoy helping others find solutions to problems.	☐	☐	☐
5. I enjoy spinning a story to entertain others.	☐	☐	☐
6. I can find pictures in things like clouds or spilled paint.	☐	☐	☐
7. I enjoy connecting one idea to another to find a new concept.	☐	☐	☐
8. When I listen to others, read, or watch something, I get ideas that go beyond the message content.	☐	☐	☐
9. I tend to compare and relate ideas and think of analogies to explain them.	☐	☐	☐
10. I enjoy creating fantasies and stories.	☐	☐	☐

Think of other things you like to do—and things you do well—that require you to see things from a different angle. Think of things that require you to separate or to relate ideas so you see them differently. You're probably much more creative than you know.

"Shall we flip a coin?"
Maybe not—50 percent of the time you lose!

PROBLEM ANALYSIS AND DECISION MAKING

Following Clear Systems

8

Suppose you coach a Little League team, and the kids' uniforms are in tatters. You call a meeting of their parents, kick the problem around, and decide to accept a local food emporium's offer to provide new uniforms. What you don't realize, however, is that the company plans to splash its advertising all over the place—which might not be so terrible, except that your kids will be labeled with the company's name, *Lem's Supreme Hot Dogs*. This is hardly the image you want the team to have. This decision, it seems, needed a bit more thought.

Decisions are made about imaginary worlds; problem solvers and decision makers must try to predict these unknowns as accurately as they can. If answers were obvious, choices would be automatic and decision making unnecessary. Gut reactions and random choices sometimes may work out, but it's much better to steer a clear course toward a decision.

In this chapter, we explore systems for steering through problem analysis and decision making. The first step is to identify and analyze problems, their causes, and their effects. Next comes generating and analyzing solution options, using clear, mutually held criteria. After examining both processes, we look at some critical issues and methods involved in making decisions. Finally, we look at the need to create a plan for implementing and assessing those decisions. Our goals for this chapter are to help you to:

1.   Make systematic analysis part of your team's work
2.   Identify and analyze problems
3.   Establish criteria for potential solutions
4.   Decide on the most appropriate action to take
5.   Develop plans to implement your decisions
6.   Plan to assess the effectiveness of your choices

PLANNING APPROACHES

All too frequently, groups do what the Little League parents in the previous example did—they sit down, talk, and make a decision. Sometimes their decision shows foresight, but sometimes it shows no vision at all. *Effective* decision making, however, seems to have certain activities in common. Researchers have identified some of these activities, and their lists often serve as step-by-step agendas or work plans that guide a team's task processes. Here we will look at some traditional sequences teams may follow, ways technology may aid the process, and the importance of maintaining flexibility in your approaches to decision making.

FOLLOWING SYSTEMATIC SEQUENCES

We're going to examine three approaches that a team might use for thorough consideration of alternatives in decision making: Simon's phases, the vigilant decision-making approach, and Dewey's reflective thinking sequence.

Remember that Chapter 5 mentioned Simon's broad categories of activities that a decision-making team goes through—intelligence, design, choice, and review. In the intelligence phase, you gather and analyze the necessary data; in design, you create and select possible solutions; in choice, you make decisions; and in review, you assess the consequences of those decisions. These are broad descriptions of activities that distinguish effective decision making, and they can be used as a guide to systematic processes.

The more important activities, however, may be more specific. Several researchers (including Dickinson & McIntyre, 1997 and Salas, Sims & Burke, 2005) have examined group decisions, both good and bad, to see what makes the difference. These researchers maintain that the quality of choices depends on the **vigilance** group members exhibit in their critical thinking and analysis during a series of smaller decisions at four stages:

1. Examining the problem
2. Clarifying objectives
3. Developing available choices
4. Examining potential consequences

These decision-making approaches are similar to the now-classic **reflective thinking sequence** identified by John Dewey (1910) as the way that individuals think through problems. As "ancient" as this approach is, it remains a useful problem-solving guide because it suggests a sequence for setting agendas for meetings and for establishing work plans for reaching team goals. According to Dewey's sequence, a group:

1. Feels something is wrong and recognizes a problem
2. Defines the problem as well as its causes and effects
3. Lists possible solutions
4. Compares the pros and cons of the possible solutions
5. Selects the best solution
6. Implements that solution
7. Reviews the effectiveness of that solution

A team might well use this list to chart its work over an extended period of time. Frequently, a group organizes an agenda for a single meeting in terms of these—or at least some of these—steps. If one meeting is sufficient to resolve the problem, such an agenda can work well as a guide to both thinking and discussion. Because problem solving is so detailed, however, and thinking often is not as orderly as this outline, the agenda may be modified considerably as the meeting moves along. That's okay, too, if it serves to remind people to think things through.

Using Computer-Supported Collaborative Work (CSCW)

The processes suggested by these traditional problem-analysis and decision-making formulas are the basis of many CSCW software platforms. These programs provide a structure for generating, storing, organizing, and evaluating data that can help all team members to see ideas visually and to track the analysis as it progresses. These programs are particularly useful for tasks that require group members to find and share information (Huang & Zhang, 2004). For example, one of the two most commonly used programs is Group Systems (http://www.groupsystems.com). This software has facilities and programs for group decision making for synchronous, same-site meetings or for asynchronous teamwork from multiple locations. Yakal

(1996) reports that "PC-based decision-support tools, that help users determine which system factors are involved, weigh the importance and priority of each and balance them to arrive at a conclusion" (p. 62).

Some research indicates that individuals participate more in groups that use a group decision support system and that they also make better decisions than they do without computer-mediated assistance, especially when particularly complex problems are involved (Dennis & Garfield, 2003). Today, decision-support systems are used to determine what price to charge a customer, whether to grant a loan or insurance policy, which delivery truck should be re-routed, or what drug to prescribe for a diabetic patient ... sometimes with no human intervention at all, but more often working beside a human expert such as a doctor (Davenport, 2004).

MAINTAINING FLEXIBILITY

With or without technological links, you need to maintain flexibility in problem analysis and decision making. All these systems treat the process as a series of stages, but in reality, people overlap, loop back, and jump forward during task analysis and achievement. A knowledge of these systematic approaches, however, can be useful in three ways:

1. To provide strategies for team work
2. To guide agenda designs
3. To remind members of essential elements so they don't miss something important when thinking through their tasks

In fact, Westcott (2007) contends that lacking a strategy and procedural guidelines is among the most significant barriers to group problem solving.

Still, you can go too far in following procedures. Members may become so task-oriented they overlook the transactional processes that build emotional and social connections among people and that allow the task processes to progress. Members also risk assuming that the systematic plan automatically guarantees clear thinking. This is not necessarily the case. Sometimes groups proceed with no detectable system and produce good decisions, while other groups meticulously follow a systematic plan and produce mediocre results (Heninger, Dennis & Hilmer, 2006).

In short, these approaches to decision making remind people of the process and help teams to stay on track—but they don't guarantee the quality of thinking. From that perspective, the remainder of this chapter guides you through a step-by-step approach to problem analysis and decision making, as depicted in Figure 8.1.

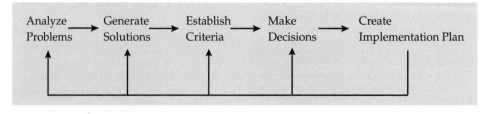

FIGURE 8.1

Problem-analysis and decision-making stages.

ANALYZING PROBLEMS

Dewey (1910) tells us the first step in analyzing a problem is to "feel difficulties." People sense that something is wrong, but what? This is similar to the difficulty students feel when they lament registration or parking problems. Sometimes there are as many explanations of just what the problem really is as there are students lamenting.

The challenge is to move from feelings to isolating the nature and scope of specific problems. This step requires all the skills covered in previous chapters: asking questions and gathering information, thinking analytically and critically, and thinking innovatively and creatively. The main issues here are to avoid compounding the problems through incrementalism, to identify what the real problems are, and to determine their causes and effects.

AVOIDING INCREMENTALISM

Identifying problems can be an extremely complex process. Problems frequently have been compounded by previous mistakes in problem solving. For example, in a process called **incrementalism** (Braybrooke & Lindblom, 1963), decisions are made in bits and pieces, responding to pressures as they are felt. This is especially characteristic of policy-making teams, which tend to react to current conditions rather than plan for future ones. Horiuchi (2006) points to NASA's reaction to the space shuttle Challenger disaster as an example of incrementalism. She notes that, "despite intense efforts and national scrutiny, [problems] resurged as indicated in the loss of the space shuttle Columbia" (p. 210). Rather than planning for future technological challenges, NASA remained reactive to past occurrences. Typically, these teams have shifting priorities, lack a clear sequence of team phases, have many issues to consider simultaneously, and so tend to be reactive rather than proactive in their decisions.

Incremental decisions create new problems, and these spur new increments of change—which makes identifying new problems, causes, and effects even more difficult. An example: A faculty-student team at your college is charged with creating a new general education program. The time limit on this project is 6 months, and the members have just started collecting information. Suddenly, the president requests a full list of problems in only 4 days. The result?

Increment 1. In a frenzy, the team whips up an intuitive list of problems and presents them.

Increment 2. The problems are not well identified, but the team now feels they are cast in stone, so it tries to work with that list.

Increment 3. Important problems are missed completely or misdiagnosed. The team makes some bad decisions, which are implemented, and new problems then arise.

Ideally, teams should not make decisions incrementally. All teams need to develop fully the processes of identifying the actual problems they need to solve and of analyzing those problems' causes and effects.

IDENTIFYING PROBLEMS

Identifying problems is not as easy as it sounds. You "feel the difficulty" first, and then you begin scanning the general area of concern for trouble spots. Next you begin to isolate problems by tracking them through the processes in which they appear, identifying how things are functioning, and comparing what you find against the ways things should work.

Let's put this in the context of a college task force charged with improving in-person registration. First, your team gets as broad a picture as possible of how the registration process works. Next you identify the more glaring issues, and then you get to work on finer analyses of those issues. You put aside issues that are not important, and you focus on issues you see as most critical to the problems.

Your analysis might begin by seeking answers to some of these questions:

- What difficulties are people feeling? What harms are being done?
- What is the scope or extent of the problem? How serious is it?
- What pre-established conditions or criteria relate to the difficulties? Are there organizational policies, procedures, objectives, criteria? Laws or rules?
- In what ways do the difficulties or harms relate to these pre-established conditions or criteria?

As you start to analyze the difficulties, you detect some specific patterns. One difficulty may be a lack of classes at the times students want them. In this case, the harms are fairly obvious: Students can't get classes or must take classes at inconvenient times and, thus, possibly have trouble completing requirements or fulfilling prerequisites for future courses. To analyze the problem, however, you also need to understand two other issues: the scope (How many students are affected?) and the conditions (college limitations, registration policies and procedures, departmental issues).

To analyze this problem, the team needs to trace through these issues and visualize them. We suggest using a **flowchart**. Creating a flowchart of the registration process helps clarify the team's thinking; the completed chart helps identify the problems. A flowchart can be used at any stage of information sharing or problem solving, but it is particularly useful for explaining processes. It can be simple or complex, and it can be created by hand or on a computer. The flowchart in Figure 8.2 (page 187) illustrates the registration process as experienced by the students in our example. Comparing this flowchart with the procedures intended by the college would show exactly where and how the problems occur. Problems usually are found where the reality deviates from the expectations.

DETERMINING CAUSES AND EFFECTS

As you track problems, you begin seeing some of the reasons for them, and exploring causes and effects can make or break a problem analysis. If you make decisions that correct the wrong cause, you're not going to solve the problem—and you may create new ones. It can be difficult to determine whether one factor causes a problem or simply happens to be associated with the effect or with some other cause.

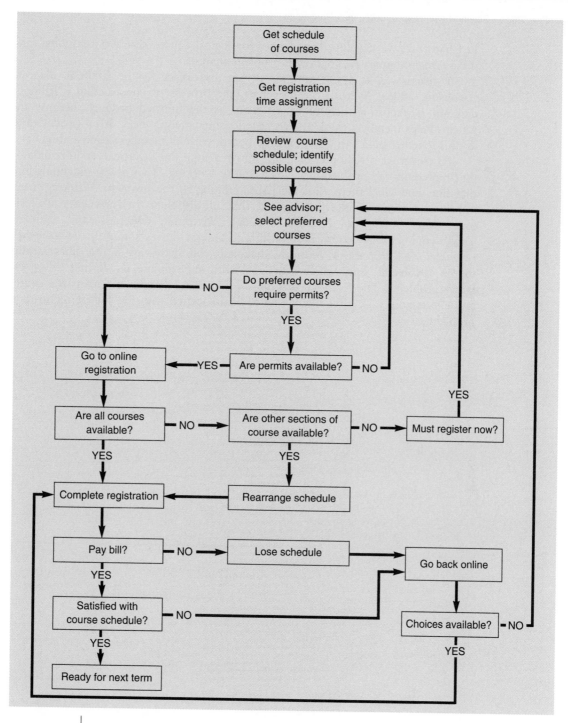

FIGURE 8.2

Flowchart of college registration process used for problem analysis.

In Chapter 7, we developed guidelines for logical cause-and-effect reasoning, and these principles must be applied to problem analysis.

A visual way to track multiple causes and effects is the **fishbone diagram** (Levinson, 2006). As with the flowchart, the process of constructing a fishbone diagram is almost as helpful to the team as the finished product, because the process helps members think and see relationships among ideas. It's a good idea to do this together on a flip chart or large board, with all members contributing.

To construct a fishbone diagram, draw a long line—vertical or horizontal—that represents the problem on which you're working. Then draw diagonals into that line, and label them with the issues relating to the problem. Working in an industrial setting, Ishikawa proposed that all problem analyses have at least four main "bones" to the "fish"—people, machines, materials, and methods. Thus, your college registration fish-bone might have *students, departments, resources*, and *procedures*. From the diagonals you then draw shorter lines parallel to the "problem" line, which you label with subordinate issues that affect the larger problems. The fishbone diagram in Figure 8.3 (page 188) maps the causes and effects your task force might find to be associated with the college registration problem.

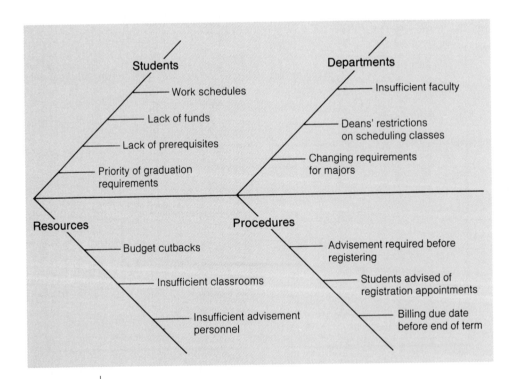

FIGURE 8.3

Fishbone diagram used to analyze a problem of insufficient class availability at college registration.

Fishbone diagrams are also well suited for computer-aided work. Specifically, the drop-down file folder organization can enhance the diagram's power and ease of use. Since each directory can contain an unlimited number of subdirectories, it can be expanded to show all the detailed information or collapsed to hide it. Subdirectories can also hold supporting information, so the team's work is easily organized by issue (Levinson, 2006).

You now have a diagram for seeing and analyzing the issues pertaining to the problem. It doesn't solve the problem, and it doesn't even prove the causes. It does, however, make all the elements visible so you can work with them.

GENERATING AND ANALYZING SOLUTIONS

After carefully analyzing a problem's causes, effects, and impact on people and operations, it's time to begin considering what actions to take. The main tasks at this stage are identifying options and setting criteria for analyzing them.

GENERATING POSSIBLE SOLUTIONS

Identifying a range of possible solutions takes time, energy, dedication, real team work—and the full creative thinking of all members. The best decisions result when all possibilities have been considered.

At this stage, you want to get every imaginable solution out in the open. This is a time to use one—or more—of the idea-generating approaches discussed in Chapter 7, such as brainstorming, the nominal group technique, and fantasy chaining. As always, hold off judgment and criticism when using these techniques until you get the ideas on the table, and don't be afraid to get silly. For now, you want quantity; later, you'll evaluate the options for quality.

ESTABLISHING CRITERIA

Arriving at quality decisions from a multitude of options depends on knowing what you require of the solution. With solutions, you can't simply assume you'll "know it when you see it." You might not. Setting up clear criteria is extremely important to your success. In a study of regularly meeting decision-making teams in a leasing company, Zack (2007) found that establishing customer evaluation criteria was a key factor in the business' success. Two years after implementing the criteria, the company "became a leader in offering highly customized services to novel markets and enjoyed one of the fastest growth rates and highest profit margins in the industry" (p. 1671).

Developing criteria can start with brainstorming a list of what conditions would be like after implementing the perfect solution. If your task is to create a project for a class, for example, your criteria might include some that meet the objectives of the assignment, others that meet the members' objectives for learning and grades, and still others that meet conditions you, as a team, have decided to include in your project.

Suppose you're on a creative team for a video production class. Your list of ideal criteria might specify that the project:

- Be original and unique
- Involve each team member in a specific role
- Deal with a controversial or timely topic
- Demonstrate skill in each area listed on the syllabus
- Have a well-written script
- Use graphics effectively
- Be cut and edited smoothly
- Achieve demonstration quality for each member's portfolio
- Serve as a foundation for next semester's project
- Be fun to do
- Earn an A for each team member

Some of these criteria are dictated by the assignment; others result from the team's own thinking about what will make a good project. The team may well add other criteria—and delete some—as it compares this list with specific project possibilities.

After you've drafted your criteria, try to visualize what—according to those criteria—the achieved solution will be like. Read about getting the picture right in Box 8.1. We've talked about the power of visualization in helping teams achieve their goals. All members need to understand the team vision, which in this case is the projected consequence of your work. Talk about the criteria to ensure every member has a mental picture of how that final result will feel, what it will provide, and how you will "know it when you see it." The phrase "a well-written script," for example, becomes a more specific criterion as the members describe the qualities of the finished product. You then have a clearer basis for evaluating possible solutions, and your common vision motivates the team's members to achieve it.

Finally—this is very important—record the criteria. Write out each criterion clearly and unambiguously, and make copies available to everyone. As you go through the decision-making process, keep those criteria in front of you—possibly in big print on a flip chart—and check all possible "winning" ideas against them.

When setting criteria, remember several issues that were raised earlier in this chapter. First, decisions are made about imaginary worlds. Second, decision-making processes often loop back. Noted psychologist Weick (1977) put it well: "If you look before you leap, you may not see anything. Action generates outcomes that ultimately provide the raw material for seeing something" (p. 113). In other words, you may want to revisit your criteria after further analysis of the possible solutions.

MAKING DECISIONS

At this point, your team has a list of possible solutions and a list of criteria a solution should meet. Decision making is intense, concentrated work. You can make it easier and more accurate by using visual charting methods to weigh each proposal

| BOX 8.1 | GETTING THE PICTURE RIGHT LEADS TO BETTER DECISIONS |

In 1996, Lee Roy Beach edited a volume that became widely regarded as the definitive work on "image theory." According to this theory, three kinds of images or mental pictures are used to make decisions:

- Principle images ... our morals, beliefs, ethics, or guiding values
- Goal images ... an idealized method of making principle images a reality
- Strategic images ... plans or tactics to carry out goals

Traditional decision theory says that in making decisions, people essentially do a cost-benefit analysis of their options and then select the best one. Image theory says that before people ever get to a cost-benefit analysis, they compare their options with these principles, goals, and strategic plans. If the options don't fit those images, either the images have to be changed or the options are rejected.

More recently, Kevin Morrell focused on business ethics in comparing the use of traditional, or "rational choice" theory, and "image" theory in decision making. He found that traditional theory is consistent only with utilitarian ethics, while image theory is consistent with both utilitarian and virtue-based ethics.

About the same time, Paul R. Falzer examined the use of image theory in making decisions about medical treatment. He discusses how image theory can assist clinicians, administrators, researchers, and policy makers in achieving a balance between evidence-based medicine and patient-centered practice.

Sources: Image theory and its applications, in *Decision Making in the Workplace: a Unified Perspective*, Lee Roy Beach (ed.), Mahwah, NJ: Lawrence Erlbaum Associates, 1996; Kevin Morrell, "Decision Making and Business Ethics: The Implications of Using Image Theory in Preference to Rational Choice," *Journal of Business Ethics* 50, 3, March 2004, pp. 239–252; and Paul R. Falzer, "Cognitive Schema and Naturalistic Decision Making in Evidence-Based Practices," *Journal of Biomedical Informatics* 37.2, April 2004, pp. 86–98.

against your criteria. Once you've completed this process, you're ready to choose—and use—one of several methods for making a final decision.

A little pragmatic planning will help this process along. Have a large-print chart of the solution options you've identified and another of your criteria right in front of the team as you work. You'll also find it helpful to chart your analysis on flip charts, a blackboard, or tacked-up butcher's paper as you go along.

ANALYSIS TECHNIQUES

We suggest two approaches to charting your solution analysis: a T-chart for comparing the pros and cons of a given plan, and a decision matrix for making comparisons among several plans.

A **T-chart** is a simple and effective way of ensuring that everyone stays focused on the comparison and that nothing is missed. It's called a T-chart because a large sheet or board is divided into a T, with the two sides labeled "Pros" and "Cons." As members make their observations, simply write each point in favor of or against a given proposal on the appropriate side. As Figure 8.4 shows, the resulting chart makes it easy to see, compare, and weigh the alternatives.

A **decision matrix** is a grid—also made large and roomy—that allows you to compare the merits of different plans. It lays out the comparisons visually and jogs

PROS	CONS
Would meet increasing needs for care for the elderly	Would take priority over needs for infant and child care
Can get partial funding through grants	Construction would disrupt hospital procedures and patient care
Land is available on west end of present facility	Grants would require matching funds
Would improve community relations	Wealthy sponsor is pushing for a new burn unit instead
Wealthy patrons have promised gifts of equipment	Would require large additions of geriatric specialists on staff
Local media are critical of Care Memorial's attention to elderly—new wing would appease them	National media attention is on inadequate care for children in this country

FIGURE 8.4

T-chart of the pros and cons of a proposal for a new geriatric wing at Care Memorial Hospital.

members' memories as they try to process enormous amounts of information. Across the top of the grid, label each column with one criterion for the ideal solution, and down the left side, label each row with a solution option. Working together, the team then fills in the cells with notes as to how each plan meets each criterion. When you've completed the grid, you have a concise, easily comprehended set of comparisons among the various proposals at hand. You can see an example in Figure 8.5.

Criterion Total Rating Relationship	Performance	Ease to Implement	Benefit/Cost
Weight	3	1	2
Alternative A 18	3 (X3) = 9	3 (X1) = 3	3 (X2) = 6
Alternative B 10	1 (X3) = 3	1 (X1) = 1	3 (X2) = 6
Alternative C 28	5 (X3) = 15	3 (X1) = 3	5 (X2) = 10
Scoring: 5 = high 3 = medium 1 = low			

FIGURE 8.5

Decision matrix grid of a proposal for a new geriatric wing at Care Memorial Hospital.

CRITICAL ISSUES

Having established and clearly visualized your criteria for the ideal solution, your team should now consider four critical issues: the applicability; the practicality; the advantages, disadvantages, and risk; and the desirability of any proposed decision or solution.

Applicability   Does a given idea or proposal meet your criteria for solving the problem or for meeting some need? The extent to which it does is that proposal's **applicability**. Questions to consider in this area include:

- Will the proposal solve the entire problem?
- If the proposal solves only part of the problem, is that a significant part?
- What must be sacrificed to use this idea?
- How does the idea compare with others regarding goal achievement?

Suppose you're on a church committee charged with raising $10,000 in matching funds to send the gospel choir to a music festival in Europe. On your brainstorming list is the ubiquitous "bake sale." Either somebody will have to bake a lot of cookies, or you'd better have some more lucrative possibilities on that list. Some proposals clearly are inadequate and are either eliminated or combined with other possibilities at this point. For those that remain, practicality becomes the issue.

Practicality   Every possible solution can raise sticky issues of **practicality**—that is, the feasibility of implementing it. Depending on the kind of team you're working with, who sponsors it, and what its purpose is, such issues might include:

- How much time will be required?
- How much money will be necessary?
- What kinds of support from others (teams, agencies, parent organizations, individuals) will be necessary?
- To what extent will each of these resources be available?
- What kinds of barriers will have to be overcome?
- Will it be possible to sell the idea to the organization or sponsoring group?

Practical drawbacks can kill an idea quickly. If money, time, or support is significantly short, or there will be insurmountable opposition from the parent organization, the idea simply won't do.

Sometimes, however, you can see ways to adapt a proposal to solve practical issues. Then weigh the adapted proposal with questions like these:

- Does overcoming the impracticality weaken the effectiveness of the plan or solution?
- Once adaptations are made to counter the impractical aspects of the plan, will that plan still be superior to others?

If a proposal is applicable and practical—if you think you can make it fly—the next considerations are the advantages, disadvantages, and risks that adopting the proposal might incur.

Advantages, Disadvantages, and Risks   Aside from simply meeting the criteria, implementing a proposed solution may bring with it extra advantages, disadvantages, or risks.

Consider what is likely to occur if the project is implemented. The immediate problem may be solved, but will the solution produce any side effects, either beneficial (**advantages**) or harmful (**disadvantages**)? Questions to think about include:

- What effects would the implemented proposal have on individuals or groups other than those it is intended to affect?
- What tangential effects would the proposal have on resources such as time, money, and supporting services?
- Would the advantages flow automatically from implementing the idea, or would they require some other action?
- Would the disadvantages be unavoidable, or would some minor modification in the proposal eliminate them?
- Are the advantages or disadvantages exclusive to this idea, or would the same ones result from other actions?
- How do the advantages and disadvantages weigh against each other?
- How do the advantages and disadvantages weigh against those of other proposed solutions?

These questions clarify the advantages and disadvantages. They also may unearth some previously unconsidered risks in the proposal. A **risk** is the chance a team takes by going ahead with an idea that might fail or produce serious, extensive, costly, or even damaging results.

Any idea that is innovative and potentially successful involves some risk. By definition, a new idea isn't backed by long experience, so it carries the possibility of failure. But without risk taking, there would be nothing new—no progress, no exciting possibilities. The reality is that people have to weigh their risks and hedge their bets. A team needs to take a hard look at the risks involved before making choices.

One classic format for estimating risks is Maier's (1963, pp. 174–177) risk technique. It involves working with a facilitator who takes the team through the following sequence:

1. Review the proposal with the team.
2. Explain that the facilitator is there not to evaluate, just to keep the process moving.
3. Explain the procedures.
4. Brainstorm all possible risks. Follow the rules for brainstorming: Don't allow evaluation; sweat out the silences. Post every concern on a flip chart or board.
5. Allow people to think about the risks between this meeting and the next, and send a copy of the brainstormed risk list to everyone.
6. Meet again to reconsider and to add new risks that may have occurred to people.
7. Discuss each risk. Is it serious? How can it be handled?
8. Cross off risks the team agrees are not serious.
9. Set up an agenda to discuss the remaining risks after members have had time to research and think about them.

As in brainstorming, the group owns each concern. Knowing that an idea doesn't belong to any one member eases apprehension about looking foolish or overanxious.

You might adapt this format to only one or two meetings if your team is on a short deadline or your risks are few. If your team needs to make major, far-reaching decisions with potentially serious risks, however, this process may take several meetings to identify those risks and to arrive at better decisions.

Desirability   No matter how perfect a proposed solution may appear in terms of the previous issues, it may rise or fall on issues of desirability. **Desirability** judgments are based on the character of the proposal and the value systems of the members.

What "good" means has been debated for many centuries, and disagreements will continue to occur as people and companies try to define ethical behaviors (Mathieson, 2007). While many guidelines for ethical decision making exist, many experts agree that the best approach is "to make the ethical component of business decision-making explicit so as to make it better" (Megone & Robinson, 2002, p. 28). This is why a team must examine the relative worth of probable outcomes as well as the values and ethical choices that impinge on their decisions.

At this point in the decision-making process, values and goals really come into play. This is when the decision makers debate how desirable, how valuable, and how worthwhile the goals are in terms of what it takes to implement a given plan.

We remember the shock several years ago when it was reported that an automobile manufacturer had considered—and rejected—a proposal to recall cars because the number of people killed as a result of a safety defect was not deemed to be large enough to justify the expense of recalling the cars. The management team had weighed numbers of human lives against the cost of a recall—and human life lost in the balance. How many lives, America wondered, would have made it worthwhile to recall those cars, and how could the management team have been so unethical and so stupid? In Chapter 12, we discuss groupthink—the analytical paralysis that allowed the decision makers to do this.

Meanwhile, as your team looks at proposals, you might do better than the automobile company by asking some of these questions:

- How desirable are the probable effects of the proposal?
- Will the proposal serve the vision of the team?
- Will the proposal serve the best interests of people it will affect?
- Will the proposal harm anyone, spiritually, psychologically, physically, economically, or socially?
- Is the proposal consistent with the personal value systems of the individual team members?
- Is any member uncomfortable with the ethics of the proposal?
- Does the proposal violate any code of ethics to which the team is bound?
- Does the proposal fulfill the spirit of any code of ethics to which the team is bound?

Even better than using this list, your team can brainstorm and refine a list of ethical criteria for itself. As you discuss ethical questions, you will find that some answers are easy: "No, that's against our values." "Yes, that's ethically defensible." Some questions, however, are not simple at all, and they represent a dilemma between two choices.

Barbara Toffler's work (discussed in Chapter 2) provides excellent guidance on this point. In her book *Tough Choices* (1986), she makes a clear distinction between *ethical issues* and *ethical dilemmas*. Toffler says an ethical issue is easy to identify as such, is not clouded by context, concerns only one person or group, addresses "right" or "wrong" for only one value, and assumes individuals can do the "right" thing. An ethical dilemma, however, arises when any of these characteristics is complicated by numbers of competing people or values, is clouded by interpretations of whether it really is an ethical question or not, or assumes people can't identify or are unable to do the right thing, despite their willingness.

Let's take an example. Someone you know offers to sell you a stolen DVD player. The issue is easy to recognize, and the context is simple. The situation affects only you and the would-be seller, and it is either right or wrong. You can choose to do the right thing. This clearly is a yes/no ethical issue.

Now, however, suppose your team believes the success of its project presentation depends on having a DVD player, and a teammate offers a "hot" one purchased for the occasion. Now the responsibility for actually buying stolen merchandise is one person removed, and the issue is not so easy to name. The context—the team, the project, the goals—is much more complicated and cloudy. More people are affected in more ways, and some members who want to do the right thing may be prevented from making that choice. The battle lines are drawn when one member says, "So what? C'mon, this has nothing to do with ethics. It's just a practical matter," and when another says, "How can you say that? It's not right to buy and use stolen property!" Now you know you have an ethical dilemma.

What do you do with an ethical dilemma? First, the team must recognize it as a dilemma. Then, having recognized it as such, you talk it out. Sometimes this means getting a more objective outsider to facilitate; sometimes the team can do it alone through shared leadership. Robinson, Davidsson, van der Mescht and Court (2007) contend that, since most people wind up making ethical decisions without the benefit of consulting an ethics expert, "it is imperative that they be equipped with a technique that enables them to consider their options and make effective choices" (p. 421).

Take time to reflect on the issues, to examine what moral perspectives each person brings to the dilemma. Consider in what ways alternative responses to the dilemma can be justified, and look at each set of reasons in the context of both individual and social codes of ethics. Above all, don't brush off the dilemma with comments like, "Everyone's entitled to an opinion," or "Value judgments are subjective." These comments can actually end the discussion prematurely, indicating that a discussion of ethical differences is pointless. In fact, there are significant benefits to ethical debates. Thinking about how to phrase an argument helps people clarify their thoughts (Mathieson, 2007).

Additionally, research indicates that the ability to make ethical decisions improves over time and with practice (Chun, 2005). Perhaps more important, though: over time, failing to talk about ethical quandaries lulls people into thinking their decisions and actions have no ethical implications. As Toffler's more recent research into the lack of ethical culture at the accounting firm Arthur Andersen demonstrates, this false sense of security prompts organizational members to engage in more problematic—and unquestioned—behaviors over time (Toffler & Reingold, 2004).

In working through ethical dilemmas, your team can learn to understand one another's points of view and to resolve the hard issues together. You're reaching for ethical choices that everyone can live with. This may mean taking more time—and a higher road—than some would prefer. But strive to achieve consensus on the issue as a team, and work out a decision with which each team member can live.

DECISION MODES

Analysis of alternatives can go on indefinitely, but at some point, the group needs to make a decision—even if that decision is to make no changes. Take time to ensure everyone clearly understands the merits and characteristics of each proposal and to clarify any questions. This lets you get second thoughts out in the open and check everyone's agreement. Then use an agreed-on method of deciding.

All too often, groups fall into making "twofer" decisions—that is, two members speak for a decision, and the silence of other members is interpreted as giving their consent. Twofer decisions may look okay at the moment, but they eventually lead to disgruntlement and lack of commitment.

A team's method of deciding affects the fairness of the decision and the members' satisfaction with that choice (Song, 2007). Therefore, consider your methods carefully. Your options include decision by consensus, majority vote, two-thirds vote, multiple ranking, and decision by authority.

Consensus Consensus decisions are ideal because they represent—at least theoretically—the full agreement of every member. In reality, consensus represents *some* degree of agreement by all members, and it may be achieved through intensive discussion and negotiation. Striving for consensus is worth the effort, even if the final decision has to be made by another method.

As noted earlier, teams with a high degree of consensus develop a stronger commitment to their decisions and are more likely to follow through on them than teams without such consensus (Lewis, 2007). Individualistic North Americans are trying hard to learn the consensus techniques of the Japanese, because these approaches clearly work so well. Japanese groups typically hammer out decisions in 'round-the-clock, patient, persuasive, exhaustive discussions until everyone agrees. This is a harrowing process, but once consensus is achieved, the implementation proceeds swiftly with the full support of all concerned.

Voting Most North Americans are accustomed to a **majority vote**—that is, more than 50 percent—as the quick and easy method to decide among alternatives. If the discussion has been thorough and everyone has had his or her say, most people will accept a majority decision. This is a big "if," however. All too frequently, a majority vote is a cop-out—a lazy way of pushing forward to a conclusion without vigilant and vigorous problem analysis. It's quicker, but it leaves more people dissatisfied and gets less cooperation than a consensus decision.

A majority vote may be a requirement if your group is part of a larger organization bound by a constitution, bylaws, and parliamentary procedures. You also may be required to have a quorum of the membership in attendance—a minimum number specified in your bylaws—and to hold a formal vote on any decision. If so, the group still needs to work hard at developing mutual understanding and agreement on the decision.

In some instances, the bylaws of a group require a **two-thirds vote**—that is, at least twice the number of votes for a proposal as against it. This voting requirement applies to major issues, such as changing the bylaws, and to any proposal that interferes in some way with the rights of any member to discuss an issue fully, such as a motion to limit debate or change the agenda.

Multiple Ranking   Multiple ranking works well when there are several choices, and it often is used with a long list of possibilities or in conjunction with the Delphi or the nominal group technique (discussed in Chapter 7). This method is time consuming and bulky because it can require several ballots.

Multiple ranking can be used for recommendations, ideas, criteria, or people. Suppose you're on a nomination committee with a list of ten possible candidates. Your group wants to recommend a slate of three for the larger organization's vote. You can winnow those ten possible candidates down to three in a fair way using multiple ranking as follows:

1. The members discuss the merits of each possible candidate.
2. Each member ranks his or her ten choices, in order, from 1 to 10.
3. The ballots are tallied.
4. Each possible candidate receives a sum of his or her rankings. For example, if candidate A receives rankings of 1, 5, 3, 3, 2, 1, 5, 5, 4, 1, then the total for that candidate is 30.
5. The three lowest totals represent the top three candidates.

Multiple ranking is a slow process. It provides something close to consensus, however, while also working efficiently through many possibilities to find the "best."

Decision by Authority   Decision by authority means that the team's decisions are only recommendations, not actions. Someone with higher status than the team members—perhaps a manager, an executive committee, or the president of an organization—has the final word. In some cases, the hierarchy is very clear: the team's function is to conduct the inquiry, do the critical and creative thinking, make recommendations, and then wait for a decision.

Some researchers contend that an authority decision is better than consensus. For example, Wernerfelt (2007) argues that authorities typically have better information and more truly representative preferences, and further contends that it is too time-consuming and expensive for the majority of decisions to be reached by consensus. Kopeikina (2006) contends that leaders make decisions consistent with their vision, and this keeps an organization moving in the right direction. On the whole, though, we would argue that leaving decisions up to the "boss" without striving for consensus can be a mediocrity trap. After all, it's easy to shrug your shoulders and just say, "Oh, well. It's the boss's problem now." To help you imagine how groupware might work in the decision-making process, read Box 8.2. Moreover, other researchers have found that consensus decisions significantly increase the communication openness within an organization, such that employees are more willing to share their views and concerns with management and thus can resolve potential problems before they occur (Breen, Fetzer, Howard & Preziosi, 2005).

This approach also fails to build a real team because the team's job often continues with implementing the decision after it is made and then assessing the results. This phase is likely to be more successful if the team has worked out its disagreements together.

BOX 8.2 | **COMPUTER-SUPPORTED GROUP DECISION MAKING**

To help you imagine how groupware might work in the decision-making process, we'll describe a meeting in the University of Hawaii at Manoa's Electronic Meeting Room (EMR). Decision sciences professor Laku Chidambaram facilitated the meeting. The goal of the meeting was to identify "uses of electronic support for intercultural meetings." A chalkboard and a large monitor were at the front of the room with Dr. Chidambaram, and a technical facilitator who managed the equipment sat to his right. Participants sat at a semi-circular desk in front of the facilitator; a keyboard, hidden from others' view, was in front of each participant on which to type ideas anonymously. These ideas then were displayed on the large monitor in front of the participants. The group followed an agenda that included:

1. *Defining the important terms for the electronic dictionary*. Once in memory, the dictionary could remind members of how they were defining their ideas.
2. *Brainstorming ideas*. As each member typed in an idea it was displayed on the monitor for everyone to examine.

3. *Adding comments or further ideas to messages already entered*. Again, each addition was displayed on the monitor for all to see.
4. *Organizing ideas into discrete categories*. During this phase, the program and the facilitator helped the group to bring a large number of ideas into ten or so possible categories by commenting (on the computer) and by ranking.
5. *Prioritizing ideas*. After an oral discussion, members voted on which ideas were most worthy of evaluating and brought the list down to a manageable few.
6. *Evaluating ideas*. At this point, participants typed in their observations and concerns, these were displayed on the monitor, and the group discussed and evaluated the ideas in light of these comments.
7. *Voting and deciding on the most important concept*. Again, participants used their keyboards to register their votes as the program tallied their responses and reported their results on the monitor.

CREATING AN IMPLEMENTATION PLAN

Our experience reveals that teams often go astray at the implementation stage. They may have really superb ideas, but when it comes to putting them into action, something slips. They miss some of the details that would have made those ideas work. Without appropriate follow-up, important decisions made in the previous phase can get lost or be implemented wrongly (Borges, Pino & Valle, 2005).

DESIGN

Implementing a proposal begins with the original goals and vision for the team's work. In other words, what will the final product look like? Keep this idea in front of you at every stage of the following steps:

1. *Brainstorm a checklist.* Include everything that must be done to implement the proposal, and ask yourselves, "Who does what, when, where, how, and from what resources?"
2. *Divide the brainstormed list by categories.* Consider issues such as:
    *   Resources needed—money, information, technological support, and permissions as well as cooperation required from authorities, agencies, and organizations
    *   Actions that must be taken to get the proposal under way—contacts to be made, communication needs, materials to be obtained, applications to be made for permissions and licenses, and arrangements to be made for space, guests, equipment, and so on
    *   Steps to achieve each action
    *   People responsible for each action
    *   Time required for each step
3. *Decide precisely who is responsible for each step.* Make sure each person commits to his or her responsibilities. Duplicate and distribute the list to all members. At implementation meetings, go over this list to check progress, and make any necessary revisions. Human beings have a touching faith in their memories; unfortunately, it is unjustified. No matter how many times a flight crew may have flown a Boeing 747, you still want the pilots on your flight to use the preflight checklist again.
4. *Create a flowchart with time factors.* If you've carefully considered the practicality issues of your plan, you already may have a clear idea of how long the implementation will take. Now, however, you need to establish the time for each individual step—and this is when reality sets in. On a flowchart, map out each step, its time allotment, and who is responsible. Some steps will overlap; in other cases, one step must be completed before another can begin. Mapping the steps develops a strategy or work plan for the entire process. Recall that Figure 8.2 shows a flowchart developed for analyzing problem sources. This same approach can be used to display a working plan, which then is used to monitor the implementation process.

ASSESSMENT

Whether your task was small or enormous, you still want to know how well you accomplished it. In Chapter 4, we talked about ways to assess your team's processes. In this chapter, we talk about ways to get feedback on how well your team's decision works after it's been implemented.

First, look at your goals, and then draft questions about their achievement. If your goal was to involve more freshmen in student activities, you need to find out how many freshmen actually participated in specific events. Intermediate questions, however, might be, how many freshmen know where the Student Activities Office is? How many activities do freshmen know about? The clearer and more specific your questions, the more directly you can answer them.

Next, devise ways of finding answers to these questions. Possible approaches include:

- Questionnaires or surveys aimed at the people affected by your project
- Tallies of actual participants compared with some benchmark figures
- Pre- and post-project tests or surveys
- Observations and assessments by objective sources

Each of these methods can yield useful information about the effectiveness of your work. But assessment cannot be haphazard; it needs to be a regular part of the process. These guidelines should help you develop an assessment plan that works:

- Everyone involved in the plan should be involved in assessing it. Where possible, assessment data should be user-generated.
- Assessment should be planned ahead of time. Methods should address the goals, instrumental objectives, and vision of the final task. When the assessment is not preplanned, people often suspect the motives.
- Assessment should be continuous. Feedback should occur on a regular basis, beginning early in the implementation period, so you can use the information to make changes quickly if things don't go as expected.

AVOID ESCALATION OF COMMITMENT

One of the major benefits to an implementation plan is avoiding escalation of commitment. Escalation occurs when a group continues to pursue a course of action just because it feels it has gone too far to quit. When faced with negative results of its decision, the group decides to simply keep going in its current direction and just "work harder," hoping that events will change course. Escalation usually happens because groups either do not have processes in place to review feedback about their program (positive or negative), or because they discount negative information they do receive (Keil, Mann & Rai, 2000). Research consistently demonstrates that groups who appropriately define their problem, carefully decide on a solution, and have a complete implementation plan can avoid this common phenomenon (Keil, Depledge & Rai, 2007).

SUMMARY

Systematic processes of analysis enable teams to arrive at good solutions. Dewey's reflective thinking sequence is a traditional approach, but teams can vary the order of the steps according to need. A systematic approach—scanning the difficulties, isolating primary issues, flowcharting processes—helps in identifying problems.

After analyzing the causes and effects with the help of fishbone diagrams, the team can generate a range of possible solutions and set criteria for the best solution. Making decisions by increments often leads to new problems, however, so a systematic examination of critical issues is needed. Critical issues include the proposed solution's applicability to the problem; its practicality; its possible advantages, disadvantages, and risks; and the desirability of its implementation. Assessing ethical issues as well as ethical dilemmas also is critical to this process.

Decisions may be made by consensus, majority vote, two-thirds vote, multiple ranking, or decision by authority depending on the context, the system, and the purpose of the group. Consensus, however, provides the best foundation for team commitment and follow-through on decisions.

Once a decision is made, the team may continue with implementation plans and use a flowchart to show who is responsible for which steps and when. The implementation plan also should include contingency adjustments and, finally, approaches to assessing and adjusting the implemented solution.

Exercises

1. Your team is a quality committee in a large corporation, and the following set of facts has been called to your attention:
   - The plant is in a rural industrial park.
   - The closest town is 10 miles away.
   - Sometimes employees who have families seem to be distracted.
   - The town has one small day-care center.
   - Two churches have preschools that operate until 5 o'clock in the afternoon.
   - The company has no maternity/paternity leave benefits.
   - Many employees live 20 or more miles away.
   - Parents of small children frequently are late or absent.
   - Parents of older children miss work on many school holidays.
   - Some personnel have left the company when they started families.
   - Recent declines in productivity have occurred primarily among people from 25 to 45 years of age—normally a productive group.
   - Morale in the company is low.

   Using this information, identify the problem or problems these facts suggest, and then analyze and diagram their causes and effects.

2. Using the cause-and-effect diagram for Exercise 1, set goals that your quality committee would like to achieve and establish criteria for considering your solution to be satisfactory. Generate possible solutions to the problems, and then create an implementation and assessment plan.

3. Observe a group or team as the members try to solve a problem, and using Form 8.1, analyze the team's processes. What worked well? What didn't? Where did the members seem to conform to what you've learned in this chapter? Where did they not? What could the members do to improve their processes?

4. Recall a time you've been in a group (school, work, family, or community) that had a problem to analyze and a decision to make. Using what you've learned in this chapter, reflect on how your experience relates to effective processes of analyzing problems, generating and analyzing solutions, making decisions, and implementing as well as assessing those decisions.

FORM 8.1 | OBSERVATION OF A GROUP'S PROBLEM ANALYSIS AND DECISION MAKING

Observe a group as it solves a problem. On the form, mark each time someone in the group contributes to a function (listed on the left) during each period of the discussion (listed on the right)—early, midpoint, or late in the discussion. If no one contributes to a particular function, then check "Never" when the discussion is over.

	Early	Mid	Late	Never
1. Suggests a system for problem analysis				
2. Defines a problem				
3. Identifies goals				
4. Analyzes causes and effects				
5. Identifies criteria for solutions				
6. Generates possible solutions				
7. Analyzes solutions				
8. Suggests decision mode				
9. Guides final decision process				
10. Designs implementation				
11. Designs assessment				

On the basis of your observations, consider:

1. Was the process systematic? What worked well? What functions needed more attention? What would a diagram or flowchart of the team's process look like?

2. Which critical issues—applicability, practicality, advantages/disadvantages/risks, desirability—did the team consider?

3. Did the team consider ethical issues or dilemmas? How did the members work through these?

4. How satisfied with the outcome did the team appear to be? How committed do you think the members were to their decision? Why?

"I just say what I mean and mean what I say, and if my teammates don't like it, tough."
Oops. Real communication just isn't that easy.

VERBAL AND NONVERBAL COMMUNICATION

Building Transactional Processes

9

"At a recent international conference," one observer recalls, "members of the Israeli delegation, who were arguing their position in a dynamic manner, complained that the representatives from Thailand showed no interest in or enthusiasm for the meeting because they 'were just sitting there.' The Thai delegates, on the other hand, thought the professors from Israel were angry because they were 'using loud voices'" (Samovar & Porter, 1995, p. 107).

Who was right? Both were—from their cultural perspectives. Each just needed to understand the other's communication style—and to learn how to adapt their own when appropriate.

Naturally, what we say to one another is important. As other chapters in this book have pointed out, the messages we choose to share with teammates create an environment in which everyone understands team norms and values, and this shared understanding is critical to team performance. However, we often neglect what is arguably one of the most important components of communication: our nonverbal cues. As communication consultant Thomas Lee puts it, "Words matter greatly. Indeed, many . . . attitudes, behaviors, and decisions reveal themselves in the presence of words. But the words count only to the extent that people regard them as true and real. For that, they look around them, and they take notice. At day's end, people may or may not hear what you say. But they will always see what you do, and seeing is believing" (2008, p. 28). That's why this chapter focuses on how members create connections and negotiate mutual meanings through verbal and nonverbal communication.

Our goals in this chapter are for you to:

1. Understand the dialectical/dialogical processes of negotiating mutual team meanings
2. Know how culture and gender relate to communication styles
3. Know how assertive, appropriate, and confirming language affects transactional processes in teams
4. Be able to discriminate communication needs in face-to-face teams as compared to virtual teams
5. Understand the role of nonverbal communication in transactional processes
6. Start using communication styles that help you share leadership effectively in a team

NEGOTIATING TEAM MEANINGS

By negotiating team meanings, we mean that teammates must trade and adapt to one another's thinking until each person can accept a shared interpretation of the ideas under discussion. People often just assume others understand the words they use in the way that they meant to use them. Alas, however, this is not always true. The more diversity you have within a team, the harder it is to be sure you're understanding one another correctly.

Sometimes negotiating meanings is fairly simple. You might say, "I think we should bring in some experts on this issue." Someone else then says, "Uh-uh, we can't afford the time or the money to bring anyone in." You respond, "Oh, no, I just meant I think we should look up some expert resources before we go any further." With this negotiation, you have successfully defined the meaning of "bringing in experts."

Often, however, negotiating meaning is more difficult. As the philosopher Mikhail Bakhtin (see Griffin, 1994, p. 207) suggests, when people communicate, they may be torn between contradicting—yet interdependent—desires or forces. Bakhtin calls this internal conflict **dialectical tension**. Simply put, a *dialectic* is the argumentation between two issues or forces, and *dialectical tension* is the conflict that people feel between two desires or needs.

For example, Baxter (1988) found that people experience tensions between wanting both integration *and* separation, stability *and* change, and expression *and* privacy. Suppose your team is discussing whether to take on a huge project. This project will demand great sacrifices of time and energy, but it will integrate the members into a superteam that may even win awards for its work. The tension between wanting an integrated team and a separate, private life might color each member's interpretation of every statement made in this discussion. To negotiate past this tension, the team must engage in dialogue.

FROM DIALECTIC TO DIALOGUE

If dialectic is the argumentation between two issues, then dialogue is the conversation through which people sculpt or negotiate meanings they can share. In the integration/separation example, Ria might say, "We'll have to meet on weekends," but Len responds, "No way." Weekend meetings will contribute to integrating the team, which may be okay with Ria because she's free on weekends. Len, however, has a conflict—he needs to be separate from the team on weekends because he's a Little League coach, a volunteer fireman, and a leader in his synagogue.

Take a look at Figure 9.1 (page 208). To negotiate through the dialectical tensions underlying each individual's responses, members must agree on what specific concepts mean for the team. Because words are abstract and individually meant, members must offer personal interpretations of ideas. As they listen, question, and analyze together, they begin to adapt to one another's understandings and negotiate team meanings with which they can work.

It's a good idea to record the most critical definitions as the team works through them. You then can refer back and redefine them as necessary. If your team is working with groupware, you may have a computer dictionary for storing negotiated terms in the computer's memory. Then, when members need to, they can bring up the previous definition on the screen and apply it to the team's analysis or, if necessary, renegotiate and revise the concept.

Dialogue often requires redefining ideas, because the more abstract a concept or demanding the tensions, the more difficult communication becomes. And the more difficult, important, and far-reaching a team's job, the more it must find ways to bring the teammates' various meanings into closer alliance.

FROM SEEING STEREOTYPES TO SEEING PEOPLE

The more diversity within a team, the richer the possibilities—and, perhaps, the greater the dialectical tension and the harder members may have to work at dialogue. This is partly because people have different communication styles, which reflect their social status, culture, and gender. Naturally, people grow up talking and acting like

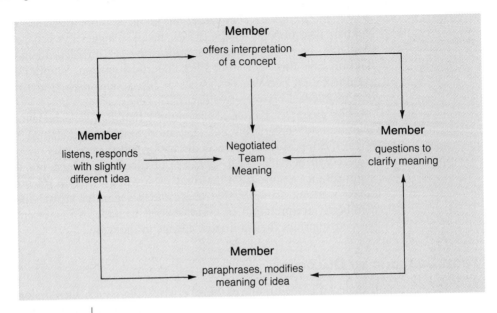

FIGURE 9.1

The process of negotiating meaning among members.

others in their identity groups, which is fine when they are with others like themselves. If they can't adapt to people from other backgrounds, however, some may judge them by their communication ("Oh, he thinks he's so smart and classy," or "Oh, she's just so dumb and crude"). Equally, people may stereotype themselves by refusing to adapt their own styles to help others better understand them.

Adapting your style and understanding the styles of others require an awareness of what cultural and gender differences may be operating. At the same time, it requires an ability to cast aside stereotypes and see people as individuals.

Cultural Differences   People from different cultures communicate in ways that reflect both the general characteristics of their culture and also the ways of their specific class within it. If you don't believe this, go to the poshest community in your state and listen to people. Then go to the most poverty-stricken area and listen again. The people in each area are just people—good and bad, smart and dumb, strong and weak—but their verbal and nonverbal communication is radically different. They've been socialized within their specific identity groups, and those identity groups are determined by their economic and social status.

In a broader sense, however, each culture holds values that influence the communication of people at all levels. People tend to assume that challenges in multicultural teams arise from language barriers, but this is only part of the picture. One area on which cultures differ that can thwart the creation of shared meaning is context. Brett, Behfar & Kern (2006) distinguishes cultures along a range between **high-context cultures** and **low-context cultures**. In this sense, *context* means the amount of information that all members of a society hold in common.

The high-context culture is collectivistic, with close family and community groupings. People know one another, and because they have a basic context for their communication, they need little verbal information. They understand one another through nonverbal cues and interpersonal empathy. Many Asian cultures are described as high-context. Their members value maintaining group harmony and saving face, so their communication is often subtle and indirect (Buchan, Johnson & Croson, 2006).

Contrast this subtlety and concern for harmony with the characteristics of a low-context culture, such as that of the United States. This type of culture is individualistic and diverse, so people within it have less context about others and less motivation to sacrifice their individual wants for the group. You can easily see how this affects communication. Residents of northeastern U.S. cities, for example, are likely to be direct, explicit, and focused on the individual goals of communication.

Given these cultural influences, you might find a Thai or a Chinese teammate counting heavily on empathy and trust but hesitating about giving information. In contrast, a North American might be objective, open, and direct—but a little low on the empathy quotient.

One of our classroom teams exemplified—and overcame—their cultural differences. This team included Tam, from Vietnam; Tom, an African American; Asad, a Pakistani; and Terry and Joan, both Caucasian North Americans. Of the low-context North Americans, Terry was subtle and facilitative, and Tom and Joan were direct and task-oriented. Asad and Tam, who were both from high-context cultures, rarely spoke and used a soft, indirect, unassertive style when they did.

At first, the more vocal North Americans did not understand the quiet Pakistani and Vietnamese members. Didn't they care? Why wouldn't they just speak up? In turn, Tam and Asad were intimidated by the North Americans with their questions and prolonged explanations. It was Terry's active, facilitative leadership (even though she was not formally the leader) that brought this team together. Terry helped the high-context members express their ideas and the low-context people tone themselves down. The result? The team became cohesive, supportive of one another, and effective in producing excellent class projects.

Gender Differences Deborah Tannen (2001) considers that men and women actually grow up in different cultures. Their communication, therefore, differs markedly in many ways. Other theorists suggest the differences are more a matter of economic class and power: those in control communicate in one way, and those who are subordinate communicate in another. There's some truth to both points of view.

Tannen, for example, says women more often use *rapport-talk* whereas men typically use *report-talk*. "For most women," says Tannen, conversation is "a way of establishing connections and negotiating relationships. Emphasis is placed on displaying similarities and matching experiences. . . . For most men, talk is primarily a means to preserve independence and negotiate and maintain status in a hierarchical social order" (p. 77).

Similarly, Wood (2001) says that stereotypically, men communicate in an *agency style* (agents of problem solving and decision making) and women use a *communality style* (nurturers and facilitators of cooperation and community) (pp. 169–170). For some time, Western researchers labeled the male, agency style as "powerful" and the female, communal style as "powerless." Truly powerful communication, however, is communication that achieves its goal. Sometimes that goal is transactional and sometimes task-oriented, but most often, the goal requires both processes. Each style, therefore, has its own power. Recent research also indicates that individuals adapt their communication style to fit the amount of power they have in social transactions rather than adapt to their particular gender or culture (Scudder & Andrews, 1995) and that, in groups, men and women are more similar than they are different in their communication styles (Grob, Meyers & Schuh, 1997).

Yet, you often will see the differences that researchers have noted. For example, many women—or anyone in a subordinate position, or either sex in some high-context cultures—are deferential and accommodating. They are prone to phrase ideas tentatively, politely, and properly and soften their statements with tag questions ("It's true, don't you think?"), fillers ("you know," "and . . ."), qualifiers ("I believe," "it seems to me"), hedges ("I'd like to," "if you would"), and hesitations ("well," "that is . . .") (Farrington, 2008).

Higher-status persons—especially Western men—frequently assume more authority and freedom, so they often speak more casually. Those in power may be more confrontational and work toward a goal with direct, declarative, and fluent language. They also are likely to be less accommodating than lower-status people, presenting more opinions, suggestions, and orientations as well as talking more, interrupting more, and overlapping comments more (Tannen, 2001).

Even Western society, however, is beginning to recognize the value of communication that builds relationships and—especially in teams—that facilitates the participation of all members. As the culture changes, we see more styles that adapt to the team and the situation.

IDENTIFYING COMMUNICATION STYLES

You never have to sacrifice your way of communicating with friends and family—but you can learn how to adapt that style to make it productive in various situations, including teamwork. Here, we describe a spectrum of productive as opposed to unproductive language styles. These are previewed in Figure 9.2.

Productive communication styles have some basic characteristics in common: The communicator is oriented toward facilitating the team to do its job. A productive style is both verbally and nonverbally responsible, confirming of others, appropriate to the team and the context, and assertive. Nonetheless, style choices may range widely and still be productive for the particular team and its circumstances. We distinguish each end of the productive spectrum like this:

- The **facilitative/equal style** focuses on transactional processes that help teammates to express ideas in a supportive climate. As such, a facilitative/equal style uses many behaviors researchers previously labeled as feminine or powerless, but it can, in fact, be very powerful.
- The **commanding/authoritative style** moves task processes forward and focuses on ensuring that the job gets done. The behaviors associated with a commanding/authoritative style are more like those previously labeled as

Productive Styles

Facilitative/Equal . . . . Commanding/Authoritative

Responsible

Confirming

Appropriate

Tactfully Assertive . . . . .Directly Assertive

Unproductive Styles

Passive-Aggressive . . . . Hostile/Divisive

Not responsible

Disconfirming

Inappropriate

Nonparticipative/Indirect . . . . .Aggressive

FIGURE 9.2

Two spectrums: productive and unproductive communication styles.

masculine or powerful, but again, this style might be either weak or strong depending on the circumstances.

The unproductive spectrum encompasses these extremes:

- The **passive-aggressive style** is nonparticipative or uses control and strategy to block transactional and task processes. We'll discuss passive aggression further in a little bit.
- The **hostile/divisive style** is counterproductive, concerned primarily with an individual's objectives or defenses, and may be aggressive. This style is not responsive to the transactional needs of the team, nor is it responsible for ensuring that task processes are accomplished. Such negative styles create defensive climates that are poisonous for team communication.

Suppose your team is frustrated by Irena's seeming irresponsibility. She has just sashayed into the meeting, late again, and interrupted a serious discussion. Here's how you might respond using each of the styles just described:

- *Facilitative/equal:* "Ah, Irena, we were just talking about Joe's idea for the project. Maybe someone could give Irena an update on it—we need everyone's opinion here."
- *Commanding/authoritative:* "Irena, please hang on for a second while we finish this thought, and then Joe can give you an update on his idea."
- *Passive-aggressive (and sarcastic):* "Aren't we lucky? Irena has graced us with her presence."
- *Hostile/divisive:* "What do you think you're doing, Irena? For crying out loud, I'm sick and tired of wasting my time in these meetings because some people are so..."

Facilitating a task can seem like solving a puzzle.

Both productive styles allow you to get the team on task and Irena into the loop without wasting time, energy, and interpersonal comfort. Both unproductive styles focus on punishing Irena rather than moving the task forward. The team may have to deal with Irena's behavior, of course, but this would be neither the time nor the place to do so. We will talk more about problems—and how to manage them—in Chapter 12.

The point is you want to use a productive style, adapting the degree of facilitation or authority you use to the people and the circumstances. Our observation has been that men and women of widely varying identity groups and power positions can do just that, adopting productive styles ranging from fully facilitative to commanding and authoritative.

USING DIALOGICAL STYLES

Ideally, transactional and task processes support and encourage authentic, inclusive, sharing negotiation of ideas and perspectives. A climate develops in which members are sensitive to one another, dialogue is supported, and defensiveness is reduced through language that is assertive, responsible, confirming, and appropriate.

SENSITIVITY

Using a productive/facilitative style relies on your ability to understand others' feelings and responses and, then, to respond facilitatively to them. Hart and Burks (1972) identified people who can do this as *rhetorically sensitive*. They are neither rigid and absolute about their own opinions, nor are they wishy-washy and ready to emulate everyone else's positions. Rhetorically sensitive men and women are productively responsive to others, flexible, assertive, and not bound by predetermined gender roles. They adapt their communication to needs as they see them (House, Dallinger & Kilgallen, 1998).

ASSERTIVENESS

In cultures where individualism is valued, as in North America, assertiveness is a respected style of communication. **Assertiveness** is communicating openly, with awareness of yourself and concern for others and what you need or want them to know. An assertive statement often is direct, but it may be very gentle and considerate of others' feelings.

It is crucially important to know what assertiveness is—and is not. Assertiveness is expressing your ideas or feelings; it is not "spilling your guts." Assertiveness is stating your position, not attacking others. Assertiveness is taking responsibility for your own communication, not allowing someone else to manipulate your responses.

Assertiveness requires the sensitivity and the ability to know what you want, to cope with risk in communication, to state a position responsibly and openly, and to understand and care about how your communication might affect others. Figure 9.3 provides an overview of assertiveness in relation to other behaviors.

The assertive person (upper left quadrant in Figure 9.3) is self-disclosing, seeks to influence others, and has high concern for others' rights. A person whose assertiveness is effective knows how to use tact and diplomacy as well. Comparing supportive to defensive groups, Gibb (1961) noted that members of supportive groups express themselves openly and nonjudgmentally. They focus on problems rather than on people, on openness rather than on strategy or manipulation, and on empathy rather than on neutrality. All these goals can be accomplished assertively *and* supportively.

The person who is self-disclosing and seeks to influence others but has low concern for their rights (lower left quadrant in Figure 9.3) may be aggressive. **Aggressiveness** is adopting a "me first" attitude, trying to control others, and demonstrating a low regard for their interests or feelings. Communication is aggressive when it is used to inflict psychological pain (Infante et al., 1992, p. 116) by attacking a person's self-concept (Infante & Wigley, 1986). Aggression actively seeks to

	Self-disclosing Influencing others	Self-protective Influenced by others
High concern for rights of others	Assertive Open climate	Passive Closed climate
Low concern for rights of others	Aggressive Hostile climate	Passive-aggressive Anxious/hostile climate

FIGURE 9.3

How assertiveness relates to other behaviors.

control the target's feelings and behavior, perhaps through a verbal—or nonverbal—"punch in the nose," malicious teasing or manipulation, or relentless verbal pushing. Aggressiveness is almost always an unproductive style of communication because it expresses hostility and divides teammates into defensive camps. Kassing and Avtgis (1999) found that aggressive communication contributed to employees' negative attitudes toward their employer and their work team, and that such communication also diminished open communication and trust.

Someone who is both highly concerned about and influenced by others (upper right corner of Figure 9.3) may behave with **passivity**. This person withholds communication and might agree falsely to appease others, subordinating her or his own nterests in fear of possible consequences. There are times that you might choose to be silent without being passive, however. The facilitative/equal style, on occasion, can withhold comment to allow teammates to explore an issue. This is not passivity; you have not withdrawn but have chosen to listen silently for the sake of the transactional process.

The person who is self-protective, readily influenced, yet not concerned about the rights of others (lower right quadrant of Figure 9.3) may behave with passive aggression. The passive-aggressive style, too, is hostile/divisive. This person uses indirect strategies to block progress or hurt someone without being caught. She or he may tease or joke with the intent to cause pain or may disregard and disconfirm others to put them in their place. Passive aggressiveness cloaks the anger in someone who feels controlled by others, resents it, and seeks to protect himself or herself but still "get" those others.

Individuals are not always the same in their responses. People are continually developing, changing, and responding—often within a single meeting. Many American businesspeople learned the hard way, for example, that it was a serious mistake to push their Japanese counterparts for an affirmative or negative answer before the Japanese folks were ready. What the Americans considered assertive, direct, powerful communication was rude, ill timed, and destructive to the Japanese sense of harmony and face. When pushed that hard, the Japanese tended to say "No" to a deal when the Americans wanted "Yes."

RESPONSIBLE LANGUAGE

All would be easier if everyone simply acknowledged their own responsibility for feelings and ideas. Suppose, for example, Sam is to bring background research on the team's topic and Harold is to get applied examples of the theory. Then, at the meeting, Sam brings excellent material—and Harold mutters aggressively, "Well, Sam-I-Am, you got the green eggs and ham and there was nothing left for me in the library. You always do this, and I'm sick of this garbage!" Harold might feel better for a moment, but you can bet Sam won't—and neither will the rest of the team.

Harold would do better with responsible language, language that owns his feelings and avoids casting blame. For example, Satir (1999) suggests using "I" to own your own feelings rather than using "you" to imply someone else caused them. Satir also suggests avoiding absolute terms such as *always* and *never*. Harold could have been more responsible by simply saying, "I'm frustrated because I couldn't find anything in the library."

Responsible language also allows room for others' ideas as well as for opinion change. You will certainly find that the use of responsible language keeps the lines of communication open. When someone appears to be quite certain about their position, others are less willing to question and challenge them. On the other hand, if they use language to show that they are actively seeking feedback and input, others are more willing to share their ideas. Qualify your statements, and recognize other points of view to keep the climate open and supportive. In our example, Sam might improve a defensive situation with a provisional comment such as "I think I was just trying to get everything the team might need." He might *want* to say, "You just waited until the last minute, Harold. Isn't that right?" Even if Sam is sure that's exactly what Harold did, he'll escalate the defensiveness and turn the meeting into a battleground if he responds with such certainty and blame.

Of course, certainty is not always negative; it depends on how it's stated, the context, and your own expertise. Researchers recently have found that people tend to see speakers as more credible when their style fits the listeners' expectations of them, and this includes the certainty or provisionalism that the speakers use. The more expert you are, the more certainty your listeners expect from you. The less expert, the more provisional they expect you to be (Smith, Hosman & Siltanen, 1998).

In general, saying "I believe" or "probably" communicates clearly, yet leaves room for people to disagree. "Always," "never," and "impossible!" cut off negotiation of ideas. Even when you have the expertise, providing support for your ideas helps to establish your credibility.

CONFIRMATION

If you're like us, you feel confirmed when someone really listens to you and responds by acknowledging your ideas and feelings. This is called a *person-centered message*, and yes, it does *confirm* a person's worth and role in the transactional process. Furthermore, someone who uses person-centered messages is seen as more persuasive (Waldron & Applegate, 1998).

But when there is no response at all, or when others outright *disconfirm* you by indicating that your comment was wrong, stupid, or insignificant, you probably feel damaged. There's a big difference between being confirmed and being rejected or disconfirmed:

- A *confirming* response indicates understanding. It may take the form of an acknowledgment ("That's a good idea"), support ("You've earned it"), clarification ("Do you mean . . . ?"), or praise ("You said that well").
- A *rejecting* response is outright dismissal. The listener may walk away without a word or interrupt you in midsentence. Sometimes you get a pseudoconfirmation ("That's great, now let's eat") or an irrelevant statement.
- A *disconfirming* response may be impersonal ("That's not my problem"), incoherent ("It's, like, you know, that's . . . well"), or incongruous, with words that say one thing and tone or actions that say another.

It's easier to be assertive and productive—to contribute to the team—when you're confirmed. Also, remember that people become defensive not only when they feel manipulated or attacked but when others seem neutral or indifferent to them. Confirming a teammate helps that person to participate fully and helps the team to develop a supportive climate.

APPROPRIATENESS

Appropriate is an overused term these days, but it's probably the only one that will do here. We're talking about using language that fits the team members, yourself, and the team context. If your words open up discussion and understanding, they're appropriate. If they close off communication or cause others to think and worry about what may be behind them, then they are not appropriate.

Choosing appropriate language depends on your sensitivity to people and your wisdom about your goals. The choice requires both heart and mind: the mind contributes the analysis, and the heart contributes the response. Appropriateness considers your listeners' level of knowledge, background, and feelings.

Appropriateness to Teammates Consider your listeners' knowledge level, and try to be clear and concrete. Satir (1999) advises avoiding indefinite pronouns such as *they* or *it*. You know how people say, "They've really done it now," or "It's a problem." Who has? What is? Be as unambiguous as you can, and if you must use terms that might be unfamiliar to your teammates give definitions.

Sometimes people forget about other people's backgrounds and feelings, and this is a sure way to set up defenses. Appropriate language is inclusive and respectful. For example, using only masculine pronouns (*he, him, his*) tends to exclude females, so why do that? Why not say "he or she" or use specific examples of one gender or the other?

Worst of all, an insensitive communicator might use cursing or *derogatory ethnic labels (DELs)* that offend teammates. A DEL attributes a set of negative characteristics to a person and his or her group, showing prejudices based on race, color, gender, sexual orientation, age, and abilities. Many people routinely (and inappropriately) use these labels as jokes, but regardless of their intention, DELs are aggressive. They hurt people and make the user look like an insensitive fool.

Appropriateness to Yourself Your language also should be appropriate to yourself. Your talk reflects your self-image, and adapting it may involve difficult choices. Once in a while, a student asks, "But isn't adapting the same thing as hypocrisy?" We believe that hypocrisy would be lying or distorting what you believe, how you feel, or who you are. Adapting, in our view, is communicating who you are and what you think in ways that allow others to receive your message.

Many excellent communicators use **code switching**: changing style to communicate more effectively with someone who may not be used to the way they normally speak. An example: You're a highly educated member of a team. A less educated member makes snide remarks about people from "ivory towers." You're proud of your education. If you say, "Ah, education means nothing. I wasted a lot of years," that's hypocritical. You don't mean it. If instead you avoid talking down and look for things you have in common with this teammate, that's an honest—and probably effective—way to break down barriers and open up communication. Answer the questions in Case Study 9.1 about using "language" effectively.

Appropriateness to the Context As you consider language choices, you need to be aware of the context in which your team is working. You could think of context in any number of ways. For example, the amount of slang or even obscenity

| **CASE STUDY 9.1** | **THE NATURAL REMEDIES COMPANY: WHEN "FAMILY" GETS TOO CLOSE FOR COMFORT** |

The Natural Remedies Company (not its real name) had 300 employees, was founded by a charismatic leader, and was strongly values driven. . . . At the time of the consulting work, revenues were about $65 million.

This organization had a strong value of "family," and employees often proclaimed, "We are the Natural Remedies Company 'family.'" This was interpreted quite literally—they hired family members, treated their staff very well, had a gym with full-time employees and a spacious cafeteria with natural foods, gave people a bottle of champagne on their birthdays and anniversary dates with company, etc. . . .

However, there was a different interpretation of this "family" value from department to department when it came to one issue: how to deal with nonperformers. Some departments didn't deal with nonperformers too much; after all, you don't fire family members. In others, they got rid of nonperformers if it was clear they weren't working out.

This inconsistency became a problem. . . . Employees resented the differences from unit to unit. . . . Competition started to heat up and . . . sales flattened. . . . The "family" value was starting to be a problem because they couldn't afford nonperformers anymore. . . .

[The new] CEO was mindful that to make a cultural change dealing with the entrenched value of "family" required bringing the workforce along, rather than simply imposing new policies. So . . . everyone in the organization met in focus groups [with the consultant] to talk about this issue (as well as a few others). The supposition was that many people in the workforce would cling to the traditional interpretation of family and resist change.

But here's what the discussions revealed: First, at least half the workforce didn't even like the notion of "family" at their workplace . . . [they] found it condescending and paternalistic. Second, 95 percent . . . believed nonperformers . . . should be treated fairly . . . but not allowed to remain. Third . . . people had been somewhat self-conscious about voicing these opinions . . . with anonymous upward feedback to

management, they could admit that they didn't feel comfortable with the family orientation anymore.

What they preferred was to adapt the family value . . . recasting it as "teamwork," "respect," and "support." . . . The company could retain the positive aspects . . . but insist upon high performance standards as well. And . . . they suggested a clear policy, rigorously followed by all departments . . . of a process in the event someone was not performing.

The result has been that the organization has put this ambivalence behind them. . . . The adaptation of values has led to a clarification of the meaning of the underlying belief in "family." And adherence to the result is more wholehearted because the process was broadly consultative across the workforce.

Questions to Consider for this Case

1. In what ways do you think the language associated with "family" helped to create and maintain this organization's culture? How did that language and culture affect the company's and employees' responses to change?

2. The employees' focus groups chose to replace the idea of "family" with the terms *teamwork, respect*, and *support*. To what extent do you think this change in language represented a real change in the culture of the organization and in the workplace of the employees? In particular, with 300 employees, how do you think the concept of "teamwork" would actually be practiced?

3. What was it about the process the consulting company used that helped employees to create a situation with which they felt more comfortable?

The Natural Remedies Company: When "Family" Gets Too Close for Comfort, Holly English, consultant and author. Copyright 2000. Values At Work, http://www.valuesethics. com/success.htm, retrieved January 30, 2003.

accepted in a team's locker room is very different from the language appropriate to a business team's boardroom. Here, however, we're talking about two types of context: The degree of pressure your team is under to complete a task and the medium you're using for communication—the open channel of face to face or the limited one of virtual reality.

High-Pressure versus Low-Pressure Tasks   Compare two corporate teams. Team A, a management team, is under the gun to produce a budget within a brief time period. Therefore, members need to keep their language task-oriented, highly focused, and very specific. Team B, however, is charged with exploring a wide range of alternatives for developing a supportive organizational culture. Its task requires creativity and imagination and language that is exploratory, feeling-oriented, and metaphorical.

Developing dialogue requires using language that enables people to interact freely, without unnecessary barriers to communication. If you and your teammates use language well, you should be able to say the following of your processes:

- We support and confirm one another so that everyone speaks and is heard.
- We respect one another's differences and adapt our communication to open up discussion.
- We take care to express our ideas responsibly and appropriately.
- We consider and refine our thinking with careful negotiation and definition of terms.

Face-to-Face versus Electronic Meetings   Much of what we have said about dialogue seems impossible to achieve with online communication, despite the fact that people now use e-mail for everything from shopping to meeting people to developing romances to conducting business. How can a virtual team become a superteam—or can it?

It seems that virtual teams can become superteams—with effort. Research has demonstrated that "virtual team members can exchange verbal information as efficiently as . . . face-to-face team members, however, their ability for nonverbal exchange is severely limited, which can contribute to increased misunderstanding" (Horvath & Tobin, 1999, p. 10).

A virtual team must cope with lack of physical cues, lack of a shared environment, and timelags of response in an asynchronous system. That means your team may:

Have to work to establish trust in one another's competence and good will. These conditions are essential in traditional and in virtual teams, but it's harder to do online than in person. Specific meetings—online, on the phone, or in person—need to focus on getting to know one another and establishing mutual respect and trust.

Need more time for some team processes. Decision making and short-term conflict management take longer for a virtual team, although long-term conflict management requires about the same amount of time (Horvath & Tobin, 1999, p. 26). Making a decision will take more messages and more time to work through the levels of analysis. To negotiate your way through a conflict without the help of nonverbal cues will require messaging that deals with both task and transactional processes, coping both with feelings and with issues.

Lose some clarity in leadership and coordination of team tasks. Traditional teams have much more opportunity to develop leadership as well as their working norms and expectations. Virtual teams lack the conditions for these developments, and so must consciously focus on creating its working relationships and guidelines (Horvath & Tobin, 1999, p. 26).

We have mentioned before one piece of advice that is given repeatedly (Creelman, 2001; Gaspar, 2001; Katzenbach & Smith, 2001). That is to meet face to face, at least at the beginning and, if possible, occasionally during the life of the team. If that isn't possible, then it helps to use telephone or videoconferencing to broaden members' perceptions of one another and ability to collaborate more fully when they are online.

Katzenbach and Smith (2001) have found that, in addition to using opportunities for face-to-face meetings, successful virtual teams do the following:

- Decide whether to have a single leader or shared leadership according to what the task requires
- Match member skills and perspectives to the tasks at hand
- Deliberately change leadership roles as needed
- Choose groupware and practice it together
- Agree on its own netiquette

The agreement on "netiquette" is essential to a team's communication. Your team needs to be together, for example, on the appropriate degree of informality or formality in messages, and members need to be particularly sensitive to the tone of their messages. What one person deems funny may be offensive to another, and what one may think is honest indignation may be seen as "flaming," with obscenity and insult.

Using a few guidelines for messaging can avoid a lot of misunderstandings and expedite your work. DeTienne (2002) offers these techniques:

Subject line: Compose a clear, specific, informative subject line.

Messages: Write audience-focused, short, concise, well-organized messages.

Typography: Don't use ALL CAPITAL letters, since this is considered rude.

Polite messages: Don't send rude or impolite messages or make personal attacks (a.k.a. flaming).

References: When responding to a previous message, refer to that message specifically.

Proofread: Review your messages before sending them; you can lose credibility and look stupid when you make spelling and grammatical mistakes; check for appropriate tone as well. (p. 47)

To save time and convey ideas about how you feel about something, your team may use "neticisms" (commonly used shorthand phrases, acronyms, or symbols on the Net), or you may work out your own shorthand for ideas. You need to be certain everyone knows the meaning of team neticisms or they'll be of no help at all. If you're going to introduce a new one, it would be a good idea to define it.

COMMUNICATING NONVERBALLY

Even silence is filled with nonverbal cues. When a team member speaks, the statement is surrounded by nonverbal hints about what those words mean—hints that are particularly important in teamwork.

How Nonverbal Cues Work

Nonverbal communication occurs when people interpret meaning from cues that accompany language or that are separate from language. People often are unaware of the nonverbal cues from their eyes, bodies, faces, and voices—even from how they use time or touch or protect their territories. Because nonverbal communication is so complex, it can be tough to interpret even one person's cues. These problems steadily increase as the team increases in size, because:

Nonverbal cues outnumber verbal cues. Every single word may come with dozens of subtle nonverbal cues. And in groups, even when only one person is speaking, everyone else is sending nonverbal cues at the same time.

Nonverbal cues may confirm or contradict a verbal message. If you say "I agree" with a warm smile and an open posture, the message is confirmed. If you say "I agree" but frown and turn away, your actions contradict your words. When this happens, people believe the nonverbal.

Nonverbal cues are not easy to decode. Even "experts" are wrong in their interpretations of nonverbal cues as often as they are right (Peterson, 2005). Even though approximately 55 percent of interpersonal messages are conveyed nonverbally (Lavan, 2002), even people who have been formally trained in detecting nonverbal clues are wrong about as often as they are right (Sundaram & Webster, 2000).

Building relationships and communication patterns in a team is something like creating a three-tiered, multidirectional system of freeways. Each road is interconnected (in some way) with the others. The interchange system and structures then affect the way the entire entity functions. If the pieces are connected properly, strength is distributed appropriately, and traffic flow is regulated effectively, the system works. A team's relational processes and traffic patterns often are regulated by nonverbal cues that establish role relationships, dominance, appropriate levels of intimacy, and emotional tone as well as timing and synchronizing communication (Mignault & Chaudhuri, 2003).

Knowing how to use and how to decode nonverbal communication can greatly enhance your effectiveness, so let's examine nonverbal ways that you can facilitate your teammates' contributions and help them understand you when you speak.

Decoding Nonverbal Messages More Accurately

No one can always interpret nonverbal cues correctly, but to increase your accuracy become a people-watcher—in your team, in your family, in your classes, on the subway. The more you watch and listen, the more sensitive you become to nonverbal cues.

Suppose, for example, your teammate widens her eyes. How do you interpret that? It depends. If she's a North American Anglo, it might mean surprise. A Chinese person might be angry; a French person, disbelieving; a Hispanic, confused; an African American, feeling innocent or intending to persuade. Or any of these people might have an entirely different meaning behind the widened eyes, depending on many influences.

So, how can do you know for sure? First, formulate hypotheses carefully; then wait and watch. (She looks closed, tight; her forehead is wrinkled; she isn't smiling. Maybe she's tense about this assignment. Maybe she's angry at someone. Wait and see.)

Second, observe people over time. One nonverbal cue won't tell you much; patterns give you a sense of how an individual uses nonverbal cues. Furthermore, nonverbal behaviors change as the team builds itself. Your teammates' postures, for instance, might indicate how they feel, but postures and hand positions of group members change over time, apparently indicating how members come to feel about the group and one another (Van Swol, 2003).

Third, look for consistency among an individual's cues and between nonverbal and verbal messages. If nonverbal cues contradict either one another or the verbal message, consider what that contradiction might mean. (She says she likes the idea, but she's frowning and tapping her fingers. Does she really not like it, or does something else concern her?)

Fourth, be aware of multiple causes. A person's nonverbal behavior may reflect many influences, including something completely unrelated to the team that might be on her mind. (She raised her voice, and she sounds shaky. Is she upset about something?)

P. Broze/ONOKY/Getty Images

What nonverbal message is being communicated by this woman, and what cues suggest what she is feeling?

Fifth, observe interactions. What kinds of transactions might have triggered an individual's nonverbal behavior? (He talked a long time, and she pushed her chair back, turned away, and stopped contributing. Is she withdrawing because he's dominating the discussion?)

Finally—ask for clarification if the verbal and nonverbal cues are contradictory or if you're puzzled by a nonverbal response. ("You say you're okay with this decision, but I hear something unhappy in your voice. Is something bothering you about it?")

BUILDING LEADERSHIP ABILITIES IN NONVERBAL COMMUNICATION

The way people see you—your competence, trustworthiness, friendliness, and coorientation with them—relates directly to your nonverbal communication (Kristof-Brown, Barrick & Franke, 2002). This means that being a skilled nonverbal communicator helps you to provide leadership, both through facilitating others' participation and through participating yourself.

FACILITATING TEAMMATES' CONTRIBUTIONS

Frequently, the best way to help your team is to facilitate the participation of other members. One way to do this is through nonverbal support or intervention.

Facilitating Turn-Taking   Sometimes less assertive members need help in getting their turn to speak. If you are sensitive to the transactional process, you will know when to use nonverbal regulators to help another person get a turn.

Your responsiveness is the foundation for regulating turn-taking. You show teammates your responsiveness by maintaining eye contact and by using posture that makes others comfortable, by adapting your position to theirs, turning toward the speaker, leaning forward.

Suppose Ian is dominating the talk and Irena has tried—unsuccessfully—to speak. Here's what you do. Break eye contact with Ian, and look at Irena. Then look back at Ian, and when he takes a breath, raise your hand in front of you. Nod toward Irena, and gesture for her to speak. You also might add a verbal message such as "Irena has something to say." You also can encourage her to talk by nodding, smiling, looking agreeable, giving a thumbs-up sign, and saying "um-hum, yeah, hmm" as she speaks.

Making Space   Another way to make your teammates comfortable is to watch for cues that they feel crowded. If they move away, turn their shoulders away, or scrunch up, you might suggest the members spread out a bit. Each person lives inside a psychological "bubble" of personal space, and when someone intrudes on that bubble, the individual begins to feel defensive and self-protective. The amount of space a specific individual needs depends on a number of things, including culture, gender, background, the activity, the relationship, and the homogeneity or heterogeneity of race or culture within a given group (Dolphin, 1988, p. 32). You might move close to someone you know or to someone who seems similar to you but be uncomfortable in close quarters with a stranger.

Equalizing Influence   With all these suggestions, be especially aware of nonverbal dominance that makes people uncomfortable or defensive. Sometimes such behavior is unintentional—it may be natural to someone who has always had power and privilege—but it often inhibits others' participation.

Women often accommodate nonverbally by adjusting posture to those of others, giving them more space, smiling more often, and speaking more gently (Wood, 2001, pp. 139–143). Women are thought to be more responsive than men. Guerrero (1997) observed, however, that men and women show responsiveness in different ways. Women maintain more eye contact and face the other person more directly, but men lean forward and imitate the other's body posture.

Male nonverbal behavior tends to be more dominant than female behavior; a man often takes more space, speaks louder, withholds "um-hums" that might encourage others to speak, uses less eye contact (except to return a stare), touches others more for power than for affiliation, and defends his territory when it seems challenged (Wood, 2001, pp. 139–143).

Nonverbal dominance moves also can trigger power struggles in the group. Such moves range from staring, crowding, leaning, and interrupting people to drowning them out with a loud voice, overwhelming them with big gestures, or touching them in dominating ways. In a multicultural setting, moves like these can be misinterpreted readily; see Box 9.1.

Similarly, teammates may find it easier to participate when all are seated at the same level. People who are seated may hesitate to speak up if someone is standing over them because an individual's elevation indicates dominance more than any other factor (Jones & LeBaron, 2002). We have observed some powerful people who, knowing this, deliberately take a low chair in a group to free others from that feeling of domination. Or, you may suggest a seating arrangement that creates a more level field for communication.

If you observe someone else dominating others, you can help to ease the strain. Suppose, for example, that Angela interrupts, stands over people, uses heavy gestures that dominate others, and touches others much too freely. You also notice

---

| **BOX 9.1** | **CROSS-CULTURAL NONVERBAL COMMUNICATION** |

Don Burleson, of Burleson Consulting, offers the following tips for facilitating multicultural teammates' contributions:

Dress and customs are very different in different parts of the world. For example, in Caribbean and Latin American countries, you show respect for a person by avoiding direct eye contact.

- **Bowing**—shows rank and status in Japan
- **Slouching**—is considered rude in most Northern European areas

- **Hands in pocket**—is disrespectful in Turkey
- **Sitting with legs crossed**—is offensive in Ghana and Turkey
- **Showing soles of feet**—is offensive in Thailand, Saudi Arabia, and Muslim nations
- **Touching**—many Asians don't touch the head, which houses the soul; a touch puts it in jeopardy

Source: Burleson Consulting website

that Carl becomes progressively quieter and shrinks away from her. What can you do?

1. You might position yourself next to Carl, find opportunities to listen to him, and find out what he'd like to say. You might ask Angela to let Carl get a word in, or you might interrupt her yourself, if necessary, and ask Carl to speak to his point. Angela may or may not take the hint, but at least you can open up the transactional process a bit.

2. You might have to speak to Angela—but do it privately, in the context of your mutual concern for the team's processes. (Saving face is important, to greater or lesser degrees, in every culture.) To keep Angela from feeling defensive, however, use all the supportive, positive, and descriptive language discussed previously.

Touching   To touch or not to touch, that is the question. Touching fills a human need. It expresses liking and affection (Collier, 1985); warmth, reassurance, and comfort (Marx, Werner & Cohen-Mansfield, 1989); support, affiliation, and power (Leathers, 1992, p. 119). Unfortunately, touch can be used to dominate. In Western cultures, the individual with the highest status and the greatest power is allowed to touch those of lower status and power, and this person also is most likely to be the one who actually touches others (Major, 1980). It isn't fair, but it's true.

Jones (1994) says, "The right touch suggests the special sensitivities to the moment that distinguish the exceptional communicator from the merely competent one" (p. 2). People working on teams must be sensitive to how much—and to what kind of—touching they do. It's important to recognize how volatile the issue of touch can be. You may touch someone's shoulder to give support, but that touch could be interpreted as domination, intimidation, disrespect—or even as sexual intent. Sexual harassment is a real issue in the workplace today. If a person believes that someone's touch is sexual in its intent, she or he has a right to complain and, perhaps, to charge sexual harassment.

Teams develop norms for touching, of course. One team expresses support with hugging and patting; another may touch no more than to shake hands. Just don't push it. A good rule of thumb is to be sure the touch is appropriate to the context. Give priority to what the other person is comfortable with, and be supportive, not exploitative. If you're in doubt on any of these issues, don't touch.

GETTING TEAMMATES TO LISTEN TO YOU

Suppose you have an idea you're really excited about, but you're also worried about an upcoming exam. If, as you explain the idea, you focus on it and the excitement you feel, your face, your body, and your voice will show your positive feelings. Your teammates will pick up on this feeling and will listen to your suggestion. If, as you explain your idea, you are distracted by your anxiety, your teammates will see a tense, anxious body. They will wonder: Are you really convinced this is a great proposal, or are you nervous and anxious about it? They will believe the nonverbal cues—even though those cues relate to an entirely different issue.

Your message needs the full support of your face, body, voice, and speech to make you interesting and believable when you speak.

Face   Your face tells people what you feel, and your body tells them how intense that feeling is. If your feelings are mixed, your cues will be, too; your face may be difficult to decode. It also can be difficult to control.

Gueguen and Jacob (2002) found in their research that there is a significant amount of agreement across cultures with regard to the meaning of individuals' facial expressions. People everywhere seem to understand such emotional expressions as happiness, surprise, fear, anger, sadness, disgust, contempt, interest, bewilderment, and determination. It's also true, however, that your upbringing and culture may allow you to express your emotions easily, whereas another person may have learned not to show feelings openly. The most important thing is to know what you want to express and to involve your entire being—face and body—in expressing it.

Gestures   Obviously, gestures can reinforce your words. Two kinds of gestures especially help to keep interest and reinforce your words:

- **Emblems** are specific gestures that are widely used and understood within a culture. Emblems can enliven, clarify, and substitute for words. In fact, emblems compose much of American Sign Language, used by people who are hearing impaired. Coaches, pitchers, and catchers in a baseball game use emblems to signify a play; irate motorists use a middle finger to signal *their* feelings. But be careful that your entire team understands the emblems you use. In the United States, for example, a palms-out gesture means "Stop," but in Greece, it's an insult. In the United States, a raised hand, palm turned toward the sender and fingers wagging, means "Come here," but in Italy, it means "Good-bye."
- **Illustrators** are mostly spontaneous ways to make a point clear and vivid by showing what you mean. You're describing teamwork, for example, and you say, "It's interdependent, interwoven, cooperative." As you say this, you weave your fingers together to help the team visualize the concept.

Voice and Speech   Nonverbal messages are created with more than just your body and your face. Your voice and the way you speak are critical to how well teammates understand you and how highly they regard your credibility (O'Sullivan et al., 1985). Speaking with vocal variety—in your inflection, rate of speech, pitch, and volume—and with clear articulation helps your teammates to listen to and understand you. Sometimes your voice and speech clarity are the only nonverbal help your listeners get from you. In teleconferences, for example, or even in settings where visibility is difficult, teammates receive little or no nonverbal information other than what comes across from your voice and speech. Even in the best setting, the expressiveness of your voice and the clarity of your speech facilitate the understanding of teammates who are visually impaired or are just learning your language.

IMPROVING YOUR NONVERBAL COMMUNICATION

Communicating nonverbal messages that support your verbal message demands self-monitoring and adapting to your listeners and your situation. You can develop stronger nonverbal communication skill through the following steps:

Ask friends and family. Have people observe you and give you feedback about your nonverbal communication. Ask about your habits, what you do, how consistent you are, and how well your nonverbal cues support your verbal messages.

Use videotaping. There's no substitute for observing yourself. Look for what you do well. Note where your nonverbal messages are clear and consistent, and listen to your voice when it provides effective emphasis and tonal qualities. Watch your listening behavior; see if you communicate interest and provide feedback for the speaker. Look for inconsistencies, contradictions, and bad habits as both a speaker and a listener.

Watch others' responses. Look for positive, negative, and comprehending responses from others. Ask how they perceived your message.

Decide what to change. Identify specific things you want to do differently. Ask yourself what you should be doing, and then practice the new behaviors.

Visualize yourself using excellent nonverbal communication. You might want to review the technique of visualization described in Chapter 2. When you visualize yourself the way you want to be, you actually start using the relevant physical mechanisms correctly (Garfield, 1984).

Use relaxation techniques before you enter a communication situation in which you will practice your nonverbal skills. Again, remember from Chapter 2 that when you relax—through deep breathing and/or muscle exercises—you develop more confidence and effectiveness in your communication.

Practice what you want to do well. Concentrate on one skill at a time (eye contact, perhaps, or vocal variety), and practice it in various contexts. After a while, this skill becomes automatic, and you can move on to another one.

SUMMARY

The more diverse a team is, the more differences teammates will need to negotiate through transactional processes. This requires working through dialectical tensions to dialogue among a variety of people whose communication styles may derive from their cultural, gender, and social background. People may stereotype themselves or others based on expectations of their power in any situation as well as on their socialization in gender and cultural styles.

We suggest that productive communication styles may vary along a continuum, ranging from a facilitative/equal style to a commanding/authoritative style. Unproductive styles may range from passive-aggressive to hostile/divisive. Although it has been labeled feminine or powerless in the past, the facilitative/equal style actually is neither. It uses verbal and nonverbal messages that develop transactional processes among teammates. The commanding/authoritative style, similar to styles previously labeled masculine or powerful, uses direct verbal and nonverbal messages that focus more on task than on transactional processes. The hostile/divisive style is centered on the individual rather than on the team, and it uses aggressiveness—or passive aggressiveness—to disrupt transactional and task processes.

At any point along the continuum from facilitative/equal to commanding/authoritative styles, productive communication is rhetorically sensitive as it uses assertive, responsible, confirming, and appropriate language. All of these language skills must be used in virtual teams, and teammates can share information effectively, but communication in a virtual team requires some special skills and efforts to offset the lack of non-verbal communication and shared time and place. An initial face-to-face, telephone, or teleconference meeting helps people develop trust and establish working norms.

In traditional teams, people must be sensitive to the difficulty of interpreting non-verbal cues, the bombardment of nonverbal cues to which team members constantly are exposed, and individual as well as cultural differences in how non-verbal cues are used and interpreted. Sensitive, able, and credible communicators develop abilities to convey consistent and credible nonverbal messages, to facilitate their teams, and to interpret their teammates' nonverbal communication tentatively and perceptively.

Exercises

1. Assess your assertiveness. Consider your experiences in groups and teams—including your family, friends, and other groups—and then answer the questions on Form 9.1. Which of your ways of dealing with things are assertive? Which are not? What would you like to change? And what can you do about it?

2. With a small group, do the following:
   a. Divide into two sets of observers: half of your group will observe verbal communication, and half will observe nonverbal communication.
   b. Have the verbal subgroup create a list of concepts that are important to effective verbal communication in a team.
   c. Have the nonverbal subgroup create a list of concepts that are important to effective nonverbal communication in a team.
   d. Report your lists to your entire group, and discuss how you could use each list to observe and evaluate a group discussion. Refine the lists, and make sure each member has a copy.

3. With your group from Exercise 2, select a group discussion program on TV. (CNN, ESPN, and PBS show several of these.) Have half of your team observe and evaluate the discussion using the list of verbal communication concepts, and have the other half observe and evaluate the discussion using the list of non-verbal communication concepts. Afterward, convene as a full group, and have each subgroup report what they saw in the discussion participants' communication.

   Now try to bring the two sets of observation together and analyze these questions:
   a. What styles of communication did the participants use?
   b. How did their nonverbal communication and verbal communication interact?
   c. What kind of climate did the participants develop?
   d. How did their communication affect the outcomes of their discussion?
   Report your findings to the class.

4. Think about your own nonverbal behavior and responses to nonverbal cues in a group. How and to what extent do you think you use nonverbal cues to protect your territory or express liking, responsiveness, or status? In your teammates' nonverbal behavior, what makes you comfortable, what makes you uncomfortable, and how do you respond?

5. Set up a group of three or four people to compare online communication to

face-to-face communication. You don't even need a chat room; just exchange e-mail addresses. Here's what to do:

a. Assume you are a virtual team and your task is to decide one of the following:

- What your team should recommend to the university administration to improve food services for students
- What your team should recommend to your student activities office to involve more students in charitable activities
- What your team should recommend to your campus security office to improve nighttime security on campus

b. *Do not* discuss the topic, even face to face. Do nothing but exchange addresses in person. Using e-mail, decide which topic you will choose, analyze it on the basis of what you know about it, and draft a recommendation.

c. *Meet face to face* to discuss the recommendation and the experience. Consider:

- What worked well in using the e-mail messages?
- What were the problems in using the e-mail messages?
- What happened when you met face to face? In what ways did the experience change?
- What steps at the beginning or during the experience would have facilitated the clarity and collaboration of the process?

d. Report the experience to the class, providing specific examples and tracking how the e-mail worked versus the face-to-face communication, and suggesting ways that would have improved the process.

FORM 9.1 | ASSERTIVENESS ASSESSMENT

When you're working with a group of people, how assertive are you? Think about the following questions:

1. If I think my rights are in conflict with others' rights, do I:
   a. Worry a lot about what they might do if I confront them?
   b. Worry more about how they will feel than how I feel?
   c. Feel too much empathy with their positions to argue?
   d. Feel empathy with their positions, yet know I have a right to my own?

2. If somebody does something that makes me angry, do I:
   a. Keep it to myself?
   b. Describe the problem without attacking the person?
   c. Keep quiet but look for a way to "get back"?
   d. Attack the other person verbally?
   e. Attack the other person physically?

3. If I want something to happen, do I:
   a. Express my preferences but allow others to have theirs, too?
   b. Look for ways to get others to do what I want without having to ask?
   c. Keep quiet, go along with others, and figure it doesn't matter?
   d. Keep quiet, go along with others, and seethe?
   e. Seethe quietly until I blow up?

4. If I must confront a difference or issue, do I:
   a. Use language that blames or manipulates others?
   b. Use language that puts the blame on myself?
   c. Use language that is direct, responsible, and problem-focused?

If you can feel empathy with others' positions and still know you have a right to your own, if you can describe the problem without attacking the person, and if you can express your preferences but allow others to have theirs, then you're on your way to being assertive. If you also can confront issues with language that is direct, responsible, and problem-focused, you are assertive.

"Yes, of course I heard you....
What'd you say?"
Teamwork really goes awry when everyone talks and nobody listens
and questions.

LISTENING AND QUESTIONING

Developing Team Dialogue

10

A meeting that's all talking and no listening can give you a headache. Reflect on this college program committee's deliberations. The members are considering whether to allow a radical group to argue its position on campus.

BRENDA:	I just don't think those people should be allowed on this campus!
NADIA:	Oh, there you go again, Brenda. Just because you hate....
MARCUS:	How about freedom of speech?
DEIRDRE:	Did you hear about that guy in the student center?
BRIAN:	Yeah. He really went nuts....
JACOB:	Right, Marcus. We've got to let them debate, because....
BRENDA:	Why? They're stupid and people would just come to watch....
DEIRDRE:	I guess he was mad because he didn't get to....
BRENDA:	Anyway! They'd just come to watch them be stupid, not to learn anything, and besides, why should groups like that be given attention?
LARRY:	What? Have we started? I'm sorry, I was reading....
NADIA:	Well, Brenda, if you feel that way, maybe you should go live in China!
BRENDA:	That's not fair! I'm just saying....
JACOB:	Hey, if Brenda feels that strongly about it....
MARCUS:	How about freedom of speech? Can we deny them access?
LARRY:	What did she say?
JACOB:	Oh, shut up, Marcus. Brenda's got a point....

What's happening here? Is anybody really listening? Poor Marcus can't get people to think about his issue—no cooperative analysis is going on—nobody's dealing with Deirdre's side trip (it might relate to the issue, who would know?). John's more interested in soothing Brenda than in resolving the problem; Nadia's more interested in making personal attacks on Brenda. We don't know what Brian's interested in, and Larry's just lost. Certainly, this committee isn't functioning well.

These people obviously need help. They are not building a positive communication climate, and far from being dialogue, their talk involves neither listening nor questioning—both of which are extraordinarily important aspects of a team's verbal and nonverbal communication. In this chapter, we explore how listening and questioning contribute to dialogue and a positive communication climate. To provide a foundation, we first identify team norms for good listening and questioning as well as barriers that can be eliminated. The heart of this chapter offers guidelines for active, interactive, empathic, and dialogic approaches to listening and questioning. Through listening and questioning—and listening and questioning some more—members engage in the cooperative analysis and argument that produce clear, valid decisions. We then finish with a view of how your leadership can guide a team to use these interactions effectively. Our goals in this chapter are for you to:

1. Understand how listening and questioning are essential to a team's dialogue, climate, cooperative analysis, and success
2. Know how to build foundations for good listening and questioning

3. Understand how to use active, interactive, empathic, and dialogic listening and questioning

4. Know how your leadership can facilitate listening and questioning transactions in your team

LISTENING AND QUESTIONING IN TEAMS

Remember the old philosophical question, "If a tree falls in the forest and no one is there to hear it, is there a noise?" A similar question applies to communication: If you speak and no one is listening, is there communication?

Active listening, as the online *BNET Business Directory* (2008) defines it, is "a technique for improving understanding of what is being said by taking into account how something is said and the nonverbal signs and body language that accompany it. This technique requires receptive awareness and response on the part of the listener." Verbal communication and nonverbal cues convey messages; listening and questioning provide the ongoing feedback necessary to negotiate what people mean. The key for effective listening lies in the fact that most speakers talk at about 150 words per minute, but listeners can process almost 400 words per minute (Feuerman, 2008). This leaves listeners with time on their hands, and how they use that time is the key to effective listening. Most of the time, "we listen at only 25 percent efficiency. That means we ignore, forget, or confuse 75 percent of what we hear" (Smith & Piele, 2006, p. 345).

CREATING DIALOGUE

Dialogue means more than simply taking turns when speaking. In a dialogue, people transact ideas as they develop meanings and insights together. Dialogue involves sharing ideas, listening, paraphrasing, questioning, adding, and changing until common meaning emerges. Sometimes people think of dialogue as involving only two people. Certainly it's easier to develop the give-and-take of authentic, open communication in private exchanges between two people. However, as you no doubt recognize, dialogue can occur on a number of levels and with a number of people simultaneously. In today's digital world, it is not uncommon for people to have dialogues with many people at once, using cell phones, instant messaging, and e-mail simultaneously.

We talk so much about dialogue, dialogic ethics, and—in this chapter—dialogic listening because these are the foundations of good team decisions. As a plaque in Lyndon Johnson's office put it, "You ain't learning nothing when you are talking" (Boyd, 2004).

This philosophy underlies everything in this chapter. Later, we'll talk about approaches to listening and questioning, including suggestions for dialogic listening. First, however, let's examine how listening and questioning influence a team's communication climate.

CREATING CLIMATES

In Chapter 9, we discussed some of the ways verbal and nonverbal communication develop supportive or defensive climates. Equally—perhaps even more—important are listening and questioning. Supportive climates occur, in part, because people listen and question in ways that develop trust and commit members to finding shared meanings. The way questions are phrased, for example, may challenge or confirm a respondent's self-worth (Eales-White, 2004).

When you know your teammates really listen to you, when they ask you questions supportively—questions that enable you to make yourself understood and to think clearly—you feel you can trust them. This trust reduces the amount of risk you must take to communicate and encourages you to share what you know openly. When others listen and ask questions that indicate your ideas are worth thinking about, they confirm you as a person. Maybe Carl Rogers (1999) speaks for all of us when he says that when somebody really listens to him, "it feels damn good" (p. 568).

Effective listening and questioning develop a climate in which people are committed to developing shared meanings. When you listen to one another, you make the effort to understand one another. When we listen actively, we are focused not on the words the person is saying, but on the meaning and intent behind those words. Your questions and responses help speakers clarify their own ideas and thoughts. This mutuality enriches the communication climate and makes it healthy.

Listening and questioning are almost absent in defensive climates. Sometimes these responses are abused, becoming tools to compete with others for attention, to win points, or to express hostility and judgment of others. When members can neither listen nor question openly, the defensive climate escalates because information is not clarified, meanings are not shared, and problems are not solved.

In these defensive conditions, a team is likely to ignore members' ideas. The team listens to no one, questions no one, and soon, not one member cares to bring in ideas or information. They feel the team just isn't worth their effort. A team that shows these signs is operating in a poor climate; it's a team whose members are blocked from listening—and don't dare to question. In a climate that bad, you're not going to find clear thinking or cooperative analysis.

CREATING COOPERATIVE ANALYSIS

As a team, you are working toward a set of goals; you have a vision; you have a task. You're trying to be vigilant. *Vigilance*, as you remember from Chapter 8, demands watchful, thoughtful interactions as you set goals and criteria, analyze your information and problems, generate solutions, and make decisions. Quality interactions involve **cooperative analysis**, a process of listening and questioning that makes it possible for team members to think together—critically, creatively, analytically—and to test the logic and validity of their arguments.

A team's advantage is its variety of viewpoints, experiences, backgrounds, and ways of seeing. But that is no advantage at all if members cannot probe one another's meanings to arrive at new or better understandings. Excellent listening and perceptive, analytical questioning accomplish that goal.

FOUNDATIONS FOR LISTENING AND QUESTIONING

There's no question that listening is essential to success as an individual, in teams, and in the workplace. As Box 10.1 illustrates, listening is valuable even in unlikely settings. We contend you can't get very far without intelligent, perceptive questioning

| BOX 10.1 | **EFFECTIVE LEADERS ARE LISTENERS** |

A couple of years ago, University of Michigan business school professor Noel Tichy watched a platoon of Army Rangers raid a terrorist camp. The enemy was heavily armed and had chemical weapons, and the Rangers were caught off guard when they realized that the terrorists had night-vision goggles and were hiding behind a fence of triple-strand razor wire. Then the radios failed. It was chaos.

The raid, staged at Fort Benning, Georgia, was only a simulation. But what struck Tichy most was the after-action review. Defying all his preconceived notions about military hierarchy, right after the simulation ended, at one o'clock in the morning, everyone sat down, from generals to privates, "all stripes off, [for] honest, candid feedback," says Tichy. The point of the exercise wasn't "to become perfect in choreographed maneuvers," but rather to "season soldiers to make split-second decisions in difficult circumstances."

Tichy argues that top-down leadership styles don't work in either the military or business world, and leaders must recognize that they, too, can learn by listening to employees. The Special Forces' transformation into a teaching organization, Tichy says, has advanced the Rangers from a purely warfighting function to an all-purpose nation-building force. In countries such as Bosnia, Afghanistan and Iraq, Special Forces have had to fight the enemy and also work with communities to rebuild schools, infrastructure and government.

Source: Shawn Zeller, "When Leaders Listen," *Government Executive,* October 1, 2004. Reprinted by permission.

as well. Without questioning, you have no way of verifying that your understanding is accurate, no way of probing ideas, and no way of creatively building new insights with another person.

Unfortunately, tests of listening do not measure an individual's ability to question. Even so, research has found that students who are good listeners are more successful than those who are not. Listening is the language activity students use most throughout their school day, and those who excel at it find rewards in better grades (Imhif, 2008).

At work, listening is one of the most important skills for entry-level positions, managerial competence, job success, career competence—and for corporate excellence (Smart & Featheringham, 2006). In fact, the higher up you go in an organization, the better listeners you will find (Boyd, 2004). In addition, good listening characteristics were the most frequently identified trait of competent managers (Kesby, 2008). Listening skills are important on a variety of levels. As Boyd (2004) put it: "Really effective salespeople may listen up to 75 percent of their communication time. Physicians who listen well have fewer lawsuits against them. There is a real connection between quality listening and success in the workplace" (p. 35).

All this means that both as an individual and as a team, you need to develop norms for listening and questioning that open up the dialogue. You also need to recognize some of the barriers that get in the way.

BUILDING TEAM NORMS

Effective listening is especially difficult in groups. In one-to-one dialogue, you might spend 50 percent of your time listening; in a group, you may listen from 65 to 90 percent of the time. With so many people interacting, it becomes harder to listen—and easier to let others take the responsibility for it (Kolb & Rothwell, 2002). That's why a team needs to develop a few clearly understood norms for members to observe in their transactions. These norms might include:

- Take turns in speaking. Pay attention to nonverbal cues indicating that others want to speak and help others get the floor. Ask for attention to others; ask others to speak; ask the team to listen when someone is being ignored.
- Listen openly and supportively; don't cut others off, put them down, or interrupt. Employees in organizations have identified good listeners as people who are open to others' ideas and who use verbal and nonverbal responses to encourage effective communication (Garmston, 2008).
- Ask questions that help others clarify ideas and information.
- Use questions supportively. Focus on content, ideas, analysis—not on the person. People rate highly "support" and "empathy" as essential behaviors for competent listeners (Drollinger, Comer & Warrington, 2006).

By observing these standards, you help create a positive communication climate. As a team member in such a climate, you are encouraged to share your ideas and feelings because you know that others really are listening and want to understand you.

BREAKING BARRIERS

Many influences can block effective listening and questioning. Listening and questioning responsively take intellectual, emotional, and physical effort, and just the sheer volume of demands on you as a listener can be a barrier in itself. As a student, you probably spend most of your classroom time listening. Think about a day when you must listen to, question, analyze, and organize material from three reports made to your team, material from two lectures, and information for three exams. Students suffer this "information overload" frequently.

Information overload and the need to organize so many ideas get in the way of processing and retaining what you hear (Savolainen, 2007). Generalized stress, anxiety or apprehension about the situation, or just being preoccupied with other things in your life can also interfere (Eales-White, 2004).

In addition to these difficulties, teams may develop norms against dialogue that build negative communication climates. Perhaps members continually interrupt one another or use questions that aren't really questions—but are nothing more than bullying, discounting, or ignoring statements with question marks at the end. Humor is sarcastic and cutting. Support is weak, and people listen only for material with which to put someone else down. In a group whose norms are poor, you frequently see people working against one another.

Defensive norms often arise from competition among members. People become motivated to score points against others, and the team can't seem to establish a norm for cooperation and mutual support. As long as that continues, a team will not develop a positive climate—nor will anybody be able to listen to anybody else.

As a team tries to build positive norms for listening and questioning, the members need to break down their own barriers to listening. Rarely are people actually taught how to listen and question in dialogue. Too often, however, people are taught how *not* to listen. Think back to your childhood, when you may have heard messages such as:

"We don't listen to those things in our family."
"Don't pay any attention to him."
"Pretend you don't notice."
"Don't take it so seriously."
"He didn't mean what he said."
"Don't give them the satisfaction of knowing that you heard them."

This type of advice is defensive. It is meant to protect individuals from discomfort, or perhaps from an attack on their sense of self, or from information that might cause psychological conflict among values, beliefs, and behaviors. All this self-protection, however, reinforces bad listening habits. For example:

Zeroing in. If you stick to one idea that you want to rebut or support, you start mentally rehearsing your responses and miss everything else the speaker says.

Stereotyping or labeling. Your preconceived labels for a speaker or a subject can close your mind to understanding another's ideas.

Judging the speaker. Focusing on an individual's presentation, teamwork, or personal attributes blocks understanding. Your attention needs to be on the message.

Reacting to loaded words. Every person reacts to some specific words, but you won't see the rest of the picture if you focus on a word you don't like.

Being disinterested in the topic. Telling yourself the topic is "boring" or "I couldn't care less" ensures you won't find anything of interest.

Being distracted. Thinking about other things ("What will I have for dinner?" or "Isn't that new student cute?") will drown out what your teammate says.

Distracting others. Making comments or carrying on side conversations keeps you from getting the message and also ensures that others don't get it, either.

Assuming interpretations or details. If you mentally fill in what the person didn't say, you may be wrong. Don't assume—ask.

Faking listening. You may be a "wide-asleep listener," nodding brightly at the speaker, but there is no significant relationship between the number of head nods and measures of listening effectiveness (Eales-White, 2004). You may be nodding your head but dreaming on, blissfully unaware.

APPROACHES TO LISTENING AND QUESTIONING

Individuals tend to be oriented toward listening in one of four ways. They are centered on the speaker, on their concern for conciseness and accuracy, on understanding the content of the message, or on time—just getting it over with. Although each orientation is justified in different situations, people tend to use one style from habit. They probably aren't even aware of what they are doing.

Gesell (2007) describes two conditions necessary for what she calls "full body listening." These are focus and acknowledgement. "Focus leads to all conversers being present, meaning they exist in the here and now. Acknowledgement leads to the communicators' connection, meaning each becomes part of a co-creation team. The distance between the communicators is no longer seen as a gap to close. It becomes a connector, filling the space between bodies like a seesaw connects the two riders on either end" (p. 22). Listeners who are really effective can adapt to a variety of situations and conversational styles (Hughes, 2002).

Some writers advise people to ask "What's in it for me?" when they are about to listen to someone. We would say that you also should ask what's in it for the person to whom you're listening, for the relationship between you, and for the team as a whole.

All four orientations can motivate your listening concurrently. For example, a member of your team may be reporting information that she or he worked hard to get. You listen intently and question probingly, because:

1. You need to understand and evaluate the information.
2. You want that person to know that his or her work is appreciated.
3. You want to build stronger bonds with your teammate.
4. Your listening, as part of the team's transactional processes, contributes to the communication climate and synergy needed for the task.

To accomplish these purposes, at times you will listen and question silently but actively. At other times, you will listen and question interactively, empathically, and dialogicly. Each of these is important. As Bucero (2006) put it, "If you want to foster involvement among your team members, you have to listen to them constantly" (p. 20). Let's talk about developing each of those approaches.

ACTIVE LISTENING

Active listening is the processing that occurs inside your head. During active listening, you are engaging with the speaker at an intellectual level. You are not asking the speaker questions, but you're analyzing and asking questions of yourself. You're "tuning in."

Active listening capitalizes on your thought speed to process information. Remember that people speak more slowly than listeners can process information. The differential can be lost to distractions, or it can be used for information processing and analysis. To use it well:

Make a commitment to listen. Volunteer to take notes in the meeting—this could make you the best listener in the room! Or tell someone who cannot attend that you will report back to them. These kinds of commitments motivate you to really listen (Boyd, 2004).

Get set physically for listening. Sit where you can see and respond to the speaker. Lean forward, maintain eye contact, and nod at appropriate times. These actions help your teammate and also help you to concentrate.

Screen out distractions. Adopt a mindset that says, "Person at work. Do not disturb." If your mind does wander, pull it back quickly. If the distracting thought is compelling, jot it down for future consideration, which frees you to get back to full listening.

Focus your listening to get main points and concepts. Don't get stuck on small details. If a detail worries you, make a quick note to clarify it later, then get your mind away from it.

Organize and key the information while you're listening. Connect thoughts logically, synthesize concepts, use key words, and make associations with ideas so they make sense to you. Connect the ideas in your mind; create analogies and metaphors, or connect ideas with familiar examples.

Analyze the information mentally. Sort through what you're hearing. Ask yourself questions about the material. Note discrepancies for future analysis, and look for the speaker's evidence, values, assumptions, and arguments.

Each of these suggestions requires a very active mind and physically attentive body without direct verbal interaction with the speaker. In a team, you often need to listen silently—but actively—as another member makes a report or develops an idea. Active listening then leads to interacting with the speaker and other team members.

INTERACTIVE QUESTIONING

Interactive questioning clarifies, probes, analyzes, and follows up on information your teammate has expressed. It requires your analytical and critical thinking skills—not, we remind you, critical of people but critical in your investigation of problems, causes and effects, information and evidence, proposals, and projects.

By asking questions of a teammate who has presented information, you can help develop a positive climate and work toward your goals. By asking questions of the team as a whole, you can clarify information that is not clear ("Can we go over that point again, please; it's not clear to me"), and you can expand information that is incomplete ("Does anybody have information on this?" "How can we find this out?").

Your questions can get people to think critically about information or ideas ("Anybody have any thoughts about this?" "How does this line up with our criteria?" "What is the logic—rationale, evidence, support, justification—behind this?"). You might ask questions to improve task processes. ("How should we approach this job?" "Anybody see a way to move ahead faster?" "How do we get around this roadblock?") Questions can also improve transactional processes ("How can we be sure that everyone's involved here?" "Any ideas on how to manage this conflict?" "Is this an ethical route to take?").

Questioning the team in this way helps all of you to stay on target, to examine information and ideas, and to ensure you are working well. Two broad categories of guidelines can help to keep you on track in your questioning.

First, ask questions that help the thinking of the team:

Test the reasoning and the evidence. With your questions, test the connections among fact, inference, and judgment. Look for fallacies and correct them, but be sure you keep the focus on the issues and not on the people.

Ask the questions that provide analysis. Phrase questions that get at cause and effect, tests of good solutions, and criteria. Focus those questions so that the issues can be discussed without putting the speaker on the defensive.

Probe for further information. Ask (tactfully) for supporting evidence. Probe for the speaker's assumptions, and ask about ethical issues or dilemmas. All these can be done in a supportive spirit of "finding out" rather than in an argumentative spirit of "winning."

Second, ask questions in ways that help the speaker answer objectively and honestly:

Listen to questions that others ask. Someone else may ask your questions. The goal is to analyze ideas and reach a shared understanding of messages, not to conduct your own personal interrogation. Don't just ask questions to hear yourself talk.

Know what you want to ask. Be clear about what you're looking for. If you're not sure, say so and ask your teammates for help. Someone else may know just what you're confused about.

Be specific. Be clear in your terms; ask only what you need to know. If you must precede the question with an example, observation, or hypothesis, keep it clear, objective, and concise. Don't make speeches that pretend to be questions.

Ask one question at a time. If you have a two-part question, preview it: "I have a two-part question. Part one is…. Part two is…." This helps the speaker answer and keeps the issues clear.

Give the speaker a hook on which to hang an answer. To clarify or confirm a point, ask for examples or definitions. Paraphrase what the speaker said, and ask if your understanding is correct. Give your own examples or analogies, and ask if these are what the speaker meant.

Ask for analysis; don't attack. When you ask about underlying assumptions, values, and ethics or about reliability, validity, and credibility of sources, relate these issues to the team's criteria, goals, and values. Don't relate them to individuals or to personal motives.

Avoid "loaded" questions. Don't make the speaker choose between equally incorrect or damning answers. For example, "Did you stop cheating on exams?" is a loaded question. Or, "Are you a liberal or a conservative?" may ask for one of two equally incorrect representations.

Active listening and interactive questioning require special skills that need thought and practice. Listening to the answers and responding to the nonverbal cues require empathy.

EMPATHIC LISTENING AND QUESTIONING

Empathy is understanding the ideas and feelings of another. Sometimes this translates into specific language, as illustrated in Box 10.2. It has been described as walking in another person's moccasins or feeling what another person feels. In sales, for example, empathy allows a salesperson to understand her customer's needs and wants, which helps her develop a bond and an ongoing relationship with that customer (Aggarwal, Castleberry, Ridnour & Shepherd, 2005).

| BOX 10.2 | TEN OBSTACLES TO EMPATHIC LISTENING |

If you find yourself saying anything like the following examples, you need to keep working on your empathic listening skills.

1. **Give Advice/Fix-It**
   "I think you should ..."
   "If I were you, I'd ..."

2. **Explain It Away**
   "I would have called but ..."
   But I didn't mean to ..."

3. **Correct It**
   "That's not how it happened ..."
   "Wait! I never said that!"

4. **Console**
   "It wasn't your fault ..."
   "It could've been a lot worse ..."

5. **Tell a Story**
   "That reminds me of the time ..."
   "I know how you feel. That happened to me too when I ..."

6. **Shut Down Feelings**
   "Cheer up. Don't be so mad."
   "Quit feeling sorry for yourself."

7. **Sympathize/Commiserate**
   "Oh you poor thing ..."
   "How can people do that?"

8. **Investigate/Interrogate**
   "When did this happen?"
   "How come you did that?"

9. **Evaluate/Educate**
   "You're just too unrealistic."
   "The trouble with them is ..."

10. **One-Up**
    "That's nothing. Listen to this!"

Source: From "Ten Obstacles to Empathic Listening" by H. Holley Humphrey, www.empathymagic.com. Copyright © 2000, H. Holley Humphrey. Reprinted with permission.

Teams need to understand the members' feelings as well as their ideas, and **empathic listening** helps them to do just that. But it's essential to know what we mean by empathic listening in a team. We don't mean the type of listening you might do in a support group, as a professional counselor with a client, or as a dear friend. Nor do we mean sympathy or, necessarily, approval. Empathy suggests understanding what another person is thinking and feeling; sympathy is an emotional response of your own (possibly pity or sorrow). Empathy might help you understand the behavior of a teammate who is drinking excessively and falling down on the job. Although you might understand the person's distress and seek to help, you can still disapprove of the drinking and recognize the problem it creates for the team.

If teammates use empathic listening and questioning to ensure the transactional processes are meeting individual as well as team needs, and if empathic listening and questioning help to identify personal or interpersonal issues as they impact the team or the task, then this approach is essential to team processes.

You can be listening and questioning empathically at the same time you're exercising active and interactive skills. It's a matter of picking up what a teammate is feeling while you're processing the information in his or her message. Integrating these listening approaches, however, may require special effort. People tend to use one style habitually, but men tend to score higher than women on listening for content while women tend to score higher than men on listening for people's feelings and emotions. In their review of the literature, Roman, Ruiz & Munuera (2005) found that women tend to be more empathetic than men, and more likely to emphasize behaviors that build positive relationships and trust. One reason gender diversity is important for teamwork is that each sex brings somewhat different abilities for developing positive climates. Traditionally, women have been socialized to nurture and develop relationships and men to compete and survive. Wood (2001) observes that, "The relatively thin ego boundaries cultivated in females partially explain why they tend to be more empathic—to sense the feelings of those close to them and to experience those feelings as nearly their own" (p. 170). Men, on the other hand, tend to be more instrumental than women, looking for objective information to solve problems and give advice rather than to establish rapport.

However, research does indicate that it can be difficult to develop empathy for people whose work styles are different from yours (Williams, Parker & Turner, 2007). This could result in miscommunication with people who are culturally different from you, or who work in a different area of your own organization. Remember, though, that empathy develops over time—you get better at it as you come to know and understand more about the other person (Aggarwal et. al., 2005). It is worth the effort to spend time getting to know more about your teammates than just their job within your group.

Empathic listening enriches your understanding and enables you to support and question the speaker in ways that facilitate the development of mutual meanings. This requires being sensitive to a given teammate's cues, being sensitive to team communication that might cause others to respond emotionally, and being careful in your own empathic responses.

To tune in to your teammates' responses, be aware of their bodies, faces, gestures, and voices as they convey emotion. Listen carefully to language that might indicate defensiveness, feeling threatened, or some emotional response to a subject. Question the teammate carefully to develop empathy. With open, supportive questions, you can develop a shared base for mutual empathy among members of the group. This includes paraphrasing what you think a teammate is saying and asking for confirmation to correct your impression. You also can ask for examples or explanations of the other person's feelings or ideas. In the proper context, you can share your own experiences to help bring about a shared empathy.

At the same time, be sensitive to potentially abrasive behaviors in the team, such as racist or sexist jokes or language, cultural slurs, offhand negative comments, or dominant behaviors. People often don't recognize how toxic such issues can be until someone hits their own, personal raw nerves. An empathic listener is alert for such unintentional or intentional insults and tries to counteract them.

With all of that, empathic listening requires great care in responding and questioning. You never know exactly how someone feels, although your observation and sensitivity may bring you close to feeling with that person. Emotional responses are complex, personal, and private. Even when you feel intensely with teammates, you have to respect their privacy, and that means being careful in communicating your empathy nonverbally and verbally. Use nonverbal communication—eye contact, body posture, face, voice—to communicate that you are "with" them, but don't push. Be sensitive to their preferences, and let others establish their own distances and degrees of contact.

Often a person sounds empathetic, with a comment such as "I know how you feel" or "I had that same experience," and then uses it as a transition for his or her own 10-minute story. Instead, carefully reflect what you think your teammate has said—"You sound as though that made you pretty angry," or "That must make you feel pretty good"—but don't project your interpretations past the speaker's own statements. Beyond using attentive body language and eye contact, Garmston (2008) suggests using phrases that help the other person to open up. One possibility is to describe the body language you see ("You're smiling a lot today!"). If someone has started to talk about an issue already, you can encourage him or her to continue ("Please go on…." "Care to talk about it?"). And still another powerful, rarely used response is silence. Your silence, along with nonverbal attentiveness, can give the other person time to consider whether and how she or he wants to talk (Feuerman, 2008).

These approaches help clarify issues that may be clouded by personal feelings or interpersonal differences. This can be important to team cohesion and to achieving the team's goals. Furthermore, along with active and interactive listening and questioning, it can contribute to listening and questioning dialogically.

DIALOGIC LISTENING AND QUESTIONING

Dialogic listening (Stewart & Thomas, 1995) and questioning bring together all the approaches we've discussed into a transaction in which the participants immerse themselves in creating and developing ideas together. In **dialogic listening,** "instead of trying to infer internal 'psychic' states from the talk . . . you join with the other person in the process of co-creating meaning between you" (p. 192).

Dialogic listening is a process of "sculpting" ideas, as if two or more people chipped away at and shaped a piece of marble until they created a three-dimensional sculpture of meaning. It involves listening, questioning, paraphrasing, and building on one another's ideas. Dialogic listening brings all the skills we've talked about into one framework that is particularly valid for team communication.

Stewart and Thomas identify four distinct features of dialogic listening:

1. The communicators are deeply in the transaction together.
2. They deal with present issues and concerns.
3. They consider the process "ours," not "yours" or "mine."
4. It is open-ended and playful, which is especially important for teams.

Remember how creativity and eliminating mind blocks rely on a group's ability to open up and play? So does this type of transaction.

In sculpting meaning, Stewart and Thomas suggest that listeners and talkers apply these conversational strategies:

"Say more." Encourage the other person to develop his or her thoughts and suggestions, to think more deeply, to identify more possibilities, and to clarify and expand ideas.

Run with the metaphor. As with the creative thinking strategies we talked about in Chapter 7, grab a metaphor and develop it, play with it, and use it for deeper analysis.

Paraphrase plus. Put the other person's statement in your own words, but develop the ideas. Then ask for a paraphrase of what you have said. As you do this, you begin to co-create new ideas together.

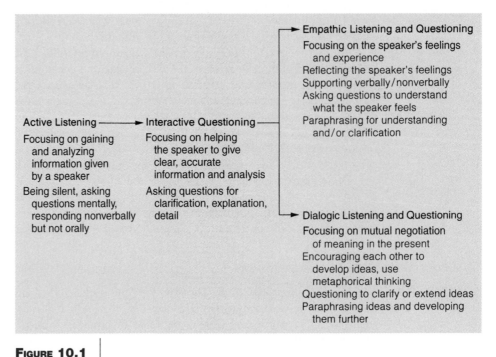

FIGURE 10.1

Relationships among types of listening and questioning

Build context. Explain your frame of reference for what you have to say, and get others to explain their contexts. Help the team understand the variables that shape each individual's meanings so you can create mutual meanings from them.

These approaches to "sculpting" meanings take time and commitment. Members have to learn how to do them together; otherwise, some people will think others are nuts. ("What do you mean, 'Say more'?" "Run where with my metaphor?"). Members may even get impatient with the process. Dialogic listening is a skill that members learn, develop, and use together because they are motivated to search for more complete, more mutual interpretations and because they want to build a team that analyzes issues effectively.

You can see in Figure 10.1 the way active listening leads to interactive questioning and how these skills can be expanded into empathic listening and dialogic listening. When you use these approaches to listening and questioning well, the transactional processes produce interpersonal understanding and team cohesiveness, understanding, and analysis, as well as creativity and ideation. They help to build a team and reach its goals.

LEADERSHIP IN LISTENING AND QUESTIONING

In Chapter 9, we talked about using verbal and nonverbal communication to help team members listen to one another. The other part of that leadership is using your listening and questioning to help the other members participate.

Unfortunately, a number of things can put blinders on people when it comes to giving and taking turns in conversation. People who are vision- or hearing-impaired can miss the cues. Or a person's background or culture may have provided a different approach to turn-taking than the other members have. For example, men in North American culture overlap and interrupt much more than women do. A person from an Asian culture, however, may have been brought up to wait—forever, if necessary—for a long pause and a signal from someone of higher status before speaking. Still another person may have been raised with a norm for interrupting loudly whenever the spirit moves. To others in the group, the Asian member may seem passive and disinterested, and the member with the norm for interrupting loudly may seem rude and unfeeling. In fact, neither one understands the norms and cues for turn-taking in the predominant culture.

It may be that the speaker, for similar reasons, is unaware of signals that others want a turn to speak. Sometimes a speaker would love to turn the floor over to someone else but goes on and on, desperately waiting for someone to interrupt, because he or she doesn't know how to stop. This speaker, and others like him, needs your help.

FACILITATING LISTENING AND TURN-TAKING

Sometimes you can ask a clarifying question tactfully to help another person get the floor. Suppose Joe looks confused. You can make a statement such as "I'm not sure I'm clear on this," and then you can turn to Joe and say, "Have you got it, or are you confused, too?" This allows Joe to express his doubts without looking like a fool. If Joe has got it—or pretends he has—that's okay. You've opened the floor to questions, and nobody loses.

If you hear a speaker floundering, that's a good time to interrupt politely ("Excuse me, Shirley—would you mind if I added something here?"). If you hear someone trying to say something and being cut off repeatedly, you also can interrupt (still politely) and turn the floor over to her or him. If it's appropriate, a little humor can work ("Hey, Toni, time out! I think Elyse has tried about ten times to say something—c'mon, Elyse, what have you got to say?").

Usually, interrupting is considered rude, thoughtless, and disruptive—but not always. Sometimes interruptions are necessary to get the floor back for other people, or interruptions may be just brief supportive statements ("Yeah, right, I absolutely agree with you!") or quick supplements ("Sure—remember what happened in class the other day?") from which the first speaker then continues his or her contribution. Additionally, interruptions can help a group remain flexible in their decision-making processes, such that their performance on novel, unfamiliar tasks is enhanced (Okhuysen & Eisenhardt, 2002).

Interrupting should be used carefully, as a way of facilitating turn-taking when other means won't work. Used excessively, interrupting is a self-centered exercise in disruption and reduces your credibility with the team.

MANAGING DISTRACTIONS

If members just are not listening to one another—they interrupt randomly, don't let a person finish his or her thought, go off on tangents, or otherwise distract each other from listening—they need some leadership. You can help bring attention back to the subject and the member who was speaking.

One way of doing this is to ask the speaker a question that focuses attention back on the content. You might say something like, "We've talked about so many things here, I need to find out where we are. Let me summarize what you've said, John." You can follow this with a brief paraphrase of what the speaker has said—which serves to get the group back in focus—and add, "Is that about right? Okay, thanks—then please go on."

If the discussion is completely out of hand and nobody is listening to anybody, ask for a time-out to talk about the team's transactional processes. You can make descriptive observations of the norms that seem to be operating, and you can try setting a new norm for turn-taking and listening. Again, this requires tact—you have to describe the problem without blaming people—but it can be done. And somebody needs to do it if a team is going to work together. That's leadership.

ADAPTING TO ELECTRONIC MEETINGS

Your work in groups and teams may occur through an electronic medium. In this case, your listening and questioning will take a different slant. Computer support is good news, bad news for listening, questioning, and turn-taking. With an electronic meeting, *listening* may become reading. In an online chat group, each individual's message goes online and shows up on the receivers' screens with a delay. You have to be patient in reading—or not reading—the responses that went online before the ones that relate to your query. This is a sort of hopscotch pattern of turn-taking, but at least you know that your question or comment is in the system.

One of the good things about an online meeting is that interruptions are few—people tend to type in a full thought at a time, and turn-taking is determined only by whose message pops up first for others to read. And, you can type in your idea instantly—no waiting while someone else is speaking and perhaps forgetting what you want to say. Furthermore, you can piggyback your idea on another person's message at any point.

On the other hand, the flow of ideas in an electronic meeting is not as rich or as full as in oral conversation. The terse, sometimes anonymous messages on a screen limit the group's ability to build on a metaphor, to fantasy chain, or to examine feelings. This is one reason that computer-assisted meetings should use direct oral communication in addition to the computer medium. The design and facilitation of this meeting is assigned to a leader, and your role (if you are not the designated leader) is to think clearly, put good ideas on the screen, and respond encouragingly to others.

SUMMARY

Listening to and supporting one another are critical to a team's communication climate, dialogue, cooperative analysis, and success. We've examined the foundations of good listening and questioning as well as barriers erected by both individuals and teams. We've also suggested that teams set norms for listening and questioning and that members develop their abilities to listen and question.

Active, interactive, empathic, and dialogic listening and questioning work together in a team. Active listening involves the concentration, commitment, and intense involvement of the listener with the speaker's content. Interactive questioning confirms, clarifies, probes, and analyzes information, and empathic listening seeks to understand and confirm teammates' feelings. Dialogic listening involves all these skills in a mutual, creative process of sculpting meanings through talking, listening, and questioning.

You can exercise leadership by facilitating turn-taking and discussion. This way, listening, questioning, and talking can be fully participative.

Exercises

1. Either with a group of which you are a member outside of class or with a class team, do the following: Using Form 10.1, have each member evaluate the group's listening and questioning behavior. Then discuss the evaluations. Where do members agree? What accounts for the disagreements? How do listening and questioning relate to the climate in the group? How do they relate to the dialogic ethics of the group's processes and decision making? What's good, what's bad, what should be improved? How?

2. Observe and evaluate a televised, taped, or live group discussion. Using Form 10.2, record the barriers as well as the barrier-reducing processes that you detect. What suggestions can you offer to improve this group's listening and questioning?

3. Practice dialogic listening and questioning. Meet with three or four other people, and select one of these topics for discussion:
   - What should be the U.S. government's role in citizens' health care?
   - What should be the United States' policy on pornography?
   - What should be the trade relationship between the United States and other countries?

   Now discuss the chosen question following these rules and procedures:

   a. One person explains her or his views on the question.
   b. Another person paraphrases the speaker's statement—not repeating it, but summarizing the meaning. Others also may paraphrase if they feel something needs clarification, or they may ask the original speaker if the paraphrase is correct.
   c. Any member now adds to the speaker's thoughts ("paraphrase plus"), creates a metaphor to take the idea further ("run with the metaphor"), or asks the first speaker to keep talking ("say more").
   d. Once another full statement is made by anyone in the group, someone must paraphrase and start the process again.

   Keep working at this process until everyone has acquired new insights into ideas, feelings, or the process itself. Then discuss these questions: What did you learn from the discussion? How, when, and to what effect did assumptions and values surface? Which points raised questions of ethical choices or dilemmas? When and how did new insights emerge? What got in the way? What barriers to thinking broke down? When and why?

FORM 10.1 | LISTENING AND QUESTIONING IN TEAMS ASSESSMENT

Individually, check off the extent to which each statement describes your team's communication. Then compare and discuss your responses.

The members of the team:	Always	Sometimes	Never
1. Listen and question cooperatively for critical analysis of issues	☐	☐	☐
2. Negotiate meanings by openly sharing values and assumptions	☐	☐	☐
3. Convey empathy and trust with sensitivity and care	☐	☐	☐
4. Play with ideas and metaphors to find meanings together	☐	☐	☐
5. Monitor turn-taking, making sure everyone gets to be heard	☐	☐	☐
6. Break down ambiguity with clear language and questioning	☐	☐	☐
7. Test the ethics of team processes by questioning and listening	☐	☐	☐
8. Help one another to clarify and elaborate ideas	☐	☐	☐
9. Use listening and questioning to help less dominant members be heard	☐	☐	☐
10. Listen to people of minority cultures and both genders	☐	☐	☐

What this team does well in listening and questioning is

What this team needs to work on in listening and questioning is

FORM 10.2 | OBSERVATION OF GROUP LISTENING AND QUESTIONING

As you watch a meeting, record each time you observe each of these barriers and barrier-reducing processes:

BARRIERS	
1. Making sarcastic, "put-down" remarks	
2. Interrupting abruptly	
3. Ignoring a person's turn to speak	
4. Asking loaded questions	
5. Stereotyping and judging a speaker	
6. Criticizing a person (rather than a problem)	
7. Creating distractions	
8. Reacting to loaded words	
9. Rebutting instead of listening	
10. Focusing on details, missing concepts	
DIALOGIC PROCESSES THAT BREAK DOWN BARRIERS	
11. Helping a member get the floor	
12. Asking questions that show empathy	
13. Giving a speaker nonverbal support	
14. Paraphrasing and confirming	
15. Asking clarifying questions	
16. Asking questions that test reasoning and evidence without attacking people	
17. Asking probing questions for information	
18. Asking questions about a speaker's context	
19. Supporting a speaker with self-disclosure	
20. Testing ethics of the team processes	

"What this team needs is a real leader!"
Okay, what is a real leader, and what does a real leader do?

Teams and Designated Leaders

Achieving Team Visions

11

It's popular, at every level of human interaction, to grouse about the deficit of leadership or the crying need for a "real leader." But what is a leader? Maybe identifying a leader is like defining pornography: It's hard to define, but you know it when you see it. We look at leaders who have changed the way we view the world—Mahatma Gandhi, Martin Luther King, Jr.—and are awestruck. We look at leaders who have ravaged human souls—Hitler, Jim Jones, Stalin—and are horrorstruck. Whether for good or evil, a few people become leaders in some incredible, powerful, overwhelming ways that move others and change some aspect of human life.

We can learn much to emulate from the great leaders of history—and much to avoid from the despots. Leading, however, occurs on far more ordinary levels than these. Many current analyses of leaders center not on the great figures of history but on executives, managers, and team leaders who guide their organizations to meet the challenges of a changing world. Back in 1991, Kinlaw observed that managers' jobs were shifting "from managing by control to managing by commitment; from focusing on individual motivation and output to focusing on team motivation and output; and from traditional functions of planning, organizing, staffing, evaluating to the functions of coaching and facilitating" (p. xix). Recent events have certainly proven this to be true. Today, in addition to developing skills to manage people they can see, managers also need to extend their leadership skills into the virtual realm—a challenging task indeed (Hoyt & Blascovich, 2003).

In Chapter 2, we defined team leadership as a function that all should share, the *verbal and nonverbal communication behavior that facilitates a team's transactional and task processes in achieving members' and the team's needs and goals.* You may wonder why we have another chapter on leaders so far along in this text. It's because we believe that teamwork is more about sharing leadership than about leaders and followers, and we wanted to develop the teamwork skills of leadership before we dealt with designated leaders. So here we are now with the leader who has been designated.

Does a designated leader do more than members of a team sharing leadership? Sometimes. A **designated leader** "directs the behaviors of group members in pursuit of common goals" (Hoyt & Blascovich, 2003). Yet, emphasizing the complexity in team interactions, many theorists contend that a team leader's most important function may be to empower other members to take on leadership roles (Carson, Tesluk & Marrone, 2007). Interesting. The leader should, then, develop shared leadership. Both views are on target, describing the activities and objectives of a good leader.

In this chapter, we look at power and at leaders—at how expectations (of themselves and of others) affect leaders and their approaches to leading. Finally, we take a look at a leader's responsibilities and how you can develop the skills to be an effective leader. This chapter will help you to:

1. Know how the position of leader relates to power
2. Identify styles and approaches to leading
3. Recognize how expectations affect a leader's success
4. Discern a leader's tasks and responsibilities
5. Learn ways to increase your effectiveness as a leader

SOURCES OF POWER

Presumably, every leader has some source of power and authority to guide others and to make decisions. Power is an emotionally charged concept, because those with power can build up or tear down people, relationships, and institutions. Because power and leaders are so intimately related, we begin by exploring what power actually is.

Pace and Faules (1994) synthesized several definitions of power into "*the capacity . . . to influence, regulate, and control outcomes*" (p. 172). This is a good definition, but we would like it even better if it said "to influence *and/or* regulate *and/or* control outcomes." Maybe that's picky, but the distinction can be important. Perhaps a teacher has the power to inform your thinking; a boss may be able to regulate the flow of your work; and someone you love might change the way you live. Or perhaps a wise mentor whom you revere might influence all three. Then, too, you have your own power—ultimately, you make the decisions to control your own life.

Everyone has some sources of power. Managers, boards of trustees, parents, teachers, police officers—all have power. So do unions, guilds, families, and secretaries who know where the secrets are hidden. A boss who can fire you has power, but so does a toddler who throws herself on the floor in a tantrum. Each can influence what you do.

On the other hand, people who theoretically have a lot of power may really have very little. We often are bemused at presidential campaigns when candidates make grandiose promises about reforms they can't deliver without congressional approval. Any individual's power, in fact, is interdependent with the power of others and with the structure of the organization (Braynion, 2004). Over time, a number of variables such as communication patterns, organizational structure, compensation and reward systems, etc. have worked together to create a unique culture within each organization that determines its norms and values. Any group is formed and works within these parameters, and they influence how people interact, norms for behavior, and even what topics are discussed (Pearce & Manz, 2005).

Within any organization, the structure of relationships influences how people interact within it. For example, we once saw a new college president demand confidential information about one faculty member from another, tenured, professor. The professor refused to provide that information because the orders conflicted with long-established personal and institutional values. The president, having no history with the organization, didn't know that previous interactions among individual members of the institution, the union, and the administration had created unwritten rules about what could—and could not—be done. The president had power, all right, but not enough to override the power of the institution itself or of the professor who acted within it.

In this example, the leader was operating under a traditional control model of power. Let's examine some other traditional and contemporary ideas about power and control.

TRADITIONAL CONTROL MODELS

Throughout history, Western societies have been structured on a win/lose, competitive basis. She or he who has power wins, thereby controlling the rest of us—or that's the theory. From this perspective, French and Raven (1959) first identified five sources of power in groups and organizations as well as among individuals:

1. **Coercive power** derives from the ability to punish. If a person can fire you, demote you, reduce your salary, or inflict emotional or physical pain on you, that's coercive power.

2. **Reward power** is the reverse of coercive power. If a person can hire you, promote you, raise your salary, give you physical or emotional pleasure or relief, help you meet your goals, fulfill your needs, or achieve your desires, that's reward power.

3. **Legitimate power** is inherent in the person's position or office. A police officer, your boss, your teacher, all have degrees of legitimate power granted by the hierarchy and structure of the system.

4. **Expert power** flows from an individual's expertise, academic credentials or certification, experience, research, and competence in a given area.

5. **Referent power** is the influence inherent in the respect and admiration that others have for an individual. A person who is perceived as credible, as wise, and as goodwilled has the power to change others as a role model, a counselor, a guru.

An additional source of power is in *communication* itself. Communication, or *discourse*, in Foucault's view (1980), creates the base of knowledge from which people reason and make decisions. In our example of the college president and the faculty member, the power to demand confidential information lay in the president's legitimate position, but the power to withhold information lay in the professor's possession of it—and in the institution's unwritten rules about what could be communicated. The power of communication arises from two choices that an individual or a group might make regarding:

1. *Whether to communicate data that could allow others to make decisions or to understand issues and processes accurately and fully*. Essentially, this involves choosing what information to share with people. When you use *rhetorical power*, sometimes called *covert power*, you may attempt to change people's perceptions through the information you choose to share—or not to share. For example, if in a meeting "someone avoids a difficult issue which had previously been raised, they are having an important effect on the course of the discussion by means of skillful use of language. So this is an indicator of rhetorical power" (Sillince, 2000, p. 1133). A manager might encourage rumors about impending layoffs to intimidate people and keep them from complaining about safety violations. Or a secretary can make or break events in an organization by finding, losing, or using information about the organization's history, personnel, and informal networks.

2. *In what manner to communicate ideas.* The way information is communicated—the words, the images, the media that are used—affects the nature and the impact of the discourse. One lawyer tried using communication power to silence his opponent with belittling language, calling her "a little mouse" and telling her to "pipe down" and "go away, little girl." The judge used legitimate power, however, to slap the attorney with a $500 fine for sexist bullying (*Rat Patrol*, 1992, p. 15).

We suppose it's all too obvious that power can be abused to manipulate others or to promote individual interests above team interests. We want to believe that most people, when faced with an ethical choice, will do the right thing. However, in response to subtle pressures from their boss, organizational norms, or an overt command, some people wind up violating even their personal codes of ethics (Verbos, Gerard, Forshey, Harding & Miller, 2007). Rewards, coercion, a sense of loyalty, and the compulsion to obey all may induce an individual to behave unethically in response to the pressure of a leader's power.

Not surprisingly, people react emotionally to the use of power, and a principled leader must recognize the potential effects of its use. In her review of the literature, Braynion (2004) found that subordinates generally react more positively to their managers' use of power when they perceive the manager to be using both his or her legitimate power and expert power/expertise. On the other hand, when managers focused only on coercive forms of power, subordinates viewed them negatively—some even categorizing their bosses as "bullies."

Ideally, a leader empowers the entire team by sharing all possible information, choices, and decisions. Some self-managing teams make decisions about schedules, employment, assignments, promotion, pay increases, and most aspects of their tasks. Much power resides in such a team.

But team power, authority, and structure vary widely, according to the type of organization, the team's stage of development, and the training of its members. In some cases, all authority to reward, to punish, and even to make decisions belongs to outside group leaders or managers. Even then, the leader and team members have information, expert, and referent power. Often, these sources of power can overcome enormous hurdles—if leaders and members know how to use them.

A student we knew used these three sources in a personal campaign to induce his college to reinstate the discontinued ice hockey team. He had no legitimate, reward, or coercive power. Instead, he used expert power (he knew his game), communication/information power (he did a lot of research to back up his proposals), referent power (he was respected by students and teachers)—and grit. He got the team reinstated against seemingly insurmountable odds by those who had all the *other* forms of power at their command and didn't really want to bother with ice hockey. His success was gratifying to see.

You probably could generate a list, right now, of the times you have seen people draw on each of these sources of power. But even though these sources of power are real, contemporary thinking about power suggests giving some of it away. See Box 11.1 for an example of this brand of leadership.

BOX 11.1	LEADERSHIP IS . . . LEADERSHIP

Dee Hock, Founder and CEO Emeritus of Visa International says,

> Control is not leadership; management is not leadership; leadership is leadership. If you seek to lead, invest at least 50% of your time leading yourself—your own purpose, ethics, principles, motivation, conduct. Invest at least 20% leading those with authority over you and 15% leading your peers. If you don't understand that you work for your mislabeled "subordinates," then you know nothing of leadership. You know only tyranny.

Source: Excerpt from "Make Yourself a Leader," *Fast Company* (June 1999), pages unnumbered.

CONTEMPORARY EMPOWERMENT MODELS

Let's talk about *empowerment*. The word is a rallying flag you'll see used in everything from organizational communication textbooks to flyers for workshops on teamwork, management, women's issues—you name it. The word may be overused, but the concept is an important issue for leaders to understand.

It's like this: When people feel powerless, they don't feel good. When they don't feel good, they aren't likely to be productive. When people feel they have some power over their own lives and actions, however, they feel a lot better. When they feel better, they are more likely to be motivated and productive. Simple.

Team empowerment occurs when the members of a group are highly motivated to perform tasks because they perceive them as meaningful, and because they have autonomy over how the tasks are done (Carson, Tesluk & Marrone, 2007). Empowered teams believe that they make an important contribution, both individually and together. **Empowerment** is what happens when leaders free people to develop self-efficacy and confidence, allowing them to have ownership of themselves and their work.

Many organizational leaders try to empower people. Unfortunately, even more do not. As usual, a canyon separates theory from reality. One study found that "nearly two-thirds of human resource managers acknowledged that their companies haven't been as employee-friendly as they've promised" (Lee, 1998, p. 19). In a recent Gallup poll, 4 out of 10 workers said they are mad when they are at work, a condition that Weisenfeld (cited in Lee, 1998) says "makes it a lot more difficult to make teams work effectively" (p. 3). This same poll found that people know their interpersonal skills are critically important—but they have trouble making them work when they are angry all the time. These findings do not translate as empowerment.

We once had a conversation with a colleague who firmly asserted the trouble with empowerment is that people who have power will never give it away. We thought about that carefully and immediately recalled instances when leaders did give away power—in fact, instances in which we, as leaders, had deliberately given away power to others. In a way, power is like love—you get it when you give it. A little song we used to sing with our kids provides the analogy: "Love is like a magic penny—hold it tight and you won't have any. Lend it, spend it, and you'll have so many—they'll roll all over the floor."

Boulding (1989) calls this synergistic effect *integrative power*, or power that brings people together, inspires loyalty, and builds a sense of mission. Andre Harrell (1996), the former head of Motown Records, reflects on this kind of power:

> When I look at some of the people I most admire—Dr. Martin Luther King, Jr., Malcolm X, Supreme Court Justice Thurgood Marshall and Motown founder Bert Gordy—I realize . . . you can intimidate people through fear, or you can motivate them through opportunity. The more you touch and empower people, the more power you have. By empowering others, these men changed the world for the better in their own unique ways.
>
> Their power sources were conviction, dedication, commitment. . . . I equate power with how many people you affect emotionally, and you can achieve that through words, deed, wisdom, and style.

Some writers contend the traditional perspectives on power reflect a male-dominant view of society, whereas a woman's conception of power involves supporting and enabling others to build something together. The way a woman looks at power may range from intrapersonal control to self-determination to a feeling of duty to empower others. Interestingly, with the current popularity of shared leadership models, both male and female managers find that the often neglected "feminine" side of managing—encouraging participation and caring about workers' individual needs, for example—are important skill sets for leaders of both genders (Aldoory & Toth, 2004).

Not only is the influx of women into the workforce changing the idea of leadership and power; so is the influence of other cultures. For example, even within the rigidly structured Japanese status system, their participative, cooperative management style has taught Western businesses a thing or two. There's still more to learn, however. Taka and Foglia (1994), comparing ethical aspects of Japanese to U.S. leadership, noted that the Japanese leadership style encourages self-realization, appreciation of diverse abilities, and trust in others. The difference is between power that focuses on controlling undesirable outcomes and power that motivates desirable growth. One is static in structure and reactive to events; the other is dynamic in process and proactive in creating an empowered work force.

APPROACHES TO LEADING

There's no one way to lead a team. There may be just about as many ways as there are leaders. Still, we can examine some major approaches to leading as they are influenced by situations and contingencies as well as by classic or contemporary theories.

SITUATIONAL-CONTINGENCY APPROACHES

This is one of those good-sense things. You can't expect one approach to work in all situations. Much research has demonstrated that adaptability is essential to effective leading (i.e., Aronson, 2001; Ralph, 2005). In contemporary organizations and teams, the need is even greater not only to understand the members and the situation but also to inspire commitment in others and adapt flexibly yourself.

Situational-contingency approaches to leading recognize that situations, tasks, purposes, members, and leaders may vary—and that a leader's behavior may need to vary accordingly (Robbins & Langton, 2004).

In today's wired business, for example, the tasks of virtual teams will dictate the best choice of leadership approach. Katzenbach and Smith (2001) describe the choices of one of the teams they studied as differentiating between "individual tasks and tools that members could achieve under clear single-leader direction, and critical collective work that demanded real-time collaboration, multiple leadership, and the disciplined behavior of a real team." They go on to note that "these options have little to do with technology, although both can certainly be enabled by groupware" (p. 3).

A designated leader, then, must choose the best approach for the task and the team, as well as for the individuals. Suppose, for example, that you head an executive committee of capable, confident people who make their own decisions. The members like it that way, and so do you. Then, one day, information comes to you about a serious, life-threatening crisis in the plant. It must be resolved immediately. Can you call a meeting and work out a decision? No, somebody might die before action is taken. For this situation, you act quickly and tell your team about it afterward. The situational contingencies dictate your style for that moment.

In their **life-cycle theory** of leadership, Hersey and Blanchard (1977) suggest that a leader's style adapts to the group's maturity, defined as "the ability and willingness of individuals or groups to take responsibility for directing their own behavior in a particular area" (Hersey, Blanchard & Natemeyer, 1979, p. 420). They classify leader communication according to the degree of maturity that members exhibit, moving from telling, to selling, to participating, to delegating.

> *Telling communication* is directive, nonnegotiable task ordering for teams with low maturity. It uses coercive and some (but not too much) reward power.
>
> *Selling communication* is more supportive, rewarding persuasion for teams with low to medium maturity. Power and direction are still centered in the leader; the focus is still on task, not transaction.
>
> *Participating communication* is for teams with moderate to high maturity and brings the members into the process as partners. It supports, encourages, and builds leader–member transactions and relationships.
>
> *Delegating communication* is appropriate to highly mature teams. It involves little direction and permits teams to make their own decisions.

In short, the leader adapts the style to the team as the team develops sufficient maturity to take responsibility for its own development and actions.

CLASSIC LEADERSHIP STYLES

Although theories change, you still see the three classic leadership styles that White and Lippett identified back in 1960 (p. 12):

> **Laissez-faire** leadership refers to a neutral, kick-back-and-let-the-folks-do-whatever-they-choose style. You must already be designated as the leader to be laissez-faire, because being this laid-back rarely gets you the position.

Tiger Woods

Because Tiger Woods' golf game is arguably the best in the world, he has significant power through expertise.

Ellen Degeneres

Ellen Degeneres is widely recognized as one of the most likeable people in the world. This important source of power helps secure her place in the competitive world of television.

In what ways are each of these people leaders? How do they affect the lives of others? What aspects do they have in common? How do they differ as leaders?

Barack Obama

President Obama's masterful speaking style and comfortable interaction with people help make him a charismatic leader.

This style works just fine for a team of real experts who want to share leadership and charge ahead. For other teams, however, productivity, quality, involvement, and satisfaction suffer.

Authoritarian (or *autocratic*) leadership is just what it sounds like. The authoritarian leader keeps tight control, runs meetings by the book, sets schedules, and may use coercive or reward power. Authoritarian leadership often increases productivity in the short term, but it also increases aggression and turnover rates among members. Some people equate authoritarianism with leadership, however, and their expectations are met by an authoritarian leader.

Democratic leadership fits the Western ideal. The democratic leader ensures that everyone is heard, guides and facilitates discussion and decision making, and shares power. Democratic leaders do three important things. First, they make sure everyone in the group feels responsible for outcomes. Second, they enhance the group's feeling of empowerment, as we described earlier. Finally, they create processes through which the team can make effective decisions. Over time, each member in the group develops the expertise (and, hopefully, the desire) to perform these roles as well, and ultimately everyone can take turns serving as both leaders and followers.

In an article titled "It's Like Prison in There," Zak (1994) reports a modern horror story when management chose the wrong sources of power and styles of leading. Here's the abstract of her report:

> When a vehicle maintenance unit of a public transit agency underwent extensive demographic diversification of its work force, original workers escalated the symbolic actions and language patterns traditionally used to establish and maintain hierarchy in the workplace. Taken literally and seen as malicious by new workers, the shop talk and horseplay became vehicles for internal power struggles that led the organization toward dysfunction and even violence. Management responded by stepping up structural control and punishment. The managers failed to acknowledge and provide for the need of newly diverse discourse communities in this work-place to negotiate a new order in which sufficient shared meaning and agreed-upon language and behaviors could be constructed. (p. 281)

The authoritarian approach used by management in this case "has been widely referred to as management by intimidation, or command and control management" (Zak, 1994, p. 281). You might want to find this article and read it. It surely highlights the reason for more creative and sensitive approaches to power and leadership.

CONTEMPORARY APPROACHES

More recently, two theories of leadership have emerged. Bass (1990) first distinguished between two of them: **transactional leadership**, which exchanges rewards for performance; and **transformational leadership**, which elevates, motivates, inspires, and develops the team. Transactional leaders set goals, clarify desired outcomes, provide feedback, and give subordinates rewards for good work. On the other hand, transformational leaders motivate their followers through more subtle—but very effective—means, and these strategies tend to result in high worker satisfaction (Sparks & Schenk, 2001).

Effective transformational leaders provide motivation by articulating a clear, detailed picture of what the future could be if the team works together effectively (Hoyt & Blascovich, 2003). You might call this **visionary leadership**. Transformational leaders "engender trust, seek to develop leadership in others, exhibit self-sacrifice and serve as moral agents, focusing themselves and followers on objectives that transcend the more immediate needs of the work group (Dumdum, Lowe & Avolio, 2002, p. 38). Many researchers have confirmed that transformational leaders use the following techniques and skills to effectively motivate their subordinates:

Charisma: Providing vision and a sense of mission, instilling pride, and gaining respect as well as trust

Inspiration: Communicating high expectations, using symbols to focus efforts, and expressing important purposes in simple ways

Intellectual stimulation: Promoting intelligence, rationality, and careful problem solving

Individualized consideration: Giving personal attention, treating people individually, coaching, and advising

We have to recognize, though, that leaders can't be all transformational, all the time. It is perhaps best to think of transformational leadership as building on transactional leadership. Both are important to ensure that teams reach their goals.

Transformational leaders tend to have personalities that are more extraverted, agreeable, and proactive than non-transformational ones (Bono & Judge, 2004). However, this link is relatively weak. Instead, it appears that a transformational leader develops through the experiences he or she has had with his or her own managers. When we work with and for people who understand and use the transformational leadership processes, we become better transformational leaders ourselves (Divir, Eden, Avolio & Shamir, 2002). In fact, employees at any level of an organization can be trained to be both more transactional and transformational (Towler, 2003).

Transformational leadership has been the most-studied leadership topic over the past few years, and the results of that research are compelling. Employees are more strongly committed to both their leaders and their immediate work groups when their leader uses a transformational style (Kark & Dijk, 2007). Similarly, workers with transformational leaders report higher job satisfaction than those without them (Dumdum et al., 2002). And, transformational leadership contributes to overall organizational success on a number of levels (Judge & Piccolo, 2004).

We have given you quite a dose of theory—sources of power, styles of leadership, contemporary approaches. To give you a clearer idea of how this all fits together, Figure 11.1 relates each of the styles and approaches we've discussed to questions of power, control, support, autonomy, and overall effect on the team.

EXPECTATIONS OF LEADERS

If only a person who became the leader could just lead—but that isn't how things work. Team members have expectations of how a leader should lead, and leaders have expectations of how they should perform. Often, however, neither of these

STYLE OR APPROACH TO LEADING	SOURCE OF POWER	CONTROL OF TEAM	SUPPORT OF TEAM	TEAM'S AUTONOMY	EFFECT ON TEAM
Situational-contingency (Hollander, 1978)	Varies	Varies by situation, leader, and members	Strong	Depends on situation, leader, and members	Enables team to meet situational needs
Life-cycle (Hersey & Blanchard, 1977)	Legitimate, and other sources as appropriate	Adapted to maturity of members—telling, selling, participating, or delegating	Adapted to maturity of members	Adapted to maturity of members	Allows members to develop through stages of ability to guide themselves
Laissez-faire (White & Lippett, 1960)	Legitimate	None	Little	Complete	Demoralizes team
Authoritarian (Ibid.)	Coercive and reward	Strong	Variable	Little or none	May increase productivity but also increases hostility and turnover
Democratic (Ibid.)	Possibly all except coercive	Loose	Strong	Extensive	Produces openness and ability to work together
Transactional (Bass, 1990)	Legitimate and reward	Exercised through negotiation	Strong	Moderate	Produces a positive climate but less productivity and commitment than with the empowering leader
Transformational (Bass, 1990)	Legitimate, referent, expert	Implemented charismatically by coaching, inspiring, providing intellectual stimulation	Strong	Maximum freedom, responsibility, and self-direction	Empowers and develops personal leadership in team members

FIGURE 11.1

Characteristics of styles and approaches to leading.

sets of expectations matches the actual task and transactional responsibilities that a leader must fulfill for a team to reach its goals.

MEMBERS' EXPECTATIONS

Group members' expectations may start with stereotypes—positive or negative—and extend to assumptions about the leader's values, beliefs, intelligence, and behaviors. You may have heard some version of these comments made about a candidate for leader of a group:

"Make him chairperson. He went to Yale." (People with high-powered educations must make better leaders.)

"Don't make him leader—he'll always be late." (People from his culture don't value time the way we do.)

"She must be voting for him because he's a hunk." (Women think with their hormones.)

"She can't be chairperson—she'll be biased." (She might select people from her ethnic group instead of sticking entirely with mine.)

Are these stereotypes old-fashioned, passé, obsolete? Yes, but they're still with us. Unfortunately, when people evaluate leaders' attributes, they tend to base their responses more on what they expect of the leader than on how the person actually behaves (Ensari & Murphy, 2003). In most cases, people evaluate leaders more favorably when the leader is considered typical of all members of the group (Platow & van Knippenberg, 2001). For example, women are still a minority in most business contexts, and this means they won't be viewed as typical group members when the group is predominantly made up of men. In these contexts, even when people are given identical performance information about male and female leaders, many say they like female leaders less and prefer not to work for them (Maher, 1997).

As Wood (2001) points out:

> The male-as-standard norm defines expected communication in professional settings. Leadership, a primary quality associated with professionals, is typically linked with masculine modes of communication—assertion, independence, competitiveness, and confidence, all of which are emphasized in masculine speech communities. Deference, inclusivity, collaboration, and cooperation, which are prioritized in women's speech communities, are linked with subordinate roles rather than with leadership. To the extent that women engage in traditionally feminine communication, then, they may not be recognized as leaders or marked for advancement in settings where masculine standards prevail. (p. 254)

What if you become a leader in the face of expectations such as these? What if people expect you to fall on your face? What happens if, contrary to expectations, you turn out to be very competent indeed? In this case, people tend to rationalize that you are the "exception to the rule." When expectations are violated by better-than-expected performance, group members may evaluate a person more highly and treat her or him with greater respect—or less hostility—than they would someone else for whom they had higher initial expectations (Giessner & van Knippenberg, 2008). This allows the members to cling to previous expectations about people like them while, at the same time, they enjoy the benefits of your effective leadership.

The message is obvious. If you fit the going stereotype of a leader and you meet members' expectations, that's great. If you don't fit the current stereotype, however, you probably have to be better than those who do. Then people will be so startled at having their expectations refuted they will think you're wonderful. And take heart; this society is beginning to understand why leaders need a variety of approaches, not just one. Old barriers are crumbling—just a tad.

LEADERS' SELF-EXPECTATIONS

While you're being a good—or better—leader, remember that your own expectations can be the heaviest burden of all. After you've exercised leadership for a while—either as a very involved member of a group or as the designated leader—

you begin to discover what you can reasonably expect of yourself and how to adapt your leadership to the members and various situations.

It helps to understand that expectations can—and probably will—clash. Suppose your self-perception is that of a nurturing, supportive person—and you're in a leader's role that requires you to be tough and assertive. You might have to negotiate those roles within yourself and learn how to live with a more complicated self-concept than you had previously. That's part of learning to be an effective leader.

Expectations can be particularly difficult for leaders who have worked in a "real" setting and now must switch their leadership to the virtual one, perhaps because they lack experience in this context. Research has shown that virtual workers whose leaders or managers also telecommute are more satisfied and productive than those whose managers are desk-bound (Hoyt, Blascovich & Swinth, 2003). However, managers whose experience is within a traditional organizational structure are going to have to change their expectations of themselves as leaders and of the entire work process. That's pretty scary, and will take a considerable adjustment, although preliminary research offers some evidence that the same fundamental principles of good leadership apply whether you're online or face to face with your subordinates (Hoyt & Blascovich, 2003).

You can't meet all expectations, and you shouldn't even try. Some expectations, in fact, are unrealistic or defeating or against your principles. Sometimes, therefore, you must violate others' expectations; that may require careful negotiation of what you expect and what others expect. For example, the founder of your team may expect you to lead it to a specific goal and rapidly produce results. Perhaps your expectation for yourself, however, is to empower team members, to lead them to lead themselves. That takes more time, of course. So you, as a leader, must manage these conflicting role expectations with communication and compromise.

It isn't always easy, but it's what you have to do.

RESPONSIBILITIES OF LEADERS

Theory is all well and good, but when it comes to actually leading your team or group, you probably want to know some specific things to do that will fulfill expectations and help you develop the team as well as achieve the tasks.

At McDonnell Douglas, for example, the leader's first responsibility is nicely summarized in a job description: "Teamplayer: Unites others toward a shared destiny through sharing information and ideas, empowering others and developing trust" (Kinlaw, 1991, p. xvi). Nanus (1992) sees four responsibilities for visionary leaders: spokesperson, direction setter, change agent, and coach (p. 15).

We'll build on that by examining a range of functions that leaders frequently—but not always, or in all ways—should fill. These fall into broad categories of linking and buffering; motivating and coaching; and managing and moving the team. Box 11.2 has some additional ideas on this topic.

LINKING AND BUFFERING

No team works in a vacuum; it has to coordinate with a parent organization and other systems and subsystems. The organization has its needs, and so does the team. Wood and Fields (2007) found that high-performance teams had leaders

BOX 11.2 | WE HAVE LOTS OF MANAGERS . . . WE NEED LEADERS

Drop your stereotypes! A few years ago, the United States Marine Corps Combat Correspondents Association gave a top award to an article titled "Leadership and Love." [The article] proposed that leadership is a subset of love and that if a person was not capable of loving and being loved, then most likely he or she was not capable of being a good leader either.

While it will offend some and puzzle others to look to the military for lessons in leadership, it is well worth ignoring the stereotypes. The United States Marine Corps' Guidebook for Marines lists eleven leadership principles.

Take responsibility . . . for your actions as well as subordinates'.

Know yourself. Be honest. Constantly seek self-improvement.

Set an example. Your conduct influences others.

Develop your subordinates. Guide but be confident in them.Be available . . . but don't take away others' initiative.

Look after the welfare of your employees. Help but don't pry.

Keep everyone well informed. Stop rumors, provide the truth.

Set achievable goals. Successes will be more easily reached.

Make sound and timely decisions; have courage to change bad ones.

Know your job. Stay abreast, learn, adjust to new ways.

Build teamwork. Assign projects to your entire staff. Train employees so they understand contributions that each makes to the entire effort. Insist that everyone pull his or her share of the load. When you do something well, celebrate it.

Source: Condensed from Patrick L. Townsend and Joan E. Gebhardt, "We Have Lots of Managers . . . We Need Leaders," *Journal for Quality and Participation*, September 1989, pp. 18–19. Published by the Association for Quality and Participation. Used with permission.

who were strong in obtaining outside support for the team as well as in tolerating the ambiguity of a team in progress. It's the leader who links the team to the organization and buffers it from interference.

Creative and research teams, especially, need autonomy to function effectively. The leader works between the team and the outside—consulting, representing, feeding back, moderating. In addition, the leader seeks the necessary time, money, materials, and information—as expediently as possible, but without sacrificing the team's integrity (Hackman & Wageman, 2005).

In a real sense, a leader's job is to act as the group's "face" when interacting with other people both within and outside of the organization. Good leaders make sure that their teams remain connected to the strategic priorities of their organization by communicating regularly with top management and other teams. Ideally, they serve as conduits for information both coming into the group from outside sources and leaving the group in the form of requests and progress reports. Through this "buffer" role, team leaders both manage their teams and manage the context in which their teams perform, helping the team meet its objectives (Pearce & Manz, 2005).

In summary, an organization expects leaders to demonstrate loyalty, perceptiveness, commitment, intelligence, innovativeness, as well as skill in managing and talent for inspiring people. Nothing much. The team expects the leader to free them to do their jobs by keeping the organization and the resources in line—a buffer, indeed.

MOTIVATING AND COACHING

The best part of being a leader is the teaching—inspiring, motivating, and helping team members to transcend their ordinary selves. The better the members get, the less they need someone to direct them—and that's what you want. A leader can encourage this process using the following approaches:

Envisioning. Listen carefully to the team; help to articulate its goals in clear, symbolic terms. Help members to see themselves as a cohesive whole and to see their goals by finding images that work for them.

Developing others' self-leadership. Identify members' strengths; suggest areas in which they can take special responsibility; encourage their leadership; and appreciate their successes.

Setting standards. People often look to a leader to set standards for both the work and the ethics of the team, so help the team to brainstorm and set standards for its processes. Express high standards of your own, and manage your own behavior to provide a model for others.

Guiding ongoing assessment. A leader often has to make self-evaluation a desirable, shared, helpful process. With the team, develop methods and criteria for assessing processes and outcomes.

Coaching. Understand the processes. Explain, encourage, and help people assume responsibility for themselves. Become an expert yourself, then coach members in how to go out and do it. When a project is to be presented, help to organize it but also coach members in their roles and encourage their success.

MANAGING AND MOVING

Members sometimes are shockingly grateful when a leader simply manages and moves the task. Yet these probably are the easiest skills to learn and to provide for a team. They include planning and following through as well as ensuring task and transactional processes.

Planning and Following Through   Somebody needs to take care of the details, but if you haven't noticed, all too often nobody does. Without a designated leader, teams must pay extra attention to delegating these tasks. With a designated leader, however, it generally is expected that she or he will perform them or delegate them specifically to other members. The following checklist can help:

- Plan meeting times, places, and arrangements.
- Make sure information and resources are available.
- Plan agendas with the team or with delegated members.
- Communicate plans by publishing and distributing notices, meeting minutes, and agendas well ahead of time.

- Contact, set up, and confirm experts, consultants, or guests for meetings.
- Write and send follow-up letters, memos, and acknowledgments.

It's all in the details. All it takes is being organized and doing it.

Ensuring Processes An empowering team leader helps the team to lead itself. An appealing—and common-sense—concept of a leader comes from Weick (1978), who uses the metaphor of a medium for the leader. The leader, as medium, helps the team organize the complex interrelationships of its transactions and work in its environment, but does so by empowering all team members rather than hoarding all the authority for themselves. Pearce and Manz perhaps said it best: "if workers, particularly those in formal leadership roles, resist the notions of self- and shared leadership, their potential may simply remain that—potential" (2005, p. 134). This is not to say that no team should have a designated leader, only that a leader alone will not make a team effective. Instead, the leader's effectiveness will be in facilitating the team's processes so that members share leadership together.

Sometimes, groups meet with a person named as **facilitator**, whose function is to plan meetings and then to help planned processes occur. A facilitator keeps group members on task and helps them work through their assigned duties in the most efficient way possible, while ensuring that good decision-making practices are in place. A good facilitator drives the meeting just as a skilled chauffeur drives a car. His or her presence helps the meeting stay on the right path and arrive at a suitable conclusion. Gifted facilitators also bring a sense of coherence to the group's activities, so that everyone leaves the meeting feeling positive about both the process and the outcome (Yoong & Gallupe, 2002).

A meeting facilitator could be a consultant, a member, or the designated leader of the group. Earlier, we discussed *focus groups*, in which a facilitator guides discussion of specific questions to arrive at data relevant to anything from changes to a college curriculum to marketing a presidential candidate in a national campaign.

Whether a person is designated as a leader or a facilitator, his or her responsibility is to ensure the transactional and task processes work. One classic, but still highly relevant set of standards to keep in mind is that suggested by Larson and LaFasto (1989, p. 123):

- Avoid compromising the team's objective with political issues.
- Exhibit personal commitment to the team's goal.
- Don't dilute the team's efforts with too many priorities.
- Be fair and impartial toward all team members.
- Be willing to confront and resolve issues associated with inadequate performance by team members.
- Be open to new ideas and information from team members.

To achieve these objectives, a leader needs specific skills in meeting facilitation. Effective facilitators will:

Facilitate participation. Encourage, motivate, and get members to participate. Ask for and give information on the problem, solution generation, evaluation, and implementation.

Define roles. Regulate participation and structure role expectations for ensuing meetings. Make sure everyone gets a chance. Keep people from dominating, and consider the differences and needs of members.

Keep discussion coherent. Make connections among ideas. When appropriate, refer to previous information or to related information from other experiences. Synthesize concepts, identify relationships, or find new interpretations or applications of ideas within the discussion topic.

Control discussion inhibitors. Keep people from sidetracking the discussion; from withdrawing or criticizing negatively; or from contributing to confusion in the group.

As the use of groupware increases, these facilitative actions are gaining in importance. Yoong and Gallupe (2002) emphasize the crucial role of facilitative leadership in making virtual meetings effective. Hertel, Geister, and Konradt (2005) propose a planning model in which leaders focus systematically on planning a virtual team's work by first analyzing who should participate, how the work should be delegated, and how social ties within the team can be developed. Almost all researchers agree that, in the beginning of virtual teamwork, all members should meet each other face-to-face (i.e., Alge, Wiethoff & Klein, 2003; Gibson & Cohen, 2003); planning and facilitating these workshops is also an important task for the team leader. Members also need feedback about both work output and processes as the team spends more time working together—another task critical for good performance (Hertel, Konradt & Orlikowski, 2004).

All the information in this chapter is great in theory—and we know from experience it also is great in practice. When you get right down to it, it's the practice that makes it possible—and also challenging, fun, fulfilling, and useful—to learn to lead. We have a few suggestions for doing just that.

LEARNING TO LEAD

Can you learn to be a leader? Yes. Learning to lead, like any other skill, is a matter of mapping out an approach and following it. We suggest these four steps:

1. Identify people you consider to be excellent leaders, coaches, mentors, or teachers. Analyze what they do that makes them so effective, and use them as models for your own leading.
2. Identify your own strengths, and build on them. Observe yourself on videotape; use the self-analysis instruments; ask for feedback. Think about your skills in terms of what you've learned here and what you've observed in your models. Practice your strengths, make them even better, and reward yourself for what you do well.
3. Identify what you would like to have as new strengths. Visualize (remember Chapter 2?) how you feel and act when you're being the kind of leader you would like to be. See yourself being an effective leader; then make it true.
4. Look for opportunities to practice leading. They can be small tasks: chair a committee, get a group together to tackle a campus problem, teach a religious

| BOX 11.3 | NATURAL LEADER |

Rayona Sharpnack [founder of the Institute for Women's Leadership] is a teacher and a mentor to some of the most powerful women (and a number of men) in some of the most important companies around, including Boeing, Charles Schwab, Compaq, and Hewlett-Packard. . . .

[Sharpnack says] for most people, leadership is about "what you need to know" and "what you need to do." But Amazon.com sells more than 1,000 books that will tell you what you need to know and what you need to do. We work on *who you need to be*, which we call the "context." It's the *being* aspect of leadership that enables breakthroughs in what people do and what they learn. . . .

Context can be an individual's mind-set or the organizational culture. It includes all of the assumptions and norms that are brought to the table.

Context is perception, as opposed to facts or data. People don't go off and design their context—they just inherit it. So take anything from racism to sexism to what you think you can and can't do. It's all pretty much inheritance. It's conversations, oral tradition, all that kind of stuff. When you slow down enough to examine those ideas, you might realize, oh my gosh! I've been operating as though everyone else knew more than I did, just because back in grade school I was put in the bluebird reading group, instead of in the faster robin group. So it might be that kind of a deep individual insight that allows you to see that your whole context has been that you're a second-rate player.

Source: From Cheryl Dahle, "Natural Leader," *Fast Company*, December 2000, pp. 268–280. Reprinted by permission.

class at your place of worship, coach a Little League team. Practice, evaluate how you did, and develop your skills.

Being a leader can be a big responsibility. Seeing your team develop its strengths, become a force to deal with, and move forward to accomplish its goals, and knowing that your leadership contributed to that—now there's a great feeling.

SUMMARY

In this chapter, we've explored the mundane to the magical sources of power, approaches to leading, expectations and behaviors of leaders, and ways to develop the ability to lead. Leaders influence transactional and task processes, effect change, and empower others to lead themselves.

A person's power may come from many sources, including the ability to be coercive or to reward, a legitimate position, expert standing, respect and reputation, or communication of information. A good leader's objective is to empower the team, but the best way to do that is with a situational-contingency approach, which means adapting to situations and, perhaps, changing style according to the life cycle of the team. Classic styles of leadership are laissez-faire, authoritarian, and democratic. Contemporary approaches focus more on empowering members to lead themselves through transformational leadership methods and on facilitating their processes.

Expectations—from yourself, the team, or the organization—affect how an individual is perceived as a leader. People's expectations of a leader may conflict with their expectations of a person as social stereotype, however, and this may affect how they perceive an individual's potential and performance as a leader.

Leaders link the team to the parent organization and outside systems and buffer the team from interference. They motivate, coach, manage, and move the business of the team through transactional and task processes.

You can learn to lead by taking on responsibilities and using role models, feedback, visualization, and practice. Remember that leaders are not just people who do things right; they are people who do the right things (Bennis, 1989).

Exercises

1. As an individual, think of someone—living or dead, a public figure, a family member, a friend, anyone—whom you consider to be a leader. Make a list of what this person is or does that distinguishes her or him as a leader. Then, with a small group of other students, share your lists. What do your leaders have in common? Where do they vary in the qualities that each of you considered important? What accounts for these variations?

2. With the same group, do the following:

   a. Decide which style or styles each person you've identified as a leader uses or used—laissez-faire, authoritarian, democratic, or situational-contingency. Are they empowering and facilitating?

   b. Examine if, why, and how the style or styles used by the particular leader was or were appropriate to his or her group and situation.

   c. Decide which responsibilities of the leader (as we've discussed them in this chapter) each of your leaders fulfills or fulfilled.

   d. If a given leader fulfills or fulfilled some responsibilities but not others, why? And why is or was that person still a good leader? (An individual can be a good leader without meeting all criteria.)

3. Recall a time when you've been the designated leader of a group, or imagine yourself in that position. Using Form 11.1, identify what you can do that makes you potentially a good leader. What do you want to work on to develop your strengths?

4. With a group to which you now belong, evaluate the group's leadership—whether or not you have a designated leader—using Form 11.2. As usual, do this first as individual members, and then compare and discuss your responses as a team. Where do you agree? Disagree? Why? What can the team do to develop strong leadership? List what you intend to do, and then reassess the leadership after a few more meetings. Has the leadership developed further?

FORM 11.1 | PERSONAL ASSESSMENT OF LEADER CHARACTERISTICS

Think about your leadership and leader potential:

1. Do you prepare yourself for the meetings and teamwork?
2. How credible are you to yourself and others?
3. Do you convey enthusiasm, involvement, and commitment?
4. Do you see and adapt to other members' responses?
5. Do you monitor and adapt your own behaviors?
6. Are you principled? Do you discuss ethical issues?
7. How well are you able to communicate with others?
8. Are you good at helping to create a supportive climate?
9. Do you sometimes emerge as leader in groups and teams?
10. What style(s) of leadership do you think you use?
11. How and when do you adapt your leadership style?
12. How do you represent the team's interests to others?
13. Are you able to motivate and coach others in teamwork?
14. How well do you help to organize and focus the group's work?
15. How good are you at planning agendas and managing meetings?
16. Do you guide members to cooperate in vigilant analysis?
17. How do you feel when you know you've provided leadership?
18. Do you enjoy working through problems with others?
19. Do you help others to think, lead, and contribute?
20. Do you help people reach mutual understanding and goals?

Your strength in any of these is a start toward leadership. Look over your responses, and find the areas in which you have leadership qualities. What can you do to strengthen them? What can you do to strengthen skills? You will be asked to be the leader at some time or another, so be ready for the challenge.

FORM 11.2 | GROUP OR TEAM LEADERSHIP ASSESSMENT

1. If there is a designated leader, identify him or her: _____

   Was she or he: Elected? _____ Appointed? _____ By whom?_____

   Why? _____

2. If there is/are emergent leader(s), identify him/her/them:

   _____

   _____

   What behaviors identify him/her/them as leader(s)?

   _____

   _____

3. If leadership is distributed among members of the team, identify individuals and what they do below:

   MEMBER   FULFILLS LEADER FUNCTION OF:

   _____

   _____

   _____

   _____

   _____

   _____

FORM 11.2 | **CONTINUED**

4. How well do you think the following are done in your team?

	Well	Okay	Poorly
Developing a team vision and image	☐	☐	☐
Coaching and motivating members	☐	☐	☐
Getting information and resources	☐	☐	☐
Linking with other organizations or parent group	☐	☐	☐
Representing the team	☐	☐	☐
Planning agendas and activities	☐	☐	☐
Communicating information about meetings	☐	☐	☐
Moving meetings efficiently	☐	☐	☐
Building a supportive climate	☐	☐	☐
Keeping communication open	☐	☐	☐
Assuring that all members are heard	☐	☐	☐
Empowering members to take initiative	☐	☐	☐
Managing conflicts	☐	☐	☐
Setting goals and criteria	☐	☐	☐
Measuring ideas against criteria	☐	☐	☐
Summarizing, orienting team to task	☐	☐	☐
Encouraging critical analysis	☐	☐	☐
Focusing on ethical and value issues	☐	☐	☐
Assessing processes and outcomes	☐	☐	☐

"Communicating in this team is like running through a minefield—anybody got a detector?"
It's possible to prevent, detect, and dismantle group mines before they blow up.

TEAM PRESSURES AND CONFLICTS

Meeting the Challenges

12

Everything a work team does follows a path toward the team's goal. Each activity moves the team forward, overcomes barriers, or deflects the team along its way. If the team encounters mines, barriers, or rocks along the path, then the members' combined efforts are essential to defuse, hurdle, and move those impediments to their progress. This is what Dennis Gouran (1982) has called "counteractive leadership" or "acts directed toward coping with obstructions in a group's goalpath. . . . Leadership functions to counteract those influences acting on a group which, if left unattended, would prevent the members from achieving their goals" (p. 150). Such negative influences can arise from team pressures on individuals and vice versa; from groupthink, which blocks good decision making; and from competition and conflict within the team.

Your leadership can help the team hurdle its barriers or avoid building them. To those ends, this chapter seeks to help you to:

1. Understand the pressures that groups put on individuals
2. Know the causes and consequences of groupthink as well as ways to prevent it
3. Recognize and manage competitive communication strategies
4. Understand and manage conflicts in your team's processes

TEAM PRESSURES

Pressures on a team and its members come from many sources, some of which we've examined already. Here, we're concerned with a kind of point-and-counterpoint set of pressures. Pressure on the team is created by individual members who deviate from what the team expects; pressure on individuals builds when other members try to get them to conform to the group's preferences.

DEVIANCE

Diversity of opinion, thinking, background—all are essential to good teamwork. But, oh, the pressure a group can put on the individual who deviates from the group. **Deviance** can be defined as words and/or behavior that violate organizational or social norms, or that doesn't conform to other's expectations (O'Leary-Kelly, Duffy & Griffin, 2000).No mold-breaking allowed.

Role expectations. Members' preconceived ideas about how people should behave may seem insignificant, but when someone violates those expectations, these ideas can take on importance to the group. Note the effect of gender as illustrated in Box 12.1. Examples include:

- Infractions of general group norms ("We dress casually, but he always wears a tie. The guy just isn't like us.")
- Violations of expected behaviors in specific roles ("A leader should be formal, but she's relaxed. She can't be a leader.")
- Breaks in social stereotypes and role expectations of gender, class, race, status, or age ("Women should be nurturing—but she's tough!" "Men

BOX 12.1	**GENDER AND ROLE EXPECTATIONS**

Two social psychologists at the University of Surrey, England, were curious about how people might have different role expectations for female versus male leaders. The researchers designed and implemented an experiment in which fifty-five subjects read how a manager solved a problem either innovatively (creating new methods) or merely adaptively (using existing methods). Then the subjects were asked to attribute the solutions to male or female managers. Innovative solutions were attributed more often to a male than a female manager, whereas adaptive solutions were attributed more

often to a female than a male manager. The researchers also found that, unlike male managers, female managers might avoid the risks associated with being innovative because they were more likely to fear the consequences of failure or mistake, the risk of criticism, and the risk of not receiving credit for their ideas.

Source: Lynne J. Millward and Helen Freeman, "Role Expectations as Constraints to Innovation: The Case of Female Managers," *Creativity Research Journal*, 14.1 (2002), 93–109.

should be tough—but he's nurturing!" "Students should be submissive—but he's assertive." Deviants, all.)

- Reversals of expectations developed over time ("Hey, you're our clown—you can't get serious on us!")

Expressing deviant opinions. When someone perceives and expresses ideas differently from the way the group's majority sees them, she or he becomes the minority voice. Often, this is the person with the guts to raise issues, to suggest alternatives, to unsettle a group's complacency. But because the majority tends to protect its decisions from minority opinion influence, members may take an irrationally strong stance against someone with deviating opinions.

Innovating. The deviant member may amplify, strengthen, and extend a position. That's *innovation deviance.* Frequently, this person's ideas on the issues are too far out in front of the rest of the group's thinking. The innovator may identify implications of an idea the team hasn't considered, suggest alternative approaches, or advocate new points of view.

Deviance isn't all bad or all good, but it certainly gets attention. A member's insistence on behaving or seeing ideas differently can spark interpersonal conflict and ethical dilemmas in team processes. The team has a set of priorities for its goals—presumably worthwhile, valuable goals. The team wants to reach those goals expeditiously, and deviance may lead to incessant arguing and random decision making. It's distracting, it's time-consuming, and it comes from people who are not "just one of the guys." There's plenty of motivation within a team to silence deviating members.

On the other side of the deviance dilemma is the dialogical ethic—that every member should be able to express opinions, feel free to participate, and be acknowledged as an individual important to the group. Silencing a member violates this ethic. Furthermore, left to itself, the majority view tends to be unoriginal and closed. Dissenting or raising controversial issues can help the team make better decisions and evaluate more options (DeDrue & West, 2001).

CONFORMITY

Because deviance puts pressure on the majority, people have an overwhelming urge to throw everyone into a pressure cooker and make them all come out the same. When people want conformity, they can really turn up the heat under the lone deviant in that pot.

Conformity is behaving in ways that are consistent with the group's norms and standards. Obviously, everyone complies with some rules and norms. If they didn't, folks would just spin out into their own orbits and there would be no society. Conformity becomes a problem, however, when people want others to conform to their preconceived ideas, whether they make sense or not—no deviance allowed. It helps to understand people's motives, methods, and strategies for pressuring others to conform as well as how people respond when under pressure.

Motives   Group members can put both subtle and overt pressure on their peers to conform—and sometimes they may not even be fully aware that they are exerting this pressure. There are a number of reasons for this:

Protection of ego or self-image. A challenge to a person's assumptions, values, beliefs, or stereotypes also may challenge his or her self-concept and values. One way to avoid dealing with that is to label the other a deviant (or whatever term is in style for people who don't quite fit). That way, a group's norms are psychologically protected as "right" (Fu, Morris, Lee, Chao, Chiu & Hong, 2007).

Instrumentalism. Disagreement slows processes, so a team may put pressure on deviating members to conform to remove barriers along the path toward their goals. This is particularly true when people are multi-tasking, because they just want to get things done in the most efficient way possible and cannot absorb additional information effectively (Knowles, Morris, Chiu & Hong, 2001).

Avoiding interpersonal conflict. Deviant behavior makes many people psychologically uncomfortable. Deviance prompts negative feelings, reduced trust, and perceptions of unfairness in other group members, which can then lead them to withdraw from the group or engage in a defensive outburst (Felps, Mitchell & Byzington, 2006).

Methods   Individuals and groups use a variety of communication strategies to get others to do what they want, and these strategies interrelate with the kinds of climates in which people function. Figure 12.1 shows some of the strategies researchers have historically identified (Cody, Woelfel, & Jordan, 1983; Hunter & Boster, 1987; Kipnis & Schmidt, 1982).

What you see in this figure probably is consistent with your own experience. People pressure others to conform by being direct or indirect, friendly or unfriendly, and persuasive or coercive. Most people prefer to use cooperative approaches. King (2001) found that people's persuasive efforts to get compliance gradually increased pressure through progressively more negative sanctions toward the deviant.

Cooperative/Supportive Strategies	Competitive/Defensive Strategies
Direct, friendly: Using assertive requests or supportively phrased orders	*Indirect, unfriendly:* Implying guilt or aversive results, lying, using intermediaries to imply threat or aversive consequences to noncompliance
Persuasive: Focusing on the desired behaviors with reasoning and evidence, identifying them with the relationship between nonconformer and persuader, with mutual values, or with mutually respected others	*Coercive:* Threatening, withholding rewards or encouragement, playing double-bind (damned if you do; damned if you don't) games
Indirect, friendly: Setting a supportive mood, hinting, using intermediaries to negotiate, saving face, offering favors or rewards without linking them directly to the desired behavior	*Direct, unfriendly:* Issuing ultimatums, giving aggressive orders, blaming, attacking, being hostile or sarcastic

FIGURE 12.1

Cooperative/supportive versus competitive/defensive strategies for gaining compliance.

Ultimately, however, groups can and do ostracize deviants who refuse to join the pack (Pech, 2001). Groups have the advantage of outnumbering the deviant, and members begin by focusing communication more on the nonconformer than on the others. At first, they're friendly, waiting for the nonconformer to become aware that she or he is out of line. Next, they may move to gentle teasing and then to ridicule and sarcasm if the deviant hasn't gotten the message. Then the members intensify their persuasive efforts. Finally, if they don't get the compliance they seek, the members outright reject the nonconformer by discontinuing communication entirely (Bormann, 1990, pp. 187–188).

Groups are inconsistent about their pressure, however. If a group expects a person to be incompetent because of role expectations, then the deviator's competence seems to surprise the group—and draws greater support than a nondeviant might. Or the group may exert pressure to conform to the previous expectation when that person proves to be competent. In one study, for example, groups treated competent dissenters from a different department in their organization less cooperatively than they did dissenters from their own departments who expressed the same ideas with the same language (Schutz & Bloch, 2006).

Culture   Low-context, individualistic cultures and high-context, collectivistic societies approach conformity differently. Low-context society members (such as North Americans) generally prefer direct strategies, whereas members of low-context groups (such as East Asian societies) are more apt to use indirect, nonconfrontational approaches. Obviously, the high-context society has more concern for group harmony than does the low-context society, and this leads to more effort to protect personal face. **Face** can literally be thought of as the face people show the world. It is how we project ourselves to be viewed by others, and in a large sense, it is our sense of personal identity (Domenici & Littlejohn, 2006). The term "facework" is used to define the negotiation used to protect people's self-face (their own image), other-face (another's image), and mutual-face (their images together or the image of their relationship). Although the idea of "face" and "facework" originates with Chinese societies, never think it is nonexistent in Western societies—quite the contrary. Just remember a time when you or someone else have scrambled to cover your mistake or to change others' perceptions of your talent, work, or intentions by "spinning" what just happened. Regardless of your culture, it is hurtful to think that others think less of you or, perhaps, your friend or group. In fact, recent research has examined differences in facework among Chinese, Germans, Japanese, and U.S. Americans. They found that the Asians were more concerned with facework than the Westerners, but all had self-face concerns. The differences lay in degree of concern for other- or mutual-face and in methods of managing the problem. Germans had more self- and mutual-face concerns and were more defensive than Americans, and Chinese had more self-face concerns and involved third parties in negotiating resolutions more than did Japanese (Oetzel, Ting-Toomey, Masumoto, Yokochi, Pan, Takai & Wilcox, 2001).

Suppose you have taken a strong stand in opposition to the rest of your team. Your Western teammates might be inclined to work together in a meeting, directly trying to persuade you to conform. The women might be more conciliatory and nurturing, the men might be more direct and confrontational. Your Asian teammates might help you spin your position more favorably or even send a friend to speak with you privately about your friendship, your common goals, and the importance of the team's success to all of you. The intermediary also might suggest—indirectly—ways you could change your mind without seeming to do so. Either approach may (or may not) induce you to change, but each has its distinct strategy and sense of individual as well as group priorities. (On the other hand, we have personal Asian American friends who are more direct and confrontational than any Westerner; we have Anglo-American friends who are indirect and subtle to a fault; and we know women who are more confrontational and men who are more subtle and conciliatory. Go figure.)

Responses   Sometimes group members' reasoning and explanations make sense, and an individual goes along because she or he is genuinely persuaded. Sometimes the individual just rolls over rather than fight the pressure. But usually it's a little more complicated than either of those alternatives.

Conformity research goes back a long way. It's been found that under some circumstances, people will change their attitudes, beliefs, or even their perceptions of reality to conform to a group's norms or opinions—even if they are correct and the group is wrong. Unfortunately, there's no guarantee that a group will be right. Groups can be mindless: members lose their individual identities and exhibit instead mindless affinity with other members. In instances of apparently insane group behavior, people forget their individual ethical principles, go along with the crowd, and do things they would never do if they had to take personal responsibility.

One explanation for this is the sense of anonymity a group can provide. "I had nothing to do with it. It was the committee's/the union's/the management's/the family's decision. The *group* did it, not I." Anonymity can protect individuals from detection and separate them from self-awareness and moral restraints. When those are gone, mindlessness can rule.

If you want historical examples of group mindlessness, look at the lynch mobs that murdered thousands of African Americans in the nineteenth and twentieth centuries, at the atrocities of the Chinese Red Guard during the Cultural Revolution, at the insanity of the Nazi Youth Movement, or at neo-Nazi groups in the United States. All relied/rely on mindlessness; on group pressure for conformity; on norms and rules; and on symbols such as uniforms, salutes, music, posters, and flags. All these can assuage individuals' confusion and need for order, deindividuate people, and enforce a mass mentality that leaves personal ethical systems far behind.

Perhaps you think that's not a danger in a task team. Sure it is. Your team's decisions can be important. And too much pressure on one lone voice can silence that voice, resulting in nobody noticing that the emperor's stark naked and leading the parade.

Dissenting voices can be heard, however, and deviating members can influence groups. Conformity need not be mindless, just reasonable and sufficient for a group to be effective. Find out what a "granfalloon" is in Box 12.2. Principled leadership and vigilance are required to achieve this ideal.

BOX 12.2 | **TEAMISM**

Everyday we confront new ideas and opinions that are different from our own. We turn to our previous experiences, our friends, our philosophies, and our heroes for answers. We might even look at the general opinion to gauge our position. Even the government might have an answer. All of these are reasonable if we seriously answer our questions and if we do not commit the errors of teamism or hiding behind a granfalloon.

The philosopher Bokonon, in Kurt Vonnegut's novel *Cat's Cradle*, defines "granfalloon" as a meaningless association or bond between two people. Examples of this are nationality, race, political party, or a major league sports franchise. I call it teamism. Whose "team" are you on?

Like being born an American, wearing gang colors or a Baltimore Orioles hat, many of these actions are not based on a philosophy, just a circumstance. If you live in Baltimore, you are an Orioles fan. If you were born an American you think America is the greatest country in the world. I think America is a pretty great place to live, but is that only because I live here? Or you might have joined the team for one reason, but find yourself defending people and ideas that don't appeal to you, as many people find with their chosen political parties. Why still defend it? Does being open to criticism make you disloyal?

Your team or granfalloon will make you do things that you wouldn't do if you were on another team. Think of the gang members killing each other of the color of a bandana. If you had grown up in another neighborhood, or gone to a different high school, you'd want to "start a rumble" with an entirely different group of "others." Republicans and Democrats have gang colors too, red and blue. If you are a red-stater, you are supposed to hate the blue-staters.

Source: Excerpt from Kevin D. Rollins, "Teamism and Granfalloons," *The Free Liberal*, May 15, 2005, www. freeliberal.com. Reprinted by permission of the author.

GROUPWARE AND VIRTUAL MEETING INFLUENCES

Interestingly enough, research indicates that "virtual teams displayed a 'group mind' more often than face-to-face teams. When we're interacting in a computer-mediated group, we don't have enough information to view others as individuals. All we see is the group and its task. Consequently, we're likely to view others and ourselves only as group members, and not as individuals (Lee, 2006). In computer-mediated groups, we simply pay more attention to the group's opinions than to our own (Postmes, Spears, Sakhel & de Groot, 2001).

With the advent of groupware, enthusiasts contend that pressure to conform will be eliminated. They think that the anonymity of participants as they type in their messages from a hidden keyboard is the answer. After all, if no one knows who wrote the message, how can the message sender feel pressured to conform or constrained from expressing an honest opinion?

Even computer-mediated groups can detect deviants, although members of smaller groups are more accurate than those of larger ones "in determining who said which comments over time" (Scott et al., 1997, p. 21). Lee (2006) suggests that it is just as likely that groupware will enhance personal and social power of some individuals as well as minimizing them. The anonymous individual, sitting alone at the keyboard, is very much aware of what powerful people want him or her to do. And that lone individual also is aware of being alone, of having no peers for support. When people are in face-to-face group meetings, nonverbal cues can help them spot allies for their own ideas and sense how others in the room are responding to counter-arguments. This can give them the courage to put alternative viewpoints forward (Lee, 2006).

GROUPTHINK

Without vigilance, the best of teams can slide into **groupthink**. Irving Janis (1982) coined this term to describe a set of behaviors consistently exhibited by high-power groups that made disastrous decisions. Groupthink, too, is a kind of mindlessness, or perhaps single-mindedness. It keeps out everything but what the group assumes—and wants—to be true. It protects people from doing the analysis necessary to make good decisions. And, sometimes, it lights the fuse for disasters.

When the *Challenger* space shuttle exploded in 1983, the nation was thunderstruck. No one understood how this could have happened. As the inquiry proceeded, it became painfully obvious that information had been available to prevent the tragedy but had never reached the top levels of the hierarchy. The goal and lift-off date were set. The public relations value of the launch was critical to the administration, and NASA officials were closed off to—and protected from—data that would have delayed the blast-off and allowed the fatal flaw to be corrected. These people were not stupid; they were both the perpetrators and the victims of groupthink.

More recently, we watched the 2003 *Columbia* space shuttle disaster in horror. Here, two days before the *Columbia* fell apart in reentry over California, a NASA safety engineer warned that the shuttle "might be in 'marginal condition' and that others in the space agency weren't adequately considering the danger of a breach near the left wheels. . . . 'We can't imagine why getting information is being treated like the plague,' the engineer wrote. . . . The board investigating the accident. . . believes the shuttle suffered a breach based on its analysis of rising temperatures inside the same wheel compartment that the engineer had cited for concern" (Bridis, 2003, pp. A1, A4). Despite the efforts of many very smart people, groupthink happened again.

Knowing how groupthink happens, what it does, and how to correct it is vital to any ongoing team with decisions to make.

How Groupthink Happens

Some conditions are like a petri dish in which groupthink can—but not necessarily must—grow. These "antecedent conditions" (Janis, 1989a) include group cohesiveness as well as the structure, situation, and leadership with which the group functions.

Cohesiveness In Chapter 4, we talked about cohesiveness as a glue among team members that can contribute to productivity but also can give members illusions about their group's effectiveness. Even when problems loom, nobody wants to sacrifice the group's cohesiveness by introducing anything that might dissolve the glue, so problems are not discussed. In fact, research indicates that group cohesion may be the single most important issue contributing to groupthink (Park, 2000).

Structure Structural conditions that make it easy to develop groupthink include homogeneity, inadequate group processes, and insulation from the outside. With homogeneity, members of groups that have high social attraction often are alike and like-minded, and thus think in narrow channels. With inadequate processes, the group lacks the norms for critical thinking that would protect the team's openness to ideas and dissent.

Larger cohesive groups with fewer individual interaction opportunities, for example, tend to make poorer decisions than smaller cohesive groups (Park, 2000). With insulation from the outside, members lack the information and the stimulation necessary to develop and to be effective.

Situation Situational stress can pressure a group into groupthink. In the face of a crisis, threat, or even competition involving extremely high stakes, members are more likely to remain closed to new or different ideas. Chapman (2006) writes that, in the presence of anxiety, people are motivated to seek agreement with others in order to feel less nervous. The more important they perceive the decision to be, the more comfortable they are when fully committed to a solution. The problem grows worse if the team's self-esteem is low because of recent failures, or it's up against an impossible task, or it faces moral dilemmas for which no alternative meets members' ethical standards. A team in this depressed situation may accept alternatives that, as individuals or under other circumstances, the members might reject.

Leadership Leaders who are directive, authoritarian, and controlling tend to push their groups into groupthink (Scharff, 2005). Such a closed leadership style encourages poor decisions by pushing for concurrence and establishing a group norm for closed inquiry. When the leader pushes the group toward consensus, without seeking input or alternative perspectives, members quickly learn that their qualms about the group's direction are not to be voiced (Erdem, 2003).

WHAT GROUPTHINK DOES

Teams that experience some—or all—of the antecedent conditions do not necessarily fall into the groupthink trap. If they do, it shows up in their decision-making processes. Members aggrandize the qualities of their team, close off their minds, and pressure themselves and one another to be unanimous. Consequently, the team fails to survey alternatives, settles quickly on one solution, and ignores any possible difficulties with it. As a result, the groupthinking team does not work out contingency plans for implementing its decision—in short, a recipe for disaster.

Here are some things to watch out for:

Illusion of invulnerability. Members feel the team is stronger than any counteracting forces. This leads them actually prefer risky decisions over conservative ones (Koerber & Neck, 2003).

Belief in the inherent morality of the group. The group assumes it has the forces of "right" on its side; therefore, anyone who is in opposition must necessarily be with the forces of "wrong." This relates directly to the next two issues.

Stereotyping members of out-groups. Feeling that the in-group is especially strong and moral is facilitated by a "we against them" mentality that stereotypes others as incompetent, inferior, or immoral.

Closed-mindedness and collective rationalizations. Members cooperate in resisting new ideas and information as well as in building rationalizations for their preconceived positions. They exclude information from experts, outside groups, and resources that could increase their understanding, and they pay attention only to those facts that support a position they favor and ignore those that weaken it.

Self-censorship. Members don't allow themselves to say—or sometimes even to think—something that counters the group's thought. Individuals rationalize their positions so they can believe in the unanimity of the group.

Pressure on dissenters. Members exert pressure to conform on anyone who expresses a dissenting thought. Leaders may reinforce this pressure by ignoring, downplaying, or even ridiculing a dissenting view.

Mindguards. Members become guards to keep the leader from hearing anything that might upset his or her point of view. They deflect messengers with bad news, and they filter, distort, and hide information that might disturb the illusions. In the past, congressional hearings have uncovered instances when officials allegedly concealed or distorted facts in their reports to a president. "Don't bother the chief" means the chief makes groupthink decisions.

Illusion of unanimity. All these issues lead to the team's illusion that they all agree, which comes around in a spiral to reinforce all the behaviors that led to that illusion in the first place (Janis, 1982, 1989a, 1989b).

These behaviors protect a team's sense of self-esteem, superiority, cohesiveness, and strength. They also create a stranglehold on the group's ability to think rationally and critically, and they can easily lead to bad decisions, as shown in Figure 12.2. It's scary when you consider that the disastrous decisions resulting in the Bay of Pigs, Watergate, Iran-Contra, and the *Challenger*—and, probably, the *Columbia*—incidents were made under the influence of groupthink (Scharff, 2005). Even as you read this, groupthink afflicts groups that make high-level decisions affecting your safety and well-being as well as that of the entire nation.

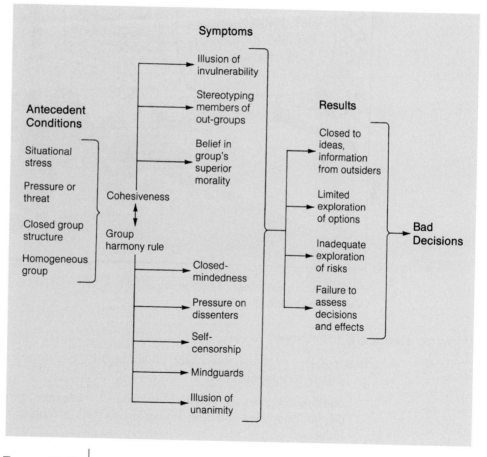

Figure 12.2

The process of groupthinking to a bad decision.

It also is vastly irritating (at the very least) when groupthink affects less earth-shaking policies and actions. We remember a group of students who got together to study for an exam. Under stress but overconfident, they failed to research their topic, ignored a professor's offer of help, and relied on one student's recollections about Plato and Aristotle. As they talked, they created a rubric of misconceptions that all the members then used as the database to write their exams. Their professors were boggled at the extent of the inaccuracies—and the students were shocked that they did so poorly. Groupthink had convinced them they had the right information.

Would an outside consultant's advice be helpful here?
Source: Reprinted by permission of Joel Pett

How to Reduce Groupthink

It is possible to avoid this blight on teamwork. We suggest you practice these groupthink-busting methods:

Norm setting. Discuss and agree to norms for openness, protecting the right of dissent, principled and open leadership, as well as transactional and task processes.

Assumption testing. Examine your discussions for assumptions about facts, values, or people. Look for illusions of invulnerability, moral superiority, or unanimity. Avoid stereotyping other groups and making assumptions about others' behaviors or values.

Information scouting. Aggressively seek outside resources, experts, and relevant information. Janis (1982) suggests inviting outside experts to each meeting and asking them to challenge team members' views. Encourage each member to discuss ideas with outside groups and to bring their responses back to the team.

Challenging. Have all members take on the role of critical evaluator and regularly challenge ideas, information, and suggestions. When considering policies, appoint someone to be a devil's advocate, arguing as persuasively as possible for the other side (Janis, 1989a).

Structure shifting. Create outside groups to work on the same issues, and compare your deliberations. When considering policies, divide the team into subgroups, meet separately, and then come back to the full team and hash out the results.

Even with these methods, a team may need to do still more to break down groupthink barriers. Janis (1982, 1989a) suggests the following:

Focus meetings. Set up special meetings to focus on single issues when policy decisions may involve serious risks.

Reviewing. Hold "second chance" meetings for people to review decisions and to raise new ideas or concerns about them.

Processing. At every stage, review and assess your transactional and task processes to ensure that everyone is heard, that pressures to conform are within bounds, and that the team is cohesive without using groupthink.

If your group is vigilant in avoiding the groupthink traps, you can develop a cohesive, productive team that investigates and analyzes issues openly, clearly, and critically. The group might be aided by use of computer group support systems (GSS), too. Miranda (1994) examined extensive research concerning antecedents and processes that often lead to faulty decisions and concluded that "when appropriately used, structural features of GSS technology may mitigate certain group characteristics that predispose [to] groupthink. They may promote more structured group interactions and better meeting management" (p. 116). Conditions in GSS such as process structuring, extended and more efficient information-processing capacity, and task focus suggest the potential for achieving greater vigilance in decision making.

COMPETITIVE COMMUNICATION

"They are playing a game. They are playing at not playing a game. If I show them I see they are, I shall break the rules and they will punish me. I must play their game, of not seeing I see the game" (Laing, 1970, p. 1).

You've no doubt felt this way at some time in your life. Have you ever seen a couple deliberately baiting each other? ("Too bad you didn't have time to fix dinner, darling." "Yes, dear, but if you'd remembered to fill the gas tank I could have gone to the store." "Right, my love, if I hadn't taken all day to repair that lock you broke." "Well, sweetheart, I wouldn't have broken the lock if you'd installed it the way my brother told you to in the first place.") As an observer, you wince each time one player scores, but you know you must pretend you don't notice. If you reveal your awareness, you know you'll be drawn in.

You may have noticed that some people seem to prefer game playing to direct communication. When someone manipulates others into playing a game, it is to gain some reward or payoff. The payoff need not be positive; it's defined in terms of what the individual needs, wants, expects, and can handle emotionally. Just like families and other social organizations, teams can get caught up in playing **games** as well. We're going to examine how team members may play games, how games affect communication climates, and how to manage games when they occur.

How People Play Games

The game-playing adult has learned to manipulate others into playing out scripts that keep interdependency with others within the person's survival range and that also provide rewards to meet his or her needs. In addition to your almost-certain gut feeling, several clues indicate that someone is playing a game. These include the *gimmick*, the *repeated script*, and the *payoff*.

> *Gimmick.* The game player often begins with a particular approach or phrase that requires others to respond as the game player wants them to. Jan comes to your study group meeting, for example, and says, "I just don't get it—I guess I'm stupid or something—I studied for hours, and I just don't get it." This is a negative self-visualization, and unhealthy, but anyone might say it at some time. Jan, however, does this frequently. This is a gimmick when it's repeated and when it leads into a script.

> *Script.* Although a script is not to be repeated word for word every time an individual puts it into action, it does have an observable general structure. As a script, it includes heroes and villains in some plot, action, and climax. If Jan wants to launch a game, she starts with her gimmick. You respond by saying, "Hey, no, really—it's easy. Just let me show you," and Jan, flaring up as she has at almost every meeting, yells, "Don't patronize me, you jerk. Just because you think I'm an idiot doesn't give you the right to put me down." When this happens, you realize that you didn't want to get into this game again, but somehow you were trapped. You'll know it's a repeated game if your mind goes back over it: "What am I supposed to say, for crying out loud? How can I make her see I don't think she's stupid?" Now, as you phrase responses to meet her requirements, you're well into the script. Are you the villain? Is she the hero? The victim? What is the plot?

> *Payoff.* As a script develops, a plot emerges—and the climax is the payoff. How can you tell what the payoff is? It may be something tangible. Sometimes people set up scripts like these so they can blow up, walk out, and not be held accountable for the work. It may be more complicated, however. Does Jan need to be a victim? Does she need to feel stupid? Does she need to be angry, find a scapegoat, and not deal with learning what she needs to learn? Perhaps figuring out the payoff should be left to psychologists. It's enough just to understand that strategic communication is going on and that there is *some*

reason for it. As a team member, your concern is to understand how the game can affect your team's climate.

How Games Affect Climate

Game playing devastates communication climates. When a group becomes trapped in a game, you can almost measure the barometric changes, humidity, temperature, and wind chill.

One key to how games affect the climate is the difference between cooperative and competitive approaches to communication. You remember that supportive climates are cooperative, open, trusting, and empathic, but defensive climates are competitive, closed, and lacking in trust and empathy. Competitive communication assumes that if there's a winner, there also must be a loser. There are only two alternatives: win or lose. Under this assumption, no one can be trusted, and any risk one person takes is calculated for the purpose of defeating another. A competitive approach means anticipating what others might do, weighing the consequences, and choosing an offensive action or a defensive counteraction. Competitive games are appropriate to sports, advocacy, debate, or chess—any enterprise in which the objectives are to hone competitive skills and win a victory.

Cooperative approaches assume the opposite on all counts—that it is possible for both (or even all) parties to win: a win-win outcome. Cooperation relies on trust and taking risks to maximize the gains for everyone. Obviously, cooperative approaches are appropriate to situations in which the objectives are to hone cooperative communication skills, to develop relationships, and to achieve the goals of all involved.

A person who takes a competitive approach to a situation that should be cooperative will manipulate others' responses to "win points." This leads to those others losing trust and becoming unwilling to take cooperative risks. The result often is that no one wins—a lose-lose outcome—and the climate is seriously damaged. Yet people repeatedly find themselves in presumably cooperative situations in which others are playing competitive games.

How to Handle a Game

You'll note that we deliberately use the term *handle*. This is because you may or may not be able to stop a game. You and the other members of the team may hate it, but the person (or persons) perpetuating the game have rehearsed the script for a long time; they're one up on you. Furthermore, everyone is feeding into it.

First, analyze the situation. You can start your analysis by answering these questions:

- How seriously is the game affecting the team? Is it slowing progress, alienating people, creating minor stress or extreme tension, or bringing work to a halt?
- How reasonable is the initiator? Can you communicate cooperatively? Is she or he so intense, so manipulative, or so involved in the game that every communication transaction is a move toward checkmate?

- How clear is the source of the game? Is it between two people? Does one person regularly open the game and bring other members into his or her transactions?
- How obvious is the payoff? Is it part of someone's not-so-hidden agenda? Is it an identifiable, concrete outcome or an individual's identifiable personal need or want?
- Is the payoff something the team can legitimately assist in providing? Is it an objective the game player can achieve with the team's cooperation, or is it unrelated to the team or inconsistent with the team's goals?

Based on this assessment, decide whether—and if so, how—to confront the issue. This decision can be guided by these general considerations:

Whether to intervene. If the game is not bothering the team much, if it's only a minor irritation or even a source of humor, then don't bother intervening. It takes time and energy to end a game. If it's a real problem, then the team needs to consider how to confront it. This requires careful leadership and communication.

Getting to the game. If the game player or players are obvious, then you know where to start. If they are rational and capable of being cooperative, then you have reason to try. If you think the payoff can be identified by discussing the problem—if you think it's something the team can help with, something unrelated to the team, or something about which the team at least can be supportive—then you have a goal to work toward.

Under these circumstances, you may want to confront the game. The criteria in Chapter 9 for cooperative communication climates and ways to use language apply here. It takes careful phrasing and supportive attitudes.

It's a mistake to say, "You're playing a game." That's direct, but it also is blaming, judgmental, and usually triggers yet another game. Instead, own your feelings. Use "I" statements, be descriptive, and be problem-oriented. Say something like, "I feel uncomfortable. I feel that something's going on here under the surface . . ." or "I'm frustrated because I feel that when you say . . . , then I have to say. . . . That feels like a game to me, and I'm uncomfortable with it."

No matter how careful you are, however, a real pro will come back with something like, "I am not playing a game! How dare you accuse me . . ." because that, too, is a game. You then need to reaffirm your position, gently yet assertively ("I didn't say you were playing a game. I only know what I feel, and I feel our communication is scripted somehow . . ."). Step by step, never casting blame, you work out an understanding of the underlying issues and a more direct way of communicating about them. For a group to work its way out of a game can be very painstaking and difficult, but it's possible if you work carefully through the confrontation approaches.

CONFLICT

Conflict often scares people. Some like a good fight, and some greatly enjoy negotiation. Many others, however, would prefer not to deal with conflict at all. The bottom line, however, is that conflict is inevitable and sometimes cyclical. The nature of the conflicts may change as groups progress toward their goals. Conflict episodes may increase, for example, when groups reach the midpoint of their lives, when issues of power, conflict, and decision emerge. The nature of the conflict may also change at the team's midpoint, moving from competitive behaviors to cooperative, problem-solving behaviors as the group moves toward its goal (Behfar, Peterson, Mannix & Trochim, 2008).

Good leadership frequently brings conflict to the fore—not for a fight, but to examine the alternatives. To make reasoned decisions, sometimes you need to see how ideas, information, and values clash. To do this effectively, you need to understand the various types and sources of conflict and how different people approach conflict. With this knowledge, you can learn ways to manage it.

TYPES OF CONFLICT

Conflict occurs when two or more people perceive their individual goals as being mutually exclusive—that is, if they perceive that accomplishing one person's goal keeps another's goal from being achieved. Differences may be negotiated cooperatively, or transactional processes may degenerate into a dysfunctional clash. That is, it gets personal.

Clearly, conflict may be either productive or dysfunctional for a team. Witteman (1991) makes the distinction this way: "Productive conflict involves the critical evaluation of ideas. In dysfunctional conflict, members either completely suspend evaluation or focus it on the behavior and personality of other members" (p. 28).

Figure 12.3 shows the bipolar characteristics of conflict. When conflict is productive, members depersonalize the process and focus cooperatively on substantive issues. Although competitive conflicts seem to be associated with personalized issues, groups can learn to differentiate the types. The groups that can distinguish between *task* and *relationship* conflict, and have strategies for dealing with each, consistently show better decision making and productivity than those who do not (Rahim, 2002).

PRODUCTIVE CONFLICT	DYSFUNCTIONAL CONFLICT
Positive	Negative
Depersonalized	Personalized
Substantive	Affective
Cooperative	Competitive

FIGURE 12.3

The bipolar characteristics of conflict.

BOX 12.3   CAN YOU BE COMFORTABLE WITH CONFLICT?

An important dimension of culture is the extent to which members identify with the group rather than themselves as individuals. Individualistic cultures place a high value on "autonomy, initiative, creativity, and authority in decision making" (Moore and Woodrow). Individual interests trump group interests, and any group commitment is a function of a perceived self-benefit.

Collectivist cultures, on the other hand, value the group above the individual. Group conformity and commitment is maintained at the expense of personal interests. Harmony, getting along and maintaining "face" are seen as crucial.

The dominant culture in the U.S., Canada, Western Europe, Australia, and New Zealand is individualistic, while collectivism predominates in the rest of the world. However, examples of both are found everywhere. In California, where the recent census found that 32 percent of the population are

Hispanic, 7 percent are African American, and 10 percent are of Asian descent, it can safely be assumed that a relatively high percentage of the workforce comes from a social environment that is collectivist.

Individualists and collectivists view conflict differently. Collectivists, who place a high value on harmony, getting along, and "face," see conflict as a sign of social failure. As a result, comfort levels with conflict situations are low. Conflict is often avoided.

While many individualists also feel discomfort with conflict, it is acknowledged as an inevitable part of life that must be dealt with. However, being in conflict with another is not necessarily something to be ashamed about.

Source: Excerpt from John Ford, "Cross Cultural Conflict Resolution in Teams," October 2001, http://www.mediate.com. Reprinted by permission of the author.

SOURCES OF CONFLICT

The source of a conflict can be simple or complex. For example, team members may experience conflicts between their responsibilities to the team and their responsibilities to other groups. Many studies concur that a significant number of group conflicts are based on differing interests in the organizations that group members represent (Schutz & Bloch, 2006). Note the influence of culture on conflict in Box 12.3. Whether between individual members, members and other groups, or groups and other groups, major sources of conflict include:

Information. If individuals have contradictory information or differ in their interpretation of the same information or ideas, they may come into conflict.

Resources. When needed resources—time, money, materials, support—are insufficient, conflict may arise over who gets what or over how to find more.

Expectations. If members' expectations—of roles, stereotypes, leadership, structure, process, goals—are not met, or if members' expectations differ, then pressure to conform and competitive behaviors may lead to conflict.

Needs. If individuals' personal needs, motivations, or agendas block or clash with those of other members or the group, then pressures to conform, game playing, and conflict may arise.

Power and control. Individuals who compete to achieve greater power, to control others' responses, or to control outcomes in the team often come into conflict.

Values, attitudes, and beliefs. Individuals who hold radically opposed attitudes, values, or beliefs may clash. The more deeply an individual holds a given value or belief—that is, the more central it is to his or her self-concept—the more threatening it is to have it challenged.

Ethics. If values clash over ethical choices, then people may come into conflict on both philosophical issues and on concrete decisions, because ethical choices often rest on deeply held concepts of self and society.

Personality. Individual personality clashes, which may be linked to any (or all) of the previous sources of conflict, can lead to affective conflict, which may compound even the most rational conflict over simple content issues.

APPROACHES TO CONFLICT MANAGEMENT

The conflict management process starts with individual styles and approaches. We're going to look at some of those, and then at some ways your self-awareness and ability to adapt your communication can help to manage conflicts as a team. Read about successful approaches to conflict and confrontation in the Harley-Davidson company in Case Study 12.1.

Individual Styles   People tend to respond to conflict on the basis of two things: how much they care about the issue at hand, and how much they care about the other party(s) with whom they disagree (Richter, Scully & West, 2005). See if you recognize your own responses to conflict in any of these:

The Collaborator operates from a cooperative, win-win perspective, bringing everyone's interests and points of view into perspective and trying to ensure that each person's goals are achieved.

The Compromiser works from a cooperative point of view, but doesn't see everyone winning as a possibility. His or her focus is on negotiating some gains for everyone.

The Accommodator assumes that situations are competitive—but that it's better to yield than to fight it out. The accommodator shifts positions to allow others to win.

The Controller has a competitive, defensive, win-lose orientation and sees conflict management as making the right moves to win points and control others' responses.

The Avoider assumes that everything is competitive, win-lose, and that loss is inevitable. This person simply avoids conflict by any means possible.

These styles relate to what psychologists call "fight-or-flight" reactions to threat. Conflict arises, and adrenalin pumps. People often can't walk out or slug it out, so they adapt their responses to civilized alternatives. A person who wants to run away may play the role of an avoider or, perhaps, an accommodator. A person

CASE 12.1 | QUALITY IS NO "EASY RIDER"

Accountability, confrontation—two success factors at Harley-Davidson . . .

The deep V-Twin engine growls. Daytona Beach Biker Week. An American icon of the open road. All are emblematic elements of a company that produces the most sought-after bikes on the planet—Harley-Davidson. But behind the mystique lies a unique culture of teamwork, accountability, and empowerment that serves as the foundation for sustained growth and profitability. . . .

[Editor Bill Brewer of *News for a Change* interviewed Vice President of Quality John Goll. Stand-out insights from Goll about Harley-Davidson's processes were:]

About HD's use of circles as organizational structure: "'Circle' illustrates a message of collaboration and synergy . . . to get away from the typical hierarchical structure . . . to get participative involvement . . ."

About consensus decision-making: [Consensus takes longer in the beginning. It takes] "practice, practice, practice, it starts to become a way in which you operate your business. Don't misunderstand, we don't do everything by consensus. I surely hope we don't do that in our fire drills."

About conflict with unions: "It's just like a marriage. You get out of it what you put into it . . . sharing the same basic principles and objectives . . . getting the upfront involvement in understanding your differences. . . . We talk about telling the truth, being fair, keeping promises, trying to respect all individuals . . . trying to encourage intellectual curiosity. You have to walk that talk and it's a tough thing to do."

About getting at the truth: "What we see more than a person not telling the truth or lying . . . [is] the suppression of information by the other individual. The confrontation associated with that I think is one of the key leadership skills for highly successful organizations."

About confrontation: "A very tough issue . . . in business . . . in family and personal life. But if we don't confront eventually whatever's being suppressed will evolve into a very unpleasant situation. If you don't confront how do you give people the opportunity to improve? We talk about business meetings that are conducted in the washrooms. If you can get them out in the open so people have the opportunity to respond to what they believe is going on, what they believe they're hearing from their peers, then they find out the reality. It's not easy."

About confrontation and Harley-Davidson's success: [A definite contribution to success through confrontation and feeling comfortable] "in saying, 'That's not the way I've seen it,' 'That's not the way you seem to be behaving lately.' It's almost like helping a person understand as opposed to making accusation that they did something wrong."

About individual performance objectives, quarterly reviews, constant dialogue, and meshing these goals with teamwork: "A good example is our PPG (Produce Product Group) circle. . . . About eight members each have a functional responsibility. . . . Each in their own area of responsibility has goals and objectives, but the key is they are tied to the goals and objectives that are established by that circle in its entirety. Those eight circle members need to define what their goals and objectives are so that the individual goals and objectives support that common purpose which naturally would relate to the vision and mission of your business."

Questions to Consider

1. How do you think the concept of circles as organizational structure relates to teamwork? How do you think Harley-Davidson's philosophy

and methods relate to traditional organizational patterns?

2. Consider concepts we've discussed throughout this text and in this chapter that relate to what Goll tells you here. What about control versus commitment strategy in organizations? Synergy and syntality? Image and culture? How about ethics?

3. What do you think an organization such as Harley-Davidson has to consider in putting

together effective teams? How would you envision a team managing a situation of game playing, conflict, or groupthink?

Source: Excerpt from Bill Brewer, "Quality Is No Easy Rider," *News for a Change*, November 1997, Association for Quality and Participation, pp. 1, 3, 7. Copyright © 1997 American Society for Quality. Reprinted with permission. No further distribution allowed without permission.

whose urge is to fight may be a controller. Either one may moderate his or her urges by working as a collaborator or compromiser.

A team may have people who use any or all of these conflict management styles. A good conflict manager can adapt to the situation; there are occasions when each response may be best. It's helpful to recognize these styles and to work on developing your own flexibility in using—and in coping with others'—styles of conflict management.

Communication Adaptation   To work with conflict situations, you need to be aware of your own strengths and limitations. It's essential to assess your strengths and build on them. It develops both self-confidence and skill.

By "self-awareness," we also mean awareness of your own feelings while you are communicating with others. During conflicts, you continually need to test your internal states as well as monitor your external communication. You need to check in with your physiological and psychological condition. Is your heart beating too fast? Are you becoming angry, or flushed? Do you have your adrenalin under control? Are you cool? Conflict management requires as much self-control as you can muster, and self-awareness helps you to recognize when you need to step in and work on your own responses. Telling yourself "I'm cool, I'm okay, I'm dealing with this" can help keep your own tendencies to fight or to flee in check as you work with others to manage a conflict.

Self-awareness is also a process of monitoring your verbal, listening, and nonverbal communication with others. It is never more important to be aware of the messages you send and their possible effect on others than during a conflict. Sometimes, particularly when stress is high, people don't hear themselves at all.

Self-monitoring takes practice, learning to listen to what you say and how you say it, and being aware of your nonverbal cues. You can watch and listen to others for feedback on what you are doing and how it is affecting them, so you can adapt your communication to convey what you want more accurately. As you monitor your own communication in a group, you can learn to modify it as well. We've written at length about transactional and task processes as well as about verbal, listening, and nonverbal communication in other chapters. Here, we stress only a few things that help to ensure effective communication during conflict management:

Concern for individuals and the team. Your coorientation with others and your concern for a win-win solution for everyone is important. You need to recognize your interests in the conflict but keep them in the broader framework of mutual solutions.

Fairness and equity. If members work for balance, justice, and fairness, they feel better about the process, understand that an ethical framework has surrounded it, and are able to adjust better to one another.

Good humor. Good humor is an attitude, a willingness to cut others a little slack. Humor can reduce anger and tension; it can point out foolishness and contradictoriness in a friendly way and bring people back to focusing on issues and away from personalities.

Sense of humor. Related to good humor—but not identical—is an ability to see the humor in a situation, to appreciate an irony, and to alleviate stress with appropriate levity. As Smith, Harrington, and Neck (2000, p. 606) put it, "in today's increasingly diverse and competitive workplace, conflict management skills and having a sense of humor are becoming requisites for every worker." It should be noted, of course, that joking around also can be used to mask aggressiveness or to avoid dealing with conflict. In that case, someone needs to identify the problem and get the team to focus on managing the issues.

PROCESSES OF CONFLICT MANAGEMENT

There are reasons for talking about conflict *management*, not *resolution*. It takes a management process to resolve a conflict. Furthermore, resolving a conflict once and for all isn't always possible. A single issue may be resolved, but when the sources of conflict remain, the potential for clash continues. A team needs, therefore, to develop skills and approaches to managing conflict through its transactional processes.

Here are some suggestions for starting the process of conflict management:

Assess its importance. Is the conflict one that can impede the team's progress, impair relationships, or impact on a decision? If so, the conflict is important.

Diagnose the conflict. What are the sources of the conflict? Where and how do goals conflict?

What is the focus? Substantive, content, task issues? Interpersonal, emotional clashes? Both?

Analyze people's interests. Do they have positions on a question, fact, or information? Are they motivated by differing needs, attitudes, values, or beliefs? What are their goals and expectations?

Analyze the ways the team normally transacts individual, task, and team issues. Are there patterns or expectations that can form a basis for managing the conflict? Are there factors that have to be dealt with before the conflict can be managed?

The answers to these questions can help you select the most appropriate strategy for managing the problem. Possible strategies include ignoring conflict, approaching it indirectly, or confronting and negotiating it.

Ignoring a conflict sometimes works, sometimes doesn't. You just have to hedge your bets when making that decision.

Managing conflict indirectly may be appropriate if interpersonal or private issues are involved or individuals are not likely to respond positively to direct confrontation. Remember, for example, that Asian groups often use intermediaries. But unlike North Americans, who seek an objective, detached person as a conflict mediator, Asians seek intermediaries who are personally involved with the parties and have more "face"—or status and respect—than the conflicting individuals have. This intermediary helps each person work out ways of saving face so that she or he can accept a resolution to the problem (Domenci & Littlejohn, 2006). Some ways of approaching a conflict indirectly include:

- Use an intermediary to negotiate privately.
- Restructure responsibilities or contacts to diminish interdependence between conflicting people.
- Suggest new, more acceptable ways of interpreting the differences.
- Confer with the conflicting parties and the leader, a member, or a consultant.

Confronting and negotiating conflict issues requires cooperative, win-win, full involvement of all members in a problem-solving approach. If this is the best strategy for your team, we suggest that you follow the diagnosis process with these steps:

1. Identify what each party to the conflict wants. Keep the focus on the issues, however, not on the people. Talk until the concerns are clear and affirmed by each person.
2. Identify in what ways both parties can get what they want, and isolate any items that seem to be irreconcilable. In their classic book *Getting to Yes*, Fisher and Ury (1981) emphasize concentrating on interests at this time, not on positions.
3. Assess the value of the achievable, mutual goals. Be creative; Fisher and Ury (1981) recommend creating multiple options that explore new approaches for mutual gain. Work for agreement that these mutual goals outweigh the irreconcilable points.
4. Talk the issues through. Eliminate unimportant differences, and isolate important ones.
5. Talk through important differences. Find all points in common within each difference, and work out compromises.
6. Agree on the solution.
7. In a substantive conflict, move on.
8. In an affective or personal conflict, create an agreement or contract as to what each party will do to manage potential problems in the future. Make the agreement positive and specific.

The last two steps may require some further explanation. If the conflict is substantive—say, over whether the team has enough money for a project—then a decision of "Yea" or "Nay" allows you to go on to your planning. But if the conflict is affective—for example, a personal conflict has arisen because I'm sarcastic and you're sensitive—then I need to agree to monitor my behavior, to be aware of your feelings, and to soften my communication. You probably need to agree to try taking me with a grain of salt, but also to tell me if you're upset before you get to the explosion point.

It's probably obvious that at each stage of this process, it is vitally important *to listen empathically and interactively, to support and confirm each other, to communicate clearly and assertively, and to maintain a cooperative, open, nondefensive climate.*

SUMMARY

In this chapter, we've called your attention to some challenges that teams face, including members' deviance from group expectations and pressures to conform. Conformity pressure can short-circuit ethics and good decision making by taking advantage of individual anonymity within the group and by silencing important contributions. Principled leadership, support from others, and competence all make it more likely that dissenters will be heard.

Cohesiveness, which is necessary for group satisfaction and productivity, can also be a problem. Too much cohesiveness, along with structural problems and situational pressures, can lead to groupthink. Under the illusion that it is superior, moral, and invulnerable, the group screens out information and analysis. Groupthink decisions can be disastrous, but clear norms for vigilant information gathering and decision making help to avoid groupthink.

Game playing, or scripted and manipulative communication, involves a starting gimmick, a predictable script that controls the communication choices, and some payoff or reward for the game player. Stopping a game requires a cooperative, win-win, trusting, supportive climate in which to examine carefully the interpersonal dynamics of the game. Sometimes getting a game under control requires a full conflict-management approach.

Productive conflict is substantive, depersonalized, and cooperative, and it can yield better analysis and decisions. Dysfunctional conflict, however, is personalized and competitive, and it can harm a group's cohesiveness, productivity, and satisfaction. Managing conflict requires diagnosing the types and sources of the conflict. As a conflict manager, you need to be self-aware and adaptive. Other important qualities include concern for individuals and for the team, fairness and equity, good humor, and a sense of humor. Appropriate management strategies range from ignoring a conflict to full-fledged confrontation.

Exercises

1. With a group in your class, go back over this chapter and list ways that a team can manage conflict. Starting with this list,

   a. Refine it into a list of the most important ideas.

   b. For each item, write a short, clear statement that describes the team's or member's behavior.

   c. From these items, create an assessment form a team can use to evaluate how well it manages conflict.

   d. Test the form by administering it to another group.

   e. Revise the form using feedback from the other group.

2. In a group, brainstorm a list of games you've seen people play in groups. Choose four or five games that all of you have seen or experienced. For each game on your list,
   Give the game a name that describes it.
   Identify the gimmick that starts the game.
   Describe briefly how the script develops.

Identify payoffs that might motivate a person to play the game.

   a. Suggest ways a group can stop or manage the game. Finally, share your game book with the class.

3. Think of a time when a group pressured you to conform to its opinions or norms. What was the situation? Who exerted the pressure? How? How did you feel? What did you do? Was there ever a time when you pressured a member to conform to a group? If so, how did you do it? What was the effect? How do you feel about pressuring others?

4. With a small group of students, review the concept of groupthink, and then create a skit that shows a decision-making group with all the relevant symptoms. In your skit, have the group arrive at an ill-considered groupthink decision. Act out your skit for the class. Ask your classmates to identify when and how groupthink was operating and what communication behaviors revealed the effects of group-think. Finally, discuss how the group in the skit could have prevented or stopped itself from the effects of groupthink.

"Just tell us what to do with this ... #@!+!"*
Sometimes a little gravel in the shoe can halt the proudest parade.

TEAM PROBLEMS AND PARTICIPATION

Managing the Obstacles

13

One of "Murphy's laws" says that if it's possible for something to go wrong, it will. Groups of people only multiply the potential for problems. To cope with this law, we suggest you anticipate what could go wrong and prevent it. But if that should fail, turn what's wrong into what's right. Make it work to your advantage. That's leadership.

The previous chapter dealt with mines and boulders on the path to the goal. This one deals with petty, annoying problems that throw gravel in your shoes and stop the team in its tracks. The trick is to manage the gravel before it turns into boulders or—maybe—to turn that gravel into "magic dust" to speed you on your way. Sometimes what seems to be a problem becomes an opportunity, and that opportunity can lead to a triumph.

Specifically, in this chapter we focus on how the interaction of individuals with teams can create problems and how teams need to work with new or different members. We also consider ways to bolster inadequate leaders and leaders in transition, as well as ways to work with organizational and system issues. Our goals for this chapter are to help you to:

1. Identify and manage individual member problems
2. Recognize and manage leader problems
3. Know how to help your team improve its processes and development
4. Understand and solve problems with the organization and systems

FIXING TEAMWORK PROBLEMS

Throughout this book, we've extolled the virtues of diversity and the value of individual contributions of team members. With these advantages, however, come problems with how teams impact on members and how members' responses impact on teams. Transactions sometimes bring out the worst in people, and their responses may be difficult for teammates to cope with. And members who are new or different may feel lost because they're unfamiliar with the road the team is traveling. Teams must know how to identify and cope effectively with these problems.

PEOPLE WHO SEEM DIFFICULT

Even the nicest people can get nasty when one annoying individual seems to block the progress of teammates who are very interdependent and concentrated on their task. One individual may dominate the others or do distracting things; another may withdraw from participation or be irresponsible about the work. Even worse, someone may be truly reprehensible—manipulative, unethical, dishonest, and mean. Even with e-messages, obnoxiousness has its way of surfacing, through sarcasm, manipulation, flaming—you get the point. When you run into any of these behaviors, it's tempting to knock the individual "upside the head." Because that's not allowed, it helps to prevent mayhem and create harmony if the team keeps these points in mind:

An individual problem is a team problem. Members are interdependent. Their transactions connect them, create the structure of their communication, and respond to pressures among members and from outside of the team. When even one person does not fully participate, the entire team suffers—and so does the task.

Something allows or encourages an individual to be a problem. According to Scholtes' (1988) classic observation, about 85 percent of problems are in the system, and only 15 percent are directly caused by individuals. He suggests, "Examine each problem in light of what the group does to encourage or allow the behavior and what the group can do differently to encourage more constructive behavior" (pp. 6–32). Is a member a pain in meetings but a pleasure elsewhere? Then perhaps the problem isn't just the person—it's something happening in the team.

The team must avoid attribution and labeling. The infamous tendency to attribute motives and characteristics to others—and then to paste a label on them—is a serious mistake. First, the label may be wrong. Second, labels divert attention from the issue. It's the problem that needs to be corrected—not the person.

The team must care about the individual. Even if you don't really like a person, you can still care about him or her, both as a team member and as a human being. If members care, they can deal with the problem.

With these perspectives in mind, let's examine some specific problems in terms of three questions:

1. *What does the person do?* Isolate the specific behaviors or actions that feed into the problem.
2. *Why does the problem happen?* Figure out how the team is involved in permitting or encouraging the problem. Resolve to correct the team's motivation and behaviors that allow or encourage the problem to continue.
3. *How can we change it?* Focus communication to change the specific behaviors of the person and the team, not to punish or isolate the individual.

A team can use these guidelines to understand and influence behaviors that dominate or distract the team, and to alleviate problems when people do not participate, or seem to be irresponsible, or behave in ethically reprehensible ways.

Dominating A dominating individual demands attention, controls the discussion, keeps others from being heard, prevents the team from concentrating on its task, and frequently creates resentment and power struggles within the team. However, this person may care about the team and its goals and be frustrated if the work isn't progressing smoothly. Burgoon and Dunbar (2000) found that, in fact, dominance behaviors interact with an individual's traits, the communication format and message goal, and the acquaintanceship of participants. The dominator, while frustrating, may have something important to contribute and bring energy and enthusiasm to the team process. How can the team benefit from this person's participation without being overwhelmed? Look at:

What the Person Does Interrupt a lot? Make too many authoritative-sounding assertions? Bully others with verbal or nonverbal communication? Always bring the focus back to his or her interests? Speak loudly? State opinions aggressively? Send too many e-mail messages? Try to analyze the behaviors specifically.

Why the Behavior Continues Does the team let this person dominate so they can avoid dealing with important issues? Are members afraid to confront the problem because of the person's power, status, or feelings, or perhaps due to the team's fear of conflict? Is dealing with the behavior too much work, so members just withdraw or give in to one person's control?

How to Change It First, the team must want to reduce the dominating behavior. If it doesn't, then it probably doesn't stop other blocking behaviors, either. The team may have to examine why it doesn't and why it should. Willingness to change goes beyond one person's behavior. It goes to team motivation and process, and it can be discussed in that context rather than in relation to one person. If the team does want to deal with the problem, then the members may be able to confront the issues.

Specific approaches should fit the person's behaviors. For example:

Interrupting. Every time the dominator interrupts, you can say, "Wait, please, I'm not finished." If she or he has interrupted someone else, step in with "Wait, please, I want to hear what so-and-so has to say."

Talking (or messaging) too much. If there's a pattern of just overwhelming the team with talk or e-messages, propose a new rule: "I think maybe we're out of balance. Let's say nobody gets more than three minutes until everyone else has had a chance to respond," or, "Let's say that after every message we check to be sure everyone else got a chance to respond," or, "Let's put a limit on how many lines we get to phrase an idea." Even if you don't enforce such a rule, it raises consciousness of the need to include everyone equally.

Authoritarian statements. You can ask (courteously) for more information or support or help to qualify his or her know-it-all statements: "Where could we get some data to support that?" "Then you'd say that it's probably—but not necessarily—true?" "So this is your opinion, but it isn't proven yet?"

Bullying and power grabbing. If the dominator uses strategies to control others, you may have to confront the problem. Using descriptive statements, say how you feel when this person dominates: "I am uncomfortable when you stand over me like that." "I am frustrated because I feel you control our meetings too much." Be ready to provide specific examples of the behaviors; ask what the team can do to keep participation in better balance; help the team negotiate its role in the transactions. Sometimes a dominating person just doesn't know how to stop, and the team can help.

Distracting   Once in a while, distracting the team is a genuine service. Humor at the right moment or a slight side trip to break tension can be a healthy contribution to transactional and task processes. But sometimes people dedicate themselves to distracting the team from its work. They may be playful distractors, like adorable puppies—or aggressive distractors, more like vicious attack dogs. One is more fun than the other, but both keep the team from the task.

What the Person Does   Does someone consistently and inappropriately play, joke around, tease, or act up constantly? Make funny faces? Tell outrageous stories? Change the subject as soon as the team gets its teeth into an issue? Does an individual pick fights? Divert attention to outside frustrations and conflicts? Take offense? Pout? Identify specifically the ways this individual distracts others.

Why It Continues   We've all been in classrooms where students gratefully egged on a clown or an irrelevant questioner who diverted the teacher from a boring lecture. We've all been in groups where it was more fun to play around, watch a fight, or advise someone on the impending breakup of her or his love life than to do the job at hand. A team may be motivated to allow distractions because members like being distracted, like having an excuse for not accomplishing much, or like to think of themselves as nice, supportive people who "understand" when a member diverts their attention. They may be uncertain or fearful about confronting the problem. In these instances, the team may encourage the distractions by not bringing the conversation back to the topic, by asking questions or giving responses that encourage the distractor to continue, or by piggybacking other distractions on top of the ones the distractor provides. What would you do in this type of situation if you were a "manager" versus a "coach" (see Box 13.1)?

How to Change It   The team needs to assess its transactional and task goals as well as processes. It then needs to commit itself to limiting distractions in order to achieve its task goals. These are issues that can be raised as matters of process, not

---

BOX 13.1 | "COACH OR MANAGER?"

So, which are you? Twelve clues to help you decide:

1. Managers believe that their job is to push people or drive them; coaches believe that they are there to lift and support people.
2. Managers believe that they should talk at people by telling, directing, and lecturing; coaches believe in engaging in dialogue with people by asking, requesting, and listening.
3. Managers believe in controlling others through the decisions they make; coaches believe in facilitating others to make decisions and empowering them to implement their own decisions.
4. Managers believe they know the answers; coaches believe they must seek the answers.
5. A manager triggers insecurity through administering a healthy dose of fear as an effective way to achieve compliance; a coach believes in using purpose to inspire commitment and stimulate creativity.
6. Managers believe that their job is to point out errors; coaches believe that their job is to celebrate learning.

7. A manager believes in solving problems and making decisions; a coach believes in facilitating others to solve problems and make decisions.
8. A manager believes in delegating responsibility; a coach believes in modeling accountability.
9. Managers believe in creating structure and procedures for people to follow; coaches believe in creating a vision and promoting flexibility through values as guidelines for behavior.
10. A manager believes in doing things right; a coach believes in doing the right things.
11. Managers believe that their power lies in their knowledge; coaches believe that their power lies in their vulnerability.
12. A manager believes in focusing on the bottom line; a coach believes in focusing on the process that creates the bottom-line result.

Source: Thomas G. Crane, *Becoming a Coach for the Teams You Lead*. Quoted by Kevin Moyer, director, Annuity Service Center, Prudential Financial, in his track session titled, "Coaching vs Managing in a Contact Centre," at the 2003 North American Conference on Customer Management.

in connection with one individual. Specific approaches to various forms of distraction include:

Playful distracting. Humor or gentle teasing may help to stop distracting behaviors. Or direct intervention, carefully, good-humoredly, and repeatedly used, can get the point across: "I think I heard a bell—recess must be over." "I'm having fun, but I know I'm going to hate myself later. We'd better get back to work." In desperation, you can simply ask the individual to change: "Susan, you're one of the funniest people I know, but I feel we aren't going to get this job done." If you're e-messaging, you might suggest a team neticism, such as, "Henceforth, I'd like to use 'lgbw' to mean, 'let's get back to work'—is that okay with everyone?"

Aggressive distracting. If someone continually picks fights and exhibits anger, something is wrong. Perhaps something going on in the team or outside of it is gnawing at this person. These distractions can ruin a team's transactional processes and climate. They must be handled with careful confrontation, using conflict-management strategies such as those discussed in Chapter 12. If you're face to face, that's one thing. If you're in a virtual team, you might have to arrange a face-to-face meeting or, at least, a telephone conference to negotiate out of the conflicts.

Nonparticipating   People who consistently stare out a window, doodle, mutter monosyllabic responses to questions, or say "Whatever" to any suggestion may not seem to constitute a major problem, but they certainly reflect and create one. Nonparticipation reveals a problem in that the team's processes obviously do not involve every member. It creates a problem because you need full participation to facilitate the team's development and task. Members may not participate for many reasons: Perhaps they've been run over one too many times when they tried to speak. Maybe they really don't care, and they're in the situation against their will. Maybe there are too many people on the team, and there's too much going on for them to break through. They could feel excluded because they are different in some way, or feel underprepared and unqualified, or shy. Or it might be they are deeply distracted by personal issues. Whatever the cause, the determined nonparticipant can become a resistant mountain to move.

What the Person Does   Watch carefully. Does the individual fail to make eye contact, close off with gestures and body position, show facial expressions that are angry, sad, or distant? Does the nonparticipant pay attention to other things while the team is working? Or does this person use gestures, body positions, facial expressions, and/or vocal inflections that seem like negative reactions to others' actions or statements? How consistent is the nonparticipation? Is it connected in some way with the task, with transactional processes, with other members, with certain topics?

Why It Continues   Groups often ignore nonparticipants because it's easy to do. They're quiet, after all. It's also easier to ignore people than to find out what's going on. If the team finds out an individual's nonparticipation is caused by a problem with the team, resolving the issue could be sticky—and people often prefer to avoid sticky issues. Finally, teams sometimes ignore nonparticipation because their efforts to involve these members meet with rejection or even resentment. Consequently, members encourage the behavior by ignoring the individual, occasionally throwing a meaningless question his or her way, and failing to develop connections with that person.

How to Change It   The team must recognize the importance of each person to its syntality and resolve to gain full participation. That means making up your mind to be aware, empathic, and inventive in meeting the needs of both the individual and the team. You can use some of the following options:

Reach out in discussions. If the person is simply shy or feels inadequate for some reason, gentle questioning may do the trick: "Jim, what do you think?" "Hey, Jim, we need you here." "Jim's had some experience with this subject. . . . Got any ideas, Jim?"

Make assignments. A member who does not volunteer may feel useless or unqualified, so it can help to assign that person—as well as other members—specific work to do for the team. Reporting and discussing the results can help that person develop confidence as well.

Connect outside the team. Somebody on the team may need to get to know the non-participant away from meetings. By showing personal concern, a teammate may find out what's happening and act as a bridge between the person and the team. When members know the individual, it may be easier to draw him or her into participating.

Manage team problems. If you observe or discover through outside discussion that the member has withdrawn because of a problem with someone on the team—or with the team itself—then members need to deal with the problem in the same, careful way we talked about in managing conflict. And they may need to change some of their own behaviors in accordance with what they've discovered.

Irresponsible   Here's the team tooth-grinder: people who don't show up, show up late, and/or don't do their share of the work. Handle those issues, and you handle many of the problems in teamwork—but these may be the toughest of all to manage. Sometimes irresponsible behavior results from other issues, so you might think about the irresponsibility of a member in light of what we've said about non-participants with legitimate problems.

What the Person Does   Someone may talk a good game about attending meetings and doing the work but then not show up and not produce. This person may make excuses, laugh it off, plead for sympathy, and/or distract the team with other issues. She or he may barrel into a meeting (albeit late) with such enthusiasm and so many ideas (unsupported by research or thinking) that the team believes the problem is now solved and this person can be relied on in the future. Be not deceived.

Why It Continues   Over and over, we've seen groups sabotaged by one or two members because the team never found the motivation to deal with his or her irresponsibility before it became a major problem. The members thought they had plenty of time; they thought it would work out; maybe they even enjoyed a hang-loose kind of norm during the early stages of the group. Sometimes they liked the person and covered for him or her, hoping for some spontaneous change of behavior. Consequently, they encouraged a team norm for lateness, absence, and lack of work. By the time the members realized their effectiveness was being damaged, it was too late.

How to Change It   The first thing is not to allow these behaviors to start. Team norms and expectations about each person's responsibility and reliability have to be set early, and people have to be serious about them. Once an individual shows a pattern of irresponsibility, the members must pay attention immediately. You have these choices:

Ignore it. This is not a real alternative. The point of being a team is to be a team, and the irresponsible person is not a teammate.

Approach it as a team problem. Take up the issue of group norms. Discuss them as a team process problem. Talk about changing and reinforcing those norms.

Talk to the individual privately. Have the leader or a member approach the individual. Use reasoning, and explain how important each member's work is to the team. Find out if outside or team causes are behind the person's behavior. If so, look for ways to manage these issues.

Confront the individual as a team. Talk about the importance of this person's work to the team. Ask for his or her suggestions as to how the problem can be solved, and try to negotiate a different behavioral pattern.

Go to a higher authority. No one wants to do this, but sometimes intervention by the boss, teacher, or group leader is needed. This obviously is getting to tough measures.

Throw the bum out. Occasionally, the situation is so desperate a team wants to evict the member. This rarely is a viable—or desirable—alternative within a team's structure or place in an organization. If the work has been brought to a standstill by one member's irresponsibility, and the team has tried every possible way to get cooperation, then the members may need to ask the individual to leave.

Most of these alternatives induce a person to behave more responsibly toward the group, but they depend on the team behaving responsibly toward both its processes and its individual members. Before the team gets desperate, it should try positive approaches. Make it clear the team cares about this person and truly wants his or her full participation.

But what if the situation does degenerate to the point of separation? The person can face the consequences from professors or managers for work not accomplished, so you must be ready to justify your actions with clear, accurate accounts of the irresponsible behaviors and the team's efforts to work cooperatively until the situation became impossible.

More realistically, if all these options fail, you need a contingency plan. To make one, think of these possibilities for working around the problem individual:

Restructure job assignments and responsibilities. Find ways the person can contribute to reaching the goal, but make his or her portion sufficiently discrete that the team can achieve its purposes without that contribution.

Redesign the project or restructure goals. That might mean eliminating some goals or methods you originally had planned or the need for some particular talent or expertise this person had been expected to provide.

We have seen teams in classes and organizations take exactly these steps. When the teams pulled together tightly to overcome the problem, they thought of creative ways to work around the irresponsibility of one or two individuals—and their final projects came out better than they might have.

"Waitjustadamminute!" you say? "That isn't fair! The lazy good-for-nothing will profit (share in the team's glory, the grade, the reward) from our work!" You're right, of course; it isn't fair. We have two responses to that. First, your objective as a team is to reach your goal with the best possible effect. If you have to see someone get something he or she hasn't fully earned, that may just be a price you have to pay.

Second, "what goes around comes around." Many Chinese believe that life is a rolling wheel: people come around through reincarnation to places they have been. So maybe you have an unsettled debt to that person from a previous existence. None of us can see the present and future effects of another's behavior, even in this life. It is enough to pull together as a team and reach your goal. If you can bring every member into full participation, that's the ideal. If you can't, then you get as close to the ideal as possible—and you reach the goal anyway.

Reprehensible   By *reprehensible*, we mean consistently unethical, dishonest, conniving, sexist, racist, bigoted, nasty. We mean someone who enjoys making other people miserable, who has no conscience that you can see, and who takes the immoral road by preference. This individual continually twists conversation into a negative rope with which he or she tries to hang the team. We hope none of your teams ever includes such a person, but once in a while, it happens.

What the Person Does   Does this person make snide comments about people? Stereotype and make belittling jokes about intellect, sex, race, disabilities, nationalities, socioeconomic classes? Use communication to manipulate and control others? Does the reprehensible one falsify evidence, lie, connive, or suggest dishonest and unethical actions? Belittle others' concerns for values and issues of fairness or justice, twist ideas into sarcasm, or cast goals as foregone failures? Does the person use "flaming" to disrupt e-mail communication? You may be having a great computerized conversation only to have it continually interrupted by repeated "flames" of insulting language. Sometimes people do the same thing in face-to-face groups.

Why It Continues   A team may fail to cope with these behaviors because members can't really believe they're happening, because the situation is too painful, or because it just seems hopeless. Members sometimes may encourage racist, sexist, or bigoted behavior by laughing at unacceptable jokes or unethical proposals. People often react this way because they don't know what else to do. They don't think of laughing at or ignoring such behavior as encouraging it—but it does.

A team needs to see such behavior as truly harmful. It's harmful to the spirit of the group, to the members whose self-concepts or values it attacks, and to the ethics and worth of the team's decisions. Once members see the harm, they can determine to stop allowing this individual to undermine their team.

How to Change It   Look at these reprehensible acts as conflict, because they strike deeply at people's values, self-concepts, roles, and ethics. Therefore, you may have to use a full conflict-management process to handle them. For starters, however, be very assertive in these ways:

Don't laugh at jokes that belittle individuals and groups. Courteously (but assertively) state your objection to them: "Could we please not have that kind of joke? I, personally, am really bothered by it." Believe it or not, this is easier to do than it seems, and sometimes it's all you need to do.

Do not let an unethical statement, suggestion, or act go unchallenged. Recognizing that another's ethical code may be different from your own and deserves respect is one thing. Tolerating behavior odious to your own is quite another, because silence often is interpreted as consent.

Become an advocate for members whom the offending member attacks, belittles, or manipulates. Protect, defend, stand up for people who are attacked. This is no time to be shy. Make it clear that such behavior is unacceptable.

Convert negativism into positivism. Assertively state your preference for looking at things from a constructive point of view. Object firmly to a norm of looking at things negatively. Explain that negative thinking poisons creativity and hurts people.

Confront the problem privately or within the team. Somebody—possibly the entire team—may need to tell the person that this behavior is reprehensible and unacceptable to the team. This may help to stem the tide.

Ignore, ostracize, or expel the individual. This is drastic, but sometimes it's the only alternative. When someone is flaming on the Internet, all you have to do is type in a message to "ignore" and you won't receive the messages. In kindergarten, you just put the kid who is acting out in the corner for a time-out. In a team, it's much more difficult. The team will have to agree to make it impossible for the person to gain recognition with the behavior. If that doesn't work, the team may have to find a way to expel the member.

System versus Personality Difficulties   Usually, the difficulties we've discussed stem from problems in the system, not in the individual. Careful assessment of the team's processes and of its relationship to other systems often helps you find ways to manage these issues. The American Psychiatric Association (1980), however, recognizes that perhaps 10 percent of the time, individuals really do have difficult personalities, "unable to adapt to the demands of particular interpersonal relationships or social roles" (DeWine, 1994, p. 256). DeWine emphasizes that "it is important to find a balance between trying to ignore these people and spending a disproportional amount of time with them" (p. 265).

In our experience, it's essential not to assume the problem is in a member's personality. The guidelines we've suggested should help you identify—and cure— any viruses in the system itself. If the problem is a personality issue, then these guidelines also should help you to cope with the individual.

MEMBERS WHO ARE NEW OR DIFFERENT

People who are similar to one another and people who start out toward a goal together develop similar maps of the territory they'll travel (see photos below). Some members, however, may join the team en route; sometimes teams change membership on a fairly regular basis. Others, even though they start out with the team, may have a different view of the trip; their cultures or subcultures make them new to the experience. This is obvious if a person is a recent immigrant, but it's also a factor for anyone who tries to participate in a group different from his or her previous experiences. Such team members may be, in essence, strangers in a strange land.

American work team

Asian work team

Teams need to be able to provide a map for the new person. To do that, they must understand about "newness"; know how to develop an intergroup ethic for communicating with team members who are new and different from the majority; and be able to design strategies for orienting new as well as not-so-new members.

Understanding Newness   When we say "new," we mean something more than having recently joined the team. Even at the first meeting of a team, anyone who enters the situation from a background different from that of most members is new to their ways. Your language, your culture, your race may be different, and those differences are obvious. What if, however, you have lived in the country all your life? You still may be almost as much a stranger as the person from across the sea.

It's like this: Everyone belongs to identity groups defined by family, religion, race or ethnicity, neighborhood, even their work or profession. In these settings, people engage in *intragroup communication*—using specific styles of speaking and interacting unique to that group (Price, Harrison & Gavin, 2006). Chen (2005) explains that a new or different member brings the communication expectations and socialization of one group—maybe their family unit, or the team in which they previously worked—to their new context. In essence, people engage in intergroup communication with their new team until they learn the language and norms and are able to engage in intragroup communication.

On the face of it, you might think these issues would not be so true of virtual teams as of traditional teams. After all, virtual teams do not have to deal with the myriad effects of differing nonverbal behaviors, and they are more focused on task than on transactional processes. Not so. The virtual team often is international, composed of people from widely diverse cultures, trying to make decisions and solve problems through differing language, communication style, and expectations that vary widely.

In traditional or virtual teams, there are the problems of a stranger entering an established group, not understanding exactly how this new group functions. The stranger inevitably feels anxious and tries to be accepted. Socialization is largely an adaptation process "by which an individual achieves some degree of fit between his/her behaviors and the new work demands created by . . . changing and uncertain work situations" (Chan, 2000, p. 4). The more established the team is, or the more homogeneous the other members are, the more developed the team's syntality is and the more difficult, uncertain, and anxiety-producing the experience may be for the stranger (Chen & Klimoski, 2003).

Developing an Intragroup Ethic   For the sake of the strangers on your team, and for the sake of the group itself, you need an ethic that provides room for everyone. If you recognize the differences among groups and cultures, you realize that even "treating others as I would have them treat me" assumes those others wish to be treated the way you would wish to be. But someone else may have different worldviews and social expectations from yours.

We like to be treated with directness, so we've always tried to treat others that way. Then we realized that directness may make some people uncomfortable. Kim and Sharkey (1995) found, for example, that the way people understand themselves and interact in a situation is related to their "concern for clarity, concern for hurting someone's feelings, and concern for negative evaluations by the hearer" (p. 21).

The relative importance of these concerns is tied to an individual's intragroup experiences. High-context cultures, such as those in Asia, teach members to be very concerned about face and about negative evaluations, which in turn might cause an individual to be more indirect than the team normally expects in asking questions or providing information. Perhaps we need to say to ourselves, "I would like others to consider how I feel and then try to treat me accordingly; therefore, I will consider how others might feel and then try to treat them accordingly."

Richard Johannesen (1996) asks whether it is possible and desirable to have an ethical code for intercultural communication. He notes Sitaram and Cogdell's proposed 35-item code of ethics for intercultural communicators (1976, pp. 245–246). This code rests, it seems to us, on two major principles:

1. A communicator should *respect* other people's religions, worldviews, norms, expectations, and their rights to behave in accordance with those bases.
2. An individual should *adapt* to others' experiences and expectations to create an open and supportive bridge between the two frames of reference.

Communicators who understand and apply these principles do not put others down or assume the superiority of their own groups. They are considerate in verbal and nonverbal communication; they seek ways of understanding; they broaden their tolerance; they adapt their communication to make the other comfortable. In our view, these principles seem basic to good transactional processes among all people, but especially among people who are strangers in any way.

Orienting Members   The need to orient new members seems obvious, but teams, committees, departments—any group you can name—forget it constantly. Never mind student or classroom groups; we've seen college departments lose valuable teachers because they took for granted that those new people could just "plug in" to the program and the department's way of doing things. The teachers' frustration led them to look for new jobs where they would fit in more smoothly. We can't emphasize this issue enough: All groups and teams, including (perhaps, especially) virtual teams need to orient new members to their goals, their current status, their ways of doing things. To ignore this leads to frustration and loss of time and effectiveness.

Orienting people involves several critical aspects:

Make sure someone takes responsibility. A designated leader or a specific member might take this responsibility. Of course, the entire team should make it an ongoing norm to provide orientation and to connect with anyone who might need that help.

Welcome and connect members to the team. The team needs to reduce the anxiety and uncertainty a stranger feels. Make a special effort to be interested, to listen, to understand, and to share yourself. This, too, seems obvious, but somehow it often gets lost in the press of the task or of already established relationships.

Design activities. Some social activities—even if nothing more than "going for coffee"—are almost essential for people to get to know one another without the pressures of the task. If the team meets only online, then phone conversations with the new member will help a lot. A newcomer often can ask the questions about team norms during outside interpersonal encounters (in person or on the phone) that she or he cannot ask during meetings.

Help people to understand group norms and characteristics. Listen carefully to find out what confuses the stranger. Trade understandings; that's the only way you can know how to help. For instance, maybe your team likes to argue and does so without rancor. Forewarn the new member so the first time it happens doesn't feel like an attack.

Don't count on members' self-perceptions. What you think is true may not seem so to someone else. For example, immigrants often see North Americans as seeming friendly, but not really being so, because their open, smiling faces don't necessarily include genuine invitations. To some cultures, real friendliness is asking people to your home for dinner, inviting them to an event, or extending help. Many new immigrants have felt confused and lonely because their expectations of friendly Americans were so different from the "Let's do lunch" attitude they found.

Introduce people to your team's substantive issues. Tell new members about the team's history, purposes and goals, plans, timelines, and projects. If you're working online, detail for her the netiquette you've developed as a team. Explain the structural factors of systems, hierarchy, leadership, responsibility, limitations, policies, and rules that affect the team. Encourage questions; provide supplementary printed material. Allow plenty of time for the person to absorb this information. In addition, provide opportunities for further questions and reinforcement later, because a new person probably cannot absorb all this information at once.

PROCESSES THAT NEED PROCESSING

In Chapter 3, we discussed planning and running meetings. As you develop a team, however, good meetings are only part of the process. You also need to stop now and then to examine the team's syntality, synergy, cohesiveness, and communication.

Here's an example of a problem in an individual's behavior or the team norms: **social loafing**, or the tendency of people to "exert less effort in groups than when working individually" (Stark, Shaw & Duffy, 2007, p. 699). People sometimes feel that, in a group, their loafing won't be detected. After reviewing seventy-eight studies on the subject, Karau and Williams (1993) concluded that people are more likely to engage in social loafing when "their individual outputs cannot be evaluated collectively, when working on tasks that are perceived as low in meaningfulness or personal involvement, when a group-level comparison standard is not available, when working with strangers, when they expect their coworkers to perform well, and when their inputs to the collective outcome are redundant with those of other group members" (p. 700).

Karau and Williams also found that social loafing is a fairly universal phenomenon, although women and members from Eastern cultures appear less likely to loaf than others. Further, social loafing appears to undermine efforts in a variety of tasks—cognitive, physical, and perceptual—and to be especially problematic in groups that lack cohesiveness.

What do you do about social loafing? Here are some suggestions:

Look for ways to use self-evaluation. Szymanski and Harkins (1993) found that self-evaluation was the most effective motivator for eliminating social loafing, and much scholarship points to the motivating effect of being evaluated by oneself, the team, or the leader (Bandura, 1987; Deci & Ryan, 1985; Harkins, 1987; Higgins, Strauman & Klein, 1986; Latane, Williams & Harkins, 1979; Schlenker, 1986; Szymanski & Harkins, 1993; Tata, 2002).

Develop tasks and processes that have value to team members. Price, Harrison, and Gavin (2006) found that members who were disinterested in their work tended more toward social loafing.

Find ways to build the team, to bring people together as a cohesive whole. Again, people with little knowledge of or interest in one another are less likely to engage in a highly synergistic approach to their task.

Social loafing is just one example of why teams must attend to their development throughout the team's life. Once in a while, a team might need to schedule a special meeting to discuss its own growth and development. Here are some ideas that can help you "process your processing":

Use assessment techniques to measure where you are. Self-assessment forms such as Form 11.1, which examines leadership in your team, can help you to identify issues and work through them. Additionally, you can find consultants' assessment schemes on the Web as well as software designs for team assessment. You can have a consultant come in to observe your group and provide feedback or take you through some team-building exercises. You also can videotape some of your face-to-face meetings or print some of your online meetings and examine the way the team interacts. Any of these methods can help you to improve the transactional and task processes of your teamwork.

Take a long-term view. Look back a month, 6 months, or a year or two. Where was the team at that point? What progress has been made? Goals seem more attainable when you see how far you've traveled, but you have to look over the entire road. Looking from meeting to meeting rarely gives that perspective. As you get a team view of how you're doing, start creating proactive ways of pulling together, of developing cohesiveness, of increasing your team's synergy.

Focus on the team's successes. Someone is always willing to remind you of your failures, so the team should remind itself of its accomplishments. Forgive us for our clichés, but think of it this way: Failures are just accomplishments waiting to happen. Successes are the foundation for the future. Keep in mind the poster that reads, "Be patient, God isn't finished with me yet." This applies to teams as well as to individuals.

Play together. We'd go so far as to say that every time we've experienced or observed an excellent team, it's been a group of people who could have fun together. Superteams work hard; they know what they're doing; they're committed to their goals. At the same time, they take time to kid around, to socialize, and to celebrate individual and team achievements. Some corporations even engage consultants to teach management how to play, because they find play contributes both to creativity and to developing excellent teams.

Renew and reinforce your team vision. Talk about what it is you envision as a team, in terms of both of your image of the team itself and your vision of what it will accomplish. Make your vision as clear and as consensual as you can; articulate it and work with it as a team. In doing this, you build relationships among members, and you build both your transactional and task processes for future work.

HELPING LEADERS HELP THE TEAM

A fine leader can help a group develop into a superteam; a poor leader can frustrate it at every step of the way. Sometimes you may need a "Meeting Doctor," as explained in Box 13.2. Teams studied by Chen, Kirkman, Kanfer, Allen, and Rosen (2007) reported lower performance and lower satisfaction with the team when team leaders could not or would not confront members whose performance was inadequate. Other researchers found that managers who set stringent goals for the team "in stone" (the "my way or the highway" managerial approach) without clarifying the team's priorities also experienced less effective teamwork (Kozlowski & Bell, 2003). Leaders often overestimate the morale, effectiveness, and satisfaction of their teams, and they may be

---

| BOX 13.2 | "MEETING DOCTOR" CURES "SICK" AGENDAS |

There are new players on the management team with a daunting list of goals. An executive retreat is in order—but the two-day agenda must be airtight. You need some expert advice.

Who you gonna call? How about a "meeting doctor"? Dr. Michael Freidman is one of a growing breed of psychologists specializing in the corporate psyche.

"I don't believe there is a *right* agenda," Freidman told *Strategic Meetings*. "A lot depends on the purpose of the meeting. If it's for long-range planning, for instance, I may do a number of exercises to help people talk about their dreams for the future. . . ."

In some cases, a group interview with top executives provides an initial springboard for ideas, generating a list of key issues or goals for the meeting. Issues are then ranked according to importance.

"With that information, I can go off with a designated person from the group and develop a set of strategies and an agenda for the actual meeting," Freidman explained.

If a corporation seems stagnant and is looking for fresh new ideas, perhaps the agenda should call for subgroups to meet and brainstorm.

The make-up of these groups is critical. "There are times when we want like-minded people to be in a subgroup," said Freidman. "Other times, we look for a mix of personalities and experience. Maybe we'll combine someone who's more of a dreamer with someone who's more financial-minded."

Ideas generated by subgroups are then brought to the larger group for discussion and consensus. And if there's no consensus? "If one person vehemently disagrees and just will not give in, I sometimes set up a 'mock-trial' situation. One person represents each side and presents a 'closing argument' to the rest of the group as a jury," he explained. Or, opposing members of the group may have to represent the other side of the issue. They'll be given time to prepare for the "trial" and research the opposing view. Often, in preparation, they'll discover new points or subtleties they weren't previously aware of.

Source: Condensed from Loren Ginsberg, "'Meeting Doctor' Cures 'Sick' Agendas," Strategic Meetings, *Corporate Travel*, Fall 1991, p. 35. Used with permission.

unaware of the stress their shortcomings place on the team. Members, however, tend to believe the leader knows what the issues are but just won't correct them. They often believe the leader's insensitivity to their frustration is due to personal ambition and a willingness to use the team to further his or her career.

Usually, a team does not have the power to replace an inadequate appointed leader. There are ways to bolster the leader, however, and to make him or her more effective and helpful to the team. Often, too, teams go through crises when one leader leaves and another takes over. Understanding how to ease such a transition can help a team to move ahead with its task effectively. Sometimes this means canceling meetings; see Box 13.3.

BOLSTERING THE LEADER

It isn't hard to know when you and your teammates should use your leadership to help an inadequate leader. You should do it when the team cannot replace the leader because she or he was appointed by a higher authority or was elected for a specific term. You should also help when his or her lack of skill or commitment is damaging your team's effectiveness or morale. If you must choose between living with frustration or making the situation better, it's usually preferable to do the latter. Why you should do it, then, is to relieve frustration, improve morale, and increase the effectiveness of your team. To bolster the leader for these purposes, your team needs to understand the reasons for his or her inadequacy and know some strategies for correcting it.

Reasons for Inadequacy   Often, a leader's inadequacy comes down to qualifications for leading. A worker or manager who is appointed as leader may not know anything about leadership. As Ibrahim and Cordes (1996) point out, a manager is not the same as a leader. "The leader works to translate visions into goals and achieve them through inspiration, cooperation and trust.... The manager uses his technical skills to supervise the work" (p. 41).

A leader who got the job because of political or personal connections also may not necessarily know how to lead. Even when a team chooses someone as leader because the members like that person, or because he or she has the most technical expertise in a given area, his or her or her leadership abilities are not guaranteed.

Sometimes, too, the circumstances make leading difficult. Burke (2006) has noted that, while many leadership failures are a result of leaders' individual behaviors, it is often the policies, norms, or culture of the organization itself that make it all but impossible for a leader to succeed. The leader may be unable to obtain resources or have no authority to make decisions, or responsibilities may be too dispersed.

The leader's own frustrations and defensiveness may intensify the problems. A person who doesn't know how to do a job and is afraid to ask for help is not likely to correct inadequacies. As a result, the designated leader may be a leader in name only. In this case, the team may find itself without resources, with meetings in shambles, with members snapping at each other, and with transactional processes a sorry mess. It may find it has no idea what its goals are, let alone how to reach them. Communication with the organization may be poor or nonexistent; members may have inadequate information, fed by rumors and speculation. The leader isn't correcting the problem—what can the members do?

BOX 13.3 | **LOUSY MEETINGS**

If you dislike attending meetings, you've got a lot of company. More than 25 million meetings are held daily in the United States, according to the Wharton Center for Applied Research. Participants consider 42 percent of their meetings (more than 10.5 million each day!) to be a waste of time.

Consider this: If you are in a meeting of ten people whose salaries range between $50,000 and $150,000, the average expense of a one-hour-and-eighteen-minute meeting (after all, how many meetings actually stay within their one hour scheduled time frame?) is about $691. A little quick math tells you that $691, times the more than 10 million "waste-of-time" meetings held in the U.S. each day, adds up to employers paying more than $7 billion dollars daily in salaries alone for their employees to waste time! However, if these employees were to spend that same time performing value-added activities, companies would realize far greater returns.

Unprepared meeting participants are a major reason for unproductive meetings. A 3M study of 3,406 people found that the problem of unprepared participants was the second highest reason of nine expressed for why respondents dislike meetings. Consider the following nine potential solutions to this problem that are most relevant to the conditions and culture of your company, or to the organizations where you give time and volunteer effort.

1. Cancel a meeting when participants are unprepared. The cancellation with the honest reason for why conveys a message about the importance of adequate preparation and contribution.
2. Call or e-mail participants to remind them of the need for their preparation and contribution to an upcoming meeting. Taking a few minutes to contact participants often raises the quality of participation.
3. Distribute the agenda prior to the meeting so that participants understand the expectations of time, date, location, length of meeting and their responsibility for preparation.
4. Establish "public" commitment for "who does what by when." Ask for commitment in the meeting. Make it obvious that you have record of that person's name and commitment.
5. Ensure that responsibility has been assigned with a definite time frame for items needing action. Establish a follow-up buddy if helpful.
6. Use nametags. This action sends the subtle message that participants are not anonymous.
7. Seek balanced contributions from participants so that no one fades into the woodwork. Consistently ask questions and structure participation to include all participants.
8. Use WOW!^{sm} (Words of Wonder) to express sincere and specific gratitude. Feeling appreciated helps motivate willing preparation and participation.
9. In evaluating the effectiveness of your meetings, include an assessment of participants' preparedness. Encourage members to be honest about the preparation and contribution that added value. Specific and fair feedback from colleagues and peers often influences future behavior.

Thomas Edison told us, "I have not failed; I've just found 10,000 ways that won't work." Fortunately, you've just read about nine solutions that we know do work. Try them and reap the benefits of increased productivity and meeting value.

Source: Reprinted with permission from http://www.execstrategies.com/Author/Articles/Gourmet_MeetingII.htm. Susan B. Wilson, susan@execstrategies.com.

Strategies for Improving a Leader's Effectiveness   Although some approaches to improving this situation are purely within the organization's realm, there are some things that teams can do for themselves by working on transactional and task processes. For example:

- Devise ways to get feedback from the task itself rather than from the leader. Use assessment as you go along; discuss your progress; design adaptations as a team.
- Find and affirm the value in the team's job. Talk about what it means to the members to do the task well; celebrate your successes as a team.
- Create cohesiveness by focusing on high performance, traditions, and connections within the team and by relying on the team itself to resolve problems and provide mutual support (Taggar & Ellis, 2007).
- Give the leader feedback. In their study of corporate CEOs, Dotlitch and Cairo (2003) remark that being a leader requires the ability to accurately read nonverbal cues, accurately communicate intended meanings, coping with your own stress while helping others reduce theirs . . . in short, it takes a lot of guesswork and assumptions about how subordinates are faring. When you communicate clearly about your work, priorities, etc. it helps your leader be a more effective manager of your entire team.

These strategies rely on shared leadership among the team members and intensive effort in both transactional and task processes. The team can do some specific things, too, to straighten out its disorganization and move the task along. These require tact and involvement, but they'll work:

Open communication paths with the leader. Make suggestions, requests, and proposals for team needs. If the leader is simply unaware of these needs, communication may be all that is needed.

Delegate among yourselves or volunteer for specific procedural and systematic tasks. Someone can draft an agenda, someone else can bring in information, and so on. Voluntary efforts can make all the difference when a leader is simply overwhelmed by responsibilities or doesn't know how to fulfill them.

Develop a group norm for each member to guide both transactional and task processes. Make sure that all ideas are discussed and considered and all tasks are assigned.

Volunteer to make outside connections the team otherwise might expect from the leader. Do this only with the knowledge and cooperation of the leader. If the team is a unit of an organization, it requires great care to get what you need without "going over the head" of a leader.

EASING LEADERS' TRANSITIONS

Occasionally, a leader may leave the team and someone else takes on the role. Even when this change is desirable, it can be unsettling to the team (see Figure 13.1). Members, uneasy and apprehensive, may speculate about what the new leader will be like, what changes she or he will make, and how this will affect their teamwork.

After surveying 385 managers in Asia, the Americas, and Europe during Fall 2006, Matt Pease and Richard S. Wellins of Developmental Dimensions International found that "at all levels, making a leadership transition is among life's most difficult personal challenges…more challenging than "coping with bereavement" or "dealing with divorce."

SOURCE: Retrieved December 22, 2008 from the world wide web: http://www.ddiworld.com/pdf/LeadershipTransitions_rr_ddi.pdf.

FIGURE 13.1

Leadership transition—one of life's most difficult personal challenges.

In the case of an organizational team, they may fear for their jobs. All this provides a rich field for rumors and frustrations.

A change of leaders also provides an opportunity for power shifts and political positioning. Teams or individual members may create coalitions to push their interests. This is not necessarily a bad thing—the changes may be good—but teams need to recognize that political strategies affect members' relationships with one another, with the team, with other subsystems, and with the parent organization.

Once the leader change is decided, it's best to limit speculation, rumor, apprehension, and politics as much as possible. If you can make the transition smooth and keep the team together, you may have more opportunities to deal with whatever moves are necessary to ensure the team's success. Some ways to smooth this transition include:

Keep rumors in perspective. Members can test rumors for their source and their probability and refuse to pass them on.

Reinforce the team's perception of itself and of how it works. Reaffirming the team's goals, reinforcing the vision, strengthening syntality, and cementing relationships all help members to feel they still remain a team as they weather the transition.

Close the old era gracefully. Call attention to what the team has accomplished, and suggest ways of "winding up" the era that is ending. People need some sense of closure when a period ends, even when they will go on immediately into a new one.

Open the new era affirmatively. You can initiate a new leader's experience by suggesting ways to orient him or her to the team, by asking questions to learn how this new person works, and by summarizing the team's accomplishments, goals, and tasks for the future. You need to incorporate the new leader into the transactional process and, at the same time, ensure that everyone understands what the task is and how and why it should proceed.

WORKING WITHIN THE SYSTEM

It can be pretty hard to develop a superteam if the group is stymied by outside conditions. The parent organization may not give your team the support, resources, autonomy, and recognition it needs to move ahead. Sometimes the parent organization provides what the team needs, but progress is stopped because the interests of other groups in some way relate to or conflict with those of the team. It's possible, however, to turn these problems around.

When the parent organization falls short of its responsibilities, a designated leader may be critically important. He or she can represent the team, negotiate, and be the public relations advocate to the organization. With or without a designated leader, however, every member can provide leadership on the inside by maximizing the effectiveness of the team processes. They also can provide leadership on the outside by conveying the team image, making contacts, and publicizing team goals and successes.

If there are problems with the organization, the team might consider these possibilities:

- As much as possible, be innovative, creative, and rely on the team.
- Chart the hierarchy and communication network of the parent organization. Identify with whom the team needs to interact to get what it needs.
- Develop a strategy for establishing cooperation with those individuals and groups.
- Look for other (external or related) systems or groups from whom you can get the support or cooperation the team needs.
- Use the personal resources of team members to make connections and get cooperation from others.

Sometimes teams can't get as far as they would like with a problem because that problem is too big or involves conflicting sides. A cooperative intergroup project may be the answer. We're not suggesting that a cooperative effort with other teams or organizations doesn't have its own problems. But it can be a creative, exciting, and challenging approach to meeting a team's goals.

An intergroup effort may join two or more units from within one larger organization, or it may bridge entirely different organizations. Such a group can be a rich experience in connecting different—even conflicting—organizational cultures to attain a mutual goal. An intergroup effort requires that the credibility of individual members and the team be demonstrated. It demands intensive, focused, analytical communication between teams.

Cross-organization or intergroup task forces can bring together corporate interests with public interests to address issues faced by all of us, large and small. It's entirely possible that intergroup projects are the only way for humankind to solve some of our overwhelming problems.

We once suggested that problems, even in small teams, may be opportunities. By analyzing your team's problems and implementing some of these suggestions, you can make your team more cohesive, stronger, and more effective.

SUMMARY

In this chapter, we've looked at some ways to deal with problems and obstacles that can halt a team's progress. Problems with difficult people—dominating, distracting, nonparticipating, irresponsible, or reprehensible team members—can be resolved by identifying the problem behaviors, understanding why the team allows them to continue, and finding ways to change them. A team also needs to orient and help members who are new or different—who feel like strangers in your midst.

Process problems require the use of team assessments and feedback, through discussion (face to face if possible), videotaping, transcripts of online meetings, assessment software, paper-and-pencil forms, and/or consultants' observation and training.

Problems with leaders may be due to inadequacy or the stress of transitions. In these situations, members can assume, redistribute, and share responsibilities in ways that support the leader and the team.

Problems with organizations need attention from designated leaders and members in representing the team, communicating, and finding ways for the team to gain support, resources, and autonomy. When other systems and subsystems have differing or conflicting goals and approaches, the solution may be a special collaborative effort that links different groups within a single organization or across different organizations.

Exercises

1. Think back over your experiences in groups—at work, at school, in activities, even in your family—and identify a group in which the leader was ineffective. Examine the situation and try to identify the reason (or reasons) the leader was unable to help the group be effective. Assuming you could not have replaced the leader, what could you and other members of this group have done to help that person and to make the group more effective?

2. Here's a situation: A nonprofit organization called Help, Inc., uses teams of employees and volunteers. On one team, there are six community volunteers plus three full-time employees. They are charged with designing and implementing community outreach programs. In three months of weekly meetings, however, many good ideas have been recorded in the minutes, but nothing has been achieved.

   Some of the difficulties in this team include:

   a. The same people never attend the meetings.

   b. The paid members never know which volunteers are going to show up at which time.

   c. Members never know when a volunteer will drop out and a new one will be put on the team.

   d. Only half the people attending know what has happened before and what the goals are.

   e. There is no sense of cohesiveness or team identity.

   The paid members are responsible for making this team effective. What are the problems and what can the paid members do about them?

3. Suppose the following people are on your team:

   Ray: Designated leader, friend of the boss, nice guy; knows nothing about the task or the team

   Lou: Spends 20 minutes of every meeting bewailing her divorce troubles

   Luke: Funny, great comic, relieves tension; keeps the team from working

   Sheryl: Smart, bright, committed to doing as little as possible; distracts the team with irrelevant comments

   Kiri: New to this country, speaks English moderately well, tries to prepare, but says nothing during meetings

   Irene: Brings attention to her own expertise and power at every opportunity; silences others' opinions with sarcasm

   What questions would you ask about their participation? Once you had answers, what would you do?

"This sounded like a good idea....
What have we gotten ourselves into?"
If your project turns into a big, public deal, your team can handle it.

GROUP FORMATS AND APPROACHES

APPENDIX **A**

Planning Public Meetings

Someday—perhaps as a student in this class—you'll be part of a team charged with creating and producing a meeting for another group. The project could be a conference, a workshop, a forum, a town hall meeting; it could be for 15 participants or 500. Teams or committees usually plan and implement these larger group activities, and chances are you'll be involved in that planning someday.

Most professions, from geological surveying to cosmetology, hold conferences or public meetings related to their work. Sometimes the meetings are, in whole or in part, electronic—using teleconferencing, videoconferencing, and so on. Whatever the type, such meetings are planned by teams in human resources, public relations, training and development, and/or communication departments. Sometimes conferences are set up by professional meeting planners—an interesting and promising career path.

The knowledge and leadership skills you've developed in this course will contribute to your success when you, either as an individual or as part of a team, plan a large group meeting. For us, knowing how to organize such programs—which we first learned as undergraduates in courses such as this—has opened doors to opportunities throughout our careers.

With the possibility that you have an immediate project to do for your class—and that you may plan public meetings in the future—this appendix provides an overview of various forms of public meetings and the goals they can achieve. It goes on to explain the types of conference and workshop sessions and methods for generating audience participation and learning. It finishes with a planning guide for all public group projects. Specifically, this appendix will help you:

1. Become familiar with a number of different public meeting formats
2. Understand the goals and various types of conferences and workshops
3. Know ways to involve audience members in large group meetings
4. Plan with your team for public group sessions

PUBLIC MEETINGS

By *public*, we mean any audience other than your team—members of a class, a church, businesses, a community—that meets together for some purpose. Such group meetings come in all sizes, varieties, and combinations of formats, and they meet a wide range of goals.

PUBLIC MEETING FORMATS

A public meeting can be boring or it can be stimulating, and the format used can influence which it will be. Some standard formats, which we'll highlight here, are forums, lectures, symposia, panels, colloquies, debates, and mediated or live performances. The meeting may use one meeting room or many; it may all be on one site, on several, and/or online. When you know the goals and requirements for your meeting, you can mix, match, and alter the formats to meet the specific objectives you have in mind.

Forum   A **forum** is an audience-participation session, guided by a moderator, in which people express and advocate ideas and opinions, ask questions, and seek information. A familiar forum is the radio or television talk show, in which the host introduces an issue and then invites the audience to express their opinions and ask questions. A forum can readily be adapted to online communication for any number of participants.

Lecture   The **lecture** or report format is used extensively in public meetings. Students, of course, know the difference between a deadly lecture and a stimulating one. An excellent lecturer who maintains a high level of interaction with the audience stimulates thinking and learning.

Often, lectures and forums are combined. For example, there may be a presentation, after which the audience participates in a forum. An audience-participation segment gives an otherwise straightforward presentation the sense of a public meeting. College faculty frequently use this format for sessions at their conventions to learn about current research, and students often adapt this format for group presentations to their classes. This format, too, often is used with videoconferencing, teleconferencing, or online feedback to involve a wider audience.

Symposium   A **symposium** presents several speakers on aspects of a topic. A moderator introduces the topic and the speakers, each of whom makes a presentation. After the speeches, the moderator usually opens a forum period (on-site or online) for the audience to question the presenters and express their own opinions.

Panel   On a **panel**, several individuals discuss a topic among themselves. A moderator introduces the participants, but the panelists do not make speeches, except occasionally for brief opening remarks before the discussion itself. The term *panel* often is used to describe any group of people appearing together, such as a panel of speakers. As a public meeting format, however, it describes a specific type of interaction that occurs among those involved.

Panel discussions need an adept moderator. They also need clear focus on an issue or question and a specific agenda to ensure the discussion moves along to some closure point. The audience typically does not get involved until a question or forum period is announced—and yet again, this format is easily used for any of the electronic conferencing media.

Colloquy In a **colloquy**, two separate groups interact, with or without an audience present. The interaction focuses on a specific topic. One group consists of experts; the other consists of nonexperts, or laypeople. The rationale is that together, the experts and the nonexperts can make sense of a complex issue. The experts bring knowledge; the nonexperts bring experience, common sense, and questions to help clarify the experts' talk.

Originally, the nonexperts (perhaps including an audience) discussed the topic and used the experts like a library, asking them for information as needed. This format only works, however, if the experts are willing to sit back and let the "amateurs" delve into their territories. That's unlikely, so the colloquy often is adapted.

Experts may give brief presentations or simply be introduced by the moderator. Then, a panel of laypeople directs questions to the experts. In a similar format, a group of journalists sometimes interviews a panel of experts on a given topic. The colloquy is a good choice when the planners want audience participation but the group's size or available time prohibits an open forum.

Colloquy is often used in television talk or information shows, and, of course, can be used in an electronic format as well.

Debate In a **debate**, speakers take turns advocating opposite sides of an issue before a judge or an audience. Each side has a specified time limit for speaking and a fixed time limit for a rebuttal of the other side's arguments. Some debate formats include time for cross-examination, during which speakers question each other before the rebuttals. You see what are at least alleged to be debates between or among candidates during every election in public facilities and/or on television and/or online. They often merge the "debate" with some variation of forum, colloquy, and/or panel presentation.

Public debates often merge into forum periods for audience involvement, and they may conclude with an audience vote. Debate can be intensely involving, even without direct audience participation. Every listener has strong opinions and knows exactly what she or he would have said if given the opportunity.

Parliamentary debate is an approach that allows many people to get directly involved in the action. This form, which requires a strong chairperson to guide the process, follows a set of rules to ensure that all sides get a hearing and that individual rights are protected. At the end, the majority decision still rules (Robert III, Evans, Honemann, & Balch, 2000).

Mediated or Live Performance Many creative approaches to public group communication involve a performance to provide information and stimulate discussion. Films, videos, plays, skits, music, dance, and demonstrations of art forms all provide excellent ways to help people focus their thinking. Performances also may be combined with other formats. For example, a theater professor occasionally sponsors an evening of play analysis. First, she has the playwright read his or her play aloud and then opens a forum. The audience asks questions and gives the writer feedback and criticism. This is a nice way to spend an evening; it entertains and instructs the audience and provides feedback and coaching for the playwright.

Public Meeting Goals

Your choice of formats depends, in part, on what you want that public meeting to accomplish—the clearer the goals, the easier your choice. Purposes may include learning, decision making, helping, social facilitating, entertaining, and publicizing, but keep in mind that many sessions have multiple goals. Think of how these goals might combine in a single meeting:

Learning. The goal may be to increase the participants' knowledge, understanding of issues, and/or skills. Lectures, panels, other presentational formats, and experiential methods (which we'll discuss later) advance this goal.

Decision making. Large group decision making most often takes place in representative bodies. New England town meetings are among the few surviving public groups determining their own laws and policies. Many private organizations, however, still use large groups, such as stockholders' meetings, to make decisions in public, although they usually diffuse influence by using proxy votes and elected representatives. In our teaching experience, we once were part of a faculty that met as a full body to make decisions. At other times, we have participated in groups of more than 300 people deciding on general directions and priorities for our college. These were intensely involving, challenging, and effective processes, but they do require leadership. Most deliberative groups, whether public or private, rely on some form of parliamentary procedure to make decisions in large meetings. Even then, they can become chaotic.

Helping. Many meetings are for people to help themselves and one another. Twelve-step programs, such as Alcoholics Anonymous, and many nondirective therapy groups fall into this category. The goal may be reached in small, informal group meetings, but large group events often are planned and implemented by members and/or by outside experts and facilitators.

Social facilitating. A meeting may be held simply to give people a chance to socialize and get to know one another, but this also can be a secondary goal combined with other objectives. Throughout this book, we've emphasized the need for a team to be aware of the system in which it works and to develop connectedness among its members. Opportunities to interact with individuals in that system in ways not directly related to work can establish bonds that enhance your potential to solve problems together.

Entertaining. A meeting, large or small, may be held primarily to entertain the participants. Mystery parties, for example, involve people in living the roles of detectives, victims, and plotters—solely for entertainment purposes. At the same time, these meetings can help the participants learn a number of skills or facts, so entertainment may be the path to reach another goal. In fact, individuals are entertained by that which involves them and satisfies some personal need. So in that sense, all public sessions should serve this purpose.

Publicizing. Although publicity rarely is the stated goal of a meeting, it may be the prime motivation for the sponsoring individual or organization. The congressman from a district adjacent to ours champions regular meetings for older constituents—lectures, panels, workshops—covering a range of interests. He may be altruistic, but he also receives exceptionally high support from that population in every election. Similarly, corporations sponsor programs for community relations purposes. One major corporation regularly sponsors art shows, career days for children, and charity events—all coordinated, planned, and implemented by one of our former students, who now is one of their public affairs officers.

CONFERENCES AND WORKSHOPS

Conventions, conferences, and workshops bring together individuals with similar interests to achieve common goals. People attend these meetings for some combination of all the objectives we've previously discussed.

A **conference** or **convention** tends to be large. People often register in advance by mail and come from widely separated locations within the same organization or field. Big meetings such as these may have a theme or focus that draws people with a common interest.

Workshops usually are smaller groups that convene to learn and develop specific areas of understanding, skills, or creative processes. They focus on learning and developmental goals, and the participants usually are highly involved. A workshop may stand alone, as the entire thrust of a group meeting, or it may be one form of session within a convention or conference.

Conferences and workshops serve a wide variety of goals and employ a range of public meeting formats. Planning them demands energy and draws from a wide range of knowledge and skills. A single person may be responsible for the plan, but that person usually needs a lot of assistance. More often than not, she or he works with a planning team. Regardless of who does the planning, the first steps are to identify the specific goals and to determine what types of sessions best meet those purposes.

GOALS

In addition to the general goals we've talked about for public meetings, workshops and conferences usually address specific goals as well. Identifying these goals and determining the priorities among them is a critical step. Large organizations may use extensive consumer research methods or focus groups to ensure that planners know the participants' needs and expectations. Even planners with a smaller audience and no budget, however, need to do everything possible to establish their own goals and those of its audience.

A workshop often addresses the following goals:

- Increase the participants' awareness of particular professional or interest group issues

- Increase the participants' knowledge and/or skills in specific areas
- Draw the maximum number of people to the event
- Allow people to network and establish professional and personal relationships
- Stimulate participants through entertainment and a variety of approaches
- Raise funds

Conferences and conventions of organizations whose members are dispersed across a wide geographical area usually have all the preceding goals, plus some of the following:

- Learn about new research or methods
- Be involved in deciding the organization's policies
- Pursue career advancement
- Meet old friends, and make new ones
- Develop slates of officers and/or elect officers
- Plan events
- Decide the organization's involvement in political or social issues relevant to its membership

Every planning decision should relate to the goals of the event. Goals of maximizing attendance and/or making a profit, for example, affect the major choices of location and theme. The planners must find the motivations for people to attend and pay the fees. Any or all of these goals influence the entire structure of the event, including the session types and arrangements.

TYPES OF MEETING SESSIONS

Large public meetings can be exciting, dynamic events from which participants emerge enthusiastic, charged to go forth to use their new ideas. Or people can leave groaning, "Boring, boring, boring." The difference is in the way the planners draw from and adapt their knowledge of group interaction to develop active, involving sessions. This takes creative, detailed, hard work.

A conference—large or small—is divided into units, or sessions, which are planned in blocks of time and designed to meet the goals that have been identified. Planning the sessions is like fitting a jigsaw puzzle together without using your fist: each piece must be selected so that all the purposes—or edges—fit together.

Types of sessions are influenced by goals, but also by conditions. For example, in a traditional, face-to-face situation, the number of people affects the number and types of sessions that are possible. Of course, with electronic conferencing, the number may or may not be so important. On-site, special interest groups and committees require space and time, and these meetings must be coordinated with other types of sessions. What these subgroups are, how many there are, how many people are involved in them, and which ones involve the same members all must be considered.

In addition, room availability, room sizes, and equipment availability affect what types of sessions are possible. Balancing the needs to socialize, to network, and to meet organizational and professional goals affects both the format and the arrangement of sessions, such as the choice among plenary sessions and various kinds of "breakout" sessions.

Plenary Sessions Plenary sessions are for all conferees to attend, so usually no other meeting is scheduled at that time. The topics are of general interest, often the conference's central theme or objective. The session usually is planned in the largest room available, sometimes with remote videoconferencing to other sites. Programs may involve speakers (someone who will be dazzlingly interesting to your audience), symposia, panels, or other formats. Naturally, planners want to make these programs so compelling that people at the conference won't want to miss them.

Plenary sessions often begin conferences; sometimes they conclude them as well. They often follow meetings of breakout groups to allow participants to share ideas they've generated in sessions with similar topics.

Breakout Sessions Breakout sessions meet simultaneously, preferably in separate rooms. These sessions may work concurrently on the same topic or issue, but more often than not, they have different programs, with panelists, presentations centered on a topic, or participative workshops related to special areas of interest. People usually have to select some sessions and miss others, although sessions may be repeated so that people have more than one chance to attend a specific program.

If you have a limited number of rooms, each of which holds a small number of people, you can survey participants before the conference regarding their first, second, and third choices for sessions. Then you can assign people to specific sessions and give them tickets to those events along with their registration materials. If you're using repeated sessions, you can arrange for everyone to experience every workshop or session.

When the goals include sharing information and ideas, breakout groups are used to generate ideas that participants later share in a plenary session. For breakout group reports, give the participants clear instructions at the beginning of the session and a format for their report. They may adapt these methods, but the instructions provide a starting point and help them focus on the goals for the session. The instructions should include the purpose of the report, its format, its time limits, and any other expectations.

Reports from small groups usually are presented orally, but visuals can enhance their effectiveness. Overhead projections or flip charts posted on walls or easels work well depending on room size. Be sure each group has the materials—pens, slides, newsprint—to prepare its visuals.

Teleconference Sessions With satellite technology, an entire conference can be planned as a **teleconference**. Programs can be developed and transmitted to any site capable of receiving the signal. For a fee, a conference location becomes a downlink in the network and provides the local audience access to the program.

So far, teleconference formats are like plenary sessions attended in person; in fact, they may serve as special plenary sessions at large conferences. Speakers or panels perform about the same as they do for live audiences, and telephone links can allow remote audiences to participate in a type of forum.

This change in medium certainly changes the message from that of a live presentation, but it has great advantages. Teleconferences save enormous amounts of time and money for participants compared with the costs of individual travel to a distant site to hear a similar presentation, potentially increasing the number who can participate. In addition, internationally known speakers who otherwise could not attend a conference can transmit a presentation by satellite. Panelists from throughout the world can be linked, just as news anchors bring in guests from multiple locations every day on their television broadcasts. The loss of face-to-face interaction nonetheless limits some of the personal and social goals of such conferences, so this method must be balanced with other opportunities to meet those needs. Here, again, planners need to consider carefully the goals of the program and determine the best ways to accomplish them. The potential of a resource is as great as the imagination using it.

AUDIENCE PARTICIPATION GENERATORS

Here's a workshop or conference presenter's nightmare: You ask, "Are there any questions?" and no one says a word. Unfortunately, this can happen even when you are most confident the group will really get involved in the topic. When you schedule time for audience participation, wisdom dictates that you also plan ways to get people started. Some approaches to help structure and enhance audience involvement include a variety of paper-and-pencil methods and small group participation.

PAPER-AND-PENCIL INSTRUMENTS

One way to enhance audience participation is to focus their attention on a specific topic in advance by means of **paper-and-pencil instruments**. Questionnaires, surveys, or pre-session attitude or information forms can be distributed before a speaker, panel, or debate. This increases involvement, because the process stimulates participants' thinking, focuses their attention, and mentally prepares them for the presentation or activity to follow.

Results can be tallied immediately, put on overhead slides, or given to facilitators or speakers to report or discuss with the participants during the presentation or activity. When this information is announced, participants are more than ready to contribute to a forum.

These methods can be very effective ways to conduct post-session surveys as well, to find out what people learned or if and how their attitudes may have changed. Results can be tallied immediately and announced or mailed to participants later.

Forms can be created easily, but they should be

- *Brief.* Ask enough, but no more than necessary.
- *Concise.* Keep each question or statement to a few words.
- *Clear.* Keep the language simple and to the point.

- *Objective*. Avoid emotionally loaded statements.
- *Easy to complete and tally*. Structure for brief, quick answers.

One useful participation generator is the agree/disagree discussion guide (Carbone, 1998). It is simple to design, easy to complete, speedy to tabulate, and can be adapted to many situations. To use this method:

1. Write a list of short statements about information the audience should learn from the experience or a list of possible attitudes, values, or beliefs about the topic.
2. Beside each statement, provide a space to check "Agree" or "Disagree." Having only two choices provides a clearer picture of the participants' perspectives and also permits quicker scoring. You can use more categories if you need more detailed information, but it complicates tallying.

This format works particularly well for conferences and workshops. Suppose, for example, your session deals with the welfare system and you have a panel of experts to discuss the topic. Prior to the panel, you ask the audience to complete an agree/disagree guide that states both facts and myths about present welfare needs and systems. What do people *believe* is true as opposed to what *actually* is true? As the panel presentation starts, two members of the team tally responses to each statement and put the results on an overhead slide. Later, the presenters can guide the discussion by referring to those responses. In this way, the audience is involved, panel members can adapt to what the audience knows and doesn't know, and participants learn more than they otherwise might.

Small Group Activities

Small group activities are great for involving members and reaching goals for learning, attitude change, and entertainment. We're going to look at three approaches to small group activities: buzz groups, role playing, and exercises.

Buzz Groups   Contrary to what you might suppose, small group activities can be used with very large audiences. You can divide the audience into small groups and have them work on specific questions for brief time periods. All groups can work on the same issue, or different questions can be assigned. This approach has earned the label of **buzz groups** because that's the sound and participant energy it generates.

One classic method of using buzz groups is called *Phillips 66*, not after the oil company but for its originator, J. Donald Phillips (1948). The "66" refers to having groups of six people discuss a topic for 6 minutes. It works like this:

1. Divide the audience quickly by having people in alternating rows turn around so that each set of three forms a group with the three immediately behind or in front.
2. Give each group a card with a question to consider and the format for reporting their ideas.
3. Allow the groups to discuss the topic for 6 minutes.

4. Ask a member of each group to report its major findings very briefly or to write them on a visual for display.

The presenters then incorporate the many groups' ideas into their presentations or go on to further exploration. If you're in a more flexible space than an auditorium, you might combine groups and have them share information before reporting out. It works.

Role Playing   Role playing puts participants in someone else's shoes. It may be as simple as asking them to respond from another's point of view to a problem or situation, either with oral responses or using a questionnaire. This reveals insights and opens discussion of new information and attitudes. We introduced role playing in Chapter 7 as a way of gaining different perspectives. Here, we will outline more fully the steps you need to conduct such a session.

Role playing involves assigning individuals parts in a situation to play in front of the group. This takes careful planning. We do it this way:

1. Design specific role definitions for each part. These might include the person's age, sex, and occupation, as well as his or her values, motivations, and attitudes relating to the situation at hand. Give each role player his or her definition to look over for a few minutes.
2. Give the role players a situation in which their interaction will demonstrate specific encounters and issues focusing on the goals for the session. Do not give the role players any more information than they would naturally have in the situation.
3. Instruct your role players to act just the way they think the person whose description they've been given would act. Reassure them that they don't have to be actors. Most people role-play remarkably well, and they usually demonstrate the points you want to make in a very natural way.
4. Stop the role play when it has demonstrated what you want it to show. Applaud and appreciate.
5. Debrief the experience. Question the audience about what they saw, ask the role players how they felt in their roles, and be prepared to bring out the important points.

Suppose, for example, that your learning objective is for the participants to understand assertiveness. You might prepare roles for assertive, passive, and passive-aggressive persons and then place each in a situation where another role player tramples on his or her rights. After your role players demonstrate their respective responses, the audience should be able to detect the mode in which each responded. The role players should be able to report how they, as their characters, felt. From there, your questions can facilitate discovery of the causes and effects of these response patterns in communication.

Exercises and Activities   Structured, experiential exercises enable people to have firsthand experiences and involve them in their learning. Such exercises, however, require preparation and guidance. Instructors need to think carefully about the kinds of experiences that will connect students to the learning they seek. Ideally, students will both learn how to complete the experience they are faced with, and be guided to then see how this new skill can be translated to a new task or environment (Auster & Wylie, 2006).

In a structured experience, participants are given a task such as a problem, game, case study, creative activity, or simulation. The participants work as individuals, in dyads or triads, or in small groups. Leaders provide instructions and guide the participants through the exercise and then through debriefing steps to help them gain insight and see possible relationships between the information and their lives.

We suggest setting up experiential learning sessions that alternate stimuli and activities. That is, alternate periods of stimulation with time for reflection, of intense involvement with time for pulling back to a safe distance, of talking with practicing, and of individual tasks with group tasks. "Through this application, students are able to gain both a comprehensive understanding of course material and the skills they need to excel within dynamic business environments" (Auster & Wylie, 2006, p. 335). This advice is consistent with our own experience. We find that alternating methods keeps energy high and learning opportunities strong.

It's the debriefing, or analyzing the activity, that provides the educational impact. Pfeiffer and Ballew (1988) outline five steps in this learning process:

1. *Experiencing.* The activity takes place; the participants respond to the structured experience.
2. *Publishing.* Participants describe their experiences, including their emotional and logical responses to the event.
3. *Processing.* The group "talks through" the interaction dynamics. The members discuss the tasks and processes they experienced and look for commonalities and differences.
4. *Generalizing.* Participants analyze what they learned in the previous steps to identify principles that may emerge from their collective experiences.
5. *Applying.* Participants seek to answer the question "Now what?" They look for ways to use the information and, perhaps, identify personal goals for change by responding to items such as "The next time I am in this situation, I will...."

Guiding structured experiences and activities requires a facilitator, not a presenter. Rather than listen to a speaker dish out information, participants help themselves to their own ideas and conclusions. The leader needs to ask the right questions, interject theoretical perspectives, and ensure that the group stays on track.

The various public meeting formats and activities we have described here all have their strengths and weaknesses, depending on your goals and your audience. Figure A.1 summarizes what each offers to participants.

FORMAT	EXTENSIVE INFORMATION	AUDIENCE INVOLVEMENT	EXPERIMENTAL LEARNING	ISSUES ANALYSIS	DECISION MAKING	LARGE AUDIENCE	SMALL AUDIENCE
Forum	X	X		X	X	X	X
Lecture	X					X	X
Symposium	X	X		X		X	X
Panel	X			X		X	X
Colloquy	X	X		X		X	X
Debate	X			X	X	X	X
Performance						X	X
Buzz Groups		X	X			X	
Role Playing		X	X				X
Structured Activity	X	X	X		X		X

FIGURE A.1

The appropriateness of public meeting formats and activities for specific purposes.

PREPARATION FOR PUBLIC MEETINGS AND CONFERENCES

Let's assume you have a meeting to plan—perhaps for your class, perhaps for your corporation. Let's go over some of the things you need to consider and the decisions you need to make. These include identifying your goals and participants, planning your program, finding your resources, rehearsing and running through programs, publicizing your meeting, and—after it has taken place—evaluating its effectiveness.

GOALS AND PARTICIPANTS

Goals for your sessions are almost inseparable from the participants' needs and expectations. You start with what you want your audience to *think*, *know*, and *be able to do* as a result of their participation in the meetings. To set these goals specifically, you also need to consider what the participants already know and what attitudes, values, and beliefs they bring.

Are they willing or reluctant participants? Some people attend meetings or workshops because they want to; others attend because it gets them out of something or because someone, usually their teacher or boss, thinks it would do them good. How much do they expect to participate? If your group expects to sit back and hear a lecture, then stirring them up may take careful planning. A group expecting involvement, however, may get impatient with any formal presentations of information.

Your goals are affected, too, by the time you have available. Your objectives will differ if you are planning a 45-minute session for your class or if you have to prepare a 3-day workshop on the same general topic. Be realistic in what you expect to accomplish.

Find out everything you can about your participants—who they are, what they know and feel, what they expect. Find out about time limits and conditions. And then get those goals articulated. Everything must come back to that.

PROGRAMS

It takes extensive work to develop a meeting plan. Before you're finished, you will have a detailed agenda; a grid displaying times, places, and responsibilities; and about three dozen checklists to be sure nothing slips up. You need to start early and make adaptations as you proceed because there are always surprises. Here we will look at things to consider in your plan and how to create the program. Key issues include

- *Presentation methods*. Format decisions depend on your goals, audience, time, and resources. Which formats will work best? Will written material be used for some information? Can you create innovative formats?
- *Participant involvement*. When and how will you use surveys, questionnaires, and the like? How can you divide participants into small groups? What planning will this take? Do you need additional space or rooms?
- *Scheduling the time*. How will the various formats fit together? Do they vary the types of activities? Are sessions intense or longer than one-and-a-half hours, therefore requiring breaks? Are the rooms distant, necessitating extra time between sessions? Will you have meal breaks? If so, are meals provided so that you can control the time, or are people on their own, which requires longer meal periods?
- *Registering participants*. How will you send necessary information ahead of time? How will the people register? How will you distribute the schedule and other information? Will you assign people to sessions? What fee will be charged?
- *Closing the session*. This takes more than singing "Kumbaya." How do you bring the ideas together? What sense of closure will the participants and the presenters need? What feedback or evaluation do you want from the participants? How fast will people need to get away?

A well-developed **meeting plan** addresses five variables: *Who will do what, when, how,* and with what *resources.* As you figure out all of these issues, it helps to put them on a meeting planning chart to see their relationships. Preparing a plan that incorporates these considerations is like fitting a model together. You need to be sure all the pieces are there, then put them in the right places to create the vision you have for the program. That gives you a program plan.

RESOURCES

Resources include personnel (those who possess the talent and skills necessary to do the tasks), facilities (space and equipment), and finances (money to pay the bills). You can't know specifically which resources you'll need until you have some idea of what will happen at the meeting. To resolve this dilemma, you need to work through the two aspects together. The resource plan needs to include, for each item, what you need and how you will get it.

Personnel   Effective meetings require many different abilities. Because few individuals have all the necessary talents, a number of people need to be involved. As planning team members, you may decide to fill these roles yourselves or to recruit outside specialists and experts. Here are some of the personnel the meeting may require:

Planners need the organizational ability to see the overall goals and to sense how all the parts fit together to achieve them.

Educators understand the goals and the participants and know how to manage activities so that learning occurs.

Facilitators guide people through a process without dominating. An effective facilitator asks the right questions, sometimes makes suggestions, and guides—without pushing—people through an agenda toward their goals. A facilitator is a helper and generally has more questions than answers.

Presenters need excellent speaking skills, whether as sole lecturers, part of a symposium, or panel members. He or she needs the ability to organize, support, and deliver ideas effectively within restricted time limits as well as to listen and question skillfully to connect with other ideas expressed during the session.

Presiders may be designated master or mistress of ceremonies (MC) but may serve more as a traffic cop than an MC. A presider directs activities, makes introductions, and provides transitions using skill and flexibility in thinking, speaking, listening, summarizing, and adapting to crises. When presiding over large group decision-making meetings, the presider also needs to know parliamentary procedure to guide an orderly process.

Leaders whose roles encompass all the others—planning, educating, facilitating, presenting, presiding—whatever needs doing at any point to help move the group toward its goal.

The planning team has to weave together carefully the talents it has available to make the most effective use of each. If you are working only with team members, assign responsibilities cautiously. Volunteers are not always the best solution; sometimes you need a person's specific abilities to fill a spot no one else can handle.

Facilities   Few concerns outweigh planning for meeting facilities, which begins with selecting the location and continues until the last conferee departs. Concerns include making enough rooms available, making sure rooms are convenient and at a comfortable temperature, having the proper equipment in place and on time, making appropriate seating arrangements, and assuring meals are available in a timely and convenient manner.

For meetings with multiple, simultaneous activities, the proximity of various rooms and the routes connecting them is critical. Whether you're dealing with a single room or an entire complex, get—or create—a map that provides the dimensions and capacities of each available space. Keep in mind that capacity depends on how the room is arranged, so you'll also need to know if tables can be added or removed or if there is immobile auditorium seating.

Space planning involves such questions as:

- Will the front of the room accommodate a table, lectern, or other necessary equipment?
- Can the participants see easily?
- Are the acoustics conducive to your format? Will panelists be heard, or will small groups be so close they drown out each other?
- Is the lighting appropriate? Can you control it for specific visuals or activities if necessary?
- Do you have any choices about the space? Can you change rooms or facilities? If multiple rooms are being used simultaneously, can you switch any around?
- How can you make the space work? Can you adapt creatively to make the best use of what you have available?

Equipment plans also must be carefully prepared. Someone should be assigned to ensure that all items are in the right place at the right time. The plan should be laid out on a grid, by time periods, and should include:

- What is needed at what time
- Where it is needed
- Where it will come from (for example, from a previous session or storage)
- Who will bring it and who will set it up
- Who will remove it when the session is over

If possible, arrange to have sessions needing the same equipment follow one another in the same room. This minimizes movement of equipment and any potential problems. Remember that somebody usually forgets something, so have a contingency plan for getting what you need at the last minute.

Finances You need to know where the funds are coming from and where they are going. Funding may come from sponsoring organizations, participants' fees, or some combination of these. If fees are a principal source, then your planning must involve careful market research to provide good estimates of attendance.

Potential expenses include speakers, transportation, equipment, space, printed materials, advertising, and refreshments. For a relatively simple class project, you may have visuals to prepare and handouts to reproduce. For a major conference, however, a day's video equipment rental and setup can cost hundreds of dollars, and fees for guest speakers can run into the thousands.

Obviously, you need a detailed budget, which should include all aspects of the program and cost projections for each. Then keep good records of actual expenditures as you create and implement the program.

REHEARSALS AND RUN-THROUGHS

Rarely do you have the luxury of fully rehearsing an all-day event, but a runthrough, otherwise known as a dry run, is something you can—and should—do.

A **run-through** means a step-by-step review of the entire meeting, including the following:

- Individual presentations can and should be rehearsed (see Appendix B).
- Although panel discussions can't be rehearsed because they would lose their spontaneity, the panelists should review their agenda and time frames and also briefly share their views or philosophies. If some members have written extensively about a topic, we recommend that other panelists review those materials.
- Moderators must be in tune with their information, their roles, and their agenda. They need to review the speakers, their backgrounds, and the program order. They must be ready to move the group, to give time signals, to intervene when one person dominates, and to provide the introductions and transitions that make the whole thing work.
- The team can practice small group activities with volunteers. At the least, facilitators should talk through the procedures to be sure they understand how to explain each step to the participants. This review also ensures that any materials and equipment needed for the activity are identified.
- The planning team should run through the schedule and review each person's responsibilities. Everyone needs to be comfortable that all team members know when and where they have tasks to perform.

Remember, audiences are unpredictable. In spite of all your planning, you probably will need to adapt as the session progresses. We recommend making contingency plans. For example, in case you have a quiet group, be sure you have extra exercises or material ready to fill that silence. In case you have a riotous group, know where to cut material for the sake of time. All this makes meeting planning and management challenging responsibilities that continue until the last guest has left.

PUBLICITY AND PUBLIC RELATIONS

What if you gave a conference and nobody came? Participants don't show up if they don't know about the event. Meeting planning should include ways to communicate with various audiences about the activity. You might use advertising, press releases, press coverage of special personalities or events, and direct contact with key people. Consider using multiple media—newspaper, radio, TV, direct mail, e-mail, fax, and telephones. With your specific audiences in mind, plan carefully what you will tell them, what methods you will use, the frequency of your messages (how many times each person gets one), and the costs involved.

EVALUATION

Evaluation should be an ongoing aspect of program planning. You want feedback from participants on their experiences and from team members on their processes.

The Participants   Your approach to feedback and reporting will vary depending on the objectives you want to achieve. You may want all participants to be informed about the feedback from every session; you may want chairpersons or workshop facilitators to have feedback specifically about their sessions; or you may want only the planners to receive feedback.

Planning for these objectives includes creating and distributing assessment forms, assigning people to be sure they're collected, and deciding how to distribute the results. In some instances, you may want the information given out during the conference or workshop; in other instances, you may send out follow-up reports at a later date.

The participants are the best source of information about the success of the sessions. They had personal goals for attending, and they experienced the activities directly. Thus, evaluating the meeting's successes and identifying possible improvements through their eyes are essential.

Develop the questions you want answered, and consider issues such as:

- What were the participants' goals, and were they met?
- What aspects of the program contributed most?
- What aspects of the program contributed least?
- What would the participants have changed?
- Would they have participated knowing what they know now?

You can create evaluation forms or use other systematic research methods, such as interviews and focus groups, to get the information. To paraphrase the classic warning of historians, if we don't study the problems in our programs and planning, we may be doomed to repeat them.

The Planning Team   As you plan an experience, the team should examine its processes as well as its success. The team's work processes can be examined by drawing from the suggestions and evaluation forms throughout this book. Remember, good team process evaluation requires open introspection by all members.

Working with a team to plan a conference or a workshop can be stimulating, challenging, exhausting, and very rewarding. We believe that such an experience—even if only planning a special workshop for a class or a floor in your dorm—is immeasurably valuable. It draws on every skill you've learned and every talent you've developed in group communication and leadership.

When it's all over, you may be disappointed with some aspects of your team experience but thrilled with others. That's just the way it is. You learn from the negatives and the positives. Once the workshop or the conference is over, though—once you've collected and analyzed your feedback, once you've finished the last bit of the job—celebrate your experiences as a team and congratulate yourselves for what you've learned and for what you've done.

"Now that we found this great material and have such brilliant ideas, how do we tell the world?"

ORAL AND WRITTEN REPORTS

APPENDIX **B**

Communicating Team Findings

How well members communicate their material may determine the team's ultimate success. As Daniels (2005) notes, "In today's world of video conferencing, PowerPoint templates, voice-mail messages, and faxed memos, it is the written and spoken word that is the heart of any presentation" (p. 39). At the culmination of each project, teams usually prepare a written report and present a brief oral report as well.

Far from being an "add-on," reporting often is the team's principal task. No matter how carefully the team has researched, processed, analyzed, created, and problem-solved, all can be diminished if the report doesn't reflect the same quality.

This appendix guides you through your report preparation tasks. It starts with those steps common to both written and oral reports: analyzing your goals and audience; gathering, selecting, and organizing information; and planning for visuals. It then takes you through specific processes for preparing and presenting both written and oral reports. The information in this appendix should increase your ability to:

1. Follow the preparation steps that oral and written reports have in common
2. Prepare manuscripts for written reports
3. Prepare and deliver effective oral presentations

COMMON PREPARATION STEPS

Although differences between oral and written reports are significant, you go through the same six steps during the early preparation:

1. Analyze the goals.
2. Analyze the audiences.
3. Gather research information.

4. Select material to be included.
5. Organize ideas to achieve your goals.
6. Plan visuals to supplement the text.

From this point, the paths diverge. A written report next moves to a rough draft; for an oral presentation, you prepare speaker's notes. First, let's look at the steps both reports have in common.

GOALS

You begin the process by clearly establishing what the report is intended to accomplish. The team's mission helps to clarify your goals, but you also need to consider the specific impact you want the report to make.

Team Mission   For ongoing teams, reports are a routine part of doing business, and their purposes and formats depend on the goals. Here are some typical teams and the routine reports they may need to prepare:

Self-managing teams may report on a weekly, monthly, or quarterly basis to keep management informed and to get resources the team needs. Such teams often use informal oral reports accompanied by specific written data.

Creative teams periodically report progress, provide concept presentations, and follow up with revised concepts and further progress reports as they move through a project. These teams seek approval and support, and they adapt formats to each report's purpose.

Management teams prepare reports to inform higher levels of management. These reports may be routine, with established, unvarying formats their audiences can recognize quickly.

A team needs to determine *in advance* whether it will prepare interim reports while working on a project or will wait for a complete report. Longer projects usually need periodic progress reports, and a team is well advised to plan and schedule preparation of these reports. Sometimes management requests an unscheduled report on very short notice, thrusting the team into panic. Better to anticipate the unanticipated.

Besides routine reporting, ongoing teams periodically make special reports, perhaps to get proposals approved or funded or to advocate significant policy and procedural changes. Regular reports should keep to the same, predictable format, but when a team's reporting goals are different, that format should be altered to ensure the audience perceives the contrast.

An ad hoc or special team may have been given no specified reporting format, or its charge may have detailed the form and content of a report. Team members need to determine the expectations of the group's originator and prepare reports that fulfill the charge. If the choice of format is left to the team, it should be based on the goals and the audience. If those receiving the report are a manageable number and in close proximity, an oral presentation may do the job. If the audience is spread all over the map, however, a written report may be essential.

Whether reports are routine or special, they significantly affect the team's impact. Marshall McLuhan's (1964) classic insight that "the medium is the message" applies: The report's format and appearance communicate something about the quality and significance of a team's work. Creative ideas are enhanced by creative reports; bland reports may seem to present dull ideas.

Specific Purpose   People often describe a writing or speaking task in terms of what they need to do: "I have a letter to write." "I have a report to prepare." "I have a speech to get ready." Such statements focus on the work to be done or on the product—a report or a speech. A better approach is to focus on the results you expect to achieve rather than on the method for achieving them.

The critical issues are, *Why* do you have a report to prepare, and *what* do you want the report to accomplish? Is it to meet course requirements and to get an A? To impress the oversight committee and get your proposal approved? Or to get management to understand and act on the team's findings?

The actual objective, then, is to effect some change in another person or group. That change may be to increase the audience's level of information and/or to get them to respond favorably to your ideas. When planning a persuasive report, the team should consider the nature and extent of the proposed changes. A report calling for a minor deviation from present procedures that will not cost much to implement differs from one proposing a costly, major transformation from present practices. Express your specific purpose in those terms. The work of preparing and presenting the report is only the means by which the objective will be achieved.

Specific purposes can include:

Increasing audience information. Teams frequently report just to provide information, and ongoing teams do this routinely. Special teams often are created purely as fact-finding bodies with the goal of gathering and analyzing information on a specific topic and then reporting their findings. In an information-sharing report, the material must be presented accurately, clearly, and in sufficient detail. You want the reader or listener to get a clear mental picture of the data and the ideas these data support.

Sometimes reports appear to be information-sharing when the true purpose is simply to document a team's work. The report may meet a legal obligation and fall into the infamous management category of CYA ("Cover Your . . .") to demonstrate that the formal requirements have been fulfilled, and the report is simply filed. For this purpose, the presentation must document the steps a team has taken and the procedures it followed to ensure compliance with regulations. The requiring agency or department usually provides guidelines that outline the critical information, and the team's task is to develop each content area accurately to be sure it is "off the hook."

Influence change. Many team reports are intended to persuade—to cause changes in attitude, policies, and behaviors. The team may need to convince its audience of three things: (1) There is a need to change established ways of doing things; (2) the team's proposals provide the most appropriate ways to satisfy that need; and (3) the proposed changes are consistent with the audience's attitudes, values, and goals. In these reports, the team can build and demonstrate its credibility by using sources, evidence and reasoning, clear structure and development of arguments, and a report style and format that demand attention.

AUDIENCES

Your team's objectives are achieved in the minds and by the actions of its audiences. You will want to consider both primary and secondary audiences, some characteristics of those who will act on your proposals, and their expectations for the report.

Primary and Secondary Audiences   Any report may address multiple audiences. The report you present to your immediate supervisor also may be presented to other levels of management, regulatory agencies, your peers or subordinates, and possibly, public audiences. A team of teachers, for example, may submit a report to the principal that proposes specific changes in the curriculum. This report may be made available to other teachers, the superintendent, the board of education, and the public through a parents' group or an open school board meeting. Although the primary audience is the principal, the potential secondary audiences are significant.

Characteristics   Although any audience may represent a wide range of demographic and psychographic characteristics, what you need to know about its members can be narrowed to three areas:

- How much do they know about the topic?
- What are their present attitudes about the subject?
- What values do they have that impact on the issues?

What the audience already knows indicates how much background you need to provide to establish a clear frame of reference for the report. Those well informed and close to the team's work require less introductory material than those who know little about the topic and the project.

Audience-Based Strategies   The audience's present attitudes affect how directly you should approach the proposal and how much support you need to develop for your ideas. If people already support the objective of the report, then reinforcing their attitudes requires less documentation and persuasion. If your team intends to sell a proposal to people who oppose it, however, then your presentation must change those attitudes with greater documentation and stronger persuasive appeals.

If your proposal is noncontroversial, you can present your recommendations in the first part of the report and follow those with supporting arguments and evidence. If the proposal runs counter to the audience's present attitudes, however, you need to establish common ground by developing evidence and reasoning to show that the proposal's goals and values are consistent with the audience's before presenting a specific plan.

Sometimes you have to show the audience how their values are compatible with those on which the proposal is based. For example, if your team proposes that the college should invest in a sports program, you might link your proposal to the president's and board of trustees' value of maintaining leadership and prestige, and/or to the economic value of potential alumni contributions, and/or to the public relations benefits that might accrue.

To do it right, you need to find out as specifically as you can what your audience's attitudes and values are. With the previous example, we can think of two different college presidents we've known. One, a former college football player whose top priority clearly was the students, would be sold on your team's proposal by an appeal to his belief that sports are good for students' growth and development. The other, whose top priority clearly was personal prestige, would see the benefit of the investment in terms of the image of the college—and of its president. In short, the appeal has to fit the audience.

Sensitivity to Issues   Whether written or oral, reports should reflect sensitivity— both in the ways ideas are developed and in the language used—to issues of gender and culture. We've seen well-meaning people destroy their presentations with thoughtless jokes, cartoons, and examples. Sexist or racist language and material offensive to members of certain cultures or subcultures reduce a team's credibility and directly affect audience responses to reports.

If you consider your choices of appeals and language in the context of dialogical ethics, it will help you avoid offending members of your audience. Remember Johannesen's (1996) six criteria for a dialogical ethic: authenticity, inclusion, confirmation, presentness, mutual equality, and supportive climate (pp. 67–68). This frame of reference ensures maintaining a high level of respect for your readers and listeners and invites them into a discussion on the topic. In turn, this creates genuine audience involvement, making the listeners partners with the team in your proposals.

Expectations   The people who establish a team expect certain things of its report. If they expect a brief report and they get a weighty tome, they may think the team is making too much of an issue. But if they expect a long report and receive a short one, they may consider the team irresponsible. Either error reduces a team's credibility.

If founders have not made their expectations clear, you may need to explore what they want. Sometimes you need to negotiate the requirements. The team's research findings may provide reasons to clarify and modify the founder's preconceived notions, creating a need to discuss the framework for a "doable," appropriate report.

RESEARCH

If your team has followed the guidelines in Part 3 of this book ("Sharing Leadership Through Task Processes"), you will have nearly completed gathering and analyzing information. As you prepare the report, however, review your material to find any gaps in information or logic. Organizing the material often shows what you do not yet know and what you must obtain to support your conclusions.

Because members have been intensely involved in the work from its inception, there is always a danger of underestimating how much explanation and support your audience will need to understand relationships that are obvious to the team. You don't want to insult the intelligence of your audience, but you don't want to overestimate their backgrounds, either.

CONTENT SELECTION

Everything the team has learned and done can't possibly go into a report. Selectivity is the key. At this stage, you need to identify the critical issues—the absolute "musts." Your guidelines for choosing go back to the first two steps in the report-preparation process: What is essential to achieve the goals based on what you have identified about the audience? The answers to this question influence every team decision about the report's content.

Two key content issues for your team to decide are (1) the main ideas and arguments to use, and (2) the type and amount of supporting material needed to develop these points. In addition, you need to select introductory and concluding material.

ORGANIZATION

The structure of a report radically affects its success. Clear organization helps audiences understand ideas; strategic organization leads to acceptance and approval.

You're no doubt familiar with the three major subdivisions of a report: the introduction, the body, and the conclusion. Contrary to the obvious order, *develop the body first*. After the body's content is firmly in place and the main points are clearly structured, then you have a basis for creating an introduction to prepare the audience for what follows and a conclusion to provide a strong close. Finally, make sure that your transitions keep all the relationships clear.

Body   People can process only a limited amount of data without experiencing information overload. Generally, people can remember from four to seven things from a truly stellar presentation, five being the "magic number."

To see what we're talking about, try reading this list: dog, red, four, two, blue, one, cat, horse, yellow, bird, green, three. Now cover it up, and repeat it aloud. Could you remember all the items after one reading? This list has more than five items, so most people would not remember all of them on the first try. Now look at the list this way: dog, cat, bird, horse; red, blue, yellow, green; one, two, three, four. How much more easily can you remember these three chunks of information, each containing logically related concepts?

Because people cannot process or remember many ideas at once, it helps to relate some ideas and separate them from others in this way:

- "Chunk" the information. Organize the ideas in neat groups of related items so audiences can process them easily.

- Be sure your presentation has no more than five major chunks.
- Be sure no major chunk has more than five subgroups or items.
- Be sure there is a clear, identifiable, and logical relationship or parallel among all the major chunks.
- Be sure there is a clear, identifiable, and logical relationship among all the items within any major chunk.

Clearly structured ideas create order and show relationships among a large number of items. The chart in Figure B.1 demonstrates these relationships. It is analogous to an outline in which the main ideas are designated by roman numerals (I, II, III) and the subpoints by capital letters (A, B, C). Laying out your ideas in this way can help you visualize relationships more clearly as you organize a report.

Main Points   The entire point of an organizational pattern is to show how ideas relate, thus making things easy for the presenter and the audience. You may be familiar with basic types of patterns from a composition or public speaking class. We cover this material here only briefly, however. For a more detailed review, see, for example, Lumsden and Lumsden (2003), Sprague and Stuart (2003), or Verderber (2003).

In presenting your main points, you could lay them out in linear order or take a more conceptual approach, developing various parts to form a whole picture. Another alternative is a psychological strategy, which moves the audience from where they are to where you want them to be.

A *linear* presentation, for example, may be chronological (taking ideas in order, from past to present to future), or it may be developmental (detailing a process from the first to the last step). A *conceptual*, parts-to-the-whole approach might present the team's proposal by examining the political, economic, and environmental issues. For a college community, this approach might look at the students, faculty, administration, and staff. A *logical-psychological* strategy might engage the audience in understanding the need, the solution, how the solution meets the need, and the advantages of the solution. Or it might move from the audience's values to how their values are being violated, to the proposed change, and then to how that change corrects the violation of those values.

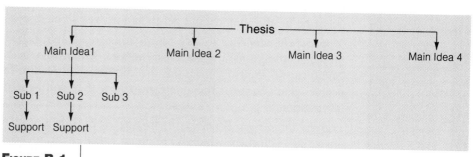

FIGURE B.1

How to "chunk" information.

Look again at Figure B.1. All the main ideas should reflect a clear and consistent relationship to one another. For example, you would not use categories of *Past*, *Present*, *Future*, and *Implications* because the first three chunks are linear and chronological, but the fourth is a parts-to-the-whole category. Mixing these two patterns upsets the relationship and makes your presentation harder for an audience to follow and comprehend.

Under each main heading, you may use different patterns without creating problems, but within each set of ideas, there should be a consistent pattern. For example, in the subpoints under *Past*, you could use a parts-to-the-whole relational pattern, selecting from the standard journalistic formula of who, what, where, when, why, how. Under the second main point, you could use another pattern, such as spatial or geographical relationships (East, South, Midwest, West). Just remember the principle: All subdivisions of any section at any level of organization should have clearly identifiable relationships.

Structures such as parts-to-the-whole, chronological, and spatial enhance an audience's understanding and are useful in reports to provide information, but they also are useful in persuasive reports. Patterns such as problem-solution or motivated sequence work especially well in persuasive messages; they also provide clear divisions for many information-sharing messages. Whether your report is written or oral, short and informal, or long and formal, applying these organizational principles helps you do two critically important things: clarify your own thinking, and assist your audience to comprehend, remember, and accept your message.

Introduction   The most common problem in preparing reports is getting started. People want to start at the beginning, with the introduction, but it's a difficult place to begin. Consider this scenario: It's the first class of a new semester, and you're seated next to someone you have never met. Shortly after the class begins, the professor asks you to introduce that person to the class. Wouldn't it be easier if you had a chance to meet the person first and find out some things about him or her? This is precisely why the introduction should be prepared *after* the body of the report has been developed. At that point, you are more familiar with what you are trying to introduce.

An effective introduction has three basic goals:

Gain the audience's attention. You need to pull the focus away from whatever might be on their minds and get them involved immediately in your topic.

Motivate the audience to stay tuned. Some years ago, Borden (1935) advised presenters to assume the audience response will always be "So what?" or "Who cares?" Starting from this assumption, you need to find ways to tell people what's in it for them and show how they will benefit from the information.

Preview the report. Whether the message is oral or written, follow the old advice to "Tell them what you're going to tell them, then tell them, then tell them what you've told them." The introduction represents the first of these; it gives your audience an idea of where your presentation will take them.

Conclusion   The conclusion also has three main objectives, which in some ways parallel those of the introduction but in reverse order:

Summarize the report. Identify the key issues you want the audience to focus on when responding to the report.

Tell the audience what to do. Should they approve your proposal or seek more information? Should they use your report as a basis for other plans? Lobby or contact legislators? Be specific. Your team has spent time developing the report, and that qualifies you to make recommendations.

Provide a strong finish. The first and last impressions are the most powerful, and you want the audience to remember your message.

Transitions   Transitions serve as bridges between ideas and as road signs that tell the audience when you are making turns or going in a different direction. To keep the audience with you, your report needs to provide signposts at every turn or connection. For example, if Main Point 1 is, "The proposal is the moral thing to do," and Main Point 2 is, "The proposal is the practical thing to do," then the transition between them might be, "We've seen that this proposal is the right thing to do morally. Pragmatically, however, is it something we can afford to do? Let's look at what it actually will cost us and at how we can pay for it." This transition reminds the audience of what it just heard, bridges the two "chunks," and previews where the presentation is going.

VISUALS

Good visuals arouse interest and hold attention by providing variety and aiding clarity, so readers or listeners get a quick, clear understanding with minimal effort. The importance of sharing information visually with your teammates, which we discussed in Chapter 5, also applies when reporting to others. When visuals supplement a message, the audience understands more of the content and, if asked to process the information to make decisions, arrives at better-quality decisions more quickly (Daniels, 2005).

With the extensive selection of graphics software available, such as PowerPoint, teams have little excuse for not using visuals in their reports—and for not making them high quality. When creating visuals for written reports, keep in mind the following criteria:

- Use different—and appropriate—forms to accomplish your purpose. Consider graphs, tables, flowcharts, diagrams, models, checklists.
- Keep the visuals simple. Break complicated information into several different chunks.
- Keep the visuals clear. Round off numbers whenever possible; create figures with plenty of room so that relationships can be seen vividly.
- Include appropriate explanatory information (legends, symbols, specifics of data collection).

As important as visuals are for written reports, they are even more significant for oral messages. You can reread a report if you have to; you can't rerun the speaker. People process more messages received through their eyes than messages received through their ears. Therefore, when the eyes are not required to look at the speaker and at his or her visuals, they wander; when the eyes wander, so does the mind. Oral presentations especially need ways to keep ears, eyes, and mind on the subject.

Posters, flip charts, videotapes, and slides are all effective ways to display visuals in oral reports, but researchers from the Wharton School concluded that visuals presented by overhead projectors achieved the most positive results. When they are done well, overhead slides have several specific advantages over most other visual aids used with oral reports:

- They can be prepared ahead of time.
- They can be created using computer software and most photocopy machines.
- They are compact and easily transported.
- They can be displayed with full room lighting.
- The speaker can face the audience while also looking at the projector.

When planning and creating visuals of any type for oral reports, be sure to make them:

Big. Be sure the visuals can be seen without effort from any point in the room. Check in advance using the equipment you plan to use.

Bold. Give the visuals life and interest. Computer programs can help you create slides with colors, graphics, appropriate humor, and interesting formats.

Brief. Use only key words or short phrases (no more than four words). Limit each slide to no more than five key ideas. For complex ideas, use multiple slides, laying one over the other if necessary to bring the "chunks" together.

As you plan the organization and content of your report, begin planning the visuals as well. Final decisions, however, must wait until the report is closer to completion. The visuals should supplement the written or oral text, not substitute for it. The two must be coordinated carefully.

PREPARATION DIFFERENCES

So far, we have talked about steps that are common to both written and oral reports, but at this point, the preparation paths diverge (Figure B.2, page 351). One path is designed to create a manuscript, the other to create a speech. You don't read and listen in exactly the same ways. Therefore, reports should not be written and spoken in exactly the same ways. Each has special requirements and requires special handling when you're doing it as a team.

WRITTEN REPORTS

The first step in moving from the organized material to a manuscript is to prepare a first draft, a rough—maybe very rough—draft. The goal is to get something

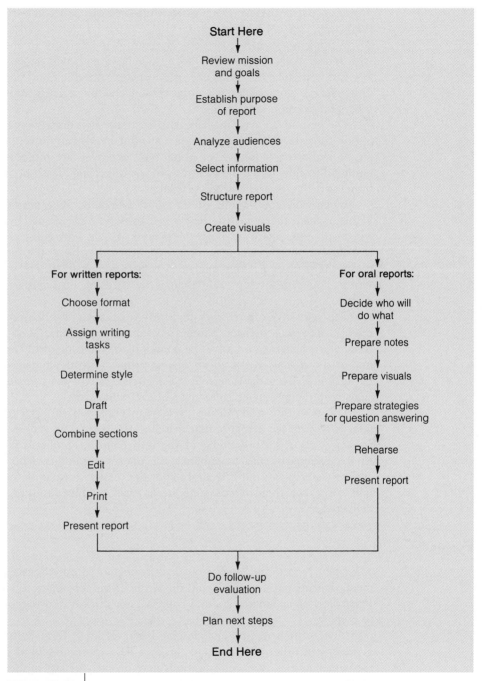

FIGURE B.2

A flowchart of processes for preparing reports.

down on paper that you can work with—rewrite and edit—to move toward the final copy.

Writing is a creative process. It requires a free flow of thought coordinated with motor skills to get ideas out of your head and onto paper. Some teams actually can write together, with one or two people speaking and one word processing. Other teams work better with one person creating a draft and bringing it to the others for revision and editing.

The best advice we can share is to write the first draft with a minimum of editing or criticism. Write or type as fast as your hands can move; don't stop to evaluate or make corrections. Evaluating and correcting are more analytical functions and tend to slow down the creative process of getting ideas out. You'll have opportunities to change and edit the text later.

When you can't think of the right words or the correct spelling, leave a blank or spell the word the best you can—and keep going. Every time you stop the creative process to turn on the analytical, you have difficulty getting the creative flow again. The more writing experience you have, the more easily you can make the transition from one process to another. If you're not an experienced writer, you can develop your abilities by focusing on one part of the process at a time.

The next step is to rework the draft yourself or turn it over to a teammate to rework. Rewrite sentences, paragraphs, or entire sections. Work to make the ideas more clear, concise, and alive. Be conscious of the tone of the report: Is it too formal or too casual? Is the vocabulary appropriate to the audience's knowledge and background? Does the tone reflect the importance of the content? Integrate the visuals with the message to maximize impact and clarity.

The rewriting and editing cycle may take you through several drafts. The goal is to prepare a report that achieves the team's objectives and purposes—to convey a clear understanding of the information, to obtain favorable responses to the proposals, and to enhance the team's credibility with the audience. To ensure the report's effectiveness, consider which format to use, how the team will work together to complete it, as well as how and to whom it will be delivered.

FORMATS

A written report can range from a brief memo to an extensive, multipage document, depending on its goals and the scope of the information you need to include. Regardless of its length, it should contain the critical information the team wishes to convey.

Most written reports include nine basic sections. These sections usually follow a prescribed order, except—and this can be important—for the placement of the recommendations. Recommendations may be early or last in the report, depending on the purposes and complexity of the information. The sections may be combined or labeled differently, but they all need to be considered for inclusion and should be structured using the principles of organization discussed earlier. If the report is only a short memo, the cover page information is included in the headings, and the table of contents is omitted.

The nine sections are

1. *The Cover Page* contains the title, who prepared the report (the name of the team and members' names), to whom it is submitted, and the date.
2. *The Executive Summary* should provide the reader with enough information to make a preliminary decision about what to do with the report. Assume the person to whom the report is addressed will read the summary to decide whether the report needs further discussion or in-depth reading or should be passed to a subordinate for more detailed review and recommendations, filed without further attention, or presented orally to another body. An executive summary is approximately 5 percent of the total report and includes a brief overview of all the major sections. Report recommendations should be detailed clearly here, and they frequently begin the summary.
3. *The Table of Contents* lists the report's major sections and subsections, including the page number on which each begins.
4. *The Background* introduces the body of the report and provides a frame of reference for what follows. It may include historical information leading to the team's formation and the report's content, and it should lead the audience to the specific goals or questions being addressed.
5. *The Procedures* describe the processes the team followed to collect information, analyze it, and prepare the report. Demonstrating sound research procedures enhances the team's and the report's credibility.
6. *The Findings or Results* present the data without bias or interpretation. Good visuals usually help clarify this information.
7. *The Discussion* interprets and explains the findings and results in terms of the report's goals. The focus here should be on the specific areas or questions that you identified in the background section.
8. *The Conclusions* present specific conclusions, which are general statements relating to the goals and providing answers to the questions raised.
9. *The Recommendations* make specific proposals. Each recommendation states who should do what, by when, and with what resources. Frequently, this section appears first; in a short report, it also can serve as the summary. In a longer report, the recommendations may appear at the beginning of the executive summary.

TEAM INVOLVEMENT

Writing a team report is a challenging job. It involves not only all the problems of group processes explored throughout this book, but also the problems of writing processes, such as differing ability levels and expectations. The team must plan well to create the best possible report.

Writing and editing a report through team meetings are difficult tasks. The overall content can be determined and conclusions as well as recommendations developed, but getting everything down in the proper format takes team time. Groupware products, however, can help cooperative groups of writers to plan—and to produce—better reports. Similarly, a new Internet-based collaborative writing tool,

Collaboratus, has been found to provide groups with better outcomes than traditional methods in terms of productivity, document quality, team relationships, and overall communication quality (Lowry & Nunamaker, 2003).

Developing a Plan Don't just jump right in—first, create an overall plan for the report, including the estimated length of each section and who will write each part. Who will put the parts together and coordinate the editing? Who will type, polish, proofread, and duplicate the report? Who will write cover letters or memos? Who will prepare supplementary materials? Recognize that some pieces, such as the summary and the table of contents, cannot be written until the process is nearing completion.

With this information in hand, assign tasks that draw on each member's expertise. For example, the person who was instrumental in a key part of the background research may be a good candidate to prepare that section. But also recognize that research skills and writing skills may not be correlated; the task has changed, and so have the skills that you need. Figure out who writes well, who edits well, who should take responsibility for the final polishing.

To complete the plan, again go back to the key elements: who will do what, by when. Set deadlines (remembering to anticipate the unanticipated). Make a pact that every piece and every draft belong to the entire team. Put all egos on hold and agree that all drafts are open to rewriting, editing, and polishing by other members. When a writer falls in love with his or her words and somebody else tries to edit them, the team—and the report—often suffer.

Determining Style Before members go their separate ways to write or edit, make some decisions about the overall tone and style of the report. What degree of formality will it have? Will it use first person *(we)* or third person *(the team)*? How will visuals be coordinated with the text? What form will they take? How will information be documented? If everyone understands these issues and incorporates them in his or her writing, then editing and integrating the parts into a cohesive report will be much easier.

We should note that the trend in today's businesses is toward more personalized, yet concise communication. As one survey of more than sixty executives found, the messages that get their attention are personalized, evoke an emotional response, come from a trustworthy source, and are concise (Crainer & Dearlove, 2004).

PRESENTATION OF THE DOCUMENT

When the report is complete, the team must make some more decisions: Who gets copies and how will they be delivered? Here are some issues and some thoughts on resolving them:

Prepare a cover letter or memo. Keep it simple. Identify the routine or special function of the report; give honest team sentiment about it, if appropriate. Make recommendations for processing it, such as meeting with team members or planning an oral presentation, and state what the team plans to do next, such as additional work, further action, or awaiting a response.

Disseminate copies to appropriate people. In an organization, every manager or supervisor in the line between the reporting team and the person (or persons) to whom the report is directed should receive a copy. Generally, it's good practice to discuss with those to whom the team reports before sending copies to anyone not in the line. Make a list together.

Decide whether to send the report or deliver it in person. The report will get more notice if delivered in person, whether by the whole team or by designated members. Personal delivery should be used only for special reasons, not for routine reports that require little or no explanation.

Plan to get feedback. Too frequently, reports sit on desks or go directly to files without the team ever hearing a word about its work. The team hardly can demand its superiors to respond, but it can plan other avenues for follow-up. For example, either in the cover letter or in person, the team can specify who will do what and when, such as by saying, "We will contact your office next Friday to see if you have specific concerns the team needs to consider."

ORAL REPORTS

Here is a classic truism in communication: "A speech is not an essay on its hind legs." Too many people write a report and then read it aloud, thereby boring the audience, reducing their credibility, and undermining their efforts. With a team report, you have special opportunities for communication because you can involve more people. This section suggests ways of planning team involvement, preparing notes, using visuals, handling questions, rehearsing, and making the presentation.

TEAM PARTICIPATION

As with a written report, the team needs to plan for each member's participation in the oral report. First, you have to decide which members will actually make presentations. Using multiple presenters adds variety and interest and demonstrates a wider range of team involvement. Too many presenters, however, looks like musical chairs, with the transitions from one to another dominating the audience's attention.

Again, draw on individual members' expertise. Look for different yet complementary presentation styles. Those who do not speak can make introductions, handle visuals, or participate during the question-and-answer period. All members can help in the rehearsal periods as well by posing as the audience and as questioners. The more all members are involved, the greater the impact the team's work will have.

Develop a work plan and agenda, specifying who will do what. Assign time limits for each speaker, and set timelines for preparing speaking notes and visuals, arranging for equipment, and holding rehearsal sessions. Make a checklist to ensure that all items are included, and check on your progress at each stage.

NOTES

Having planned the organizational structure and content of an oral presentation, speakers now need to prepare notes. We strongly recommend that you do not write a manuscript or read aloud from the report—that's deadly. Once you set precise words on paper, you will have difficulty ever getting away from the script. A manuscript also places extra burdens on the speaker. Reading or memorizing takes much more preparation and skill than working from notes, and it usually results in a less effective performance than a well-prepared extemporaneous presentation. An extemporaneous presentation is thoroughly prepared and rehearsed, but it does not tie you to specific wording. It allows you to be flexible and adaptive to the audience and the situation.

Put your notes on cards no larger than 4 by 6 inches if you may be speaking without a podium—and no more than 5 by 8 inches if you're certain you will be using one. Larger note cards or thin paper tend to rattle and flutter during the speech—very distracting.

Use only key words in notes, not full phrases or sentences, and use large print that will be easy to see even if nervousness clouds your vision. Start every new subdivision on a new note card; it helps maintain a better sense of your organization during the actual presentation.

Now, practice using the notes by letting them serve as reminders while you talk out loud about the ideas. You'll find that talking the speech—rather than writing it—casts it into more natural oral language, making it more comfortable for your listeners to hear and easier for you to remember and deliver. If, after repeated practice, you find that the key words don't serve your memory well, add something—or change the words until they work for you.

VISUALS

We've already discussed planning and preparing visuals. To present them well, you need to consider these issues: Will the speaker handle his or her own visuals, or will another member reveal each as needed? Where will the focus point or screen be located? Will everyone be able to see it easily? Will audience members need to keep shifting their focus away from the speaker to see the visuals?

Here are a few other things to remember when using visuals:

- Visuals should supplement the speaking, not supplant it. Use visuals to help focus the audience's attention on the ideas and to reinforce the oral message.
- Talk to the audience, not to the visual. A rule to guide you is "touch-turn-talk": *Touch*—identify the visual area you want the audience to focus on; *Turn*—redirect your attention to the audience by engaging them with direct, individual eye contact; and *Talk*—only then begin the oral message, not while you're still looking at the visual.
- Reveal only what you want the audience to focus on. If you have a list of items, disclose only one at a time. When you have finished with a visual, turn it off, cover it, or remove it so the audience doesn't continue thinking about it and miss what follows.

QUESTIONS AND ANSWERS

Some folks might not believe this, but questions are a presenter's best friends. Prepare for them with enthusiasm. Questions let you know if your message has been understood correctly, allow you to respond to the audience's concerns or objections, and provide additional opportunities to enhance the team's credibility. Questions, therefore, help you achieve the report's goals. You need to anticipate questions that may be asked and plan how you will respond to them.

Anticipating Questions   If you examine the contents of your report and consider your audience, you will see points that may raise questions or objections. During rehearsals, too, each member can note places where questions may pop up. You should, of course, adapt the presentation to anticipate questions, but the limitations of time and space prohibit covering everything in such detail that no questions will ever be asked. Therefore, as a team, discuss ways to handle the ideas and information during a question-and-answer period at the end of the report.

Team members sometimes develop expertise in specific subject areas, but all members should be familiar enough with the report to field most questions. It helps to prepare a concise, easily used supplementary file with information you may need when answering questions. This file might include sources, specific statistical data, synopses of research, or technical details of a plan.

Handling Questions   The speaker's and the team's credibility are enormously enhanced by masterful question answering. The skills are fairly simple but impressive in action:

1. *Be professional and courteous*:

   - Assume that questions are well intentioned, but even if they are not, treating them as if they are puts the ball in your court.
   - Listen intently and concentrate fully on the question.
   - Be friendly and cooperative in providing information.
   - If the question is idiotic, stupid, or hostile, don't get defensive or sarcastic—stay cool and friendly. Sometimes you can bridge the question: start with what the questioner said and move it to your ground. Your credibility increases; hers or his diminishes.

2. *Make the questions work for you*:

   - Unless a question is both loud and terse, restate it for the audience before you answer.
   - If the questioner asks a long, involved question, take a moment to analyze it. Then restate it more concisely for the audience.
   - If the question really involves two or more questions, separate them and state your intention to answer them separately.
   - If the questioner makes a speech instead of asking a question, don't agree or argue. Listen courteously, and then phrase a question from it or ask the speaker to rephrase.

- If you already answered the question, don't mention that fact. Just answer it again.

3. *Make sure your answers are effective*:

- Answer all questions as concisely and directly as possible.
- If your answer is complicated, organize it into concise chunks and preview the way you intend to answer.
- If another team member can answer the question more effectively, hand it off—but only if you have agreed to do this beforehand.
- If you don't have an answer, say so; don't fake it. If appropriate, promise to get the answer and get back to the questioner. If it's in your file, another member can look it up as the session proceeds.

Rehearsal   Now that you have an oral report prepared and a plan for presenting it, you are ready for the next three preparation stages: practice, practice, and practice. Nothing substitutes for good rehearsals. Use the team as a full staff of coaches.

Here are some guidelines to help you get the most from your practice time:

Rehearse out loud. Looking over notes and thinking through the speech serve as practice for only part of the actual presentation. Moving from idea coding to transmitting is a significant leap in the communication process. Silent rehearsal is like practicing for a three-ball juggling act with only two balls.

Rehearse in sections. You don't always have to go from beginning to end. It may be more productive to work repetitively on short sections with which you're having difficulty. In 10 minutes, you might run through an entire speech once, but you could work through a 20- to 30-second segment twenty times.

Rehearse at the presentation site if possible. Get the whole team there and bring friends to serve as audience members. The more closely you can replicate the actual setting, the more your practice helps you adapt to the presentation's complex circumstances.

Rehearse with your visuals. Apply the guidelines presented earlier for using visual aids. Get a sense of the time you need to move from one to another. Among other things, get a feel for how the visuals actually help relax you as a speaker. After all, the audience's focus is diverted from you from time to time, reducing some tension, and your own movement from audience to visual to notes actually helps your body relax.

Rehearse handling questions. Have other team members or friends ask questions, and practice giving clear, concise responses. Use the rehearsal to identify potential question areas. Anticipate hostile or trick questions so you can get a feel for your answers.

Rehearse with videotape. Observing yourself on videotape will give you excellent information, and if you can combine your assessment with that of a skilled observer to coach you, so much the better. Concentrate on what you do well. When you identify things to improve or change, consider specific ways to do so. Don't just say, "My hands are awkward," and then glue them to your sides. Awkward might be better.

Rehearse your feelings and responses. Visualize yourself in front of the audience being comfortable and effective. What are you doing? What is the audience doing? How are they responding? Most of us have no difficulty thinking the worst; we focus too little on the best. Create clear, moving mental pictures of you succeeding in the presentation and gaining the audience response you desire.

Play these images back in your mind in full living color; concentrate on your emotional responses as the successful presentation proceeds.

PRESENTATION

Despite extensive preparation, the actual presentation likely will be a time of nervousness and anxiety. Having your team there provides moral support, but there still is a lot at stake. The credibility and reputation of the team and its members will be enhanced or diminished by the experience. The presentation can affect careers in the workplace or grades and friendships in school, so some apprehension is reasonable and natural. The challenge is to manage the nervousness and use its energy to enliven your performance—"Get all those butterflies to fly in formation."

The first challenge is to be sure everyone and everything is on hand. Someone should have a checklist, marking off people as they arrive and handouts, visuals, and equipment when they are in place. It's easy to overlook something.

The second challenge is to prepare yourself. Consciously work to relax your throat, shoulders, and neck. Breathe slowly and deeply. Get involved in activities and conversations that occur before your turn to speak. Visualize yourself in front of the audience moving successfully through the performance. Most important, focus your thoughts on your purpose—you have a message to share with this audience.

When your turn arrives, move to the front and take a few seconds to settle in before you begin. Engage individuals in the audience, eye to eye. Smile; be friendly. When you speak, direct your conversation to one person at a time, moving around the room so all are included as you share the team's ideas.

Be flexible. One strength of an extemporaneous presentation is that you can adapt. If someone stops you to ask a question that covers one of your points, you can answer the question, skip over that point in your presentation, and save that time for other items or more questions. The goal is to have the audience understand and, if appropriate, to approve the team's report. Adapting your presentation—even if that means missing something you intended to cover—is okay as long as you achieve your objective.

FOLLOW-UP AND EVALUATION

After presenting your report—written or oral—the team should examine how well it achieved its goals and what it needs to do next. The practical outcome of your report gives you part of the answer. Did it meet the expectations of your audience? Did you get approval of the report or support for your proposals? You can enhance this information by using a simple evaluation form at the end of your presentation to get feedback from your audience. This method is fairly subtle and anonymous—and it can give you additional information you might need.

As a team, assess how well you did and plan your next steps. Does the team still have work to do? Is a follow-up report expected? Does the team, or do individual members, still have agendas they want to address? Does the report have consequences that may lead the team in new directions?

We know from our own experience that creating an oral or written presentation as a team is an especially challenging and gratifying project to undertake. Congratulate yourselves—you deserve it!

GLOSSARY

Active listening Engaging a speaker mentally, giving nonverbal feedback, silently analyzing and questioning information.

Ad hoc A meeting or a group set up to focus specifically on one issue.

Adaptive structurational process A process whereby, as members interact, groups produce and reproduce structures or rules and norms that guide behaviors; the behaviors that reflect these rules are seen in systems of interaction.

Advantages Beneficial side effects that might result from implementing a proposal.

Agenda An ordered list of events used to guide a meeting.

Aggressiveness Communicating low regard for others' rights or feelings by directly expressing hostility and/or the intent to control their responses.

Applicability The degree to which a proposal meets criteria for solving a problem.

Assertiveness Communicating openly, with concern for others' rights and feelings, what one needs or wants them to know.

Assumption An untested belief, often unconscious and usually unstated, that something is a fact.

Asynchronous meeting Team communication in which messages are entered on individuals' personal computers and are reviewed at different times.

Authoritarian A leadership style that is directive, controlling, and often relies on coercive or reward power.

Brainstorming A group process for thinking of as many ideas as possible without immediate evaluation.

Breakout sessions Small groups that meet simultaneously during a conference or workshop.

Bureaucratic organization Organization relying on procedure and protocol.

Buzz groups Small groups into which a large audience is divided for brief discussions, after which they report to the audience at large.

Cause-and-effect reasoning Inferring that one occurrence causes another on the basis of observing a relationship between the two.

Charge The purpose or objectives given to a group that provide the foundation for setting that group's goals.

Claim The conclusion or argument that is inferred on the basis of data and reasoning.

Code switching Using a different style to communicate more effectively with someone who may not be receptive to the way you normally speak.

Coercive power The ability to punish others as a method of getting them to perform in desired ways.

Cohesiveness The degree to which team members are attracted toward one another and to the group, making their involvement important to them.

Colloquy A public meeting format involving two types of groups: one of experts, the other of nonexperts or laypeople. The nonexperts use the experts as resources on the topic.

Commanding/authoritative style A communication style that concentrates on task processes, on making sure the job gets done. Behaviors associated with a commanding/authoritative style are more like those previously labeled masculine or powerful, but depending on the circumstances, this style might be either weak or strong, feminine or masculine.

Communication The process of using verbal and nonverbal cues to negotiate a mutually acceptable meaning between two or more people within a particular context and environment.

Competence The degree of expertness, qualification, authoritativeness, and skill a person demonstrates.

Conference A large meeting that brings together individuals with similar interests to achieve common goals.

Conflict Opposed positions in which two or more people perceive that accomplishing one's goal keeps another's from being achieved.

Conformity Behaving in ways consistent with a group's norms and standards.

Consensus Decisions that represent the agreement of every member of a group.

Convention A large meeting, like a conference, that brings together individuals with similar interests to achieve common goals.

Cooperative analysis A process of listening and questioning that engages team members in thinking critically, creatively, and analytically and testing the logic and validity of their arguments.

Coorientation Other people's sense that you are similar to them, that you are concerned for their well-being, and that you share their interests, values, objectives, and needs.

Coorientational accuracy The correctness of one person's understanding of another's position.

Creative team People who bring specific talents together to conduct research, formulate ideas, and carry through an entire original project.

Creative thinking Brain activity that is synthetic, artistic, innovative, global, visionary, intuitive, and imaginative.

Credibility Individuals' perceptions of another's competence, objectivity, trustworthiness, coorientation, and dynamism.

Cybernetic processes Methods of feedback and assessment that help open systems with their own development and improvement.

Debate A public meeting format in which speakers take turns advocating opposite sides of an issue before a judge or an audience.

Decision by authority Someone with higher status makes the final decision after hearing the team's report and/or recommendations.

Decision making The culmination of information-gathering and problem-analysis processes to arrive at specific policies or actions to be implemented.

Decision matrix A grid for comparing the merits of different plans by categories of criteria.

Deductive reasoning Drawing a conclusion about a specific case from a general or universal statement.

Delphi technique A method of group analysis that involves a wide range of people without holding meetings.

Democratic A leadership style that ensures everyone is heard, facilitates discussion and decision making, and shares power.

Designated leader The person charged with organizing, structuring, and empowering teams to achieve their tasks.

Desirability The analysis of value, worthwhileness, and ethics involved in the possible implementation of a proposal.

Deviance Behaving in ways or expressing opinions that do not conform to others' expectations.

Dialectical tension A pull within and between individuals because they are torn between contradicting, yet interdependent, desires or forces.

Dialogical listening A process of "sculpting" meaning through listening, questioning, paraphrasing, and building on each other's ideas.

Disadvantages Undesirable side effects that might result from implementing a proposal.

Drive-reduction theories Theories based on the idea that people are motivated to act in ways that reduce their personal drives or needs.

Electronic meeting room (EMR) A room set up for conferencing through computer, video, and/or telephone connections and/or for face-to-face groupware meetings.

Emblems Specific gestures that are widely used and understood within a culture.

Empathic listening Understanding what others feel and helping identify personal or interpersonal issues that have an impact on the team.

Empowerment Opening possibilities and providing pathways for people so they can use their own power to develop self-efficacy and confidence.

Ethical dilemma A situation in which the team must apply standards and make decisions between two real choices involving ethical issues.

Ethical issue A situation in which one individual can address what is right or wrong on only one value and can make a decision to "do the right thing."

Ethics Value judgments concerning degrees of right and wrong, goodness and badness, in human conduct.

Experiential exercises Structural activities that provide learning opportunities that participants can apply to personal or workplace situations.

Expert power Influence based on an individual's expertise, credentials, experience, research, and competence in a given area.

Face A person's sense of social identity, or the way people present themselves publicly.

Facilitative/equal style A communication style that focuses on transactional processes that help teammates express ideas in a supportive climate. As such, a facilitative/equal style uses many of the behaviors researchers previously have labeled feminine or powerless yet can, in fact, be very powerful.

Facilitator A person who guides group members through task and transactional processes to achieve a goal.

Fallacy An inference from data to a claim that circumvents sound, logical reasoning.

Fantasy chaining An imaginative, creative process of linking ideas together, like a play.

Fishbone diagram A diagram used in problem analysis for identifying and visualizing cause-and-effect relationships.

Flowchart A diagram, useful in problem analysis, showing the stages, directions, and choices from beginning to end of a process.

Focus group A group of representatives from a specific population who, with the help of a professional facilitator, discuss questions relating to anything from marketing a new product to evaluating a general education curriculum.

Forum A public meeting guided by a moderator in which audience members express and advocate ideas and opinions, ask questions, and seek information.

Games Patterns of behavior that manipulate others through a gimmick that leads into a script that, in turn, results in a payoff for the game player.

Governance groups and committees Representatives of larger populations or organizations and subgroups who consider issues, gather information, make proposals, report, make decisions, and/ or enact legislation.

Group Two or more persons interacting with one another in such a manner that each person influences and is influenced by each other person.

Groupthink A mindlessness in which a cohesive group screens out anything but what it assumes—and wants—to be true.

Groupware Any computer software designed to enable groups to work together electronically.

Health care team Professionals who coordinate the delivery of all aspects of care and/or rehabilitation to a given patient.

High-context culture A culture that is collectivistic, with close family and community groupings, so people know about one another and have a basic context for their communication.

Hostile/divisive style A communication style that is counterproductive, concerned primarily with an individual's objectives or defenses, and often aggressive or passive-aggressive. This style is not responsive to the transactional needs of the team, nor does it help with accomplishing task processes.

Illustrators Mostly spontaneous ways to make a point clear and vivid by showing what you mean.

Incrementalism A decision-making process in which the decisions to correct immediate situations create new problems that, in turn, affect consequent decisions.

Inductive reasoning Drawing a general conclusion from specific instances of an occurrence.

Inference A mental connection from data to a conclusion.

Information gathering Research and inquiry as either the sole or partial responsibilities of a team or group.

Innovative organization An organization that encourages creativity in its members.

Instrumental objectives Interim steps the group or team must achieve in order to reach its goals.

Interactive questioning Applying analytical and critical thinking skills to clarify, probe, analyze, and follow up information expressed by others.

Laissez-faire A leadership style that is neutral and uninvolved.

Leadership Verbal and nonverbal communication behavior that influences a team's transactional and task processes in achieving the members' and the team's needs and goals.

Lecture A presentation by a speaker, often followed by a forum session with audience participation.

Legitimate power Authority residing in a person's position or office.

Life-cycle theory A leadership style that adapts to a group's maturity, or members' abilities and willingness to take responsibility for directing their own behaviors.

Low-context culture A culture that tends to be individualistic and diverse, so that people have less experience in common for their communication.

Majority vote Results of a ballot in which more than 50 percent of the members who vote favor one candidate or one side of an issue.

Management team Managers who meet to coordinate employee groups, solve problems, make decisions, allocate resources, and so on.

Meeting plan A full plan for a public meeting that includes an agenda, times, places, responsibilities, and checklists.

Metaphorical thinking A creative process that phrases comparisons between two things as if one thing were the other, thereby suggesting new relationships and ideas.

Midpoint crisis The midpoint of a team's existence, when members recognize their time is half over, conflicts must be managed, and work must be completed.

Mind locks Assumptions about how people should be or act that close off the ability to think creatively.

Monochronic culture A culture in which people generally attend to one thing at a time; characteristic of most of North America.

Multiple ranking Ranking issues or candidates through several ballots to eliminate choices until a final decision is reached.

Nominal group technique (NGT) An orderly process for getting full participation in generating and discussing ideas within a group.

Nonverbal communication Cues accompanying language or separate from language that people may interpret as having meaning.

Objectivity The ability to look at both sides of an issue, to suspend personal biases, and to be reasonable and dispassionate.

Organizational culture The distinguishing realities, beliefs, values, norms, expectations, and responses that develop as people work together in an organization and that guide their behaviors.

Panel A public meeting format in which several individuals discuss a topic among themselves.

Paper-and-pencil instruments Questionnaires or surveys used to ascertain people's knowledge or attitudes about a topic.

Passive-aggressive style Behavior that expresses anger and hostility indirectly through strategies that block progress or hurt someone else.

Passivity Seeming indifferent or agreeable and hiding feelings to avoid dealing with others' responses.

Perception The process by which people sense, select, and interpret stimuli.

Person-centered messages Communicating in ways that recognize another's uniqueness, goals, feelings, and concerns.

Personal agenda The personal needs, wants, or goals an individual brings to working with a group or team.

Plenary sessions Meetings of all conferees at a conference or convention.

Polychronic culture A culture in which people do many things at once; characteristic of most of Latin America.

Practicality The feasibility of implementing a proposal.

Primary source A direct, original source of information, such as a newspaper report, research study, or interview.

Principled leader One who uses ethical standards to facilitate dialogical processes and decision making in a group.

Proactivity Reaching beyond the circumstances of the moment and creating opportunities.

Problem analysis Investigation of a problem—its scope, impact, causes, effects—possibly leading to recommendations for solutions.

Project charge See *Project team.*

Project team People of varied backgrounds and skills who work together to accomplish a specific task from beginning to end.

Punctuated equilibrium Periods of seeming inertia broken by bursts of energy and change in the development of a team.

Qualifiers Modifiers that indicate the degree of certainty of a given conclusion.

Quality teams Employees who work in a group to improve quality in any area of the organization.

Quality management (QM) An approach to management that seeks participation from all in the organization to improve continuously the quality of their products and their services.

Questions of fact Discussion questions seeking objective, testable, verifiable answers about matters of past or present conditions and data.

Questions of policy Discussion questions seeking answers to what positions or actions should be adopted.

Questions of prediction Discussion questions seeking to forecast future conditions of facts, values, and/or policies.

Questions of value Discussion questions that weigh the worth, ethicality, and relative importance of a concept, act, or policy.

Referent power The influence inherent in the respect and admiration others have for an individual.

Reflective thinking sequence The classic analysis of the steps people take in thinking through a problem: sensing a problem, defining it, listing possible solutions, comparing pros and cons, selecting the best solution, implementing it, and reviewing its effectiveness.

Reinforcement theories Explanations of human behavior as the tendency to continue rewarded behaviors and to discontinue punished behaviors.

Reservation Recognition of possible arguments against a conclusion or claim.

Reward power The ability to provide for others' needs or wants as a way of motivating their performance.

Risk The chance a team takes in going ahead with an idea that might fail or result in serious damage.

Role playing A structured experience in which participants enact a scenario using adopted roles to examine feelings and interactions from a perspective different from their own.

Roles Sets of behaviors a person uses to fulfill specific expectations of his or her function or character in a situation.

Run-through A step-by-step review or rehearsal of an entire session.

Secondary source An information source that paraphrases, repeats, and/or quotes another source.

Self-managing team (SMT) People who work together and are responsible for all aspects of their efforts, including personnel, budget, work and project planning, coordinating with other teams and departments, and self-assessment.

Self-monitoring The ability to get feedback and adapt one's behavior in relationship to others' cues.

Situational-contingency Leadership approach that adapts a leader's style to variations in situations, tasks, purposes, and members.

Social exchange theory An explanation of how an individual chooses a behavior by weighing a prediction of the outcome against his or her minimally acceptable outcome and how that would compare to other possible alternatives.

Social loafing The tendency for people to put out less effort when working as part of a group than when working alone because they feel less accountability and responsibility.

Staff group People who work together in some capacity and meet regularly to discuss information and policies.

Study group People who get together to help one another learn about a given topic.

Subsystem A small group or unit that operates as part of a larger system.

Superteam A high-performance team that achieves extraordinary results.

Support group People who help one another cope with issues affecting their lives.

Supportive organization An organization with infrastructure supporting team processes

Symposium A public meeting format in which a moderator introduces the topic and the speakers, each of whom then makes a presentation.

Synchronous meeting When members meet at the same time, possibly through computers, the telephone, and/or videoconferencing.

Synergy The energy that moves a team; the fusion or interactive combination of the drives, needs, motives, and vitality of the members.

Syntality A group's "personality," reflecting the way members interact, the way they share ideas and solve problems, and the way they feel about and respond to one another.

Systems theory Describes the systematic, interdependent relationships, processes, and structures of interrelated subsystems and systems.

T-chart A chart divided into a T for comparing the merits of an idea, with pros on one side of the vertical divider and cons on the other.

Task force A group specifically appointed to gather information, solve problems, and/or make recommendations regarding an issue.

Task processes Specific interactions that focus on gathering and sharing information, analyzing problems, designing solutions, analyzing and testing evidence and reasoning, and making, implementing, or evaluating decisions.

Team A diverse group of people who share leadership responsibility for creating a group identity in an interconnected effort to achieve a mutually defined goal within the context of other groups and systems.

Team culture A group's way of being, acting, and doing that derives from the larger society, the parent organization, the various cultures or subcultures of the members, and the members' interactions.

Team image An identifying set of characteristics unique to a given team.

Team vision A mutual understanding that includes—but goes beyond—goals and objectives to a totality the team visualizes will be the result of its work.

Teleconference A meeting by telephone, computer, or video that allows people to confer from dispersed locations.

Transactional leadership A leadership style that motivates others by exchanging rewards for performance.

Transactional processes Give-and-take interactions that carry communication about individuals, the team, and the task processes concurrently.

Transformational leadership A leadership style that elevates, motivates, inspires, and develops members to create the team and to fulfill the vision and goals of the team and the organization.

Trustworthiness Other people's confidence in a person's honesty, sincerity, and consistency of ethical behavior.

Two-thirds vote Ballot results with at least twice the number of votes for an issue as against it.

Value A personal, internal understanding about the worthwhileness and importance of an idea, action, or way of being.

Videoconferencing A technologically supported meeting using cameras, computers, and at times, satellites that allows people at multiple locations to participate.

Vigilance Team members' intense dedication to critical thinking and analysis that produces quality choices at every stage of decision making.

Visionary leadership A characteristic found in all high-performance teams, this style gets others to develop and share an uplifting view of the future and to work to bring it about.

Virtual meeting A meeting conducted electronically without face-to-face interactions.

Virtual team A group that conducts its interactions electronically using virtual meetings.

Visualization A mental picture of the way a person will feel and act in a situation.

Warrant The rationale behind an inference that links evidence or data to a conclusion or a claim.

Workshops Small groups that convene to learn and develop specific areas of understanding, skills, or creative processes, usually with high involvement by participants.

REFERENCES

Aggarwal, P., Castleberry, S. B., Ridnour, R., & Shepherd, C. D. (2005). Salesperson empathy and listening: Impact on relationship outcomes. *Journal of Marketing Theory and Practice, 13*, 16–31.

Ahuja, M. K., & Galvin, J. E. (2001). Socialization in virtual groups. *Journal of Management, 29*, 1–25.

Alge, B. J., Wiethoff, C., & Klein, H. J. (2003). When does the medium matter? Knowledge-building experiences and opportunities in decision-making teams. *Organizational Behavior and Human Decision Processes, 91*, 26–37.

Amabile, T. M., Burnside, R. M., & Gryskiewicz, S. S. (1999). *User's manual for KEYS: Assessing the climate for creativity*. Greensboro, NC: Center for Creative Leadership.

American Psychiatric Association. (1980). *Diagnostic and statistical manual of mental disorders* (3rd ed.). Washington, DC: American Psychiatric Association.

Ancona, D. G. (1990). Outward bound: Strategies for team survival in an organization. *Academy of Management Journal, 33*, 334–365.

Anderson, C. A., & Martin, M. M. (1995). The effects of communication motives, interaction involvement, and loneliness on satisfaction: A model of small groups. *Small Group Research, 16*, 118–137.

Bandura, A. (1987). *Social foundations of thought and action: A social cognitive theory*. Englewood Cliffs, NJ: Prentice-Hall.

Bandura, A. (1997). *Self-efficacy: The exercise of control*. W. H. Freeman: New York.

Barge, J. K. (1989). Leadership as medium: A leaderless group discussion model. *Communication Quarterly, 37*, 237–247.

Bass, B. M. (1990, Winter). From transactional to transformational leadership: Learning to share the vision. *Organizational Dynamics*, pp. 19–31.

Baxter, L. A. (1988). A dialectical perspective on communication strategies in relationship development. In S. Duck (Ed.), *A handbook of personal relationships*. New York: Wiley.

Begley, S. (2006, October 20). Critical thinking: Part skill, part mindset and totally up to you. *Wall Street Journal*, p. B1.

Behfar, K. J., Peterson, R. S., Mannix, E. A., & Trochim, W. M. K. (2008). The critical role of conflict resolution in teams: A close look at the links between conflict type, conflict management strategies, and team outcomes. *Journal of Applied Psychology, 93*, 170–188.

Benne, K. D., & Sheats, P. (1948). Functional roles of group members. *Journal of Social Issues, 4*, 41–49.

Bennis, W. (1989). *Why leaders can't lead*. San Francisco: Jossey-Bass.

Bergiel, B. J., Bergiel, E. B., & Balsmeier, P. W. (2008). Nature of virtual teams: A summary of their advantages and disadvantages. *Management Research News, 31*, 99–110.

Bligh, M. C., Pearce, C. L., & Kohles, J. C. (2006). The importance of self- and shared leadership in team based knowledge work: A meso-level model of leadership dynamics. *Journal of Managerial Psychology, 21*, 296–318.

BNET Business Dictionary (2008). *Business definition for: Active listening*. Retrieved April 17, 2008, from the World Wide Web: http://dictionary.bnet.com/definition/active+listening.html.

Borden, R. C. (1935). *Public speaking as listeners like it*. New York: Harper & Row.

Borges, M. R. S., Pino, J. A., & Valle, C. (2005). Support for decision implementation and follow-up. *European Journal of Operational Research, 160*, 336–351.

Bormann, E. G. (1990). *Small group communication: Theory and practice* (3rd ed.). New York: Harper & Row.

Bormann, E. G., Knutson, R. L., & Musolf, K. (1997). Why do people share fantasies? An empirical investigation of a basic tenet of the symbolic convergence communication theory. *Communication Studies, 48,* 254–276.

Bostrom, R. N. (1990). *Listening behavior: Measurement and application.* New York: Guilford.

Botero, C., Carrico, S., & Tennant, M. R. (2008). Using comparative online journal usage studies to assess the Big Deal. *Library Resources & Technical Services, 52,* 61–68.

Boulding, K. (1989). *Three faces of power.* Newbury Park, CA: Sage.

Boyd, S. D. (2004, February). The human side of business: Effective listening. *Agency Sales Magazine, 34*(2), pp. 35–37.

Braybrooke, D., & Lindblom, C. E. (1963). *A strategy of decision.* New York: Free Press.

Braynion, P. (2004). Power and leadership. Journal of Health Organization and Management, 18, 447.

Breen, V., Fetzer, R., Howard, L., & Preziosi, R. (2005). Consensus problem-solving increases perceived communication openness in organizations. *Employee Responsibilities and Rights Journal, 17,* 215–224.

Brew, F. P., & Cairns, D. R. (2004). Styles of managing interpersonal workplace conflict in relation to status and face concerns: A study with Anglos and Chinese. *International Journal of Conflict Management, 15,* 27–56.

Bridis, T. (2003, February 22). Shuttle worried NASA Worker. *Tribune,* pp. A1, A4.

Brown, M. T. (1990). *Working ethics: Strategies for decision making and organizational responsibility.* San Francisco: Jossey-Bass.

Bruneau, T. (1988). The time dimension in intercultural communication. In L. A. Samovar, & R. E. Porter (Eds.), *Intercultural communication: A reader* (5th ed.) (pp. 282–292). Belmont, CA: Wadsworth.

Bucero, A. (2006, July). Listen and learn. *PM Network, 20*(7), pp. 20–22.

Burgoon, J. K., & Dunbar, N. E. (2000). An interactionist perspective on dominance-submission: Interpersonal dominance as a dynamic, situationally contingent social skill. *Communication Monographs, 67,* 96–121.

Burke, R. J. (2006). Why leaders fail: Exploring the dark side. *International Journal of Manpower, 27,* 91–100.

Business Wire (2007, October 3). Survey finds Fortune 500 companies lost

$250 million per year from poor business intelligence. *Business Wire,* New York.

Carson, J. B., Tesluk, P. E., & Marrone, J. A. (2007). Shared leadership in teams: An investigation of antecedent conditions and performance. *Academy of Management Journal, 50,* 1217–1234.

Cattell, R. B. (1948). Concepts and methods in the measurement of group syntality. *Psychological Review, 55,* 48–63.

Chaney, L. H., & Lyden, J. A. (1998, May). Managing meetings to manage your image. *SuperVision, 59*(5), pp. 13–15.

Chapman, J. (2006). Anxiety and defective decision making: An elaboration of the groupthink model. *Management Decision, 44,* 1391–1404.

Cheek, M. (1993, September). Study examines how culture affects groupware adoption. *IEEE Software,* pp. 88–89.

Chen, G. (2005). Newcomer adaptation in teams: Multilevel antecedents and outcomes. *Academy of Management Journal, 48,* 101–116.

Chen, G., & Klimkoski, R. J. (2003). The impact of expectations on newcomer performance in teams as mediated by work characteristics, social exchanges, and empowerment. *Academy of Management Journal, 46,* 591–607.

Chen, Z., Lawson, R. B., Gordon, L. R., & McIntosh, B. (1996). Groupthink: Deciding with the leader and the devil. *Psychological Record, 46,* 581–681.

Chidambaram, L. (1995, May 25). *Electronic support for intercultural meetings.* Unpublished lecture and demonstration at the Pacific Asian Management Institute & Center for International Business Education & Research, College of Business Administration, University of Hawaii at Manoa.

Chun, R. (2005). Ethical character and virtue of organizations: An empirical assessment and strategic implications. *Journal of Business Ethics, 57,* 269–284.

Cody, M. J., Woelfel, M. L., & Jordan, W. J. (1983). Dimensions of compliance-gaining situations. *Human Communication Research, 9,* 99–113.

Cohen, S. G., & Bailey, D. E. (1997). What makes teams work: Group

effectiveness research from the shop floor to the executive suite. *Journal of Management, 23,* 239–290.

Coleman, D. (1992, August). Computer programs call meetings to order. *HR Focus,* p. 10.

Collier, G. (1985). *Emotional experience.* Hillsdale, NJ: Erlbaum.

Cooper, R. B. (2000). Information technology development creativity: A case study of attempted radical change. *MIS Quarterly, 24,* 245–276.

Cordes, K., & Ibrahim, H. (1996, February). Educating for diversity. *JOPERD: The Journal of Physical Education, Recreation & Dance, 67* (2), p. 41.

Creelman, D. (2001). Interview: Gina Walker and Virtual Teams. *HR.com.* Retrieved August 10, 2001, from the World Wide Web: http://www.hr.com/hicom/general/pf.cfm?.

Cummings, T. (1978). Self-regulating work groups: A socio-technical synthesis. *Academy of Management Review, 80,* 625–634.

Davenport, T. (2004, October). Decision evolution. *CIO, 18*(1), pp. 1–7.

Day, D. V., Gronn, P., & Salas, E. (2004). Leadership capacity in teams. *Leadership Quarterly, 15,* 857–880.

de Bono, E. (1970). *Lateral thinking: Creativity step by step* (rev. ed.). New York: Harper & Row.

de Bono, E. (1994). *de Bono's thinking course* (rev. ed.). New York: Facts on File.

De Bruin, W. B., Parker, A. M., & Fischoff, B. (2007). Individual differences in adult decision-making competencies. *Journal of Personality and Social Psychology, 92,* 938–956.

Deci, E., & Ryan, R. (1985). *Intrinsic motivation and self-determination in human behavior.* New York: Plenum.

DeDreu, C. K. W., & West, M. A. (2001). Minority dissent and team innovation: The importance of participation in decision making. *Journal of Applied Psychology, 86,* 1191–1201.

DeNisi, A. S., Hitt, M. A., & Jackson, S. E. (2003). The knowledge-based approach to sustainable competitive advantage. In S. E. Jackson, M. A. Hitt, & A. S. DeNisi (Eds.), *Managing knowledge for sustained competitive advantage* (pp. 3–33). San Francisco: Jossey-Bass.

Dennis, A., & Garfield, M. J. (2003). The adoption and use of GSS in project teams: Toward more participative processes and outcomes. *MIS Quarterly, 27,* 289–323.

DeTienne, K. B. (2002). *Guide to electronic communication: Using technology for effective business writing and speaking.* New Jersey: Prentice Hall.

Dewey, J. (1910). *How we think.* Boston: D. C. Heath.

DeWine, S. (1994). *The consultant's craft: Improving organizational communication.* New York: St. Martin's.

Dickinson, T. L., & McIntyre, R. M. (1997). A conceptual framework for teamwork measurement. In M. T. Brannick & E. Salas (Eds.), *Team performance assessment and measurement: Theory, methods, and applications* (pp. 19–43). Mahwah, NJ: NEA.

DiLiello, T. C., & Houghton, J. D. (2006). Maximizing organizational leadership capacity for the future: Toward a model of self-leadership, innovation, and creativity. *Journal of Managerial Psychology, 21,* 319–337.

DiLiello, T. C., & Houghton, J. D. (2008). Creative potential and practiced creativity: Identifying untapped creativity in organizations. *Creativity and Innovation Management, 17,* 37–46.

Dolphin, C. Z. (1988). Variables in the use of personal space in intercultural transactions. *Howard Journal of Communications, 1,* 23–38.

Domenici, K., & Littlejohn, S. W. (2006). *Facework: Bridging theory and practice.* Newbury Park, CA: Sage.

Drollinger, T., Comer, L. B., & Warrington, P. T. (2006). Development and validation of the Active Empathetic Listening Scale. *Psychology & Marketing, 23,* 161–180.

Dotlitch, D. L., & Cairo, P. (2003). *Why CEOs fail: The 11 behaviors that can derail your climb to the top and how to manage them.* San Francisco: Jossey-Bass.

Duggan, E. W., & Thachenkary, C. S. (2004). Integrating nominal group technique and joint application development for improved systems requirements determination. *Information & Management, 41,* 399–411.

Eales-White, R. (2004). Eliminating perception gaps. *Industrial and Commercial Training, 36,* 234–237.

Earley, P. C., & Gibson, C. B. (1998). Taking stock in our progress on individualism-collectivism: 100 years of solidarity and community. *Journal of Management, 24,* 265–304.

Eberle, B. (1971). *SCAMPER.* Buffalo, NY: DOK.

Ellingson, J. E., & Wiethoff, C. M. (2002). From traditional to virtual: Staffing the organization of the future today. In R. H. Heneman & D. B. Greenberger (Eds.), *Human resource management for virtual organizations* (pp. 141–177). Greenwich, CT: Information Age.

Erdem, F. (2003). Optimal trust and teamwork: From groupthink to teamthink. *Work Study, 52,* 229–233.

Felps, W., Mitchell, T. R., & Byington, E. (2006). How, when, and why bad apples spoil the barrel: Negative group members and dysfunctional groups. *Research in Organizational Behavior, 27,* 175–222.

Feuerman, C. (2008, March). Listening as leadership. *Principal Leadership, 8*(7), pp. 64–65.

Fisher, B. A. (1970). Decision emergence: Phases in group decision making. *Speech Monographs, 37,* 53–66.

Fisher, B. A. (1986). Leadership: When does the difference make a difference? In R. Y. Hirokawa & M. S. Poole (Eds.), *Communication and group decision-making* (pp. 197–218). Beverly Hills: Sage.

Fisher, R., & Ury, W. (1981). *Getting to yes: Negotiating agreement without giving in.* New York: Penguin.

Fletcher, C., & Baldry, C. (2000). A study of individual differences and self-awareness in the context of multi-source feedback. *Journal of Occupational and Organizational Psychology, 73,* 303–319.

Forster, N. (2000). The myth of the international manager. *International Journal of Human Resource Management, 11,* 126–142.

Foucault, M. (1980). In C. Gordon (Ed.), *Power/knowledge: Selected interviews and other writings 1972–1977.* Brighton, England: Harvester Press.

French, J. R. P., & Raven, B. (1959). The bases of social power. In D. Cartwright (Ed.), *Studies in social power* (pp. 150–167). Ann Arbor: University of Michigan, Institute for Social Research.

From the Editor's Desk (April, 1999). *Harvard Management Update 4,* pp. 4, 11.

Fu, J. H., Morris, M. W., Lee, S., Chao, M., Chiu, C. Y., & Hong, Y. (2007). Epistemic motives and cultural conformity: Need for closure, culture, and context as determinants of conflict judgments. *Journal of Personality and Social Psychology, 92,* 191–207.

Furst, S., Blackburn, R., & Rosen, B. (1999, August). *Virtual teams: A proposed research agenda.* Unpublished paper presented to the Organizational Communications and Information Systems Division of the Academy of Management.

Garfield, C. A. (1984). *Peak performance: Mental training techniques of the world's greatest athletes.* Los Angeles: Tarcher.

Garmston, R. J. (2008, Spring). Raise the level of conversation by using paraphrasing as a listening skill. *National Staff Development Council, 29*(2), pp. 53–54.

Gaspar, S. (2001, September 24). Virtual teams, real benefits. *Network World.* Retrieved January 28, 2003, from the World Wide Web: http://www.nwfusion.com/careers/2001/0924.man.html

Gauss, J. W. (2000, August). Integrity is integral to career success. *Healthcare Financial Management, 54*(8), p. 89.

George, J. M., & Zhou, J. (2001). When openness to experience and conscientiousness are related to creative behavior: An interactional approach. *Journal of Applied Psychology, 86,* 513–524.

Gersick, C. J. G. (1988). Time and transition in work teams: Toward a new model of group development. *Academy of Management Journal, 31,* 9–41.

Gesell, I. (2007, Fall). Am I taking to me? The power of internal dialogue to help or hinder our full-body listening. *The Journal for Quality and Participation, 30*(3), pp. 22–23.

Giacobbi Jr., P. R. (2002, July). Survey construction and analysis Part I: How to conceptualize and design a survey. *Athletic Therapy Today, 7*(4), pp. 42–44.

Gibb, J. R. (1961). Defensive communication. *Journal of Communication, 11,* 141–148.

Gibbs, R. W., Gould, J. J., & Andric, M. (2006). Imagining metaphorical actions: Embodied simulations make the impossible plausible. *Imagination, Cognition, and Personality, 25,* 221–238.

Gibbs, R. W., Lima, P., & Francuzo, W. (2004). Metaphor is grounded in embodied experience. *Journal of Pragmatics, 36,* 1189–1210.

Giessner, S. R., & van Knippenberg, D. (2008). "License to fail": Goal definition, leader group prototypicality, and perceptions of leadership effectiveness after leader failure. *Organizational Behavior and Human Decision Processes, 105,* 14–35.

Gouran, D. S. (1982). *Making decisions in groups: Choices and consequences.* Glenview, IL: Scott Foresman.

Graham, E. E., Barbato, C. A., & Perse, E. M. (1993). The interpersonal communication motives model. *Communication Quarterly, 41,* 172–186.

Gratton, L., & Erickson, T. J. (2007). 8 Ways to Build Collaborative Teams. *Harvard Business Review, 85*(11), pp. 100–109.

Griffin, E. (1994). *A first look at communication theory* (2nd ed.). New York: McGraw-Hill.

Grob, L. M., Meyers, R. A., & Schuh, R. (1997). Powerful/ powerless language use in group interactions: Sex differences or similarities? *Communication Quarterly, 45,* 282–303.

Guerrero, L. (1997). Nonverbal involvement across interactions with same-sex friends, opposite-sex friends, and romantic partners: Consistency or change? *Journal of Social and Personal Relationships, 14,* 31–58.

Hackman, M. Z., & Johnson, C. E. (1996). *Leadership: A communication perspective* (2nd ed.). Prospect Heights, IL: Waveland.

Hall, E. T. (1994). Monochronic and polychronic time. In L. A. Samovar & R. E. Porter (Eds.), *Intercultural communication: A reader* (7th ed.) (pp. 264–270). Belmont, CA: Wadsworth.

Hamid, J. A. (2008). Knowledge strategies of school administrators and teachers. *International Journal of Educational Management, 22,* 259–268.

Hamilton, A. (1995, March). From copies to conferencing: Kinko's copy shops offer video. *PC World,* p. 180.

Harkins, S. (1987). Social loafing and social facilitation. *Journal of Experimental Social Psychology, 23,* 1–18.

Harrell, A. (1996, November). My kind of power. *Essence, 27,* 102.

Hart, R. R., & Burks, S. M. (1972). Rhetorical sensitivity and social interaction. *Speech Monographs, 39,* 75–91.

Hastings, C., Bixby, P., & Chaudhry-Lawton, R. (1986). *The superteam solution: Successful teamworking in organisations.* Aldershot, England: Gower.

Heath, R. G., & Sias, P. M. (1999). Communicating spirit in a collaborative alliance. *Journal of Applied Communication Research, 27,* 356–376.

Hellweg, S. A., Samovar, L. A., & Skow, L. (1994). Cultural variations in negotiation styles. In L. A. Samovar & R. E. Porter (Eds.), *Intercultural communication: A reader* (7th ed.) (pp. 286–293). Belmont, CA: Wadsworth.

Heninger, W. G., Dennis, A. R., & Hilmer, K. M. (2006). Individual cognition and dual-task interference in group support systems. *Information Systems Research, 17,* 415–424.

Hermann, N. (1988). *The creative brain.* Lake Lure, NC: Brain Books.

Hersey, P., & Blanchard, K. H. (1977). *Management of organizational behavior: Utilizing human resources* (3rd ed.). Englewood Cliffs, NJ: Prentice-Hall.

Hersey, P., Blanchard, K. J., & Natemeyer, W. E. (1979). Situational leadership, perception, and the impact of power. *Group and Organization Studies, 4,* 418–428.

Hertel, G., Konradt, U., & Orlikowski, B. (2004). Managing distance by interdependence: Goal setting, task interdependence and team-based rewards in virtual teams. *European Journal of Work and Organizational Psychology, 13,* 1–28.

Herzberg, F., Mausner, B., & Snyderman, B. B. (2003). *The motivation to work.* Transaction Publishers: New Brunswick, NJ.

Higgins, T., Strauman, T., & Klein, R. (1986). Standards and the process of self-evaluation: Multiple affects from multiple stages. In R. Sorrentino & T. Higgins (Eds.), *Handbook of motivation and cognition* (pp. 23–63). New York: Guilford.

Holmes, J. (2007). Making humor work: Creativity on the job. *Applied Linguistics, 28,* 518–537.

Holmes, J., & Marra, M. (2002). Having a laugh at work: How humor contributes to workplace culture. *Journal of Pragmatics, 34,* 1683–1710.

Holt, R. R. (1964). Imagery: The return of the ostracized. *American Psychologist, 19,* 254–264.

Horiuchi, C. (2006). Training a "new" consciousness. *Administrative Theory and Practice, 28,* 208–224.

Horvath, L., & Tobin, T. (1999). *Twenty-first century teamwork: Defining competencies for virtual teams.* Unpublished paper presented at the 1999 Academy of Management Conference Shared Interest Track Organization Development and Change.

House, A., Dallinger, J. M., & Kilgallen, D. (1998). Androgyny and rhetorical sensitivity: The connection of gender and communicator style. *Communication Reports, 11,* 12–19.

Huang, X., & Van de Vliert, E. (2006). Job formalization and cultural individualism as barriers to trust in management. *International Journal of Cross Cultural Management, 6,* 221–242.

Huang, W., & Zhang, P. Z. (2004). An empirical investigation of the effects of GSS and group process on group outcome in small group decision-makings. *The Journal of Computer Information Systems, 45,* 23–29.

Hudson, K. M. (2001). Transforming a conservative company one laugh at a time. *Harvard Business Review, 79,* 45–53.

Huff, L., & Kelley, L. (2003). Levels of organizational trust in individualist versus collectivist societies: A seven-nation study. *Organization Science, 14,* 81–90.

Hughes, L. (2002, September/October). How to be a good listener. *Women in Business, 54*(5), p. 17.

Hunter, J. E., & Boster, F. J. (1987). A model of compliance-gaining message selection. *Communication Monographs, 54,* 63–84.

Ibrahim, H., & Cordes, K. (1996). Leader or manager? *JOPERD—The Journal of Physical Education, Recreation & Dance, 67,* 41–43.

Imhof, M. (2008). What have you listened to in school today? *The*

International Journal of Listening, 22, 1–12.

Infante, D. A., Riddle, B. L., Horvath, C. L., & Tumlin, S. A. (1992). Verbal aggressiveness: Messages and reasons. *Communication Quarterly, 40,* 116–126.

Infante, D. A., & Wigley, C. J., III. (1986). Verbal aggressiveness: An interpersonal model and measure. *Communication Monographs, 53,* 61–69.

Ishikawa, K. (1982). *Guide to quality control* (2nd rev. ed.). Tokyo: Asian Productivity Organization.

Jaffee, S., & Hyde, J. S. (2000). Gender differences in moral orientation: A meta-analysis. *Psychological Bulletin, 126,* 703–726.

Jaksa, J. A., & Pritchard, M. S. (1994). *Communication ethics: Methods of analysis* (2nd ed.). Belmont, CA: Wadsworth.

Janis, I. L. (1982). *Groupthink* (rev. ed.). Boston: Houghton Mifflin.

Janis, I. L. (1989a). *Crucial decisions: Leadership in policymaking and crisis management.* New York: Free Press.

Janis, I. L. (1989b). Groupthink: The desperate drive for consensus at any cost. In J. S. Ott (Ed.), *Classic readings in organizational behavior* (pp. 223–232). Belmont, CA: Wadsworth.

Jassawalla, A., Truglia, C., & Garvey, J. (2004). Cross-cultural conflict and expatriate manager adjustment. *Management Decision, 42,* 837–849.

Johannesen, R. L. (1996). *Ethics in human communication* (4th ed.). Prospect Heights, IL: Waveland.

Jones, S. E. (1994). The right touch: Understanding and using the language of physical contact. Kresskill, NJ: Hampton Press.

Kanter, R. M. (1983). *The change masters: Innovations for productivity in the American corporation.* New York: Simon & Schuster.

Kanter, R. M. (1990, Nov–Dec). From the editor: Thinking across boundaries. *Harvard Business Review,* 9–10.

Karau, S. J., & Williams, K. D. (1993). Social loafing: A meta-analytic review and theoretical integration. *Journal of Personality and Social Psychology, 65,* 681–706.

Katzenbach, J. R., & Smith, D. K. (2001, Fall). The discipline of virtual teams *Leader to Leader (22,* 1.

Leader to Leader Institute). Retrieved January 28, 2003, from the World Wide Web: http://www.pfdf. org/leaderbooks/121/fall2001/Katzenbach.html

Katzenbach, J. R., & Smith, D. K. (1993). *The wisdom of teams: Creating the high-performance organization.* Boston: Harvard Business School Press.

Keil, M., DePledge, G., & Rai, A. (2007). Escalation: The role of problem recognition and cognitive bias. *Decision Sciences, 38,* 391–421.

Keil, M., Mann, J., & Rai, A. (2000). Why software projects escalate: An empirical analysis and test of four theoretical models. *MIS Quarterly, 24,* 631–664.

Kelley, H. H., & Thibaut, J. W. (1978). *Interpersonal relationships.* New York: Wiley.

Kennedy, G. A., & Ball, H. (2007). Power break: A brief hypnorelaxation program to reduce work-related fatigue and improve work satisfaction, productivity, and well-being. *Australian Journal of Clinical & Experimental Hypnosis, 35,* 169–193.

Kephart, W. M. (1950). A quantitative analysis of intragroup relationships. *American Journal of Sociology, 55,* 544–549.

Kerr, S. (1975). On the folly of rewarding A, while hoping for B. *Academy of Management Journal 18,* 769–782.

Kesby, D. (2008). Day-to-day leadership. *Human Resource Management International Digest, 16,* 3–26.

Kijkuit, B., & van den Ende, J. (2007). The organizational life of an idea: Integrating social network, creativity, and decision-making perspectives. *Journal of Management Studies, 44,* 863–882.

Kim, M. S., & Sharkey, W. F. (1995). Independent and interdependent construals of self: Explaining cultural patterns of interpersonal communication in multicultural organizational settings. *Communication Quarterly, 43,* 20–38.

King, P. E. (2001). Automatic responses, target resistance, and the adaptation of compliance-seeking requests, *Communication Monographs, 68,* 386–399.

Kinlaw, D. C. (1991). *Developing superior work teams: Building quality and the competitive edge.* Lexington, MA: Lexington Books.

Kipnis, D., & Schmidt, S. M. (1982). *Profiles of organizational influence strategies: Influencing your subordinates.* San Diego, CA: University Associates.

Knowles, E., Morris, M. W., Chiu, C. Y., & Hong, Y. (2001). Culture and the process of person perception: Evidence for automaticity among East Asians in correction for situational influences on behavior. *Personality and Social Psychology Bulletin, 27,* 1344–1356.

Koerber, C. P., & Neck, C. P. (2003). Groupthink and sports: An application of Whyte's model. *International Journal of Contemporary Hospitality Management, 15,* 20–28.

Kolb, J. A., & Rothwell, W. J. (2002). Competencies of small group facilitators: What practitioners view as important. *Journal of European Industrial Training, 26,* 200–203.

Kopeikina, L. (2006). The elements of a clear decision. *MIT Sloan Management Review, 47,* 19–20.

Kozlowski, S. W. J., & Bell, B. S. (2003). Work groups and teams in organizations. In W. C. Borman, D. R. Ilgen, & R. J. Klomoski (Eds.), *Comprehensive handbook of psychology, Vol. 12: Industrial and organizational psychology* (pp. 333–375). New York: Wiley.

Krebs, D., & Adinolf, A. A. (1975). Physical attractiveness, social relations, and personality style. *Journal of Personality and Social Psychology, 31,* 245–253.

Kruger, P., & Mieszkowski, K. (1998, September). Stop the fight! *Fast Company,* pp. 93–111.

Laing, R. D. (1970). *Knots.* London: Tavistock.

Larson, C. E., & LaFasto, F. M. J. (1989). *Teamwork: What must go right/what can go wrong.* Newbury Park, CA: Sage.

Latane, B., Williams, K., & Harkins, S. (1979). Many hands make light the work: The causes and consequences of social loafing. *Journal of Personality and Social Psychology, 37,* 823–832.

Leathers, D. G. (1992). *Successful nonverbal communication: Principles and applications* (2nd ed.). New York: Macmillan.

Lee, D. (1998, November 2). All the rage. Careers, *Los Angeles Times,* Business Part II, pp. 3, 19.

Lee, E. J. (2006). When and how does depersonalization increase conformity to group norms in computer-mediated communication? *Communication Research, 33,* 423–447.

Lembke, S., & Wilson, M. G. (1998). Putting the "team" into teamwork: Alternative theoretical contributions for contemporary management practice. *Human Relations, 51,* 927–945.

Levinson, W. A. (2006, December). Bringing the Fishbone Diagram into the computer age. *Quality Progress, 39*(12), p. 88.

Lewis, C. (2007, April/May). Manage your team toward consensus. *The British Journal of Administrative Management,* p. 29.

Lieberman, D. A. (1991). Ethnocognitivism and problem solving. In L. A. Samovar & R. E. Porter (Eds.), *Intercultural communication: A reader* (6th ed.) (pp. 229–234). Belmont, CA: Wadsworth.

Ling, W., Chia, R. C., & Fang, L. (2000). Chinese implicit leadership theory. *Journal of Social Psychology, 140,* 729–737.

Lumsden, D., Knight, M. E., & Gallaro, D. (1989). Assessing learning outcomes: Opportunities for institutional renewal. *Journal of Staff, Program and Organization Development, 7,* 181–185.

Lumsden, G., & Lumsden, D. (2003). *Communicating with credibility and confidence: Diverse people, diverse settings* (2nd ed.). Belmont, CA: Wadsworth.

Mackin, D. (2008). The difference between a team and a group. Sideroad.com. Retrieved February 3, 2008, from the World Wide Web: http://www.sideroad.com/Team_Building/difference-between-team-and-group.html.

Maher, K. J. (1997). Gender-related stereotypes of transformational and transactional leadership. *Sex Roles, 37,* 209–225.

Maier, N. R. F. (1963). *Problem-solving discussions and conferences: Leadership methods and skills.* New York: McGraw-Hill.

Major, B. (1980). Gender patterns in touching behavior. In C. Mayo & N. M. Henley (Eds.), *Gender and nonverbal behavior* (pp. 15–37). New York: Springer-Verlag.

Maslow, A. H. (1970). *Motivation and personality* (2nd ed.). New York: Harper & Row.

Mathieson, K. (2007). Towards a design science of ethical decision support. *Journal of Business Ethics, 76,* 269–292.

McClelland, D. C. (1989). That urge to achieve. In J. S. Ott (Ed.), *Classic readings in organizational behavior* (pp. 82–89). Belmont, CA: Wadsworth.

McLuhan, M. (1964). *Understanding media: The extensions of man.* New York: McGraw-Hill.

Megone, C., & Robinson, S. (2002). *Case histories in business ethics.* London: Routledge.

Merritt, A. C. (2000). Culture in the cockpit: Do Hofstede's dimensions replicate? *Journal of Cross-Cultural Psychology, 31,* 283–301.

Messina, A. (2007). Public relations, the public interest, and persuasion: An ethical approach. *Journal of Communication Management, 11,* 29–52.

Metcalf, C. W., & Felible, R. (1992). *Lighten up: Survival skills for people under pressure.* Reading, MA: Addison-Wesley.

Michaelson, L. K., Watson, W. E., & Black, R. H. (1989). A realistic test of individual versus group consensus decision making. *Journal of Applied Psychology, 74,* 834–839.

Miranda, S. M. (1994). Avoidance of groupthink: Meeting management using group support systems. *Small Group Research, 25,* 105–136.

Mitchell, R. (1999, June). How to manage geeks. *Fast Company,* pp. 175–180.

Moore, R. M. (2000). Creativity of small groups and persons working alone. *Journal of Social Psychology, 140,* 142–143.

Myrsiades, L. (2000). Meeting sabotage: Met and conquered. *The Journal of Management Development, 19,* 870–884.

Nanus, B. (1992). *Visionary leadership: Creating a compelling sense of direction for your organization.* San Francisco: Jossey-Bass.

Natale, S., & Ricci, F. (2006). Critical thinking in organizations. *Team Performance Management, 12,* 272–277.

Newstrom, J. W. (2002). Making work fun: An important role for managers. *SAM Advanced Management Journal, 67,* 4–21.

Ng, K. Y., & Van Dyne, L. (2005). Antecedents and performance consequences of helping behavior in work groups: A multilevel analysis. *Group & Organization Management, 30,* 514–540.

Nguyen, N. T., Basuray, M. T., Smith, W. P., Kopka, D., & McCulloh, D. (2008). Moral issues and gender differences in ethical judgment using Reidenbach and Robin's (1990) Multidimensional Ethics Scale: Implications in teaching business ethics. *Journal of Business Ethics, 77,* 417–430.

Nichols, B. (2005, March 23). Players use power of visualization. *ESPN.com.* Retrieved January 23, 2008, from the World Wide Web: http://sports.espn.go.com/golf/index.

Northouse, P. G. (2004). *Leadership theory and practice.* Thousand Oaks, CA: Sage.

Oetzel, J., Ting-Toomey, S., Masumoto, T., Yokochi, Y., Pan, X., Takai, J., & Wilcox, R. (2001). Face and facework in conflict: A cross-cultural comparison of China, Germany, Japan, and the United States. *Communication Monographs, 68,* 235–258.

O'Leary-Kelly, A. M., Duffy, M. K., & Griffin, R. W. (2000). Construct confusion in the study of antisocial behavior at work. *Research in Personnel and Human Resources Management, 18,* 275–303.

Opper, S., & Fersko-Weiss, H. (1992). *Technology for teams: Enhancing productivity in networked organizations.* New York: Van Nostrand Reinhold.

O'Sullivan, M., Ekman, P., Friesen, W., & Scherer, K. (1985). What you say and how you say it: The contribution of speech content and voice quality to judgments of others. *Journal of Personality and Social Psychology, 48,* 54–62.

Pace, R. W., & Faules, D. F. (1994). *Organizational communication* (3rd ed.). Englewood Cliffs, NJ: Prentice-Hall.

Park, W. W. (2000). A comprehensive empirical investigation of the relationships among variables of the groupthink model. *Journal of Organizational Behavior, 21,* 873–887.

Patel, V. N., & Riley, A. W. (2007). Linking data to decision-making: Applying qualitative data analysis methods and software to identify mechanisms for using outcomes data. *Journal of Behavioral Health Services & Research, 34,* 459–474.

Pearce, C. L., & Manz, C. C. (2005). "The new silver bullets of leadership: The importance of self and shared leadership in knowledge work." *Organizational Dynamics, 34,* 130–140.

Pearson, J. C., Turner, L. H., & Todd-Mancillas, W. (1991). *Gender and communication* (2nd ed.). Dubuque, IA: W. C. Brown.

Pech, R. J. (2001). Termites, group behavior, and the loss of innovation: Conformity rules! *Journal of Managerial Psychology, 16,* 559–574.

Petty, R., & Guthrie, J. (2000). Intellectual capital literature review: Measurement, reporting, and management. *Journal of Intellectual Capital, 1,* 155–176.

Pfeiffer, J. W., & Ballew, A. C. (1988). *Using structured experiences in human resource development.* San Diego, CA: University Associates.

Phillips, K. W., Northcraft, G. B., & Neale, M. A. (2006). Surface-level diversity and decision-making in groups: When does deep-level similarity help? *Group Processes & Intergroup Relations, 9,* 467–490.

Phillips, J. D. (1948). Report on Discussion 66. *Adult Education Journal, 7,* 181–182.

Piaget, J., & Inhelder, B. (1969). *Psychology of the child.* New York: Basic Books.

Pil, F. K., & Cohen, S. K. (2006). Modularity: Implications for imitation, innovation, and sustained advantage. *Academy of Management Review, 31,* 995–1011.

Platt, L. (1999, Sep/Oct). Virtual teaming: Where is everyone? *Journal for Quality and Participation, 22,* 41–43.

Poole, M. (1983). Decision development in small groups. III: A multiple sequence model of group decision making. *Communication Monographs, 50,* 321–341.

Poole, M. S., Hollingshead, A. B., McGrath, J. E., Moreland, R. L., & Rohrbaugh, J. (2004). Interdisciplinary perspectives on small groups. *Small Group Research, 35,* 3–16.

Poole, M., & Roth, J. (1989a). Decision development in small groups. IV: A typology of group decision paths. *Human Communication Research, 15,* 323–356.

Poole, M., & Roth, J. (1989b). Decision development in small groups. V: Test of a contingency model. *Human Communication Research, 15,* 549–589.

Porter, R. E., & Samovar, L. A. (1994). An introduction to intercultural communication. In L. A. Samovar, & R. E. Porter (Eds.), *Intercultural communication: A reader* (7th ed.) (pp. 3–26). Belmont, CA: Wadsworth.

Postmes, T., Spears, R., Sakhel, K., & De Groot, D. (2001). Social influence in computer-mediated communication: The effects of anonymity on group behavior. *Personality and Social Psychology Bulletin, 27,* 1242–1254.

Potter, D., & Andersen, M. P. (1976). *Discussion in small groups: A guide to effective practice.* Belmont, CA: Wadsworth.

Price, K. H., Harrison, D. A., & Gavin, J. H. (2006). Withholding inputs in team contexts: Member composition, interaction processes, evaluation structure, and social loafing. *Journal of Applied Psychology, 91,* 1375–1384.

Rahim, M. A. (2002). Toward a theory of managing organizational conflict. *International Journal of Conflict Management, 13,* 206–235.

Rampersad, R. (2007). Enhance self-effectiveness by breathing and silence exercises. *Training & Management Development Methods, 21,* 401–406.

Rao, S. S. (1995, March 14). Meetings go better electronically. *Financial World,* pp. 72–73.

Rat patrol. (1992, August). *Working Woman,* p. 15.

Ratliffe, S. A. (1995, May). Exploring SCA's place in electronic networks. *Spectra,* pp. 4, 12.

Remmers, F. L. (1998). A beginner's guide to the internet. In C. Lynch (Ed.), *Your key to success: Kean University* (pp. 99–104). Needham, MA: Simon & Schuster.

Richmond, V. P., & McCroskey, J. C. (1995). *Communication: Apprehension, avoidance, and effectiveness* (4th ed.). Scottsdale, AZ: Gorsuch Scarisbrick.

Richter, A. W., Scully, J., & West, M. A. (2005). Intergroup conflict and intergroup effectiveness in organizations: Theory and scale development.

European Journal of Work and Organizational Psychology, 14, 177–203.

Robert, H. M., III, Evans, W. J., Honemann, D. H., & Balch, T. J. (Eds.). (2000). *Robert's rules of order* (10th ed.). Cambridge, MA: Perseus.

Robinson, D. A., Davidsson, P., van der Mescht, H., & Court, P. (2007). How entrepreneurs deal with ethical challenges—An application of the Business Ethics Synergy Star technique. *Journal of Business Ethics, 71,* 411–423.

Rodriguez, C. M. (2005). Emergence of a third culture: Shared leadership in international strategic alliances. *International Marketing Review, 22,* 6795.

Rogers, C. (1999). A way of being. In J. Stewart (Ed.), *Bridges not walls* (7th ed.) (pp. 564–573). Boston: McGraw-Hill.

Roman, S., Ruiz, S., & Munuera, J. L. (2005). The influence of the compensation system and personal variables on a salesperson's effective listening behavior. *Journal of Marketing Management, 21,* 205–230.

Romero, E. J., & Cruthirds, K. W. (2006). The use of humor in the workplace. *The Academy of Management Perspectives, 20,* 58–69.

Rubin, R. B., Perse, E. M., & Barbato, C. A. (1988). Conceptualization and measurement of interpersonal communication motives. *Human Communication Research, 14,* 602–628.

Rubin, R. B., & Rubin, A. M. (1992). Antecedents of interpersonal communication motivation. *Communication Quarterly, 40,* 305–317.

Salas, E., Sims, D., & Burke, C. S. (2005). Is there a "Big Five" in teamwork? *Small Group Research, 36,* 555–599.

Samovar, L. A., & Porter, R. E. (1995). *Communication between cultures* (2nd ed.). Belmont, CA: Wadsworth.

Satir, V. (1999). Paying attention to words. In J. Stewart (Ed.), *Bridges not walls* (7th ed.) (pp. 93–98). Boston: McGraw-Hill.

Savolainen, R. (2007). Filtering and withdrawing; Strategies for coping with information overload in everyday contexts. *Journal of Information Science, 33,* 611–631.

Scharff, M. M. (2005). Understanding WorldCom's accounting fraud: Did groupthink play a role? *Journal of Leadership & Organizational Studies, 11,* 109–118.

Scheidel, T. M., & Crowell, L. (1964). Idea development in small group discussion. *Quarterly Journal of Speech, 50,* 140–145.

Schlenker, B. (1986). Self-identification: Toward an integration of the private and public self. In R. F. Baumeister (Ed.), *Public self and private self* (pp. 21–62). New York: Springer-Verlag.

Scholtes, P. R. (1988). *The team handbook: How to use teams to improve quality.* Madison, WI: Joiner Associates.

Schultz, B. G. (1996). Improving group communication performance: An overview of diagnosis and intervention. In L. R. Frey, D. S. Gouran, & M. S. Poole (Eds.), *The handbook of group communication theory and research* (pp. 371–394). Newbury Park, CA: Sage.

Schutz, W. C. (1966). *The interpersonal underworld.* Palo Alto, CA: Science and Behavior Books.

Schutz, P., & Bloch, B. (2006). The "silo-virus": Diagnosing and curing departmental groupthink. *Team Performance Management, 12,* 31–43.

Scott, C. R., Timmerman, C. E., Quinn, L., & Garrett, D. M. (1997, November). *When the virtual honeymoon ends earlier for some than others: User differences and the declining benefits associated with repeated usage of a computerized group decision support system.* Paper presented at the annual conference of the National Communication Association, Chicago, IL.

Scudder, J. N., & Andrews, P. H. (1995). A comparison of two alternative models of powerful speech: The impact of power and gender upon the use of threats. *Communication Research Reports, 12,* 25–33.

Shalley, C. E., Gilson, L. L., & Blum, T. C. (2000). Matching creativity requirements and the work environment: Effects on satisfaction and intentions to leave. *Academy of Management Journal, 43,* 215–223.

Simon, H. A. (1977). *The new science of management decision* (rev. ed.). Englewood Cliffs, NJ: Prentice-Hall.

Sitaram, K. S., & Cogdell, R. T. (1976). *Foundations of intercultural communication.* Columbus, OH: Charles E. Merrill.

Skow, L., & Samovar, L. A. (1991). Cultural patterns of the Maasai. In L. A. Samovar & R. E. Porter (Eds.), *Intercultural communication: A reader* (6th ed.) (pp. 87–95). Belmont, CA: Wadsworth.

Smart, K. L., & Featheringham, R. (2006). Developing effective interpersonal communication and discussion skills. *Business Communication Quarterly, 69,* 276–283.

Smith, S. C., & Piele, P. K. (2006). *School leadership: Handbook for excellence in student learning* (4th ed.). Newbury Park, CA: Corwin Press.

Smith, V., Hosman, L. A., & Siltanen, S. A. (1998). The effects of powerful and powerless speech styles and speaker expertise on impression formation and attitude change. *Communication Research Reports, 15,* 27–35.

Smith, W. J., Harrington, K. V., & Neck, C. P. (2000). Resolving conflict with humor in a diversity context. *Journal of Managerial Psychology, 15,* 606–623.

Song, F. (2007). The effect of the consensus-making on intergroup trust and reciprocity in strategic interactions. *American Marketing Association Conference Proceedings, 18,* 25–32.

Sprague, J., & Stuart, D. (2003). *The speaker's handbook* (6th ed.). Belmont, CA: Wadsworth.

Staples, D. S., & Zhao, L. (2006). The effects of cultural diversity in virtual teams versus face-to-face teams. *Group Decision and Negotiation, 15,* 389–406.

Stark, E. M., Shaw, J. D., & Duffy, M. K. (2007). Preference for group work, winning orientation, and social loafing behavior in groups. *Group & Organization Management, 32,* 699–723.

Stasser, G. (1999). A primer of social decision scheme theory: Models of group influence, competitive model testing and prospective modeling. *Organization Behavior and Human Decision Processes, 80,* 3–20.

Stasser, G., Vaughan, S. I., & Stewart, D. D. (2000). Pooling unshared information: The benefits of knowing how access to information is distributed among group members. *Organizational Behavior and Human Decision Processes, 82,* 102–116.

Stewart, J., & Thomas, M. (1995). Dialogic listening: Sculpting mutual meanings. In J. Stewart (Ed.), *Bridges not walls* (6th ed.) (pp. 184–201). New York: McGraw-Hill.

Sullivan, J. J., Albrecht, T. L., & Taylor, S. (1990). Process, organizational, relational, and personal determinants of managerial compliance-gaining strategies. *Journal of Business Communication, 27,* 332–355.

Szymanski, K., & Harkins, S. G. (1993). The effect of experimenter evaluation on self-evaluation within the social loafing paradigm. *Journal of Experimental Social Psychology 29,* 268–286.

Taggar, S., & Ellis, R. (2007). The role of leaders in shaping formal team norms. *Leadership Quarterly, 18,* 105–119.

Tajfel, H., & Turner, J. C. (1986). The social identity theory of intergroup behavior. In S. Worchel & W. G. Austin (Eds.), *Psychology of intergroup relations* (2nd ed.). Chicago: Nelson-Hall.

Taka, I., & Foglia, W. D. (1994). Ethical aspects of "Japanese leadership style." *Journal of Business Ethics, 13,* 135–148.

Tangirala, S., & Ramanujam, R. (2008). Employee silence on critical work issues: The cross level effects of procedural justice climate. *Personnel Psychology, 61*(1), pp. 37–68.

Tannen, D. (2001). *You just don't understand: Women and men in conversation.* New York: Quill.

Taormina, R. J. (2008). Interrelating leadership behaviors, organizational socialization, and organizational culture. *Leadership & Organization Development Journal, 29,* 85–102.

Tata, J. (2002). The influence of accounts on perceived social loafing in work teams. *The International Journal of Conflict Management, 13,* 292–308.

Tierney, P., & Farmer, S. M. (2002). Creative self-efficacy: It's potential antecedents and relationship to creative performance. *Academy of Management Journal, 45,* 1137–1148.

Tierney, P., & Farmer, S. M. (2004). The Pygmalion process and employee creativity. *Journal of Management, 30,* 413–423.

Toffler, B. L. (1986). *Tough choices: Managers talk ethics.* New York: Wiley.

Toffler, B. L., & Reingold, J. (2004). *Final accounting: Ambition, greed, and the fall of Arthur Andersen.* New York: Random House.

Toulmin, S. (1958). *The uses of argument.* Cambridge, England: Cambridge University Press.

Toussaint, L., & Webb, J. R. (2005). Gender differences in the relationship between empathy and forgiveness. *Journal of Social Psychology, 145,* 673–685.

Traver, R. (1998). What is a good guiding question? *Educational Leadership, 55,* 70–77.

Triandis, H. C., Brislin, R., & Hui, C. H. (1988). Cross-cultural training across the individualism-collectivism divide. *International Journal of Intercultural Relations, 12,* 269–298.

Tuckman, B., & Jensen, M. (1977). Stages of small-group development. *Group and Organizational Studies, 2,* 419–427.

Useem, J. (1999, December 20). The art of lying: Can it be a good thing? *Fortune Small Business, 140,* 278A.

van Engen, M. L., & Willemsen, T. M. (2004). Sex and leadership styles: A meta-analysis of research published in the 1990's. *Psychological Reports, 94,* 3–18.

van Ginkel, W. P., & van Knippenberg, D. (2007). Group information elaboration and group decision making: The role of shared task representations. *Organizational Behavior and Human Decision Processes, 105,* 82–97.

van Mierlo, H., Rutte, C. G., Vermunt, J. K., Kompier, M. A. J., & Doorewaard, J. A. C. M. (2007). A multi-level mediation model of the relationships between team autonomy, individual task design, and psychological well-being. *Journal of Occupational and Organizational Psychology, 80,* 647–664.

Vengopal, K., & Mridula, K. (2007). Students' learning and thinking styles. *Journal of the Indian Academy of Applied Psychology, 33,* 111–118.

Verderber, R. F. (2003). *The challenge of effective speaking* (12th ed.). Belmont, CA: Wadsworth.

Volkema, R. J., & Niederman, F. (1996). Planning and managing organizational meetings: An empirical analysis of written and oral communications. *The Journal of Business Communication, 33,* p. 275.

von Oech, R. (1983). *A whack on the side of the head: How to unlock your mind for innovation.* New York: Warner.

Wageman, R. (2001). How leaders foster self-managing team effectiveness: Design choices vs. hands-on coaching. *Organization Science, 12,* 559–577.

Waldron, V. R., & Applegate, J. L. (1998). Person-centered tactics during verbal disagreements: Effects on student perceptions of persuasiveness and social attraction. *Communication Education, 47,* 53–66.

Walker, C. (1998a, September 21). Finding data in multiple haystacks. (Dataware II Knowledge Query Server document management software) [Product Announcement]. *PC Week,* p. 20.

Walker, C. (1998b, October 5). The team approach: New software raises the bar on knowledge management. (Intraspect Software's Knowledge Management Server 2.0) [Product Announcement]. *PC Week,* p. 14.

Wallace, K. R. (1955). An ethical basis of communication. *Speech Teacher, 4,* 1–9.

Walton, M. (1986). *The Deming management method.* New York: Perigee.

Weick, K. E. (1977). Enactment processes in organizations. In B. M. Staw & G. R. Salancik (Eds.), *New directions in organizational behavior* (pp. 267–300). Chicago: St. Clair.

Weick, K. E. (1978). The spines of leaders. In M. M. Lombardo, & M. W. McCall (Eds.), *Leadership: Where else can we go?* (pp. 37–61). Durham, NC: Duke University Press.

Wernerfelt, B. (2007). Delegation, committees, and managers. *Journal of Economics & Management Strategy, 16,* 35–51.

Westcott, D. (2007, August). Have you adequately defined your situation? *Quality Progress, 40*(8), p. 80.

White, R. K., & Lippett, R. O. (1960). *Autocracy and democracy.* New York: Harper & Row.

Williams, H. M., Parker, S. K., & Turner, N. (2007). Perceived dissimilarity and perspective taking within work teams. *Group & Organization Management, 32,* 569–597.

Winter, A., & Winter, R. (1997). *Brain workout: Easy ways to power up your memory, sensory perception, and intelligence.* New York: St. Martin's.

Witteman, H. (1991). Group member satisfaction: A conflict-related account. *Small Group Research, 22,* 24–58.

Wittenbaum, G. M., & Park, E. S. (2001). The collective preference for shared information. *Current Directions in Psychological Science, 10,* 70–73.

Wolff, S. B., Pescosolido, A. T., & Druskat, V. U. (2002). Emotional intelligence as the basis of leadership emergence in self-managing teams. *Leadership Quarterly, 13,* 505–522.

Wood, J. T. (2001). *Gendered lives: Communication, gender, and culture* (4th ed.). Belmont, CA: Wadsworth.

Yakal, K. (1996, January 23). To do or not to do: Two business-oriented decision makers. (Avantos Performance Systems DecideRight; Arlington Software Which & Why 3.11) [Software Review]. *PC Magazine,* p. 62.

Yoong, S. P., & Gallupe, R. B. (2002, Spring). Coherence in face-to-face electronic meetings: A hidden factor in facilitation success. *Group Facilitation, 4,* 11A.

Zack, M. H. (2007). The role of decision support systems in an indeterminate world. *Decision Support Systems, 43,* 1664–1674.

Zak, M. W. (1994). "It's like a prison in there": Organizational fragmentation in a demographically diversified workplace. *Journal of Business and Technical Communication, 8,* 281–298.

Zorn, T. E. (1991). Construct system development, transformational leadership and leadership messages. *Southern Communication Journal, 56,* 178–193.

NAME INDEX

SUBJECT INDEX

Note: Page numbers followed by *f* refer to figures